Numbers

Numbers

Translated by Ed van der Maas

A. Noordtzij

ZONDERVAN
PUBLISHING HOUSE
OF THE ZONDERVAN CORPORATION
GRAND RAPIDS, MICHIGAN 49506

THE BIBLE STUDENT'S COMMENTARY—NUMBERS
Originally published in Dutch under the title *Korte Verklaring der Heilige Schrift,* by J. H. Kok, B. V. Kampen, The Netherlands.

Copyright © 1983 by The Zondervan Corporation
Grand Rapids, Michigan

Library of Congress Cataloging in Publication Data

Noordtzij, A.
    Numbers.

    (Bible student's commentary)
    Includes text of New International Version English text of Numbers.
    Includes bibliographical references.
    1. Bible. O.T. Numbers—Commentaries. I. Bible. O.T. Numbers. New International. 1983. II. Title. III. Series: Korte verklaring der Heilige Schrift, met nieuwe vertaling. English.

BS1265.3.N56   1983   222'.14077   82-23676
ISBN 0-310-43980-9

The translation used in *The Bible Student's Commentary* is the *Holy Bible, New International Version* (North American Edition). Copyright © 1978 by New York Bible Society.

Designed and edited by Edward Viening

Printed in the United States of America

83 84 85 86 87 88   /   9 8 7 6 5 4 3 2 1

Contents

Publisher's Note

The publisher would like to call attention to a feature in this book that might raise some questions. It concerns Noordtzij's approach to the question of how Israel's religious thought world relates to that of the cultural environment of which it was a part, and how God's revelation through Moses relates to both. The question is raised in the interest of the general integrity of this series of commentaries, a series that has rightly been commended by many evangelical scholars.

Noordtzij gives due recognition to the fact that God's revelation to Israel often serves to correct or to overcome erroneous notions that Israel may have held in common with its pagan neighbors. This is a helpful insight. God's revelation to man always involves an element of condescension and of accommodation. And in the case of Israel it also involved an element of correction and purification of notions previously held.

Human beings, by virtue of their creaturehood, are inevitably religious beings, but their religion has been deformed and falsified (see Rom. 1:18ff.). When God's special revelation is imparted, these deformations are being rectified. To the extent that Israel held certain erroneous notions in common with its pagan neighbors, it too needed such rectification. (See also the discussion of Geerhardus Vos of the word "holy" in his *Biblical Theology,* where it is rightly recognized that there is a certain concept of holiness that is commonly held throughout the ancient Near East, only to receive its true and proper meaning as it is used in connection with the one and only God, the God of special revelation and Scripture.)

But there are also several points in Noordtzij's commentary where the emphasis lies not so much on correction and rectification, as on accommodation. Noordtzij assumes that there was a common thought pattern that Israel shared with the other nations. He refers to this pattern as being "dynamistic" in nature. The word "dynamistic" is derived from the

Greek word *dunamis* (power, force). Dynamistic thinking sees the universe as dominated by forces, or powers, more or less conceived impersonally, controllable by clever manipulation, and sometimes by magic. Such thought patterns can still be found on some of the islands of the South Pacific and elsewhere. Modern code words often used to describe these forces are *mana* and *taboo*.

Related to the above are also Noordtzij's frequent references to the presence of alleged demonic influences whose presence must somehow be counteracted by a law that was given. (Noordtzij's failure to make the proper distinctions leads him to suggest at a certain point that a law given by God to Israel through Moses was meant "to prevent the person from inhaling through his mouth and nose further demonic influences.") Here again the suggestion of accommodation in the process of revelation leads to rather illegitimate results when the nature of the spirit world is taken into account.

A final point, related to the above, is Noordtzij's treatment of words such as "holy," "clean and unclean." In "dynamistic" thought these notions are often understood in a material sense. Noordtzij likewise treats them in this fashion.

It is important to make careful distinctions, here, as well as elsewhere. Undue simplification can easily occur within the scope of a succinct note of this kind. Noordtzij's concern to point to a certain uniqueness inherent in the notions of the holy, the clean and the unclean, should be appreciated. The Old Testament idea of the holy often associates itself with extreme danger and with the need for proper caution in the handling of the holy things. Holiness moreover attaches itself to material objects. Touching these can even result in some sort of transference, or else in severe punishment such as sudden death.

But the fact that holiness attaches itself to things does not make this notion as such a materialistic one. In this respect there is definite discontinuity between the holiness concept prevalent in the ancient Near East and that which prevails within the pale of special revelation. Israel is to be holy because its God, who redeemed it from the bondage of slavery and sin in Egypt is holy. Just as there is a discontinuity between that God and the gods of the other nations, so there is a discontinuity in the holiness notion found in Israel's religion, normed as it is by revelation, and the other religions where this norm is not to be found.

Preface

I dedicate this book to the memory of my parents: to my father, who struggled against the influence of Wellhausen, and who saw "Eastern rays of light on the Western view of the Scriptures" (the title of one of his addresses), but who did not live to see how the discovery of the ancient Near Eastern world caused a complete reversal in the evaluation of the writings of the Old Testament; to my praying mother, whose prayer life was of such great value for my own life. Next to God I owe it above all to them that now, in my seventieth year, I can look back on a richly blessed life. I was sixteen years old when first I picked up the Hebrew Bible, which is still the object of my scholarly endeavor. That was during the time of the rise of the school of Wellhausen, which seemed to overcome all opposition and appeared to be able to provide adequate answers to all questions concerning the Old Testament. Since then our God has begun to disclose to us the world of the ancient Near East, and is making it increasingly clear that the direction the school of Wellhausen took with such great assuredness was in reality a false trail, and that the solution to the problems of the Old Testament it proposed does not do justice to the facts. These facts, which have been made available in almost overwhelming abundance by the invaluable work in the fields of archaeology, philology, and the history of religions, are now at the disposal of those who have set out to show, on scholarly grounds, that the church of all ages was not in error when it heard in the Old Testament the voice of the God and Father of our Lord Jesus Christ. I thank my God that I was allowed to see this.

A. Noordtzij

Introduction

I. *Title*

The Palestinian Synagogue, following the example of the Septuagint (LXX), divided the first book of the Bible into five parts; since A.D. 160 these five parts or books have been known collectively as "the Pentateuch," i.e., "the fivefold (book)." "Numbers," our name for the fourth of the five books, is derived from the LXX via the Vulgate. The Semitic custom was to use the first word(s) of a book as its title. The translators of the LXX, however, wanted to give each book a title that would reflect its contents; they therefore called the fourth part of the Pentateuch *Arithmoi,* i.e., "Numbers." The Western church initially adopted this title in its Latinized form (*Arithmi*), but, while the other Greek titles (Genesis, Exodus, Leviticus, Deuteronomy) were retained, this title was later translated into Latin (*Numeri*). The Syrian church also translated the name of the fourth book (*Sifrå de menjånå,* "Book of Numbers"). This title was translated into English (Numbers) in the KJV and has since been the name by which the book is known in the English-speaking world. It is possible that the name *Arithmoi* (and hence *Numeri*) is based on the title that, according to Eusebius, was common in Jewish circles: *sefer misparim* (Book of Numbers); another Jewish name was *ḥomeš hapikkudim* ("the fifth part of the Pentateuch of the numbered"). The synagogue itself uses the first words of the book as its title: *wayyedabbēr,* "And He Spoke," or (to avoid confusion with the opening words of Deuteronomy, *'elle hadebarim,* "these are the words") the fourth word of the book: *bamidbar,* "In the Desert."

The title "In the Desert" actually reflects the contents of the book better than "Numbers," since only chapters 1–4 and chapter 26, which deal with the counting of the various tribes, contain many numbers. The main body of the book, however, takes us through the desert or wilderness from Mt.

Sinai to Kadesh, and hence around the territories of Edom and Moab to the Transjordan region where the people rest for a time in the fields of Moab across from Jericho, ready to enter Canaan as "the Lord's people." The entire book is thus set "in the desert."

II. *Content*

Beginning with Exodus 25 the author of the Pentateuch describes the cultic development of Israel as the Lord's people. This theme is continued in Leviticus and in Numbers 1:1–10:10, where additional laws are given relating to the cultus. First, the results of the census are reported to show how the Lord had fully realized His promise of Genesis 12:2; 13:16; et al. (ch. 1). Then the arrangement of the camp and the marching order are given (ch. 2) to show that the Lord is a holy and inaccessible God. In chapters 3–4 the position of the Levites is described, both in relation to the priests, whom they were to serve, and in the framework of Israel's cultus. The regulations in chapters 5–6 cover a number of unrelated topics: the purity of the camp (5:1–4), the return of, or restitution for, that which had been wrongfully taken (5:5–10), how to deal with a wife suspected of unfaithfulness (5:11–31), the Nazirite vow (6:1–21), and the priestly blessing (6:22–27). After a detailed description of the offerings of the leaders of Israel at the dedication of the tabernacle (ch. 7), specific instructions are given for the setting up of the lamps (8:1–4) and the consecration of the Levites, who are to serve from age twenty-five until age fifty (8:5–26). Because some were unable to celebrate the Passover at the appointed time, instructions are given for the celebration of a second Passover (9:1–14). And finally, since Israel will shortly depart from Mt. Sinai, the signs for the breaking up and the setting up of the camp are explained (9:15–10:10).

The second main division of the book (10:11–20:13) covers Israel's journey to Kadesh and their stay there. First, Israel's departure is described (10:11–36), after which five events that take place on their journey to Kadesh are chronicled: the disaster at Taberah (11:1–3), the misery of Kibroth Hattaavah (11:4–35), Miriam's leprosy (12:1–16), the twelve explorers (13:1–14:38), and the unsuccessful attack on Canaan (14:39–45). Then follow several ritual laws concerning supplementary offerings (15:1–16), the cake from the first of the ground meal (15:17–21), offerings for unintentional sins (15:22–31), gathering wood on the Sabbath (15:32–36), and the tassels on the garments (15:37–41). The ritual laws are interrupted by two historical chapters dealing with the rebellion of Korah, Dathan, and Abiram (ch. 16) and the budding of Aaron's staff (ch. 17). The laws then continue with regulations concerning the duties and rights of, and the offerings for, the priests and Levites (ch. 18), and the water of cleansing (ch. 19). The second division concludes with the narrative concerning Miriam's death and Moses' sin at Meribah (20:1–13).

The third main division (20:14–36:13) takes Israel from Kadesh to the fields of Moab. First we are told of the journey to the Transjordan region (20:14–21:9), which includes Edom's refusal to let Israel cross its territory (20:14–21), Aaron's death (20:22–29), the attack of the Canaanites (21:1–3), and the bronze snake (21:4–9). Then follows the journey to, and battles in, the Transjordan region (21:10–22:1). The journey is outlined (21:10–20), and the defeat of Sihon (21:21–31) and Og (21:32–22:1) are described. Balaam's encounter with Israel is reported in detail (22:2–24:25). Balaam, who is summoned twice by Balak of Moab (22:2–21), is forced by the Angel of the Lord to obey only His will (22:22–35). When Balaam meets Balak (22:36–40) the latter wants Balaam to curse Israel (22:41–23:6), but Balaam blesses the Lord's people three times (23:7–24:9). After Balak gives vent to his displeasure Balaam predicts Israel's glorious future in his fourth oracle (24:10–19). Three oracles of Balaam are added; they concern Amalek, the Kenites, and Asshur and Eber (24:20–25). Immediately after the story of Balaam we are told how Israel allowed itself to be seduced to worship the Baal of Peor; the Lord's punishment follows, but His anger is averted by the action of Phinehas. Israel is commanded to treat the Midianites from that time forth as enemies (ch. 25). In view of the conquest of Canaan a second census of Israel is required (ch. 26), whereby the future division of Canaan is also mentioned (vv. 52–56), and the inheriting of property by women is regulated (27:1–11).

After Moses is told of his impending death and Joshua is appointed his successor (27:12–23), regulations are given concerning the daily offerings and the special offerings for the festivals (28:1–30:1), and concerning the validity of vows made by women, both married and unmarried (30:2–17). After this interruption the historical narrative continues. First, the battle against Midian is reported (31:1–12) and attention is given to the treatment of prisoners and the cleansing of the army (31:13–24); then follows a discussion of the division of the living spoils (31:25–47), and the offerings of the officers (31:48–54). Next we hear of the division of the Transjordan region at the request of Gad and Reuben (ch. 32); the request is initially refused by Moses (32:1–15), but later, when Gad and Reuben insist (32:16–19), it is granted (32:20–27) and implemented (32:28–38). Four verses are added, describing how the half-tribe of Manasseh also settled in the Transjordan region (32:39–42).

A list of the sites where Israel camped on its wilderness journey (33:1–49) provides a summary of the past years, after which all attention is focused on the future. First, the manner in which Canaan must be occupied and divided is determined (33:50–34:29). After the command to drive out all the inhabitants of Canaan (33:50–56) the boundaries of Canaan are given (34:1–12) as well as further instructions for its division (34:13–29), which include the allotment of forty-eight cities to the Levites (35:1–8). Rules for the selection of the six cities of refuge are also given (35:11–15), as well as regulations as to who may seek asylum in these cities (35:16–34).

The Book of Numbers ends with regulations that limit the right of marriage of women who have inherited land (36:1–12), and closes with a subscript (36:13).

III. *Observations*

1. The Book of Leviticus is clearly a continuation of Exodus 25ff.: it contains laws and regulations dealing almost exclusively with the cultic life of Israel (the only historical sections are 10:1–7 and 24:10–16). The Book of Numbers, by contrast, consists largely of historical information concerning Israel's experiences on its journey from Sinai to the fields of Moab; only the first part of Numbers (1:1–10:10) is clearly a continuation of Leviticus. In only two instances is a historical connection given between an event and the laws that follow: the institution of the second Passover (9:1–14) and the instructions concerning the division of the spoils after the campaign against Midian (ch. 31). It is not possible to find a satisfactory answer to the question as to why a given law or regulation is found in its present context rather than elsewhere. It is different with the historical narratives: there we find three groups whose various elements are closely related. The first group is found in 11:1–14:45, where six events give an impression of Israel's journey from Sinai to Kadesh. The second group is found in 16:1–17:13 and consists of the story of the rebellion of Korah, Dathan, and Abiram and their followers (16:1–50), followed by the budding of Aaron's staff (ch. 17). This second group falls in the thirty-eight-year period of wandering that followed the rebellion at Kadesh. The third group, finally, is found in chapters 20–25, and takes us from Kadesh to the fields of Moab; the story of the encounter between Balaam and Israel is prominent in this group (22:2–24:25).

2. On the one hand Numbers is related to Exodus-Leviticus in that the first part (1:1–10:10) focuses on the further development of Israel as the Lord's people and on the task assigned to the Levites in this development. On the other hand Numbers is related to Deuteronomy in that, after the survey of the wilderness journey, the focus in the final chapters (33:50–36:13) is entirely on the future; in these chapters we find only regulations

concerning the conquest of Canaan, the theme that dominates Deuteronomy (Deut. 4:1; 6:1; 7:1–2; etc.). Therefore the division of the Pentateuch into five books has, where Numbers is concerned, ignored the clear intention of the author, since 1:1–10:10 is a continuation of Leviticus and 33:50–36:13 forms an introduction to Deuteronomy.

3. While the laws incorporated in Numbers all deal with the cultus (special grain and drink offerings, 15:1–16, offerings for unintentional sins, 15:22–31, the daily offerings and the festival offerings, chs. 28–29), they focus, more so than those in Leviticus, on the rights of the priests (ch. 18), the organization of the Levites (chs. 3–4; 8:5–26; 35:1–8), and the Nazirite (6:1–21), as well as on the cleansing of someone who has touched a dead body (ch. 19). Nevertheless, the inclusion of a variety of other laws in Numbers shows that the Lord's instruction (*tora*), which was intended to govern Israel's life in the broadest sense, considered every aspect of life important; thus, we find on the one hand regulations concerning the validity of vows made by women (ch. 30), the right of succession and marriage of heiresses (chs. 27, 36), and the cities of refuge (35:9–34), and on the other hand regulations concerning such matters as the setting up of the lamps (8:1–4), the use of the trumpets (10:1–10), and the tassels on the corners of the garments (15:37–41). All things were to be made subservient to the ultimate goal the Lord envisioned when He made Israel His people (cf. my *Gods Woord,* pp. 326ff.).

4. The historical references in Leviticus are very few: only in 7:38; 25:1; and 26:46 is mention made of the Lord speaking to Moses "on Mount Sinai," and "after the death of the two sons of Aaron" in 16:1 refers back to the narrative in 10:1–7. Numbers, by contrast, contains a number of dates that give the regulations and events a specific place in the framework of Israel's wanderings through the wilderness. These dates are:

1:1 "on the first day of the second month of the second year after the Israelites came out of Egypt," i.e., one month after the tabernacle had been set up (Exod. 40:2, 17), "in the Desert of Sinai."

7:1 "when Moses finished setting up the tabernacle."

9:1 "in the first month of the second year after they came out of Egypt."

9:15 "on the day the tabernacle . . . was set up."

10:11 "on the twentieth day of the second month of the second year," i.e., shortly after 1:1, "the Israelites set out from the Desert of Sinai."

20:1 "in the first month."

The first five dates all fall in the second year after the Exodus when Israel camped at Sinai. However, they are not given in chronological sequence, since 7:1 and 9:15 both refer to an event that took place one month before 1:1. According to the Jewish exegete Rashi (A.D. 1040–1105) the purpose of this arrangement was so that the Book of Numbers would not begin with an event that reflected negatively on Israel. But, apart from the fact that Numbers cannot be viewed as a separate work, the events in chapters 7 and 9 cannot be said to disgrace Israel: chapter 7 describes the offerings of the leaders at the dedication of the tabernacle, and 9:1–14 deals with the desire to celebrate the Passover in spite of ceremonial uncleanness.

The sixth date (20:1) falls in the fortieth year after the Exodus when Israel wanted to travel from Kadesh to the Transjordan region through Edom (21:14). This follows from a comparison of 20:22 and 33:38–39 and from 20:1 (see commentary on 20:1).

The thirty-eight years of Israel's wanderings, punishment for their refusal to enter Canaan from Kadesh (ch. 14), thus fall between the first five and the sixth dates. Of this period we are only told of the rebellion of Korah, Dathan, and Abiram (ch. 16), the budding of Aaron's staff (ch. 17), and Moses' sin (20:7–12). The school of Wellhausen concluded from the paucity of information that the author knew little or nothing about those years; but this ignores the fact that the Old Testament does not give us a history of Israel, but rather a history of God's revelation. Periods during which little or nothing happened that would be important for a knowledge of that history are simply passed over in silence.

IV. *The Historical Perspective of Numbers*

As stated earlier, Numbers takes us from the setting up of the tabernacle to the end of the wilderness journey. It begins at the point where the service of the Lord could begin in the "Tent of Meeting" (cf. my commentary on Lev. 1:1) that had been consecrated by the descending of the glory of the Lord in the form of the "cloud." The earliest event recorded in Numbers thus takes place on the first day of the first month of the second year after the Exodus (7:1; 9:15). Exactly one month later the census is commanded (1:2). There is no military purpose behind this census, however; it implements the command given in Exodus 30:11ff. to count the people in connection with the "atonement money." The purpose of the census is therefore strictly cultic.

Three weeks later Israel leaves Sinai, where it had become a national community of "servants of the LORD" (10:11). They travel north to Kadesh, where they arrive at an unspecified time, but certainly in that same year (cf. Deut. 2:14). From Kadesh (the present Ain Qadeis, approximately sixty miles southwest of the southern tip of the Dead Sea) explorers are sent out to gather information for a possible attempt to invade Canaan from the south (ch. 13). But the people allow themselves to be swayed by the vast majority of the explorers and refuse to enter Canaan; they even consider returning to Egypt (14:4). Only after the Lord pronounces judgment on their refusal (14:26–35) do the people summon up their courage and attempt to invade Canaan, but this time in spite of Moses' warning that the Lord will not be with them; the result is defeat at the hands of the Amalekites and Canaanites (14:39–45).

Wiener seeks a connection between this event and the reference to the "destruction" of "Israel" on the stele of Merneptah ("The Exodus and the Southern Invasion," *Nieuwe Theologische Studiën*, 1927, pp. 71–81; cf. my *Gods Woord*, pp. 306–7). This event would then have taken place north of Kadesh. But apart from the fact that Wiener's attempt to place Israel's exodus during the reign of Merneptah (1225–1215 B.C.) must be considered a failure, he overlooks the fact that the Israel to which Merneptah referred lived in Canaan in an area between Ashkelon and Janoam near Lebanon (see commentary on 21:3).

Others see in 14:39–45 the recollection of a supposedly successful attempt on the part of some of the tribes, among them Simeon and Levi with the Kenites and Calebites, to penetrate Canaan from the south (e.g., C. T. Burney, *Israel's Settlement in Canaan,* 1921; C. Steuernagel, *Die Einwanderung der israelitischen Stämme in Kanaan,* 1901). Not only is the view, originally proposed by E. Meyer, that there were at least two entries into Canaan, one from the south and one from the east, in direct conflict with the Old Testament tradition, but it would also be unparalleled if in Numbers 14:39–45 a victory would have been transformed into a defeat. Johannes de Groot correctly observes that "he who mistrusts this [the Old Testament] tradition on salient points must abandon the possibility of any reconstruction" (*Jozua,* 1931, p. 15).

Numbers is silent about the years following the defeat. In the chapters that lie between the defeat and the journey toward Edom (15:1–20:13) no mention is made of the place where the laws were given (15:1–41; 18:1–19:22) or where the rebellion of Korah took place (16:1–50). The incident of the man who gathered wood on the Sabbath is merely said to have taken place "while the Israelites were in the desert," and 20:1 states that Miriam died when "in the first month the whole Israelite community arrived at the Desert of Zin, and they stayed at Kadesh." Only a comparison of 20:22 and 33:36ff. shows that Miriam's death took place shortly before Aaron's death in the final year of the wanderings.

The generally accepted idea, based on Deuteronomy 2:14, is that during the entire thirty-eight-year period Israel wandered from one oasis to the next in the manner described in Deuteronomy 2:1–34. But apart from the fact that Deuteronomy 2:14 says only that thirty-eight years elapsed between Kadesh and the Zered Valley (by the Arnon), this view is untenable because the oases on the Sinai peninsula are few and far between. Most likely Kadesh remained their home base during all those years; there the tabernacle was set up and the annual festivals were celebrated, while the various tribal and family units moved around independently.

Israel finally leaves Kadesh for good and travels east (Num. 20:14) until it reaches the territory of Edom. Edom occupied the mountainous region east and west of the Wadi Araba, the long valley that stretches from the Dead Sea to the Gulf of Aqaba; it is barren and infertile, especially its western part (cf. Gen. 27:39: "away from the earth's richness, away from the dew of heaven above"). The shortest route from Kadesh to the Transjordan region goes, of course, directly through Edom. Since they are refused passage (20:14–21) Israel must go south in the direction of Ezion Geber (see commentary on 33:36) and then again north along the eastern border of Edom in the direction of Moab. All we hear about this journey in the Book of Numbers is the report of Aaron's death (20:22–29), the attack by the Canaanites (21:1–3), and the bronze snake (21:4–9). Tradition places Mt. Hor somewhere northeast of Kadesh, based solely on the words "the . . . king of Arad" in 21:1; but on the basis of Hebrew idiom these words must be considered a later addition. According to tradition, then, Israel went from Kadesh first in a northeasterly direction; but after Edom's refusal there was no reason for this. We must therefore seek Mt. Hor between Kadesh and Ezion Geber, i.e., to the south.

In 21:10 we suddenly find Israel in the region east of Moab. Israel then goes across the Arnon toward the Pisgah mountains (21:10–20), whereupon Sihon of Heshbon refuses to let Israel pass, which results in the destruction of his kingdom, and later also in the destruction of Og of Bashan, whose kingdom bordered on that of Sihon to the north (21:21–22:1). E. Meyer (*Die Israeliten und ihre Nachbarstämme*, p. 74) tried to deny the existence of the Amorite kingdom of Sihon, but F. M. Th. Böhl (*Kanaanäer und Hebräer*, 1911, p. 62) has correctly pointed out that this assertion is untenable (see also H. Gressmann, *Mose und seine Zeit*, 1913, p. 307). The complete lack of data makes it impossible to determine whether it existed only for the span of one generation as Böhl assumes. The minor kingdoms of Og and Sihon were probably the sad remnants of the once strong Amorite state that had been gradually reduced by the Hittites advancing from the north. The fact that the victories over Sihon and Og are mentioned so frequently in the Bible (see commentary on 21:27–30) can readily be explained by the fact that these were the first victories of Israel over nations whose military power was comparable to that of the city-kings of Canaan, and therefore contained a rich promise for the future.

V. *Moses*

The historical sections of Numbers clarify on several points Moses as we know him from Exodus. The person of Moses presents problems to anyone who accepts to any degree the approach of the school of Wellhausen. The consistent application of the evolutionary concept that guides this approach makes it necessary to downgrade as much as possible both the period in which Moses lived and his work in order to make him fit into the evolutionary scheme. Consequently, a number of scholars have tried to get rid of him. According to E. Meyer the question whether or not the mythical figure of Moses is based on a historical person is without meaning for historical research, and therefore falls outside its scope (*Die Israeliten und ihre Nachbarstämme,* 1906, p. 451, n. 1). According to Hölscher (*Geschichte der israelitischen und jüdischen Religion,* 1922, pp. 64ff.) Moses was not a historical person. Wellhausen does speak of Moses, but does so more as a postulate than as a historical person (*Israelitische und jüdische Geschichte,* 2nd ed., p. 29). And his answer to the question as to what we actually know about him is, "Probably [!] the most historical element in what we know about him is the connection between the oldest Israelite sanctuary, the ark, and Moses." According to him Moses left "nothing positive" behind. A new era did not dawn with Moses but with Amos. And Kuenen writes, "Under Moses' influence Israel took a step forward, but it was only one step" (*De Godsdienst van Israel,* I, p. 291). R. Smend speaks in a similar vein (*Lehrbuch der alttestamentlichen Religion,* 3rd ed., p. 43): Moses accomplished virtually nothing beyond the unity of Israel. To G. Beer, Moses was primarily a finder of springs, a snake charmer, and diviner, and as such (!) a fully credible figure in the context of the steppe (*Mose und sein Werk,* 1912). To C. Toussaint, Moses was a magician and miracle worker (*Les origines de la religion d'Israel,* 1931, pp. 229ff.). According to R. Kittel the historicity of the man Moses is *ernstlich nahegelegt,* but can only be proven by means of a historical postulate: the formation of a nation does not happen without an individual playing a key role.

Small wonder that among adherents of the school of Wellhausen the picture remains vague. Gunkel says that Israel has never again produced a man who equaled Moses from either a religious or a political standpoint, yet he also fails to give a clear concept of what Moses accomplished. He limits himself to Moses' adoption of the legal customs of the Midianites and of the name of the god of the Midianites, Jahweh, whose "heroic" character corresponds to that of Moses.

When we set aside these attempts to reduce Moses to a more or less mythical figure, ill-defined and without any outstanding characteristics, and ask what kind of personality we encounter in Numbers, then we see immediately that Moses is portrayed as one to whom nothing human was alien. He is wholeheartedly committed to his people, for whose continued existence he prays when the Lord threatens to destroy them at Kadesh and promises to make Moses into a new nation (14:13ff.). He also prays for them when they overwhelm him with accusations (21:7); he prays for those who were led astray by Korah and his followers (16:22), and he prays for his people when their complaining kindles the Lord's anger (11:2). He tries to talk Korah, Dathan, and Abiram and their followers out of their rebellious plans (16:8–12) and attempts to keep Israel from their ill-advised attempt to invade Canaan from the south in order to escape the Lord's judgment (14:42). How he would like to see his entire people grow up into prophets of the Lord (11:29)!

But not even this man is always consistent. On some occasions his patience with his people seems infinite. Against Miriam he leaves his defense to the Lord (12:3); he does the same in Kadesh when the people grumble against him (14:5), and when Korah and his followers accuse Moses of setting himself above the Lord's people (16:5). Yet when Dathan and Abiram claim that he wants "to lord it over" the people (16:13), Moses becomes very angry and asks the Lord not to accept their offering (16:15). And when the people complain that he has brought them into the wilderness on purpose so that they could die there he inveighs against the people ("you rebels") and gives in to his anger even to the extent that he forgets the Lord's command to speak to the rock so that it will "pour out its water" and hits the rock twice (20:10–13). The hot-tempered character of his youth!

"A very humble man, more humble than anyone else on the face of the earth" (12:3), he was yet not an entirely consistent man, not even toward the Lord his God. True, he is favored over thousands and ten thousands, and the Lord speaks to him "face to face" and allows him to see "the form of the Lord" (12:7–8). Usually Moses is the Lord's "servant, faithful in all (His) house" (12:7). And when the Lord's judgment strikes him and destroys his hope of leading Israel into Canaan himself he bows under that judgment, aware of his sin (27:16). But when the complaints of the people about all they lack in the wilderness make the Lord angry with Moses because his leadership is inadequate and because he dares to bring such complaints to the Lord, then Moses presumptuously reproaches the Lord and asks Him three questions, followed by the request that the Lord kill him unless the situation improves (11:10–15). On this occasion he even dares to suggest that the Lord has given him instructions to provide meat that are impossible to carry out (11:21–23)!

A gifted person, but not without shortcomings! A weak moment is, in my opinion, when Reuben and Gad request that they be allowed to settle in the Transjordan region (ch. 32): Moses fails to say what he should have said, viz., that the Lord's promise concerned Canaan, i.e., the land west of the Jordan, but not the land east of the river. He reprimands Reuben and Gad, yet implies rather unmistakably under what conditions he might be able to grant their request (see commentary on ch. 32). Numbers (like Exodus) does not idealize Moses. He is and remains a man of flesh and blood, radically different from the mythical heroes of antiquity. We even get a taste of his sense of humor in what he says to Korah about his brother Aaron: "Who is Aaron that you should grumble against him?" (16:11). Here he speaks of his brother as of an obliging, even weak man who certainly did not deserve to be pushed out of his privileged position by Korah and his followers. And he displays this sense of humor at a time when, as never before, Israel's leaders are in full rebellion against Aaron and himself!

Moses was a person with strengths and shortcomings, who is nevertheless portrayed as a unique personality in Israel's history. In 12:6 he is called a "prophet" (*nabi'*, one who is spoken to), but among Israel's prophets he occupies a special position. It is said of the seventy elders that "they prophesied, but they did not do so again" (11:25), but for Moses being a prophet was not a temporary ecstasy but meant personal communication with God. He towers high above even the great prophets of later times, prophets like Isaiah and Jeremiah. The distance that lies between Moses and the other prophets is the distance between the "mediator" (cf. Gal. 3:19) whose self-giving put its stamp on Israel and those who were called to prevent this stamp from being eradicated.

So much for the portrait of Moses in the historical sections of Numbers. In the legal sections Moses' personality is of course in the background, but we nevertheless gain more of an idea of his importance for his people in these sections. Here we see him as the builder of the entire social structure of Israel. He determines the position the priests and Levites would from that day forth occupy in Israel (chs. 3–4; 8:5–26) and regulates their source of income (ch. 18; 35:1–8). He gives the necessary regulations for the offerings (15:1–31; chs. 28–29), regulates the purity of the camp (5:1–4) and of marriage (5:11–31), and stipulates what must be done when the Nazirite vow is made and fulfilled, and when it is temporarily interrupted (6:1–21), and how a person can once again become ceremonially clean after contact with a dead body (19:1–22). Israel's jurisprudence is also regulated by him, including the right of sanctuary (35:9–34), restitution (5:5–10), the validity of vows by women (30:2–17), the division of the spoils (ch. 31), and the succession and marriage of heiresses (27:1–11; 36:1–13). And finally he gives instructions for the conquest of Canaan (ch. 32; 33:50–34:29).

Moses' whole life as portrayed in Numbers is dominated by the deep awareness that he stands in the service of the God of the covenant who, because He is holy, asks of His people a manner of life in which His holiness can reveal itself, and who makes Himself known as the God who is essentially different from all other gods, unique, and therefore beyond any visible representation. Moses gained this awareness because the Lord showed Himself to Moses as He has to no one before or since, speaking with him "face to face" (12:8), continuously leading Moses through His special revelation that gave him the guidelines for his life's work.

VI. *The Origin of Numbers*

Like the other parts of the Pentateuch, Numbers does not constitute a literary unit in that its various elements do not date from the same time period. This will be clear to anyone who seriously considers the facts that present themselves to us in the Book of Numbers. Thus, e.g., the instructions concerning the arrangement of the camp and the marching order (ch. 2) cannot possibly have been given in its present form; both the number of men in the various divisions and the names of their leaders are out of place in such instructions and are a more recent addition. The same is true of 3:1–4:49, which deals with the Levites; it is rather obviously composed of several elements that originally were unrelated, but were arranged to form a unit by means of the repeated "the LORD said to Moses (and Aaron)." The author's purpose was, of course, to provide as clear a picture as possible of the task of the Levites under the supervision of the priestly family of Aaron in the Tent of Meeting during the wilderness journey. The last three oracles in the story of Balaam are undoubtedly of more recent origin (24:20–24). The report of Israel's battle with Og of Bashan (21:33–35) was added later from Deuteronomy 3:1–3. The conquests of the eastern half-tribe of Manasseh (32:39–42) did not take place until after Moses' time, and the rebuilding of the cities mentioned in 32:34–38 did, of course, take some time. The arrangement of the names of the men under whose supervision the land of Canaan was to be divided (34:16–29) is post-Mosaic; with the exception of Caleb they are listed in the order, from south to north, of the territories that the tribes would later occupy. The statement "while the Israelites were in the desert" indicates that 15:32–36 was written after the wilderness journey. The same is true of the quotation from the *Book of the Wars of the LORD* (21:14–15), which is of post-Mosaic origin, and of the song in 21:27–30, which is taken from an older collection of songs as the phrase "that is why the poets say" indicates.

The same can also be observed in the legal sections. According to 8:23–26 the service of the Levites began at age twenty-five; but 4:3, 23, 30 set the age at thirty. These laws cannot date from the same time, and those in chapter 4 are probably of more recent origin. The composite character of chapter 19 is obvious. Verse 10b concludes "the requirement of the law" (v. 2); verses 11–13 are a supplement to verses 2–10, and verses 14–22 (which have again their own heading, "this is the law") elaborate on the preparation of the water of cleansing mentioned in verses 11–13. In chapter 35, which deals with the cities of refuge, verses 16–29 are a later addition, based on Deuteronomy 19:1–13. This is supported by the fact that 35:25, 28 are the only instances in the Pentateuch where the high priest is called *kohen haggadol;* in Leviticus 21:10 he is called (literally) "the highest priest of his brothers," and elsewhere "the priest who is anointed" (Lev. 4:3, 5), or merely "the priest" (Lev. 13:2; Num. 3:6). The term *kohen haggadol* undoubtedly reflects more recent usage (Josh. 20:6; 2 Kings 12:10; 22:4, 8; etc.). Also, the calendar of feasts in chapters 28–29 presupposes that of Leviticus 23, while both in turn are based on an older calendar.

There are still other indications that force us to conclude that Numbers is not a literary unit but acquired its present form over a period of time. In Numbers, as in Leviticus (see my *Leviticus,* Introduction, sec. III), a distinction is made between the "native-born" (i.e., Israelite) and the "alien" (i.e., someone of non-Israelite origin who lives among Israel in accordance with Israel's way of life); cf. 9:14; 15:13, 15, 26, 29–30; 19:10; 35:15. This distinction would only make sense when Israel already lived in Canaan. The same is true of the distinction between the ordinary shekel and the "sanctuary shekel" (3:47, 50; 7:13, 19, 25, 31, 37, 43, 49, 55, 61, 67, 73, 79, 85–86; 18:16). While Israel lived in the desert there was, of course, no need for this distinction. But as soon as Israel became part of the larger context of the nations in Canaan with its more complex social and commercial relationships, the need for this distinction forced itself on them. Also, the reference to "the fields of Moab" as lying "across from the Jordan of Jericho" (22:1; NIV: " along the Jordan across from Jericho") could only have been written by someone who lived west of the river.[1]

Many sections of Numbers, on the other hand, presuppose that Israel is

---

[1] See Publisher's Note.

living in the wilderness. This is true in the first place of those sections that deal with Israel's camp (1:52; ch. 2; 4:5, 15; 5:2–4; 10:2–6, 34; 11:1, 9, 26–27, 30–32; 12:14–15; 15:35; 19:3, 7, 9, 14; 31:12–13, 19). Outside the camp the red heifer for the water of cleansing must be slaughtered and burned (19:4, 7, 9). The tabernacle is sometimes simply called "the Tent" (3:25; 9:17; 11:24, 26; 12:10; 18:3–4), which is never the case outside the Pentateuch (1 Kings 1:39; 8:4; 2 Chron. 5:5 refer to the tent set up by David on the threshing floor of Araunah, 2 Sam. 24:18–25). The tabernacle is also called "the dwelling place" (*mishkan,* translated "tabernacle" in the NIV; 3:25–26, 36, 38; 4:26; 7:1, 3; 9:15; 10:21; 16:9; and 16:24, 27, emended text), a term that is found rarely outside the Pentateuch (Josh. 22:19; 1 Chron. 21:29; 2 Chron. 1:5; 29:6), and "the sanctuary" (10:21; NIV: "the holy things"; 18:1; 19:20), which is elsewhere used only of the temple. Furthermore, the tabernacle is not only called "the Tent of Meeting" (3:25, 37–38; 4:4, 23, 28, 30–31, 35, 39, 43, 47; 7:5; 8:19, 22, 24; 18:6, 21, 23, 31), but also "the Tent of the Testimony" (9:15; 17:7–8; 18:2), a term found elsewhere only in 2 Chronicles 24:6.

The law concerning the institution of the second Passover as formulated in 9:9ff. reflects entirely the frame of reference of the wilderness period. No mention is made of the requirement that the blood of the Passover lamb be applied to the doorposts, which makes sense only if this law was given to a nation that wandered in the wilderness and lived in tents.

The way in which 12:6 speaks of the manner in which the Lord revealed Himself to a prophet points to the first beginnings of Israel's prophetism. At that time the Lord revealed Himself only by means of dreams and visions (the latter are even equated with "riddles" in v. 8); but the Lord speaks to Moses while he is in a fully conscious state. In the later development of Israel's prophetism dreams and visions become increasingly less important, and we hear only of false prophets claiming these experiences while the true servants of the Lord such as Elijah, Elisha, Isaiah, and Jeremiah enjoy what is presented here as the exclusive privilege of Moses.

Indeed, the whole setting of the Book of Numbers is the desert. I realize that the school of Wellhausen considers this merely "embellishment"; elsewhere I have stated why I cannot agree with this view (see my *Leviticus,* Introduction), and I shall therefore not cover the same ground here. Suffice it to point out that the ongoing discoveries of the ancient Near East force the proponents of the source hypothesis to acknowledge increasingly that the Book of Numbers, as well as the rest of the Pentateuch, contains much more "ancient material" than they were formerly willing to admit. Throughout the commentary I present many proofs of this; a brief summary follows here.

Wellhausen called the names of the leaders in 1:6–16, also found in chapters 2, 7, 10, deprecatingly *Dutzendnamen,* commonplace names, that followed a much more recent pattern (*Prolegomena,* 3rd ed., p. 366); it is now recognized that they have a decidedly pre-Jahwistic character and are definitely based on ancient tradition (Hommel, *Die altisraelitische Ueber-lieferung,* pp. 299ff.). The arrangement of Israel's camp and the marching order as found in chapter 2 make sense only during the wilderness period: only then was such an arrangement of the tribes (found also in ch. 7 and in 10:11–28) possible. Later, Reuben and Dan no longer had a position of leadership in Israel and Reuben no longer had contact with Simeon, nor Judah with Issachar and Zebulon.

The thinking behind the law concerning jealousy (ch. 5), which speaks of a divine judgment by means of holy water whose disintegrative power was increased by holy dust, is purely dynamistic[2] and very ancient (pre-Mosaic), as a number of parallels from primitive peoples and from the nations of antiquity show.

In 4:16 the daily offering (*tamid*), which consisted only of a burnt offering (28:3ff.) is called *minha.* This term originally referred to a gift to the deity or to someone of superior status, and in Israel's system of offerings is later used exclusively to indicate the grain offering (cf. 4:16 NIV), so that *ola* (burnt offering) and *minha* (grain offering) together encompass all the different offerings (1 Sam. 2:29; 3:14; etc.). If the *tamid* is here called *minha* it can only mean that this was written when Israel's system of offerings was still in its beginnings, i.e., during the wilderness period.

The concept expressed in 10:10 is very old: the sound of the trumpets over the burnt offerings and fellowship offerings must remind the Lord, as it were, of Israel, so that He will accept these offerings and bless Israel. This concept is unique in the entire Old Testament and dates from the time when the "forefathers lived beyond the river" (Josh. 24:2) when, in keeping with the ancient Near Eastern custom, the trumpets were blown to keep the demonic forces at a distance.

Also very old is the idea in 16:46 that the smoke of incense can protect the assembly against the effects of the "wrath" that has come upon them. This is why Moses instructs Aaron to stem the resulting "plague" by means of a cover of smoke. This illustrates the original meaning of the Hebrew *kipper* (lit. "cover"), which elsewhere means "atonement" (as the NIV translates it in 16:46).

The methods followed in the preparation of the water of cleansing (ch. 19) are undoubtedly pre-Mosaic in origin and date from a time when the

---

[2]See Publisher's Note.

forefathers served "other gods." Similar practices are still found in religions that practice magic. The same kind of thinking is also found in chapter 5 and in Leviticus 14:49–52.[3]

Finally, it is striking that the women in the Book of Numbers enjoy a much greater degree of freedom than was true in later times. This is illustrated by Miriam, who does not stand in awe even of a man like Moses (ch. 12), and by the daughters of Zelophehad, who venture to bring the question of the right of succession personally to the authorities of Israel (ch. 27). This would not have been possible in later times (cf. also the change in the position of women reflected in the difference between Deut. 5:21 and Exod. 20:17). The law in chapter 30, which deals with the validity of vows made by women, is undoubtedly a step backward in this respect.

The facts presented above force me to conclude that for the most part the contents of Numbers (even as those of Leviticus; see my *Leviticus,* Introduction) can be explained without any difficulty on the basis of the situation as it existed during Moses' time. But, again like Leviticus, Numbers also presents a number of indications that more than once after Israel settled in Canaan the need was felt to adapt the regulations from Moses' time to the new situation.

But it does not follow that we can trace this development, in spite of the impression to the contrary given by the school of Wellhausen. Although it is clear that e.g., chapters 3–4 consist of various elements that originally did not belong together, we are not in a position, given the data presently at our disposal, to trace the origin and date of these various elements with any degree of probability. Unless we acquire further data we must therefore be satisfied with the conclusion that the Book of Numbers, although it is based largely on Mosaic data, did not acquire its present form until after Moses' time, perhaps not until the time of Israel's kings.

---

[3]See Publisher's Note.

Numbers
Commentary

Part One

At Mt. Sinai
(1:1–10:10)

A comparison of 1:1 and 10:11 shows that in this section the author of the Pentateuch deals with the final days of Israel's stay at Sinai, from the first through the nineteenth day of the second month (Ziv; cf. 1 Kings 6:1; our April/May) of the second year after the Exodus. Exodus 40:34ff. states that the glory of the Lord filled the tabernacle so that its services could begin. In Leviticus the author of the Pentateuch presents a body of laws that regulate the service of the tabernacle. And in Numbers 1:1 the author takes us to the month following the descent of the "cloud" that made the tabernacle the Lord's dwelling place (Exod. 40:2, 17, 34–35). He thus places the laws of Leviticus in the preceding month, so that in Numbers 1:1 the setting up of the tabernacle and the arrangements for the service in the sanctuary have been regulated; the first topic is now the arrangement of Israel's camp, whose sanctifying center is the tabernacle (chs. 1–2), followed by the task of the Levites as the servants of the priests (chs. 3–4); their consecration is further described in 8:5–26. Several laws are found in this first section: the requirement that the camp be kept ceremonially clean (5:1–4) and three laws that are entirely unrelated to their context (5:5–6:27). Chapter 7 and 9:1–14 refer back to the dedication of the tabernacle.

The Census
(1:1–54)

1. *The Command to Count the People* (1:1–4)

1:1–4 *The LORD spoke to Moses in the Tent of Meeting in the Desert of Sinai on the first day of the second month of the second year after the Israelites came out of*

Egypt. He said: "Take a census of the whole Israelite community by their clans and families, listing every man by name, one by one. You and Aaron are to number by their divisions all the men in Israel twenty years old or more who are able to serve in the army. One man from each tribe, each the head of his family, is to help you."

The events of this chapter take us into the "Desert of Sinai," where the Israelites set up camp "in the third month after (they) left Egypt" (Exod. 19:1), i.e., two months after the night of the Passover (Exod. 12:3) and one month after the giving of manna (Exod. 16:14ff.). Israel stayed here for one full year.

In spite of the efforts of Gunkel, Gressmann, and Meyer to place Mt. Sinai east of the Arabah, i.e., the valley that stretches from the Dead Sea to the Gulf of Aqaba in northern Arabia, and of Kittel and Jirku to place Sinai in the immediate vicinity of Kadesh Barnea, I agree with others (e.g., Böhl on Exod. 3:2) that we must maintain the traditional identification of Mt. Sinai with the Jebel Katarin on the southern point of the Sinai peninsula.

"The Desert of Sinai": the rendering "desert" with all its connotations is, strictly speaking, inaccurate; it is based on the LXX, which always uses *erēmos* ("desert") for the Hebrew *midbār*. *Midbār* is the designation for a region or territory to which the flocks can be driven (*dabar*) and that is suitable for grazing. It is the type of terrain we usually call "steppe": it provides an abundance of grass during the rainy season, but dries out during the summer months since the limy subsoil does not retain any moisture. This is why we repeatedly hear of Israel's flocks and herds, and why more than one law presupposes agricultural activity. At the time of Numbers Israel was a seminomadic people.

The Lord (concerning the name Jahweh, see my commentary on Lev. 1:1) now speaks *in* the Tent of Meeting (cf. Num. 7:89; Deut. 31:14), rather than *from* it (Lev. 1:1). Moses is thus also in the Tent and receives the command to count the Israelites. Moses and Aaron, with the help of one man from each tribe (vv. 3–4) are to count only the adult males, i.e., those who are at least twenty years old and thus "able to serve in the army" (v. 3).

The purpose of this census is not stated. It has been suggested that it had a military purpose, and the census is then related to Moses' expectation of an imminent invasion of southern Canaan (e.g., P. Heinisch, *Numeri,* p. 19). This view is based on the verb *paqad* ("number, muster"), the age limit of those who are to be counted, and especially on the words in verse 3, "who are able to serve in the army" and "by their divisions." But Exodus 30:14, where we find both *paqad* and the minimum age limit, proves that this view is incorrect. There the men are counted in connection with the atonement money that is from that day on to pay for the daily offerings of the community. Since Exodus 30 does not state that the census was carried out, it makes sense to assume that the census of Numbers 1 is the implementation of Exodus 30:14. This is also indicated by the fact that Exodus 38:26, which states what those who were "numbered in the census" (RSV) each had to contribute to the building of the sanctuary, gives the same grand total as Numbers 1 and therefore refers to the census of Numbers 1. Only then can we understand why Aaron played a role in the actual census (v. 3; cf. also the plural in vv. 2, 4–5, 18), which would not make sense if the census had a purely military purpose. See also chapter 26.

The census did use, of course, an existing pattern, i.e., the pattern of military organization. This is why verse 3 says, "to number by their divisions all . . . who are able to serve in the army." This does not imply that verse 3 (in contrast to verse 2, which calls for a counting of all men) speaks of a military mustering of all those who are twenty years old or more. Nor does verse 3 provide a basis for Edelkoort's supposition (*Numeri*, p. 90) that chapter 1 originally described a census that was later "made into" a military mustering. In verses 20–46 the expressions used in verses 2–3 are found side by side.

2. *The Assisting Family Heads* (1:5–16)

1:5–16 *"These are the names of the men who are to assist you:*
    from Reuben, Elizur son of Shedeur;
    from Simeon, Shelumiel son of Zurishaddai;
    from Judah, Nahshon son of Amminadab;
    from Issachar, Nethanel son of Zuar;
    from Zebulun, Eliab son of Helon;
    from the sons of Joseph:
      from Ephraim, Elishama son of Ammihud;
      from Manasseh, Gamaliel son of Pedahzur;
    from Benjamin, Abidan son of Gideoni;
    from Dan, Ahiezer son of Ammishaddai;
    from Asher, Pagiel son of Ocran;
    from Gad, Eliasaph son of Deuel;
    from Naphtali, Ahira son of Enan."
These were the men appointed from the community, the leaders of their ancestral tribes. They were the heads of the clans of Israel.

Here the names are given of the family heads who are to help Moses and Aaron with the census; the same names are found in chapters 2, 7, and 10:11–28. The list of leaders in 13:2 contains different names. This indicates, in my opinion, that "leader" (*nasi'*, lit. "one lifted up," v. 16) refers to the head of a family or clan rather than to a "prince" (v. 16 KJV) or "ruler." This is also indicated by the fact that in 3:32 Eleazar is called literally "the ruler of the rulers" (NIV: "the chief leader") of the tribe of Levi. The order of the tribes is not always the same. In 1:5–16 Leah's children come first, followed by those of Rachel, while Zilpah's sons (Asher and Gad) are placed between those of Bilhah (Dan and Naphtali); the reverse is true in Genesis 49 and Deuteronomy 33 (where Simeon has already been absorbed into Judah): there Bilhah's sons are placed between Zilpah's two sons. The reason for this arrangement is not clear to me, especially since in verses 20–46 Gad is placed after Simeon, which is also the case in chapters 2, 7, 26, and in 10:11–28. See also the commentary on 13:4–16a.

Not one of the names of these leaders contains the name Jahweh. They do, however, contain the usual names for the deity also found elsewhere in the Semitic world: *el* (god), *abi* (father), *ahi* (brother), *šur* (rock). It is even possible that the name of Naphtali's leader, Ahira, contains the name of the Egyptian sungod *Re* or *Ra*. The vocalization of the second part of the names Zurishaddai and Ammishaddai could suggest that we find at least in those names the purely Israelite name of God, *Shaddai*. But we must seriously consider the possibility that this is a later vocalization that replaces *šadu*, which brings to mind *šadu rabu* ("great mountain"), an epithet of the ancient Babylonian chief god Enlil (see J. Hehn, *Die biblische und babylonische Gottesidee,* 1913, pp. 267f.). Be this as it may, the names of these leaders are the same as, or related to, ancient Babylonian names such as Ilisami'a, Iliyada'a, Abi'ali, Ahikariba, Ammiamara, Amminadbi, Mardukshadua, Sinshaduni, etc. This places Wellhausen's assertion that these names do not in any way resemble genuine ancient proper names (*Prolegomena,* 3rd ed., p. 371) in a strange light. Although these names are rarely found elsewhere in the Old Testament, there is no doubt as to their being genuine (see further F. Hommel, *Die altisraelitische Ueberlieferung,* 1897, pp. 299ff.; H. Ranke, *Early Babylonian Personal Names,* 1905).

3. *The Census* (1:17–19)

1:17–19 *Moses and Aaron took these men whose names had been given, and they called the whole community together on the first day of the second month. The people indicated their ancestry by their clans and families, and the men twenty years old or more were listed by name, one by one, as the LORD commanded Moses. And so he counted them in the Desert of Sinai.*

With the help of these leaders Moses and Aaron now call together the whole "community" (*ēda*) in order to carry out the command of verse 2.

Due to a lack of data we are not sure of the exact meaning of the term "community" (see my commentary on Lev. 4:13–21). In 27:21 it is distinguished from "all the children of Israel" (KJV). Perhaps it refers to the legal representatives of the tribes and of the tribal subdivisions, called "clans and families" in verses 2 and 18. Their assistance then would facilitate the gathering of the census data.

4. *The Results of the Census* (1:20–46)

1:20–46 *From the descendants of Reuben the firstborn son of Israel:*
All the men twenty years old or more who were able to serve in the army were listed by name, one by one, according to the records of their clans and families. The number from the tribe of Reuben was 46,500.

From the descendants of Simeon:
All the men twenty years old or more who were able to serve in the army were counted and listed by name, one by one, according to the records of their clans and families. The number from the tribe of Simeon was 59,300.

From the descendants of Gad:
All the men twenty years old or more who were able to serve in the army were listed by name, according to the records of their clans and families. The number from the tribe of Gad was 45,650.

From the descendants of Judah:
All the men twenty years old or more who were able to serve in the army were listed by name, according to the records of their clans and families. The number from the tribe of Judah was 74,600.

From the descendants of Issachar:
All the men twenty years old or more who were able to serve in the army were listed by name, according to the records of their clans and families. The number from the tribes of Issachar was 54,400.

From the descendants of Zebulun:
All the men twenty years old or more who were able to serve in the army were listed by name, according to the records of their clans and families. The number from the tribe of Zebulun was 57,400.

From the sons of Joseph:
From the descendants of Ephraim:
All the men twenty years old or more who were able to serve in the army were listed by name, according to the records of their clans and families. The number from the tribe of Ephraim was 40,500.

From the descendants of Manasseh:
All the men twenty years old or more who were able to serve in the army were listed by name, according to the records of their clans and families. The number from the tribe of Manasseh was 32,200.

From the descendants of Benjamin:
 All the men twenty years old or more who were able to serve in the army were listed by name, according to the records of their clans and families. The number from the tribe of Benjamin was 35,400.

From the descendants of Dan:
 All the men twenty years old or more who were able to serve in the army were listed by name, according to the records of their clans and families. The number from the tribe of Dan was 62,700.

From the descendants of Asher:
 All the men twenty years old or more who were able to serve in the army were listed by name, according to the records of their clans and families. The number from the tribe of Asher was 41,500.

From the descendants of Naphtali:
 All the men twenty years old or more who were able to serve in the army were listed by name, according to the records of their clans and families. The number from the tribe of Naphtali was 53,400.

These were the men counted by Moses and Aaron and the twelve leaders of Israel, each one representing his family. All the Israelites twenty years old or more who were able to serve in Israel's army were counted according to their families. The total number was 603,550.

As stated above, in verses 20–46 the tribes are listed in the same order as in verses 6–15, with the exception of Gad, who here occupies the third instead of the eleventh position, immediately after Simeon. The LXX places Gad again after Asher, but this is probably an "emendation."

With great precision and with constant repetition of the same expressions, as is customary in an official document (cf. ch. 7), the total number of men twenty years of age and older in the various tribes is given. When these numbers are added up their total comes to 603,550, at least if we follow the LXX and translate *'elef* as "thousand." This same total is also found in 2:32 and in Exodus 38:26 (see above). The 22,000 male Levites should be added to this according to 3:39. Similar numbers are also found elsewhere when *'elef* is taken to mean "thousand." Exodus 12:37 then speaks of "about six hundred thousand men on foot, besides the little ones" (small male children? NIV: "women and children"). Numbers 11:21 also speaks of "six hundred thousand men on foot"; but this does not include the whole nation according to our Western way of figuring. In Israel "the people" consists only of the men (cf. Edelkoort, *Numeri*, p. 91; J. Pedersen, *Israel*, 1926, p. 56). These figures thus all agree. The total of the second census (26:51) is 601,730 men, again assuming that *'elef* means "thousand."

But statements such as Exodus 23:29–30 and Deuteronomy 7:22 (where we hear of the necessity of driving out the inhabitants of Canaan gradually, since otherwise the land would lie fallow and the wild animals would "multiply around you," i.e., there would not be enough people left to cultivate the land) suggest a much smaller total than follows from the figure of around 600,000 men twenty years of age and over. Based on this figure the total number of Israelites (men, women, and children) would have been around three million (according to others five million), while the land west of the Jordan only had about 1.5 million inhabitants in 1940. Also, how do we then explain a statement such as Deuteronomy 7:7 where Israel is said to be "the fewest of all peoples"?

Furthermore, Israel's fear of the Philistines and Canaanites, expressed in Exodus 13:17; Numbers 14:1ff.; and Joshua 7:5 would not be easy to understand if they did indeed consist of several million souls. And the battle with Amalek (Exod. 17:8ff.) with its prolonged uncertainty as to the final outcome does not suggest that Israel was already capable of raising 600,000 armed men at that time.

It is also certain that the Sinai peninsula (which I take here to include the area up to the line from El-Arish to the Dead Sea) consists largely of mountainous wilderness areas and steppe, so that in 1917 its total population was about ten thousand. Apart from the availability of space, it certainly could not have fed several million people (cf. Exod. 16:3–4). Even the oases of Kadesh Barnea have neither sufficient room nor food for that many people.

Finally, it is difficult to comprehend how several million people with all their livestock (Exod. 12:38; 17:3; 19:13; 34:3; Num. 14:33; 32:1) could have crossed the Red Sea in one night (Exod. 14:21ff.), or how Moses could even consider being the sole judge for such a large number of people (Exod. 18:16).

The school of Wellhausen declared these numbers to be the product of the imagination of authors who lived long afterward, an attempt to present the past in as glorious a light as possible. But apart from the view of the Scriptures on which this assumption is based, it fails to explain the unanimity of Israel's testimony and also the curious fact that in the list in Numbers 1 Ephraim and Manasseh, the strongest tribes of the northern kingdom, are the smallest while Simeon, which was soon absorbed into Judah and is no longer mentioned in Deuteronomy 33, is here the third-largest of Israel's tribes; also, Dan, which was allotted a small territory (Josh. 19:40–46) and had serious problems during the period of the judges (Judg. 18) is second only to Judah in numbers here. We find something similar in the list in Numbers 26. There Benjamin, the smallest tribe in the days of Saul (1 Sam. 9:21) and an appendage of Judah in the time of the kings, is only slightly smaller than Judah, while Ephraim and Simeon (the third-largest tribe in Num. 1) are the two smallest tribes. If Wellhausen was correct, the numbers in chapter 1 and chapter 26 would not differ to such an extent. The list in chapter 26, when compared with the list in chapter 1, shows a numerical decline for the tribes of Simeon (37,100!), Ephraim and Naphtali (8,000 each), Gad (5,150), and Reuben (2,770), while the other seven tribes show various degrees of growth: Manasseh (20,500!), Asher (11,900), Benjamin (10,200), Issachar (9,900), Zebulon (3,100), Judah (1,900), and Dan (1,700).

It is not surprising that, given these facts, the conviction is growing that it is not very possible to consider these figures the invention of a later generation; "the construction is much too complicated for this" (Edel-koort, *Numeri,* p. 91). Böhl (*Exodus,* p. 123) suspects that the figure 603,550 is based on a purely artificial calculation, the product of gematria, i.e., calculations based on the numerical value of the letters of a word or of a series of words, in this case of the words *r˘ōs kŏl 'adat benē yisra'el,* "the number of the whole community of the children of Israel" (v. 2). It is true that the numerical value of *benē yisra'el* is 603, and of *rŏ'š kŏl* (without the *'alef*!) is 550. Unfortunately, 603,550 is supposed to be the numerical value of the whole set of words, not of a part of it; the value must be increased by 474 if the whole phrase is counted. It is also unfortunate (for Böhl's view) that gematria is of relatively recent origin, dating from the Hellenistic period when the Hebrew letters were used to indicate numbers. And finally, even if Böhl were correct, he would only have explained the total in Numbers 1, but not those in chapter 26, Exodus 12:37, and Numbers 11:21.

Attempts have been made from a Bible-believing perspective to resolve the problem presented by the size of Israel as given in Exodus and Numbers. Keil used various considerations and calculations, while e.g. Gispen (on Exod. 12:37) tries to resolve the problem by stating that "ancient history mentions other migrations of enormous numbers of people and movements of large armies, and we have no reason to doubt the accuracy of those reports." Yet this is not the point. The only question of importance is whether the rest of the scriptural data concerning the numerical strength of Israel in the Mosaic and post-Mosaic period do indeed point to a nation of several million people as Numbers 1 and 26 seem to indicate.

The problem hinges on the question whether we are to follow the LXX when it translates *'elef* as *chilias* ("thousand"). I am convinced that this is not the case. In several instances in the Old Testament *'elef* refers without question to a tribal division, similar to the Scottish "clan," which can of course vary greatly as to its numerical strength. I refer to Numbers 1:16;

10:4; Joshua 22:21, 30; Judges 6:15; 1 Samuel 10:19 (cf. v. 21); 23:23; Micah 5:2; and perhaps also Isaiah 60:22. The head of such an *'elef* was the *'alluf* (Zech. 9:7; 12:5). *'Elef* in the sense of "clan" is also found on tablet 2 from Ras Shamra as *'elp*. There is no question that the translators of the LXX did know this meaning of *'elef;* in 1 Samuel 10:19 they render it "tribe."

But there is more. Quite a few statements in the Old Testament present us with impossibilities if we insist on translating *'elef* as meaning "thousand." In my commentaries on the Books of Chronicles I have given several proofs of this (see my commentary on 1 Chron. 21:4–6; 2 Chron. 11:1; 13:3; 14:8; 17:14–18; 25:5–6; 26:12–13; 28:6, 8). Similar cases are also found in the other historical books of the Old Testament. Thus, in Judges 20:21, 25 we read (if we maintain that *'elef* means "thousand") that 22,000 + 18,000 Israelites fell; verse 35 of that same chapter speaks of 25,100 Benjamites who were struck down, and that while Benjamin occupied a mountainous region of approximately 2,000 km² (770 sq. mi.): twelve men fell per square kilometer (32 men per sq. mi.) in one day! I also refer to 1 Samuel 4:2, 10; 13:5; 2 Samuel 8:5; 10:6, 18; 24:9; 1 Kings 20:30; many more instances could be added.

These two facts (*'elef* meaning "clan" elsewhere and the impossibility of translating "thousand" consistently) led Flinders Petrie (*Egypt and Israel,* 1923, pp. 40ff.) to attempt to prove that *'elef* in Numbers 1 and 26 indicates a family living in the same tent. Thus, Numbers 1:35 reads "the number from the tribe of Manasseh was 32 *'elef* and 200," which would then mean that Manasseh had thirty-two tents in which two hundred people lived, which comes to an average of six people per tent: father, mother, and four children. And when in verse 25 it is said of Gad that there were 45 *'elef* and 650 this means an average of fourteen people per tent, which would allow for grandparents and shepherds or for members of the non-Israelite groups of Exodus 12:38. In chapter 1 the total number of Israelites (without the Levites) would be 5,550, living in 598 tents; the total in chapter 26 would be 5,700 people in 596 tents.

But Flinders Petrie overlooked several things. In the first place, in each of the tribal totals the hundreds are connected with the *'elef* numbers by the conjunction "and," which means that they should be added together. Second, the figures in Numbers 1 and 26 explicitly refer only to "all the men in Israel twenty years old or more" (1:2–3; 26:2). And finally, both 1 Samuel 10:19, 21 and tablet 2 from Ras Shamra show that *'elef* could never be limited to the occupants of a tent. The following illustration shows that Flinders Petrie's argument leads to rather distorted explanations. Numbers 16:49 states that 14 *'elef* and 700 died from the "plague." This then would mean 14 tents with 700 occupants. But since this would mean fifty people per tent he gives the following explanation of Numbers 16:49: fourteen families died, a total of about 130 persons, as well as 750 members of other families. This is obviously an arbitrary explanation.

The counting of the Levites (Num. 3) presents an even greater problem for him. Here he finds 7 *'elef* 500, 8 *'elef* 600, and 6 *'elef* 200. This would mean 7 tents with 500 persons, 8 with 600, and 6 with 200, i.e., an average of 71, 75, and 33 occupants per tent. And what about the number of firstborn males: 22 *'elef* 273 (3:43)? Flinders Petrie therefore puts the counting of the Levites in the time of the judges when the 5,550 Israelites who according to him wandered in the wilderness had grown to 300,000.

I cannot agree with his solution. We must take *'elef* in the sense of "clan" or "family" as our starting point rather than the meaning "tent," for which there is no proof. We must also remember that in case of war not only was one's own clan called up, but the help of neighboring clans was also enlisted, so that the army consisted of several "clans" (*'alafim*); cf. Judges 6:34–35; 12:2. Not until the time of the kings did something like a standing army develop with the royal guard as its nucleus (1 Samuel 14:52; 2 Sam. 10:7); its commanders were the "mighty men" or the "Thirty" (2 Samuel 23:8, 18 NIV margin; 1 Kings 1:8). And as the expansion under Solomon forced the tribal organization into the background and replaced it with a division into regions, each headed by a district governor (1 Kings 4:7–19), the meaning of *'elef* changed and became a fixed number, similar to our terms "batallion" and "company." Thus we find besides "commanders of hundreds" (2 Kings 11:19) as "army officers" (2 Kings 25:23) also "heads of *'alafim*," not in its old sense of "heads of clans" of Israel (Num. 1:16; 10:4; Josh. 22:21, 30) or of Manasseh (1 Chron. 12:20), whose function had been primarily social (Exod. 18:21, 25; Deut. 1:15; 1 Sam. 8:12; 22:7; 1 Chron. 26:26; 27:1), but in the sense of "commanders" of the *'alafim*. The *'elef* thus solidified over the centuries into our concept "thousand" (Num. 31:14, 48, 52, 54; 2 Sam. 18:1; and especially in Chronicles: 1 Chron. 13:1; 15:25; 28:1; 29:6; 2 Chron. 1:2; 25:5). In exactly the same way did the German *Sippen* of the days of Frederic the Great (in which the women were included) develop into *Hundertschaften* and *Tausendschaften,* organized bodies of one hundred and one thousand men respectively. Similarly, the concepts "detachment," "company," and "battalion" did not come to represent fixed numbers of soldiers until Napoleon's time.

We must conclude, therefore, that we cannot translate *'elef* simply as "thousand." We can no longer determine how large the ancient *'elef* was, and thus can only represent it by "*x*." According to the census of Numbers 1

Israel did not have 603,550 men (not counting Levi) twenty years of age and older, but 603 x x + 550, and according to the census of Numbers 26, 601 x x + 730 men in that age bracket.[1]

5. *The Levites Not Counted* (1:47–54)

1:47–54 *The families of the tribe of Levi, however, were not counted along with the others. The LORD had said to Moses: "You must not count the tribe of Levi or include them in the census of the other Israelites. Instead, appoint the Levites to be in charge of the tabernacle of the Testimony—over all its furnishings and everything belonging to it. They are to carry the tabernacle and all its furnishings; they are to take care of it and encamp around it. Whenever the tabernacle is to move, the Levites are to take it down, and whenever the tabernacle is to be set up, the Levites shall do it. Anyone else who goes near it shall be put to death. The Israelites are to set up their tents by divisions, each man in his own camp under his own standard. The Levites, however, are to set up their tents around the tabernacle of the Testimony so that wrath will not fall on the Israelite community. The Levites are to be responsible for the care of the tabernacle of the Testimony."*
The Israelites did all this just as the LORD commanded Moses.

The Levites are not to be included in the census. In verses 19–46 "the descendants of Levi" are omitted, and here the reason is given: the Levites

---

[1] Another solution has been proposed by George E. Mendenhall (*Journal of Biblical Literature,* 1958): "The census lists . . . consist of an enumeration of the number of units (*'alafim*) into which each tribe is subdivided, and following that, the total number of men to be levied from each tribe" (p. 66).

An unavoidable implication of any solution based on a meaning of *'elef* other than "thousand" is that the grand totals in Numbers 1:46; 2:32; 26:51 (and in Exod. 38:24–28) are inaccurate and were added at a later time when the original meaning of *'elef* was no longer current. If *'elef* does not mean "thousand," then the *'alafim* and the hundreds in the census lists should be added separately, which gives a total of 598 *'elef* and 5,550 in Numbers 1; this can be converted to 603 *'elef* and 550 only if *'elef* equals one thousand (or if *me'ot* is assumed to refer to a subunit of the *'elef* rather than meaning "hundred"; but even then the *me'ot* would have to be one-tenth of the *'elef* for the totals to be correct).

This conversion problem becomes even more acute in Exodus 38:25–32. The total number of Israelites is the same as in Numbers 1 (603,550). Each of these gives one-half shekel "atonement money," which comes to a total of 301,775 shekels, or 100 talents and 1,775 (1 *'elef* and 775) shekels. If *'elef* is indeed less than 1,000, then the talent must have contained fewer than 3,000 shekels; this is extremely unlikely, since in the ancient Near East the talent in some societies contained more, but never fewer than 3,000 shekels.

Also, if *'elef* is indeed a number smaller than 1,000, it would appear that it was larger than 750. According to 4:36 the total number of Kohathites was 2 *'elef* and 750. If the *'elef* consisted of fewer than 750 individuals one or more *'alafim* could have been subtracted from the 750 and added to the 2 *'elef*. If *'elef* were 751, then the total number of Israelites would only be reduced by about 25 percent to 453,266. If the arguments against the original number of Israelites (603,550) are valid, they would still apply to the reduced figure (tr).

occupy a unique position in Israel because they are to be "in charge of the tabernacle" as explained in verse 50 and in more detail in chapter 3. It is incorrect to claim, as Edelkoort does, that the Levites were not included in verses 19–46 because the census had a military purpose, and that these verses were added when the census had become a military mustering. The census, as we have seen, was related to the atonement money that was to be offered by Israel. Those in charge of the tabernacle were, of course, exempt from this: according to verse 52 they do not belong to "the Israelites" (lit. "the sons of Israel"); cf. also 2:32f.; 3:11–13.

The reason, then, for not counting the Levites is that they are in charge of the tabernacle. They must take care of moving the sanctuary (v. 51) and they are to guard it (vv. 50b, 53). The latter has a dual purpose: first, to protect the tabernacle from profanation by "unauthorized" persons, which would result in death for the offender; and second, to protect the people against the dangers that could result from a failure to respect the sacred—if this were to happen "wrath" (*qesef*) would fall on the whole community (v. 53b), which would mean destruction and death (cf. 17:13; 18:5; Josh. 9:20; 22:20). The Lord wants His holiness to be respected. Israel must be deeply aware of the fact that the dwelling of the holy God in the midst of His people brings its own unique dangers with it. See also commentary on chapter 3.

The Arrangement of the Camp and the Marching Order (2:1–34)

2:1–34 *The LORD said to Moses and Aaron: "The Israelites are to camp around the Tent of Meeting some distance from it, each man under his standard with the banners of his family."*

On the east, toward the sunrise, the divisions of the camp of Judah are to encamp under their standard. The leader of the people of Judah is Nahshon son of Amminadab. His division numbers 74,600.

The tribe of Issachar will camp next to them. The leader of the people of Issachar is Nethanel son of Zuar. His division numbers 54,400.

The tribe of Zebulun will be next. The leader of the people of Zebulun is Eliab son of Helon. His division numbers 57,400.

All the men assigned to the camp of Judah, according to their divisions, number 186,400. They will set out first.

On the south will be the divisions of the camp of Reuben under their standard. The leader of the people of Reuben is Elizur son of Shedeur. His division numbers 46,500.

The tribe of Simeon will camp next to them. The leader of the people of Simeon is Shelumiel son of Zurishaddai. His division numbers 59,300.

The tribe of Gad will be next. The leader of the people of Gad is Eliasaph son of Deuel. His division numbers 45,650.

All the men assigned to the camp of Reuben, according to their divisions, number 151,450. They will set out second.

Then the Tent of Meeting and the camp of the Levites will set out in the middle of the camps. They will set out in the same order as they encamp, each in his own place under his standard.

On the west will be the divisions of the camp of Ephraim under their standard. The leader of the people of Ephraim is Elishama son of Ammihud. His division numbers 40,500.

The tribe of Manasseh will be next to them. The leader of the people of Manasseh is Gamaliel son of Pedahzur. His division numbers 32,200.

The tribe of Benjamin will be next. The leader of the people of Benjamin is Abidan son of Gideoni. His division numbers 35,400.

All the men assigned to the camp of Ephraim, according to their divisions, number 108,100. They will set out third.

On the north will be the divisions of the camp of Dan, under their standard. The leader of the people of Dan is Ahiezer son of Ammishaddai. His division numbers 62,700.

The tribe of Asher will camp next to them. The leader of the people of Asher is Pagiel son of Ocran. His division numbers 41,500.

The tribe of Naphtali will be next. The leader of the people of Naphtali is Ahira son of Enan. His division numbers 53,400.

All the men assigned to the camp of Dan number 157,600. They will set out last, under their standards.

These are the Israelites, counted according to their families. All those in the camps, by their divisions, number 603,550. The Levites, however, were not counted along with the other Israelites, as the LORD commanded Moses.

So the Israelites did everything the LORD commanded Moses; that is the way they encamped under their standards, and that is the way they set out, each with his clan and family.

Here we find the description of the manner in which Israel was to set up camp and of the order in which they were to travel during the wilderness journey. This regulation is based on a command from the Lord (v. 2) since in Israel, which is henceforth to live and act as "the LORD's people," nothing is to be left to human caprice or arbitrariness. Because this section, unlike chapter 1, has a military purpose, I prefer to translate *paqad* here as "muster" rather than "number"; thus, e.g., verse 4 reads, "His division, that is, those who were mustered thereof, were 74,600."

Of course, this command was not given in its present form. Neither the number of those of who were mustered nor the names of the leaders is appropriate in a general regulation like this. They were added later, when these arrangements had been established by many years of actual use. This

29

follows not only from verses 32–34, but also from the structure of the whole chapter. I prefer therefore to translate the references to the numbers and the leaders in the past tense, rather than in the present tense; thus, e.g., verses 3–4: "On the east, toward the sunrise, the divisions of the camp of Judah are to encamp under their standard. The leader of the people of Judah *was* Nahshon son of Amminadab. His division *numbered* 74,600."

These regulations also make it clear that the only reason for Israel's existence lies in the Lord's service that now, after Sinai, acquires its cultic form. This is why the Tent of Meeting, which was entrusted to the care of the Lord's servants, the Levites, is the dominant center both when Israel is encamped and when it marches. Two groups of three tribes each are to precede the Tent and two groups of three tribes each are to follow it when Israel is on the move; in the camp three tribes are to set up camp on each of its four sides. Of course, we do not have to take this arrangement of the camp in an absolute sense. The terrain and especially the availability of water had to be taken into consideration. This is also implied in "some distance from it" in verse 2. And it was of course very important that when Israel stayed in one place for a longer period of time the various camps were not set up too close together in view of their large herds and flocks (Exod. 12:38; 17:3; 19:13; 34:3; Num. 3:41; 20:4, 8, 19; 32:1). But on the other hand, the distance between the tribes should not be too great, especially since an attack by some Bedouin tribe was always a possibility as the experience at Rephidim shows (Exod. 17:8–13).

The order of the tribes in chapter 2 is the same as in chapter 1, except that the first group of three in chapter 1 (Reuben, Simeon, Gad) takes second place in chapter 2 after Judah, Issachar, and Zebulon. This is in line with Genesis 49:8ff. where Judah is clearly designated as the one who inherits the promise; for that same reason Judah must camp east of the tabernacle to protect the entrance of the sanctuary, which faced east.

Each group had its own standard; each tribe and each family could be identified by its own banner. The rabbis had already lost the knowledge of what these standards and banners looked like; they thought of twelve pieces of cloth, each in the color of one of the twelve precious stones that decorated the breastpiece of the high priest (Exod. 28:17–21). Isaiah 11:10, 12 also refer to such banners. The Egyptians also had banners: the pharaoh had his own standard, as did his larger and smaller military units. The Egyptian banners were carried by officers and each consisted of a pole with a symbol or representation of one of the various gods. Assyrian and Babylonian sculptures also show such banners (see Gressmann, *Altorientalische Texte und Bilder,* 2nd ed., plates CCXV No. 537f., CCXIX No. 548).

It is striking that besides Judah and Ephraim, both of whom occupied a position of leadership throughout Israel's history, Reuben and Dan are also among the leaders of the four groups of three tribes. Reuben's prominence was soon overshadowed by that of Dan in the Transjordan region (Deut. 33:6; Judg. 5:16; cf. also Num. 32:2 KJV, "Gad and Reuben"), and the tribe was relegated to a forgotten existence (see commentary on ch. 32). Dan was put under so much pressure by the Amorites from the Gibeonite league of cities and by the Philistines who bore down on them from the west that part of the tribe was forced to resettle elsewhere (Judg. 1:34–35; 18:1ff.).

The composition of the various groups is also interesting. Reuben is grouped together with Simeon, with which it had no contact at all after the conquest. Similarly, Judah lost all contact with Issachar and Zebulon, and the combination of Dan, Asher, and Naphtali is also remarkable.

All this points to the fact that we do not have a later tradition here. During the period of the kings no one would have come up with a grouping like this; it makes sense only during Israel's wilderness journey.

Attempts have been made to establish parallels between the arrangement of Israel's camp and that of Egyptian army camps. This is right only to the extent that the royal tent stands in the center of the camp. But while in the Egyptian camp the officers' tents are placed around the royal tent for protection (see Erman-Ranke, *Aegypten,* pp. 635f.), the Tent of Israel's king is protected by the tribes camped around it.

Verse 17 states that the marching order is to be the same as the camping order, i.e., Judah's group first, followed by Reuben's group. Then follow the Levites with the tabernacle, while the groups of Ephraim and Dan bring up the rear. But in 10:17, 21 we are told that on the journey from Sinai to Kadesh Judah went first, then the tabernacle was taken down and the Gershonites and the Merarites with the tabernacle joined Judah, while the Kohathites took the "holy things" (KJV: "sanctuary") after Reuben had left, and Ephraim and Dan again come last. It has been suggested that this is a different tradition, but this is in my opinion incorrect (see commentary on 10:17). Verses 32–34 finally summarize the contents of chapters 1 and 2, which are thus a unit.

The Levites
(3:1–4:49)

Chapters 3 and 4 describe how the command given in 1:48–54 was carried out. As we shall see, these chapters are rather obviously composed of a number of separate sections that originally did not belong together but were arranged into a unit by the repeated formula "the LORD said to Moses (and Aaron)'' (3:5, 11, 14, 44; 4:1, 17, 21; cf. also 3:40). The purpose of this arrangement is to present a clear picture of the task of the Levites to be performed at the Tent of Meeting under the supervision of the priestly family of Aaron during the wilderness journey. Repetitions were unavoidable as evidenced by, e.g., 3:18, 21; 3:20, 33; 3:41, 45. Cf. also 4:4–15, 24–28, 31–33 with 3:31; 3:25–26; 3:36–37.

1. *Aaron's Sons* (3:1–4)

3:1–4 *This is the account of the family of Aaron and Moses at the time the L*ORD *talked with Moses on Mount Sinai.*

*The names of the sons of Aaron were Nadab the firstborn and Abihu, Eleazar and Ithamar. Those were the names of Aaron's sons, the anointed priests, who were ordained to serve as priests. Nadab and Abihu, however, fell dead before the L*ORD *when they made an offering with unauthorized fire before him in the Desert of Sinai. They had no sons; so only Eleazar and Ithamar served as priests during the lifetime of their father Aaron.*

Since the Levites were to assist the Aaronic family this section begins with the latter. The introduction (cf. vv. 1 and 2) proves that this section was not written by one author. The first superscription, ''This is the account of the family of'' (lit. ''And these are the generations of'') is the same formula that is also found no fewer than ten times in Genesis; Genesis 2:4 shows that it introduces not merely a given genealogy (Gen. 5:1; 10:1; 11:10; 25:12; 36:1; also Ruth 4:18; 1 Chron. 1:29), but emphasizes the history of those listed. These verses therefore were originally the beginning of a larger whole, a history of the priests. Here reference is made only to the premature death of Aaron's eldest sons, Nadab and Abihu (Lev. 10:1–5) and to the fact that they did not have any sons, explaining why the Aaronites consisted of only two families. Attention is also drawn to the fact that Eleazar and Ithamar performed priestly functions already during their father's lifetime. In verse 3 they are called ''anointed priests,'' which is not entirely clear. In Leviticus 4:3, 5, 16 only the high priest is called ''the anointed priest,'' and Exodus 29:7 and Leviticus 8:12 mention only the anointing of Aaron; on the other hand, Exodus 28:41; 30:30; 40:15 indicate that Aaron's sons were also anointed. Böhl (*Exodus,* p. 177) assumes that ''initially only the high priest was considered worthy of this royal honor, which was later claimed also by the other priests.'' Edelkoort (*Numeri,* p. 93), on the other hand, considers it probable that originally all priests were anointed, ''but after the fall of the kingdom this privilege was accorded only the high priest who in more than one respect assumed the position of the king.'' In other words, Edelkoort's view is the opposite of

Böhl's. As I explained in my commentary on Leviticus 8:10–13, I believe that while each new high priest, like each new king, was anointed, this was not true of the ordinary priests; they were apparently considered to be anointed in the high priest—they "shared in his anointing."

2. *The Levites to Be Subordinate to the Priests* (3:5–13)

3:5–13 *The Lord said to Moses, "Bring the tribe of Levi and present them to Aaron the priest to assist him. They are to perform duties for him and for the whole community at the Tent of Meeting by doing the work of the tabernacle. They are to take care of all the furnishings of the Tent of Meeting, fulfilling the obligations of the Israelites by doing the work of the tabernacle. Give the Levites to Aaron and his sons; they are the Israelites who are to be given wholly to him. Appoint Aaron and his sons to serve as priests; anyone else who approaches the sanctuary must be put to death."*

The Lord also said to Moses, "I have taken the Levites from among the Israelites in place of the first male offspring of every Israelite woman. The Levites are mine, for all the firstborn are mine. When I struck down all the firstborn in Egypt, I set apart for myself every firstborn in Israel, whether man or animal. They are to be mine. I am the Lord."

After the introductory verses, verses 5–13 describe the relationship between the Levites and the Lord's priests, the Aaronic family. Verse 6 states that the Levites are to "assist" (lit. "serve"; kjv: "minister unto") Aaron, i.e., the high priest in whom all the priests are included; hence the phrase "Aaron and his sons" in verse 9; 8:19; 18:6–7. The Levites are "given" to the priests "to do the service of the children of Israel in the tabernacle" (8:19 kjv; cf. also 16:9). In verse 6 they are called "the tribe of Levi" (cf. 1:49) and in verse 15 literally "the children of Levi" (kjv; also in verse 17; 4:2). Elsewhere they are referred to as "the Levites" (3:9, 12, 20, 32, 39, 41, 45–46; 4:18, 46; also in 1:47, 50–51, 53). The Aaronites and Moses were also from the tribe of Levi (Exod. 2:1; 6:20), so strictly speaking the name "Levites" is not entirely accurate, since one cannot say that the tribe as a whole is to serve the priestly family that itself belongs to the tribe. But the use of "the tribe of Levi" and "the children of Levi" in referring to the assistants of the priests is understandable since with the sole exception of the Aaronic family the entire tribe did serve in that capacity. Thus, the Lord can speak to Aaron of "your fellow Levites" (18:2). The word "Levite" thus became an official title for the assistants who were given to the priests when we hear, e.g., of the cities of the Levites (Lev. 25:32f.; Num. 35:4, 6–8) or of the command to Israel to take care of the Levites (Deut. 12:12, 18f.; 16:11) who did not receive an inheritance (Josh. 14:3f.;

18:7). Cf. also Numbers 18:24; Judges 17:7, 13; Ezekiel 44:10 (but see 44:15: "the Levites, descendants of Zadok"), 45:5; 48:11; and various references in Chronicles.

The school of Wellhausen claimed that the Levites were not a tribe but rather an order of priests, founded by Moses and Aaron (Moses is then turned into an Ephraimite!); the name Levite then became the official title of the servants of the priests of Jerusalem when, after Josiah's reformation, the local sanctuaries were disbanded and their priests were made subservient to the priesthood of Jerusalem, which claimed the exclusive title of "Aaronites." This was then sanctioned by Ezekiel 44:6ff. and systematically worked out in the so-called Priestly Codex.

The first claim is in direct contradiction to the Old Testament data and does not deserve a rebuttal. The second one does not do justice to either Ezekiel or 2 Kings 23. Ezekiel 44:6ff. eliminates the established distinction between "priests" and "Levites" and recognizes only the Zadokite priests as Levites, as does 43:13 (see my commentary on Ezek. 43:19 and 44:9–16). And in 40:55ff. Ezekiel refers both to those who serve "at the altar" and those who take care of "the house" as priests; we find something similar in 2 Kings 12:9; 22:4; 25:18, where the doorkeepers are called "priests." And while 2 Kings 23 does speak of the destruction of the local sanctuaries and of the transfer of their priests to Jerusalem, verse 9, which is often quoted as proof for the supposition that the latter became the servants of the priests in Jerusalem, does not in fact say this. Actually, the temple of Jerusalem was too much involved in the general degeneration for its priests to consider themselves superior to the priests of the other sanctuaries; nor would Josiah have supported them in this idea, which would ultimately have jeopardized his reformation. I maintain, therefore, that the distinction between priests and Levites was given when the cultus was organized.

The task of the Levites is related to both the priests and the people as a whole. They are called to be totally subservient to the priests, to whom they were "given," and to function as their servants (vv. 6, 9). Their task in relation to the people, from whom they were "separated" (16:9), is indicated but not specified. But comparison with 18:23 shows that their calling as it relates to the people is to prevent by their faithful service a judgment of God over Israel (see also 1:53; 8:19). In the Lord's service at the tabernacle they are therefore servants to all (vv. 6f.). But the bringing of offerings is the exclusive prerogative of the priests (v. 10); the task of the Levites in the tabernacle is limited to taking care of "the furnishings" (v. 8). This "taking care of" is not further specified, but 4:5–33 indicates that it is related to the transportation of the tabernacle when the camp is moved.

"Anyone else who approaches the sanctuary must be put to death" (v. 10b), lit.: "and the unauthorized stanger who comes near shall be put to death"; this expression is also found in 1:51; 3:38; 16:40; 18:4, 7. The meaning of "unauthorized stranger" varies; in 1:51; 3:38; 18:4 it refers to the non-Levite who performs the task of a Levite. But here and in 16:40; 18:7 the lawgiver refers to the non-Aaronite who might want to serve at the altar. A sharp distinction is therefore made here between the Aaronite and the Levite. This distinction began to fade only in the days of Hezekiah and Josiah, when the Levites are charged with the slaughtering and preparing of the Passover lambs (see my commentary on 2 Chronicles 30:15–20 and 35:7–15). The means by which the offender must be put to death is not specified, which allows for two possibilities: either a legal execution or an ordeal. The latter seems more probable in view of Israel's dynamistic thinking[2] (see my *Leviticus,* Introduction, sec. VII). The Lord's holiness opposes those who touch sacred objects or perform sacred rites without divine authorization (see also 2 Chron. 26:16–21).

Verses 11–13 explain why the Levites were not counted along with the rest of Israel (1:47), why their camp had to be located close to the tabernacle (2:17), and why the Levites were given to the Aaronites as servants (3:6, 9). The Levites take the place of Israel's firstborn, who belong to the Lord, so the Lord has the right to give them to the Aaronites as servants.

The Lord's claim to the firstborn of man and animal is of essentially the same nature as His claim to the firstfruits of the field. He is the Lord (*'adon*) and master (*ba'al*) of the land and of everything on it. Man may enjoy its fruits only after he has given Him the first and best portion of it. The farmer gives Him the fruits that ripen first, the strongest, i.e., male (Exod. 22:29–30a; 23:19; 34:26; Lev. 2:14; 19:23–25; 23:9–14; Num. 18:12; Deut. 12:17; 14:23; 26:2ff.). The shepherd gives the male firstborn of the flock and man must give the firstborn son (Exod. 13:2, 11–13; 22:29b–30; 34:19f.; Lev. 27:26; Num. 3:12; 18:15; Deut. 15:19). All this "belongs to me" (Exod. 13:2; 34:19; Num. 3:12). The idea that the male offspring of field and orchard, flock and man belongs to the deity is not unique to Israel but is found throughout Semitic antiquity. Here again the Lord breaks new ground by banishing from this concept anything contrary to His Being. The "consecrating" (Exod. 13:2) or "giving over" (Exod. 13:12) or "offering" (Num. 18:15) of "the first offspring of every womb, both man and animal" is subject to certain rules. In the case of unclean animals the firstborn must be redeemed or sold (Lev. 27:27; Num. 18:15). Exodus 13:13; 34:20 mention only the firstborn donkey, apparently be-

---

[2]See Publisher's Note.

cause the donkey and the ox were at that time the common domesticated animals; the donkey is thus mentioned as representative of a larger class (cf. Exod. 20:17; 21:33; 22:4, 9–10; 23:4–5, 12; Deut. 5:14; 22:3f.). The proceeds from the sale go, of course, to the sanctuary, i.e., to the priests. In the case of the male firstborn of clean animals the priests are allowed to eat all the meat rather than only the breast and the right thigh as was true in the case of the regular fellowship offerings (Num. 18:18).

But the firstborn male child must not be sacrificed (although Israel was familiar with this practice, Mic. 6:7); this is a unique trait of Israel's religion, since in the Semitic religions child sacrifices were considered to be the most efficacious kind of sacrifice. In Israel the firstborn male child was not to be sacrificed but redeemed for five shekels (Lev. 27:6; Num. 3:46ff.; 18:16; cf. also Exod. 34:20; Num. 8:16–19). It was the uniqueness of this law that was to arouse the curiosity of the younger generation; hence Exodus 13:14–15, which explains that this law is based on the fact that the Lord spared the firstborn of man and animal in Israel when He killed those of the Egyptians, and made them His property. The same thought is also implied by the context in Exodus 34:18–20.

Here the assurance is added that the Levites have taken the place of Israel's firstborn sons and that the Levites are therefore the Lord's special possession. Therefore the Lord has the right to decide freely what is to happen to them and to make them the helpers of His priests. This has been interpreted as an "artificial construction" (e.g., the Dutch Leyden Version; Edelkoort, *Numeri,* p. 94), based on the fact that the firstborn still had to be redeemed (Exod. 13:13; Num. 18:15). But the counting of the firstborn sons and of the Levites happened only once, while each new generation produces, of course, firstborn sons who are then to be redeemed. In order that the Lord's right to the firstborn males be not abrogated in any way, both the number of firstborn males and the number of Levites must be determined.

3. *The Number and Task of the Levites* (3:14–39)

Verses 14–39 contain not only the counting of the Levites but also a variety of statements concerning the responsibilities of the various groups of Levites as to the care of the tabernacle. This indicates that several sources have been combined here, some repetition was unavoidable.

3:14–16 *The Lord said to Moses in the Desert of Sinai, "Count the Levites by their families and clans. Count every male a month old or more." So Moses counted them, as he was commanded by the word of the Lord.*

Only the male Levites a month old or more are to be counted; the age limit is the same as that of the non-Levite children (3:40, 43; 18:16). The latter had to be redeemed, however (Lev. 27:6).

3:17–20 *These were the names of the sons of Levi:*
Gershon, Kohath and Merari.
These were the names of the Gershonite clans:
Libni and Shimei.
The Kohathite clans:
Amram, Izhar, Hebron and Uzziel.
The Merarite clans:
Mahli and Mushi.
These were the Levite clans, according to their families.

The three main divisions of the tribe of Levi and their clans are listed by way of introduction. This list corresponds to Genesis 46:11; Exod. 6:16–19; 1 Chronicles 6:16–19; 23:6–7, 12, 21. Gershon, Levi's firstborn, heads the list, followed by Kohath, even though the latter as the patriarch of the Aaronites is the more important.

A. *Number and task of the Gershonites* (3:21–26)

3:21–26 *To Gershon belonged the clans of the Libnites and Shimeites; these were the Gershonite clans. The number of all the males a month old or more who were counted was 7,500. The Gershonite clans were to camp on the west, behind the tabernacle. The leader of the families of the Gershonites was Eliasaph son of Lael. At the Tent of Meeting the Gershonites were responsible for the care of the tabernacle and tent, its coverings, the curtain at the entrance of the Tent of Meeting, the curtains of the courtyard, the curtain at the entrance to the courtyard surrounding the tabernacle and altar and the ropes—and everything related to their use.*

The two clans of the Gershonites consist, according to the census figures, of 75 *'elef* (see commentary on 1:20–46) males; their leader was Eliasaph. In the arrangement of the camp their place is "behind" or west of the tabernacle, which faced east. They are responsible for the care of "the tabernacle and tent" (v. 25); here, as in 4:25, a distinction is made between the two. The "tabernacle" refers to the sanctuary proper, the wooden frame with its coverings, while the "tent" includes the fenced-in courtyard (cf. Exod. 33:7; Num. 11:24). Elsewhere the two terms are bracketed together: "the tabernacle, the Tent of Meeting" (e.g., Exod. 39:32; 40:2, 6, 29). Since verse 36 indicates that the Merarites were responsible for the wooden frames the author must refer here to the curtains of the tabernacle (Exod. 26:1–6) rather than to the tabernacle as a whole;

this is stated explicitly in verse 26 and 4:25. They are to care, furthermore, for the coverings that go over the wooden frame of the tabernacle proper, here called "tent" (see Exod. 26:7–14) and the curtain at the entrance to the tent (cf. Exod. 26:36). The exception was the curtain of the Most Holy Place, which was entrusted to the care of the Kohathites (v. 31). They are also responsible for "everything related to their use," i.e., the pegs and ropes used to stretch and anchor the curtains and coverings (Exod. 35:18). They had two carts with four oxen at their disposal for the transportation of these items (Num. 7:7).

B. *Number and task of the Kohathites* (3:27–32)

3:27-32 *To Kohath belonged the clans of the Amramites, Izharites, Hebronites and Uzzielites; these were the Kohathite clans. The number of all the males a month old or more was 8,600. The Kohathites were responsible for the care of the sanctuary. The Kohathite clans were to camp on the south side of the tabernacle. The leader of the families of the Kohathite clans was Elizaphan son of Uzziel. They were responsible for the care of the ark, the table, the lampstand, the altars, the articles of the sanctuary used in ministering, the curtain, and everything related to their use. The chief leader of the Levites was Eleazar son of Aaron, the priest. He was appointed over those who were responsible for the care of the sanctuary.*

A more important task is assigned to the Kohathites who were divided into no fewer than four clans. According to verse 28 they numbered 8 *'elef* and 600 men. But according to verse 39 the total number of Levites was 22 *'elef*, while the sum of the numbers in verses 22, 28, and 34 comes to 300 more. One of these numbers must thus be inaccurate. The most likely solution is that in verse 28 *šš* ("six") was written instead of *šlš* ("three"), so that verse 28 originally spoke of 8 *'elef* and 300 men (see also commentary on verse 39).

The sons of Kohath are to camp on the south side of the tabernacle. They are not only responsible for the curtain of the Most Holy Place (Exod. 26:31), but more important, also for the most holy objects in the tabernacle: the ark, the table, the lampstand, the altar of burnt offering, the altar of incense, and all the holy vessels and utensils required for their use (Exod. 25:29, 38; 27:3). These vessels and utensils are listed in more detail in 4:7, 9, 14.

Edelkoort (*Numeri*, p. 95) concludes from the fact that the altars were also entrusted to the care of the Kohathites that no distinction is made here as yet between priests and Levites. But he overlooks the phrase "used in ministering" (lit. "with which they minister"); "they" refers to the priests rather than the Levites as proven by the fact that the verb *šrt* ("to minister'') is used without object (as is the case here) when it refers to the priests (see Exod. 28:35; 30:20; 39:26; 1 Kings 8:11; etc.), but with object when it refers to the Levites (see 1:50; 3:6; 8:26; 16:9; 18:2; see also 4:9 kjv). It is therefore incorrect to claim that verse 32 is a more recent addition, designed to clarify that the Levites are indeed the servants of the priests. This statement concerning the supervision over the service of the Levites, assigned to Eleazar, is inserted here rather than after verse 37 where it logically belongs because the Aaronites came from the family of Kohath (see Exod. 6:18, 20). A more specific task given to Eleazar is mentioned in 4:16. Concerning the relationship between these verses and 4:5–15, see commentary on the latter.

C. *Number and task of the Merarites* (3:33–37)

3:33–37 *To Merari belonged the clans of the Mahlites and the Mushites; these were the Merarite clans. The number of all the males a month old or more who were counted was 6,200. The leader of the families of the Merarite clans was Zuriel son of Abihail; they were to camp on the north side of the tabernacle. The Merarites were appointed to take care of the frames of the tabernacle, its crossbars, posts, bases, all its equipment, and everything related to their use, as well as the posts of the surrounding courtyard with their bases, tent pegs and ropes.*

The least significant aspect of the care of the tabernacle falls to the Merarites; they numbered 6 *'elef* and 200 men and camped on the north side of the tabernacle. They are responsible for the wookwork of the tabernacle and the courtyard: the frames, crossbars, posts, bases, and everything related to them. They have the use of four carts and eight oxen for the transportation of these materials (7:8).

The school of Wellhausen has attempted to reduce the tasks assigned to the Levites in verses 21–37 to the product of a redactor's imagination on the assumption that the tabernacle is merely a fantasy from a much later time. But this ignores the fact that the work that had to be done in and around the temple was of an entirely different nature. The description given here fits only the wilderness period.

3:38 *Moses and Aaron and his sons were to camp to the east of the tabernacle, toward the sunrise, in front of the Tent of Meeting. They were responsible for the care of the sanctuary on behalf of the Israelites. Anyone else who approached the sanctuary was to be put to death.*

Only Moses and Aaron and his sons are allowed to camp on the east side of the tabernacle as an ''honor guard'' to guard the entrance to the Tent of Meeting. Moses, although he is Aaron's brother, is not authorized to perform the cultic duties that are the exclusive prerogative of the priests; nevertheless, he is allowed to camp on the east side of the tabernacle. This minor trait also points to the wilderness period.

3:39 *The total number of Levites counted at the LORD's command by Moses and Aaron according to their clans, including every male a month old or more, was 22,000.*

The total number of Levites given in this verse is 22 *'elef*. As stated above, the numbers in verses 22, 28, and 34 add up to 22 *'elef* and 300. Theoretically the total in verse 39 could have been rounded off, but verses 43 and 46 argue against this. The rabbinical view, repeated by a number of commentators, that the numbers in verses 22, 28, and 34 include 300 Levite firstborn is unacceptable if only because 300 firstborn among the total number of Levites would be too small a number by far. The error probably lies in the total of the Kohathites.

4. *The Excess Number of Firstborn* (3:40–51)

3:40–51 *The LORD said to Moses, "Count all the firstborn Israelite males who are a month old or more and make a list of their names. Take the Levites for me in place of all the firstborn of the Israelites, and the livestock of the Levites in place of all the firstborn of the livestock of the Israelites. I am the LORD."*

So Moses counted all the firstborn of the Israelites, as the LORD commanded him. The total number of firstborn males a month old or more, listed by name, was 22,273.

The LORD also said to Moses, "Take the Levites in place of all the firstborn of Israel, and the livestock of the Levites in place of their livestock. The Levites are to be mine. I am the LORD. To redeem the 273 firstborn Israelites who exceed the number of the Levites, collect five shekels for each one, according to the sanctuary shekel, which weighs twenty gerahs. Give the money for the redemption of the additional Israelites to Aaron and his sons."

So Moses collected the redemption money from those who exceeded the number redeemed by the Levites. From the firstborn of the Israelites he collected silver weighing 1,365 shekels, according to the sanctuary shekel. Moses gave the redemption money to Aaron and his sons, as he was commanded by the word of the LORD.

The counting of the firstborn males of Israel now follows, and the results show that their number exceeds that of the Levites by 273. Verse 12 indicates that these 273 could not be replaced by Levites. They must therefore be redeemed with money since they belong to the Lord and the Lord's service does not allow for child sacrifices. In verse 47 and 18:16, as well as in Leviticus 27:6, the price is set at five shekels, but with the added specification that it must be the "sanctuary shekel," which weighed more than the ordinary shekel (16.37 grams of silver instead of 14.55 grams).

While 1:46 speaks of 603,550 male Israelites twenty years of age and older, verse 43 indicates that there were only 22,273 firstborn males (see commentary on 1:20–46 concerning these numbers); this has been thought strange and has led to numerous calculations. Keil thought that figure included only the firstborn who were born during the preceding year, thus *after* the Exodus from Egypt, but this is eisegesis; also, the figure 22,273 would then be much too high. Others think that the figure refers to the firstborn who were born during the preceding six years, or to those less than six years old, or less than sixteen years old. It seems to me that these attempts do not take the text very seriously. Those who refuse to attempt various calculations to explain the total make it easy on themselves by declaring the totals fictitious (Baentzsch) or by assuming that "we have here undoubtedly a very young section of the Pentateuch" (Edelkoort), which apparently amounts to the same thing. The one question that is not raised in all of this is what is meant by the "firstborn." Theoretically there are three possibilities: the firstborn is 1) the eldest son of the father; 2) the eldest son of the mother, whereby we must keep in mind the polygamous nature of Israel's family life which allowed for more than one firstborn son in a given household; or 3) the firstborn son of both father and mother, which would include only the first son of the first wife. The first option seems to be eliminated by verse 12 (cf. also Exod. 13:2, 12, 15; 34:19), which includes only the male child that (lit.) "opens the womb." The second possibility is also excluded since whenever we hear of a "firstborn" it is always the firstborn of the father who, even in a polygamous setting, can have only one firstborn (cf. e.g., Jacob, Num. 1:20; 26:5; Esau, Gen. 36:15; Gideon, Judg. 8:20; David, 2 Sam. 3:2). This leaves only the third option, which excludes all those "eldest sons" who are not the first male child born in a family.

The total number of firstborn males, 22,273, appears in a somewhat different light when we keep the preceding in mind. I also refer back to my comments concerning the total of 603,550 male Israelites twenty years old and more (commentary on 1:20–46); the totals for the firstborn and for the Levites must, of course, be interpreted on the basis of *'elef* being less than one thousand.

The question has been raised how it was determined which of the 22,273 firstborn had to be redeemed and who was to pay for their redemption: their parents or their clan. The author does not deal with the practical implementation of this regulation; he only points out that the redemption money (1,365 shekels) was handed over to the priests by Moses (v. 51). The Talmud (Sanhedrin 17a) claims that Moses determined by lot who had to be redeemed.

Verse 41 speaks of the redemption not only of the firstborn males of Israel by the Levites, but also of the firstborn of Israel's livestock by the firstborn of the livestock of the Levites. The basis for this command is verse 13, where we find the words "I am the LORD." This phrase is also used in the so-called Holiness Laws (Lev. 21–26), but there is no connection between Numbers 3 and those laws; "I am the LORD" is used to remind Israel of the holiness of the firstborn. The author understandably considers the redemption of the firstborn children more important than the redemption of the firstborn of the livestock, and no further mention of the latter is made in this section. The objection has been raised against the law of the redemption of the firstborn of the livestock that the other laws concerning them (Exod. 13:2, 12–13; Deut. 15:19–23) would no longer have a *raison d'etre* because the firstborn had already been redeemed. But again (see above on vv. 11–13), this overlooks the fact that we are dealing here with a unique event that does not in any way invalidate the law of the redemption of future firstborn animals. See also commentary on 18:17.

5. *The Census of the Levites and Their Tasks* (4:1–49)

This chapter shows indications of being a composite. While verses 2–3, 22–23, and 29–30 contain the Lord's command to count all the men in the three main Levite clans (Kohath, Gershon, Merari) from thirty to fifty years of age "who come to serve in the work at the Tent of Meeting," the results of the census are not given until verses 34–49. Verses 4–20, 24–28, and 31–33 describe the task assigned to each of these three groups in the transportation of the tabernacle, a matter not mentioned at all in the Lord's command. These verses must therefore be from a different hand, inserted here by the author of the Pentateuch who wanted to give a summary of the number *and* task of the Levites during the wilderness period.

Verses 3, 23, 30 contain both the age limit for the Levites ("from thirty to fifty years of age") and the phrase "who come to serve in the work at the Tent of Meeting." This is similar to 1:3, 20, etc., "all the men . . . who are able to serve in the army." The same root (*šb'*) is used in both phrases ("serve" and "serve in the army"). This indicates that the obligation of the Levites was in principle the same as that of the other tribes: the Levites also have a *saba'*, a "military" duty.

A Levite must not be younger than thirty or older then fifty years, i.e., he must be in the prime of his life. In 8:24–25 the age limits are given as twenty-five and fifty. The LXX reads "from twenty-five to fifty" in this chapter. The author of Chronicles sets the lower age limit at twenty and does not give an upper limit (1 Chron. 23:24, 27; 2 Chron. 31:17; Ezra 3:8); these references refer to the time after David and apparently reflect a change necessitated by the additional duties in the temple after it became a royal sanctuary.

The order in which the three clans are listed differs from that in chapter 3, where they listed in the order of birth of the three sons of Levi; here the order is based on the relative importance of their respective tasks, and the Kohathites are thus mentioned first.

A. *The Kohathites* (4:1–20)

4:1–15 *The LORD said to Moses and Aaron: "Take a census of the Kohathite branch of the Levites by their clans and families. Count all the men from thirty to fifty years of age who come to serve in the work in the Tent of Meeting.*

"This is the work of the Kohathites in the Tent of Meeting: the care of the most holy things. When the camp is to move, Aaron and his sons are to go in and take down the shielding curtain and cover the ark of the Testimony with it. Then they are to cover this with hides of sea cows, spread a cloth of solid blue over that and put the poles in place.

"Over the table of the Presence they are to spread a blue cloth and put on it the plates, ladles and bowls, and the jars for drink offerings; the bread that is continually there is to remain on it. Over these they are to spread a scarlet cloth, cover that with hides of sea cows and put its poles in place.

"They are to take a blue cloth and cover the lampstand that is for light, together with its lamps, its wick trimmers and trays, and all its jars for the oil used to supply it. Then they are to wrap it and all its accessories in a covering of hides of sea cows and put it on a carrying frame.

"Over the gold altar they are to spread a blue cloth and cover that with hides of sea cows and put its poles in place.

"They are to take all the articles used for ministering in the sanctuary, wrap them in a blue cloth, cover that with hides of sea cows and put them on a carrying frame.

"They are to remove the ashes from the bronze altar and spread a purple cloth over it. Then they are to place on it all the utensils used for ministering at the altar, including the firepans, meat forks, shovels and sprinkling bowls. Over it they are to spread a covering of hides of sea cows and put its poles in place.

"After Aaron and his sons have finished covering the holy furnishings and all the holy articles, and when the camp is ready to move, the Kohathites are to come to do the carrying. But they must not touch the holy things or they will die. The Kohathites are to carry those things that are in the Tent of Meeting."

The Kohathites are entrusted with the care of the "most holy things" (v. 4). These include the two altars (Exod. 29:37; 30:10) and the ark, the table, the lampstand, and all their utensils (Exod. 30:26ff.). The following verses further specify the duties of the Kohathites.

When the camp is to be moved the priests must prepare the tabernacle for transport. The ark and the table require three coverings, the lampstand and the altars two, which indicates the relatively lesser degree of "holiness" of the latter. This is perfectly understandable, since the ark speaks of the Lord's dwelling in the midst of Israel and the table of His continuous presence. The coverings include *tahash* skins (NIV: "sea cow"). We do not really know what animal is meant (KJV: "badger"; RSV: "goat"; ASV: "seal"), but since the Egyptian *tchs* refers to a type of chrome leather, I prefer the translation "fine leather" in verses 6, 8, 10–11, 12, 14. The KJV rendering "badger" is incorrect, since the badger is not found in the Sinai region. The ASV rendering "seal" is based on the Arabic, and the NIV rendering "sea cow" agrees with Dillmann, Baentzsch, and Kautzsch. Also mentioned are "blue" cloth (vv. 6, 9, 11–12) and "purple" and "crimson." The color red had a special meaning for Israel, as indeed for the whole ancient Near Eastern world: it is the color of blood and is therefore eminently suitable for warding off all kinds of demonic forces.[3] Red also played a role in healing, since illness was viewed as the result of demonic influences. It is still the color of penance and mourning in the Roman Catholic church. See Eva Wunderlich, *Die Bedeutung der roten Farbe,* 1925.

Verse 6 states that after the ark has been readied for transport the carrying poles must be put in place. But according to Exodus 25:15 the poles were not supposed to be removed. However, the practical demands of wrapping the ark necessitated the temporary removal of the poles. There is thus no contradiction between verse 6 and Exodus 25:15. Concerning the poles for the table (v. 8) and for the golden altar of incense (v. 11), see Exodus 25:27–28; 30:4–5.

The lists of the "holy things" here and in 3:31 both omit the basin for washing (Exod. 30:17ff.), which was anointed with holy anointing oil (Exod. 30:26–28) and was therefore also "most holy" (see also Exod. 40:11; Lev. 8:11). The Samaritan Pentateuch and the LXX both include the basin here, but only the Samaritan Pentateuch includes it in 3:31, which indicates in my opinion that it is a later addition. I do not know why the basin is not mentioned in 3:31 or in 4:4–14. The explanation cannot lie in the fact that it was less "holy" than the objects that *are* mentioned, since this would contradict Exodus 30:26–28; 40:11.

After the priests have carefully wrapped the holy things so that they are

---

[3]See Publisher's Note.

completely covered, the Kohathites can begin their task, which consists only of carrying these objects (v. 15a). The reason for the limited nature of their task is given in verse 15b: "they must not touch the holy things or they will die." The same thought is also found in 18:3, while 4:20 is even stronger: the mere looking at the holy things will result in death.

The remark has been made that this not only negates the unique nature of the service of the Kohathites, but also makes the service of the Levites in the tabernacle impossible, since they could not avoid seeing or touching the holy things in the course of their service. But this argument carries weight only if the contents of the Pentateuch are divorced from the historical context the Pentateuch itself presents and the service of the Levites is viewed from the perspective of its later development. The Pentateuch indisputably sees the Levites only as the carriers of the tabernacle and of the holy things of the cultus. In the service of the priests (1:50–51) they care for the tabernacle (1:53), a responsibility that would otherwise have fallen to the firstborn sons of the Israelites (8:19). This "care of the tabernacle" is a duty performed "*at* the Tent of Meeting" (or "*in front of* the Tent of Meeting," 3:7) rather than *in* the tabernacle, and concerns the "furnishings" (vessels and utensils) of the tabernacle (3:8). Their work "of the tabernacle" (3:7) or "at the Tent of Meeting" (7:5; 16:9; 18:4, 6, 21, 23) is limited: it consists of "serving and carrying" (4:47). But because the Lord Himself charged them with this responsibility it is "the work of the Lord" (8:11) and woe to him who considers it unimportant! (see ch. 16).

The position of the Levites does not change until later, when they assume responsibilities *in* the temple. This may be related to the fact that during the period of the judges the dividing line between priests and Levites is more or less obliterated, while at the same time the ancient Semitic custom, also known to Israel, that the head of a family or the representative of a larger or smaller group had the right to bring sacrifices exerted its influence (see my commentary on 1 Chronicles 23:1–3). It should be clear, however, that it is unjustified to interpret the regulations concerning the service of the Levites in the Pentateuch in the light of later developments.

Furthermore, the special character of the service of the Kohathites, which consisted of carrying the "holy things," is not in any way negated by the fact that these things were completely covered before the Kohathites were allowed to approach them. We must see this in the light of Israel's understanding of the nature of "the holy." As I explained in several places in my commentary on Leviticus (e.g., Introduction, sec. VII), Israel had a dynamistic[4] perspective, of which a number of indications are also found in

---

[4]See Publisher's Note.

Numbers. With regard to the Lord's holiness this means that he who approaches it, or enters, so to speak, its immediate sphere of influence, will feel this "holiness" enter into him, either destroying him if he is unauthorized, or "sanctifying" him and ennobling him. This holiness, which pervades the tabernacle and especially the objects such as the ark, the table, the lampstand, and the altars, is not rendered ineffective by the coverings applied by the priests. While these coverings make it impossible to see and touch the objects, and thus protect the unauthorized individual against their destructive power, they cannot interfere with the sanctifying influence on those who do the work of the Lord in His service. And thus the privilege accorded the Kohathites remains undiminished. To them and to no one else "the care of the most holy things" is entrusted; only they "carry on their shoulders the holy things" (7:9).

4:16 *"Eleazar son of Aaron, the priest, is to have charge of the oil for the light, the fragrant incense, the regular grain offering and the anointing oil. He is to be in charge of the entire tabernacle and everything in it, including its holy furnishings and articles."*

Verse 16 adds to the description of the task of the Kohathites the fact that they were under the supervision of Aaron's eldest son, Eleazar. The Gershonites and Merarites were supervised by Ithamar (vv. 28b, 33b). Verse 16 in part parallels 3:32; the second half of the verse indicates that Eleazar was in charge of the entire tabernacle, which means that Ithamar was under him. But verse 16 also complements 3:32 by listing four items for which Eleazar was specifically responsible: the oil for the light (Exod. 27:20), the fragrant incense (Exod. 30:34ff.), the anointing oil (Exod. 30:22ff.), and the "regular grain offering." The latter refers to the daily burnt offering, described in Exodus 29:38ff., which is called "the regular burnt offering" (KJV: "continual burnt offering") once in Exodus (29:42) and twelve times in Numbers (see chs. 28–29). As in Leviticus 6:13 and Nehemiah 10:34, it is here not called *'ola* ("burnt offering") but *minha,* a term frequently used for "grain offering" in Leviticus (see Lev. 2) that originally was the general term for "offering" (see my commentary on Lev. 2:1–3).

4:17–20 *The Lord said to Moses and Aaron, "See that the Kohathite tribal clans are not cut off from the Levites. So that they may live and not die when they come near the most holy things, do this for them: Aaron and his sons are to go into the sanctuary and assign to each man his work and what he is to carry. But the Kohathites must not go in to look at the holy things, even for a moment, or they will die."*

In these verses the priests are enjoined to give precise instructions to each of the Kohathites so that, in the carrying out of their duties, they would not approach the holy objects too soon. This would put them in danger of seeing these objects, or of even catching just a glimpse of them. The indwelling holiness, which cannot allow any profanation and therefore punishes with death those who see or touch without being authorized to do so (cf. 1 Sam. 6:19), would then exert its destructive power against the Kohathites. This would destroy "the Kohathite tribal clans" (v. 18), lit. "the tribe of the families." This use of "tribe" for a subgroup is also found with reference to the tribe of Benjamin (Judg. 20:12; 1 Sam. 9:21), but it seems to me unfounded to draw from this usage the conclusion that "the redaction is relatively recent" (Edelkoort, *Numeri,* p. 98) as long as it cannot be proven that *shebet* ("tribe") did not refer to a subgroup until much later.

Note that this warning is addressed to the priests. Daily dealings with the holy things can gradually lead to a lack of awareness of the dangers to sinful man inherent in them. Hence the "offenses against the priesthood" (18:1).

B. *The Gershonites* (4:21–28)

4:21–28 *The Lord said to Moses, "Take a census also of the Gershonites by their families and clans. Count all the men from thirty to fifty years of age who come to serve in the work at the Tent of Meeting.*

"This is the service of the Gershonite clans as they work and carry burdens: They are to carry the curtains of the tabernacle, the Tent of Meeting, its covering and the outer covering of hides of sea cows, the curtains for the entrance to the Tent of Meeting, the curtains of the courtyard surrounding the tabernacle and altar, the curtain for the entrance, the ropes and all the equipment used in its service. The Gershonites are to do all that needs to be done with these things. All their service, whether carrying or doing other work, is to be done under the direction of Aaron and his sons. You shall assign to them as their responsibility all they are to carry. This is the service of the Gershonite clans at the Tent of Meeting. Their duties are to be under the direction of Ithamar son of Aaron, the priest."

The command to count the Gershonites differs from verses 2, 29 in that the order of the words "clans" and "families" is reversed, as was also the case in 3:15. Their task is described in more detail here than in 3:25–26. Note that here again a distinction is made between "tabernacle" and "tent" (see commentary on 3:25). The "outer covering of fine leather" (NIV: "of hides of sea cows," see commentary on 4:2–15) is specifically mentioned here. Verse 27 (cf. vv. 18, 32) states that the Gershonites may perform their duties only as instructed by the priests, who must assign them their specific tasks (''you'' refers to the priests rather than to Moses and Aaron as some suggest). Any error on their part involves potential danger. Ithamar is the supervisor of the Gershonites and of the Merarites (v. 33).

C. *The Merarites* (4:29–33)

4:29–33 *"Count the Merarites by their clans and families. Count all the men from thirty to fifty years of age who come to serve in the work at the Tent of Meeting. This is their duty as they perform service at the Tent of Meeting: to carry the frames of the tabernacle, its crossbars, posts and bases, as well as the posts of the surrounding courtyard with their bases, tent pegs, ropes, all their equipment and everything related to their use. Assign to each man the specific things he is to carry. This is the service of the Merarite clans as they work at the Tent of Meeting under the direction of Ithamar son of Aaron, the priest."*

These verses do not have an introduction similar to verses 1 and 21. The census of the Merarites is commanded in words similar to those of verses 2–3 and 22–23. The MT reads ''count'' as a singular, referring to Moses; the LXX has a plural, indicating Moses and Aaron (cf. v. 1). Here (as in vv. 2, 29) ''clans'' precedes ''families.'' The task of the Merarites is described as in 3:36–37. Ithamar is their supervisor (cf. v. 28; also 7:8).

D. *The total number of eligible Levites* (4:34–49)

4:34–49 *Moses, Aaron and the leaders of the community counted the Kohathites by their clans and families. All the men from thirty to fifty years of age who came to serve in the work in the Tent of Meeting, counted by clans, were 2,750. This was the total of all those in the Kohathite clans who served in the Tent of Meeting. Moses and Aaron counted them according to the LORD's command through Moses.*

The Gershonites were counted by their clans and families. All the men from thirty to fifty years of age who came to serve in the work at the Tent of Meeting, counted by their clans and families, were 2,630. This was the total of those in the Gershonite clans who served at the Tent of Meeting. Moses and Aaron counted them according to the LORD's command.

The Merarites were counted by their clans and families. All the men from thirty to fifty years of age who came to serve in the work at the Tent of Meeting, counted by their clans, were 3,200. This was the total of those in the Merarite clans, Moses and Aaron counted them according to the LORD's command through Moses.

So Moses, Aaron and the leaders of Israel counted all the Levites by their clans and families. All the men from thirty to fifty years of age who came to do the work of serving and carrying the Tent of Meeting numbered 8,580. At the LORD's command through Moses, each was assigned his work and told what to carry.

Thus they were counted, as the LORD commanded Moses.

Verses 34 and 46 indicate that "the leaders of the community" do the counting, along with Moses and Aaron. These are, of course, the men referred to in 1:17, 44 whose names are given in 1:5–16. The result of the census is that the three groups (the Kohathites head the list; elsewhere the Gershonites are mentioned first: Exod. 6:16; Num. 3:17; 1 Chron. 6:1) consist of 2 *'elef* and 750, 2 *'elef* and 630, and 3 *'elef* and 200 males between the ages of thirty and fifty (concerning *'elef,* see commentary on 1:20–46). The total number of eligible Levites is thus 8 *'elef* and 580. Since the total number of Levites a month old or more was 22 *'elef* (3:39), the percentage of men between thirty and fifty is roughly the same as was found in Europe in 1940 (52 percent). Only the number of eligible Merarites is exceptionally high (3 *'elef* and 200 out of 6 *'elef* and 200). The census of the eligible Levites in the days of David resulted in a total of 38 *'elef* (see my commentary on 1 Chron. 23:3).

Verse 49 (which requires no fewer than three emendations) is intended as a subscript to chapters 3 and 4.

Various Laws
(5:1–6:27)

Here the author of the Pentateuch interrupts the historical narrative and inserts five unrelated laws; only the first of these (5:1–4) relates to the camp of chapters 1–4.

1. *The Purity of the Camp* (5:1–4)

5:1–4 *The Lord said to Moses, "Command the Israelites to send away from the camp anyone who has an infectious skin disease or a discharge of any kind, or who is ceremonially unclean because of a dead body. Send away male and female alike; send them outside the camp so they will not defile their camp, where I dwell among them." The Israelites did this; they sent them outside the camp. They did just as the Lord had instructed Moses.*

This law requires the banishment from the camp of those who, from our perspective, suffer from a more or less serious illness (infectious skin diseases or leprosy, Lev. 13–14; bodily discharge, Lev. 15) and of those who have touched a dead body (Num. 19). This law is essentially alien to our Western way of thinking but, as I have explained in a number of places in my commentary on Leviticus, Israel shared the conviction of the entire ancient Near Eastern world that sin and death are the result of demonic[5] forces. Consequently, anyone who is under the influence of these forces

---

[5]See Publisher's Note.

and is thus ill, or who touches someone who through death has fallen completely into their power, is no longer fit to participate in the cultic life, which has the purpose of seeking the life forces through communion with the deity. But when the demonic forces have attached themselves to an individual in the form of unclean matter, he himself becomes a source of defilement and is therefore a danger to his environment. Such defilement is like a contagious disease that is transmitted from one individual to the next and that can make a smaller or larger group unfit for participation in the cultic life. The only remedy is to banish the source of contamination. To us this seems cruel, but in the ancient Near East, where the practice of medicine consisted of the expulsion of demonic forces by means of magical formulas (hence the criticism in 2 Chron. 16:12), this was the only possible solution. It is applied without hesitation, otherwise the cultic life, whose aim was survival, would become an impossibility, and that would jeopardize the very existence of the nation.

Since there was no room in Israel for magical formulas (Exod. 22:18; Deut. 18:11), those who were ceremonially unclean had to be banished; otherwise the entire camp would be defiled—an unthinkable situation when the Lord and His sanctuary occupy the central place in the camp! If Israel is to survive as a nation the cultus must be preserved and the sending away of those who are ceremonially unclean is thus a necessary requirement. They are "sent away," i.e., into the desert, where the possibilities of dying are many.

As stated, this law affects three groups of people. In the first place, those who suffer from *sara'at* (traditionally rendered "leprosy"), a term that, according to Leviticus 13, refers to a group of more or less serious skin diseases (see my commentary on Leviticus, especially the introductory comments on ch. 13). Second, those who suffer from a bodily discharge resulting from a disease of the internal sexual organs of both men and women (Lev. 15). And finally, those who have touched a dead body. The first group is referred to in Leviticus 13:46 (cf. 2 Kings 7:3; 15:5). The banishment of the second group is not mentioned in Leviticus 15; there the man is ceremonially unclean only until evening, the woman for seven days during her monthly period, and the woman with a discharge for seven days after she is healed. The third group is also mentioned in 31:19, but not in the broader law in 19:11–13. This inconsistency is probably due to the fact that our passage under discussion deals exclusively with the camp, which according to Deuteronomy 23:9–14 was subject to exceptionally strict regulations. The rabbis claimed that there were three camps: the camp of God, the camp of the Levites, and the camp of the rest of the people; those who suffered from infectious skin diseases were required to stay outside all three camps, while those who had a discharge could not enter the first two, and those who had touched a dead body could not enter the camp of God. There is no basis whatsoever for this view; it shows that the ethos that underlies this law had become entirely alien to the rabbis.

2. *Restitution for Wrongdoing* (5:5–10)

5:5–10 *The L*ORD *said to Moses, "Say to the Israelites: 'When a man or woman wrongs another in any way and so is unfaithful to the L*ORD*, that person is guilty and must confess the sin he has committed. He must make full restitution for his wrong, add one fifth to it and give it all to the person he has wronged. But if that person has no close relative to whom restitution can be made for the wrong, the restitution belongs to the L*ORD *and must be given to the priest, along with the ram with which atonement is made for him. All the sacred contributions the Israelites bring to a priest will belong to him. Each man's sacred gifts are his own, but what he gives to the priest will belong to the priest.'"*

This law is intended to complement Leviticus 6:1–7, which deals with the wrongful taking of something that had been entrusted to a person by its owner, or of something the owner himself had lost. The accused has first of all committed perjury as the phrase "unfaithful to the LORD" indicates (see Lev. 6:2–3). But the individual is apparently burdened with guilt. He must, according to this law, voluntarily confess his sin to the priest (this is assumed but not explicitly stated in Lev. 5:14). Full restitution must be made and one-fifth of the value of that which was taken (the value was apparently determined by the priest) must be added by way of penalty (cf. Lev. 5:16; 27:13, 19, 27, 31).

Up to this point the law is basically parallel with Leviticus 6:1–7, but in verse 8 a new element is presented. Assume that the victim had died in the meantime; in that case the full value plus twenty percent must be given to the victim's *go'el,* his closest relative. If the victim has no close relatives restitution must be made to the Lord, i.e., to the priest.

This last thought leads the lawgiver to a new law that is only tangentially related to the preceding. In verse 8 he speaks only of one specific source of income for the priests; in verse 9 he refers to "the sacred contributions." These include everything that was brought to the sanctuary but was not to be placed on the altar (Lev. 22:2–3, 15; Deut. 12:26). Everything that is given to the priest (this probably refers in the first place to the firstfruits) becomes his personal property after the Lord has received His share. The owner's right to give the remainder to whomever he wants remains unchanged. A related subject is covered in Leviticus 7:7–9, which deals with the priest's share of the burnt and grain offerings.

3. *The Woman Accused of Unfaithfulness* (5:11–31)

This section deals with what the old Anglo-Saxons called an *ordal:* a trial by ordeal. This form of justice was found in the ancient Near East, among the Germanic tribes, and in India; it is still used by numerous African tribes and in the Malayan archipelago, and was not unknown even in the Christian West (witch trials!). This legal process seeks to prove guilt or innocence by means of divine intervention (or what is considered such) in a case that cannot be decided on the basis of the testimony of witnesses. The decisive point in the proceedings is an act performed by the accused or an act to which the accused voluntarily submits. The ordeal retained a place in the divine revelation of the Old Testament. The reason for this lies in the organic character of the divine revelation (see my "The Old Testament Revelation of God and the Ancient Oriental Life," *Bibliotheca Sacra,* 1913), as well as in Israel's judicial system, which did not have legal processes like ours. Trial by ordeal is applied in Exodus 22:8; Numbers 16:6–7; 1 Kings 8:30–31; another form of divine decision, the casting of lots, is found in Joshua 7 (Achan) and 1 Samuel 14 (Jonathan). Psalm 109:18b and Proverbs 6:27–29 allude to this form of justice, as does (perhaps) Exodus 32:20.

Here the ordeal is part of the investigation into the guilt or innocence of a woman whose husband suspects her of infidelity. The case is described in terms that lack the exactness required in our legal processes: sometimes the woman is presumed innocent, at other times guilty (cf. v. 12 and v. 14; also vv. 19–22 and vv. 27–28). This, of course, opens up the possibility of looking for two sources if one is so inclined. B. Stade (*Zeitschrift für alttestamentliche Wissenschaft,* 1895, pp. 157–78) spoke of two redactions, and J. A. Brewer (*American Journal of Semitic Languages and Literatures,* 1914, pp. 36–47) thought he was able to discern three.

Three further preliminary comments: in the first place, Israel does not see the case at issue as a purely judicial matter, or even as a primarily judicial issue. Rather, it is a religious matter as the repeated use of the phrase "she has defiled herself" (e.g. v. 27) shows: she has become "unclean" and has therefore lost her right to a continued position in the cultic-religious life of Israel (cf. Lev. 18:20).

Second, the only case discussed here is that in which the questioning of witnesses did not bring certainty concerning guilt or innocence. If guilt could be established by the testimony of witnesses, Israel's law knew of only one penalty: the death penalty for both parties involved (Lev. 20:10; Deut. 22:22).

And finally, a comparison between this law and the Babylonian and Middle Assyrian laws dealing with the same problem shows that the conception is simpler here. The Code of Hammurabi deals with two different cases. In the first the husband suspects his wife of infidelity; the wife's oath is sufficient to prove her innocence and she may return to her husband (§131). In the other case it is not her husband who makes the accusation, but others point the finger at her. She then must submit to an ordeal by throwing herself into the river (§132). If she drowns, her guilt has been proven; if not, "the river has shown (her) to be innocent" (see §2). The Middle Assyrian law also distinguishes between two cases. If an individual accuses someone else's wife of infidelity but cannot prove his case he shall be flogged, condemned to forced labor, and castrated (§ 18). If, on the other hand, the accuser has no witnesses the woman must submit to the water ordeal: she must "go to the river" (§17). Israel's law is not only simpler, but also more severe: the mere suspicion on the part of the husband requires that the woman submit to the ordeal. See also N. Wahrmann, *Das Ermittelungserfahren gegen eine des Ehebruchs Verdächtige,* 1933.

A. *The suspicion* (5:11–14)

5:11–14 *Then the LORD said to Moses, "Speak to the Israelites and say to them: 'If a man's wife goes astray and is unfaithful to him by sleeping with another man, and this is hidden from her husband and her impurity is undetected (since there is no witness against her and she has not been caught in the act), and if feelings of jealousy come over her husband and he suspects his wife and she is impure—or if he is jealous and suspects her even though she is not impure, then he is to take his wife to the priest.'"*

The husband has become suspicious and believes that his wife has been unfaithful. The basis for this suspicion is not stated; the lawgiver is not concerned with the many possibilities in this area. All he says is, "a spirit of *qin'a*" has come over the man" (v. 14), i.e., the force that brings the *qin'a* up out of the heart where man's actions are born. The rendering "jealousy" (v. 14) is not entirely accurate. The word *qin'a* indicates resistance against that which is contrary to the demands of one's own being. One of those demands is faithfulness, since the wife belongs to the husband. And the man believes that this demand has not been met, hence his resistance. He does not have proof, and the possibility remains that his suspicions are unfounded. The ordeal must now decide the matter.

B. *The woman placed before the Lord* (5:15–18)

5:15–18 *"'He must also take an offering of a tenth of an ephah of barley flour on her behalf. He must not pour oil on it or put incense on it, because it is a grain offering for jealousy, a reminder offering to draw attention to guilt.*

---

*" 'The priest shall bring her and have her stand before the L*ORD*. Then he shall take some holy water in a clay jar and put some dust from the tabernacle floor into the water. After the priest has had the woman stand before the L*ORD*, he shall loosen her hair and place in her hands the reminder offering, the grain offering for jealousy, while he himself holds the bitter water that brings a curse.' "*

The man brings the woman suspected of unfaithfulness to the priest. He must also take an offering "on her behalf" (lit. "he shall bring her offering for her," cf. KJV). This offering consists of one-tenth of an ephah (about two quarts) of barley flour; it differs from the usual grain offering (see Lev. 2:1; 6:15) in that neither oil nor incense is added. It is thus similar to the sin offering of the very poor, which consisted of a tenth of an ephah of fine flour (Lev. 5:11), and is actually even less, since fine flour is twice as expensive as barley flour (2 Kings 7:1).

Attempts have been made to explain this offering, explicitly called "the grain offering for jealousy" in verses 15, 18, on the basis of Exod. 23:15; 34:20, where it is forbidden to appear before the Lord empty-handed. But the lawgiver himself provides the explanation: it is "a reminder offering to draw attention to guilt." In other words, the offering serves, so to speak, to bring the legal case between husband and wife before the Lord for a decision. The word "reminder" (cf. 1 Kings 17:18; Ezek. 21:23f.; 29:16) expresses the idea that this grain offering will "draw (the Lord's) attention," a carry-over from the time when offerings were still perceived as food for the deity[6] (see my commentary on Leviticus, Introduction, sec. VII). It is not likely that it is the woman who is to be reminded, since the question is precisely whether or not she is guilty.

In verse 16 we read that the priest now takes over and remains in charge throughout the rest of the proceedings. First he places the woman suspected of unfaithfulness "before the LORD." Exactly what this expression means is not clear to us, since the same expression is used also for the burning of the lamps *in* the sanctuary (Exod. 27:21), the bringing of offerings *in front of* the sanctuary (Lev. 15:14), the slaughtering of animals before the altar (Lev. 1:5), and the placing of the staffs in front of the ark (Num. 17:7). But to me it seems unlikely that the woman would be allowed to enter the sanctuary; rather, she was to stand *in front of* the sanctuary so that the Lord, who "dwells" in the tabernacle, can see her and show her His power.

In verse 17 we read that the priest takes the "holy water," an expression found only here. The LXX reads "pure living water" which, judging from the combination of adjectives, looks like a later paraphrase for the benefit

---

[6]See Publisher's Note.

of Greek readers. In the Old Testament we hear only of "living," i.e., running water (Gen. 26:19; Lev. 14:5, 50). We are not informed where this holy water comes from; tradition claims that it was taken from the basin for washing. It probably was something similar to the *mu ellu* ("clean water") of the Babylonians: water free from any ceremonial impurity that was suitable for use in religious ceremonies and that could expel evil forces. In any case, both the water and the dust are "holy" because they are in the sanctuary. The holiness of the holy place radiates out and is imparted to anyone and anything in it. Israel originally shared this ancient material concept of "holiness," as well as the ritual conception of "sin,"[7] with the rest of the ancient Near Eastern world. The addition of the "holy" dust to the "holy" water doubles the "holiness" of the water and makes it all the more suitable for use in the ordeal. This addition of dust from the floor was possible only in the tabernacle during the wilderness period; in Solomon's temple, which had a floor of cypress wood (1 Kings 6:15), and in Herod's temple, in which the floor was covered with marble slabs, the dust had to be brought in from the court of the priests (Sota 2. 2). This mixture of water and dust is now placed in a jar made of clay, i.e., unglazed, since it will later be destroyed (cf. Lev. 6:28a).

We see in verse 18 that after these preparations are completed the priest again approaches the woman and undoes her hairknot so that her hair hangs loose. The purpose of this is not entirely clear. It has been suggested that the loosening of the hair was originally a hair offering, but we find no trace of this in Israel (see also commentary on 6:5). Others believe that it was done to prevent the knot from interfering with the efficacy of the bitter water. Although it is true that some nations did attribute some kind of magical power to the hairknot, there are no indications that Israel shared this concept. I do not see a form of humiliation in this act. Rather, we should think of Leviticus 13:45; 21:10. The loose hair is a sign of what we call mourning: the woman suspected of adultery and thus of ceremonial uncleanness is made unrecognizable to the forces of death (see Lev. 13:45). Only then is the "reminder offering" placed in her hands—it becomes one with her (cf. 6:19; Exod. 29:24; Lev. 8:27f.) and thus draws God's attention to her. At the same time the woman, by allowing the offering to be placed in her hands, indicates that she is willing to submit to the ordeal (see also v. 22).

---

[7]Sin is seen as "any deviation from the prescribed ceremonial actions" (*Gods Woord,* p. 89).

C. *The decision* (5:19–28)

5:19–28 " 'Then the priest shall put the woman under oath and say to her, "If no other man has slept with you and you have not gone astray and become impure while married to your husband, may this bitter water that brings a curse not harm you. But if you have gone astray while married to your husband and you have defiled yourself by sleeping with a man other than your husband" —here the priest is to put the woman under this curse of the oath— "may the LORD cause your people to curse and denounce you when he causes your thigh to waste away and your abdomen to swell. May this water that brings a curse enter your body so that your abdomen swells and your thigh wastes away."

" 'Then the woman is to say, "So be it."

" 'The priest is to write these curses on a scroll and then wash them off into the bitter water. He shall have the woman drink the bitter water that brings a curse, and this water will enter her and cause bitter suffering. The priest is to take from her hands the grain offering for jealousy, wave it before the LORD and bring it to the altar. The priest is then to take a handful of the grain offering as a memorial offering and burn it on the altar; after that, he is to have the woman drink the water. If she has defiled herself and been unfaithful to her husband, then when she is made to drink the water that brings a curse, it will go into her and cause bitter suffering; her abdomen will swell and her thigh waste away, and she will become accursed among her people. If, however, the woman has not defiled herself and is free from impurity, she will be cleared of guilt and will be able to have children.' "

The priest then takes the water, which is now "the bitter water that brings a curse" (vv. 18–19, 24, 27) and thus has disintegrative and life-destroying power (compare this with the "cup of the LORD's wrath" that features so prominently in the preaching of the prophets, e.g., Isa. 51:17, 22; Jer. 25:15, 17, 28; et al.) He holds the water in his hand and recites the incantation, after which the woman declares that she will accept the verdict of the bitter water by saying "so be it" (lit. "amen, amen"; cf. Deut. 27:15ff.; Neh. 5:13). The priest then writes the words of the incantation "on a scroll" (papyrus?), after which the writing is washed off "into the bitter water." The incantation with its disintegrative power thus enters the "holy" water, which is doubly "holy" because it is mixed with "holy" dust. The thought expressed here is that that which is written is dissolved in the water and imparts to the water the power inherent in the words so that the water can accomplish that of which the words speak (we must remember that to Israel and the ancient Near Eastern world words were more than sounds; they had power). The water thus has a triple "charge." This dissolving of holy words in water was also practiced in ancient Babylonia and is still known in the Islamic world (see e.g., J. Köberle, *Natur und Geist,* 1901, pp. 165f.).

The actual words of the incantation are found in verses 19–22. Verse 21 strikes us as somewhat surprising in that it interrupts the incantation. The usual explanation is that we have here the intentional synthesis of two "recensions" that are supposed to make up this law (v. 21b = v. 22a). But if this were correct we would expect verse 21 to follow verse 22. Rather, it seems to me that the lawgiver, faced with an ancient traditional incantation in which the expected effect is unquestionably ascribed to the bitter water, has added the element that was missing from the standpoint of Israel's thinking. This addition must make clear that the decision was not made by any magical powers residing in the water, the dust, and the words, but by the Lord's will, which was based on a moral norm. Thus the bitter water of pre-Israelite times when the forefathers "lived beyond the River" (Josh. 24:2), which was effective due to a power of its own, has become an instrument used by the Lord, who has been asked for a judicial verdict by the accuser. This addition to the ancient incantation could accomplish the intended modification of the meaning of the incantation only if it was inserted there where the incantation states what will happen to the woman if she is found guilty. The consequences for the woman are thus stated twice (vv. 21b, 22a), which is no great difficulty; the repetition would emphasize to the woman the dire consequences of the drinking of the bitter water if she was indeed guilty.

The formula itself clearly leaves open the possibility of guilt as well as of innocence. If the woman is innocent she can drink the water without suffering any consequences at all. But if she is guilty "(her) thighs will waste away and (her) abdomen will swell." And because she refused to admit her guilt her name will be remembered in Israel and used, not as a blessing (cf. Gen. 48:20) but as a curse; the name is the person's essence, and because of her action it can now be used to cause destruction of life and dissolution (cf. Isa. 65:15; Jer. 42:18). It is not quite clear to what the "swelling of her abdomen" and the "wasting away of the thigh" refer; some think of dropsy, or a similar disease of the ovaries that would cause the woman to look continually pregnant while she slowly wastes away. Or, perhaps we must understand this to mean that the guilty woman is pregnant, but her pregnancy results in a miscarriage because the bitter water destroys the fetus that was conceived in adultery. In any case, the law of retribution applies if the woman is guilty; if she is innocent she will become pregnant and be blessed with children.

Two things remain to be done: the drinking of the water and the bringing of the grain offering. The sequence is clearly stated in verse 26: the offering precedes the drinking. The nature of the offering requires that it come first: it is a grain offering, presented to the Lord by a ceremonial waving of the offering. It is then placed at the disposal of the priest by the Lord (see my commentary on Lev. 7:28–34), who places it on the altar where it is burned. By bringing this reminder offering to the altar the Lord's attention is drawn to the woman's case and He is asked to render a verdict. Also, the woman can only take the jar of bitter water *into* her hands after the offering for jealousy has been taken *from* her hands. The fact that the drinking of the water is mentioned (v. 24) before the manner in which the grain offering is to be brought can be explained from the fact that this was the focal point of the entire procedure. It appears to me that it is incorrect to see this as an indication of a "double recension," as some have suggested.

Verses 27 and 28 describe the consequences of the drinking of the water for the woman, both when she is guilty and when she is innocent. If she is guilty the bitter water will come in contact with that which her union with the man with whom she committed adultery has placed in her body; the "holiness" of the water as well as the *modus operandi* that was imparted to the *'ala* ("curse"; see my commentary on Lev. 5:1) will cause the destructive power of the *'ala* to have its effect. No indication is given as to what happens to her after she is found guilty. If the woman is innocent the bitter water will have no adverse effects; she is thus cleared of any guilt and God will bless her with children.

D. *Subscript* (5:29–31)

5:29–30 *"'This, then, is the law of jealousy when a woman goes astray and defiles herself while married to her husband, or when feelings of jealousy come over a man because he suspects his wife. The priest is to have her stand before the* Lord *and is to apply this entire law to her.'"*

These verses reiterate when this law can be applied. Verse 29 is based on the assumption that the woman is indeed guilty, verse 30 on the assumption that the husband's jealousy led to this procedure.

5:31 *" 'The husband will be innocent of any wrongdoing, but the woman will bear the consequences of her sin.'"*

In verse 31 follows the assurance that the husband will be innocent of wrongdoing regardless of the outcome of the ordeal. The reasoning behind this is apparently that he has done nothing but defend his own right to the marital fidelity of his wife. He will go free, "but the woman will bear the consequences of her sin," i.e., she will be guilty (see my commentary on Lev. 5:1).

The psychological impact of this process on the woman is clear. If she is innocent, the absence of any consequences of the drinking of the water constitutes a public exoneration and proof of her faithfulness to her husband. If she knows herself to be guilty she has to look forward to several months of anguish that will undermine her health and keep her from any further unfaithfulness.

Jewish tradition says that this law was abrogated by rabbi Jochanan ben Zakkai in the first century A.D. because divorce was so prevalent in his day; this throws a strong light on references such as Matthew 12:39; 16:4.

4. *The Nazirite* (6:1–21)

6:1–2 *The Lord said to Moses, "Speak to the Israelites and say to them: 'If a man or woman wants to make a special vow, a vow of separation to the Lord as a Nazirite.'"*

Our word "Nazirite" is derived from the passive participle *nazir* of the Hebrew verb *nazar*, "to set apart"; it has come to us via the Greek adaptation (*nazaraios*) and the Latin *nazaraeus*. The individual who is "set apart" can be a prince (Gen. 49:26; Deut. 33:16; cf. NIV margin), he can be "set apart," i.e., dedicated to the Lord for life (Samson, Samuel), or he can dedicate himself to the Lord for a specific period of time. This chapter deals with the latter.

The Nazirite vow, like circumcision (Gen. 17:10–14), is not something new that is here introduced to Israel. The lawgiver did not need to explain what the Nazirite vow was (v. 2)—also in this respect Israel was part of the ancient Near Eastern world where the making of various vows was a common practice. His purpose was to regulate the Nazirite vow and make it suited to the henceforth unique character of Israel. This is why the Nazirite vow is immediately described as "a vow of separation to the Lord" (v. 2): it may be made only to the Lord. The motivation that leads to the vow is not discussed; only the act as such is important (see my commentary on Lev. 4:1–2).

Anyone who makes this vow, whether it be man or woman (the latter of course subject to the restrictions of 30:3ff.), must know the regulations that are to govern his or her life for the duration of the vow. First, the obligations the vow entails are listed (vv. 3–8); then guidelines are given for the situation where the Nazirite is involuntarily defiled and his consecration is thus nullified (vv. 9–12); and finally, the lawgiver states what must be done at the end of the predetermined period for which the vow was made (vv. 13–20). The law closes with a subscript.

A. *The obligations of the Nazirite* (6:1–8)

The obligations concern drinking (v. 3), eating (v. 4), care of the hair of the head (v. 5), and complete avoidance of any contact with a dead body (vv. 6–7).

6:3–4 " 'He must abstain from wine and other fermented drink and must not drink vinegar made from wine or from other fermented drink. He must not drink grape juice or eat grapes or raisins. As long as he is a Nazirite, he must not eat anything that comes from the grapevine, not even the seeds or skins.' "

The first rule is that the Nazirite must abstain from wine and *shekar.* The KJV renders this word "strong drink," which might give the mistaken impression that it refers to distilled drink or liquor. It is an imported intoxicating drink made from grain, honey, dates, or fruit and is sometimes made stronger by adding spices (Isa. 5:22). Furthermore, the Nazirite must not drink vinegar made from wine or *shekar;* this vinegar appears to have been a refreshing rather than intoxicating drink (see Ruth 2:14). This prohibition thus shows how seriously the lawgiver takes the requirement to abstain from intoxicating beverages. This is also indicated by the requirement that the Nazirite must not drink "grape juice" (some have thought that this refers to grape preserves; see König, *Wörterbuch*), nor eat grapes, whether fresh or dried (raisins), nor any other part of the grapevine, including the tips of the tendrils (still considered a delicacy by some).

What is the reason for this prohibition? The priests were also required to abstain from wine and *shekar* (but not from vinegar and grape juice); the rest of the prohibition is unique to the Nazirite, however. This has been interpreted as reflecting the Nazirite's aversion to the civilized agrarian life in Canaan. But if this were correct Naziritism would have developed *after* the settlement in Canaan as a result of the protest within Israel against the nature worship of the Canaanites and of the desire to protect the Jahweh religion by an emphasis on the nomadizing wilderness life (thus Wellhausen's school). Assuming that it could be proven that Naziritism dates from the times after the conquest (which is not the case), we are faced with three problems. In the first place, nowhere in the Old Testament are the Recabites with their wilderness ideal (Jer. 35:1ff.) seen as proponents of the pure worship of Jahweh, nor do they see themselves as such. They constitute a cultural rather than religious movement. We do not hear of any contact between prophets and Recabites, nor do we hear of any prophet who became a Recabite. Second, any proof for a connection between Naziritism and the Recabites is lacking. And in the third place, Israel's religion is not based on any kind of opposition to culture; rather, Israel's prophets oppose the adoption of Canaan's *religion,* which permeated Canaanite culture.

The only explanation for the prohibition of certain kinds of drink and food lies in the use that was made of intoxicating beverages (and primarily of the products of the grapevine) in the religions of the ancient Near East. Hosea 3:1 indicates the central place of the grapevine in those religions. And Isaiah 28:7 shows how prophets sometimes reached a state of excitement induced by wine in order to receive revelations. All mystery religions, whose purpose is union with the deity, use orgiastic drunkenness to achieve their goal. Wine and strong drink are always the most suitable means to achieve "ecstasy," i.e., to step outside oneself and to come in contact with the "sphere of the deity." This must not be true of the Nazirite: he is to be consecrated to the Lord. No other powers than those of the Lord may be seen in him. It is a very serious sin to tempt a Nazirite to drink wine (Amos 2:12).

6:5 *" 'During the entire period of his vow of separation no razor may be used on his head. He must be holy until the period of his separation to the LORD is over; he must let the hair of his head grow long.' "*

The second prohibition concerns the hair on the Nazirite's head; it must be allowed to grow freely and must not be touched by a razor. The hair on his head is his *nezer* (from the same root as *nazir,* see commentary on v. 1), his "dedication" (v. 18), "the symbol of his separation to God" (v. 7). See also Jeremiah 7:29.

The Old Testament occasionally makes reference to nations whose people did unusual things to their hair. Thus, Jeremiah speaks of people who live in the desert and who "clip the hair by their foreheads" (Jer. 9:26, NIV margin), i.e., who shave the temples and leave only a pluck of hair on top (see also Jer. 25:23; 49:32; NIV margin). And we know that the ancient Arabs and the worshipers of Tammuz brought hair offerings (J. Wellhausen, *Arabisches Heidentum,* pp. 124, 128f.). There was thus a religious reason behind the shaving of the hair. In Leviticus 19:27ff. special ways of cutting hair are put on the same level as divination and sorcery, and the section also contains a reminder of the unique character of Israel's religion; cf. also Leviticus 21:5–6. Israel is forbidden to do this, except during times of mourning when not only the beard (Isa. 15:2; Jer. 41:5) but also the head may be shaved (Isa. 3:24; 22:12; Jer. 16:6; Ezek. 7:18; Amos 8:10; Mic. 1:16); only the priests are not allowed to do this even in mourning (Lev. 21:5; Ezek. 44:20).

The regulation against the shaving of the head has been interpreted as proof for the supposition that the hair was allowed to grow so that it later could be offered; the burning of the hair (v. 18), rather than the fellowship offering would then be the real offering (e.g. J. Benzinger, *Hebräische Archaeologie,* 3rd ed., 1927, p. 358). However, this view overlooks two things: if the hair were indeed an offering the priest rather than the Nazirite would have to bring it; and in the Islamic world allowing the hair to grow is proof even today of serving God in a special way, and pilgrims let their hair grow on their journey to Mecca.

Others (e.g., Edelkoort) see in this prohibition a reminder of the nomadic lifestyle. But the Egyptian and Syrian monuments always depict the Canaanites and Israelites with long hair and beards, which shows that it is not related to nomadism.

I see in this prohibition therefore nothing more than the logical implication of the fact that the Nazirite's hair was the visible symbol of his separation to the Lord. And he must therefore shave his head when the vow is interrupted or fulfilled (vv. 9, 18).

6:6–8 *" 'Throughout the period of his separation to the LORD he must not go near a dead body. Even if his own father or mother or brother or sister dies, he must not make himself ceremonially unclean on account of them, because the symbol of his separation to God is on his head. Throughout the period of his separation he is consecrated to the LORD.' "*

The third requirement for the Nazirite is that he must not defile himself with a dead body. Even if one of his closest relatives—parents, brothers, and sisters—were to die, he has to avoid any contact with the dead body. His obligation to God, which he has voluntarily assumed, must take precedence over his normal obligations toward his family. In this respect more is asked of the Nazirite than of the priest (Lev. 21:1–4); only the high priest was subject to the same regulation (Lev. 21:11f.). This third requirement, by implication, excludes any other kind of defilement as well.

A twofold reason is given for this prohibition: "the symbol of his separation to God is on his head" (v. 7) and "he is consecrated to the LORD" (v. 8; cf. v. 6). To understand this third requirement we must remember Israel's concept of illness and death, which was similar to that found elsewhere in the world of the ancient Near East. Both illness and death are considered the result of demonic influences[8] that made the sick person ceremonially unclean and the dead body a source of defilement; both made the service of the Lord impossible (see commentary on ch. 19).

---

[8]See Publisher's Note.

B. *Interruption of the vow due to defilement* (6:9–12)

6:9–12 *" 'If someone dies suddenly in his presence, thus defiling the hair he has dedicated, he must shave his head on the day of his cleansing—the seventh day. Then on the eighth day he must bring two doves or two young pigeons to the priest at the entrance to the Tent of Meeting. The priest is to offer one as a sin offering and the other as a burnt offering to make atonement for him because he sinned by being in the presence of the dead body. That same day he is to consecrate his head. He must dedicate himself to the LORD for the period of his separation and must bring a year-old male lamb as a guilt offering. The previous days do not count, because he became defiled during his separation.' "*

The Nazirite does not have to withdraw from everyday life, which means that he can be faced with painful surprises. Someone dies very unexpectedly at home or on the road, and he has not been able to keep himself from being defiled. He has thus come in contact with demonic forces that are, so to speak, concentrated in the deceased; the requirement of holiness (i.e., of being controlled by and filled with only the Spirit of the Lord, the source of his holiness) has been violated. This violation is of such a serious nature that two opposing forces are now active in him: the sanctifying power of the Lord and the desecrating power of the demonic forces.[9] This violation did not involve the Nazirite's will, but from Israel's perspective the will is not the determining factor (as it would be to us): only the fact of his defilement matters (for a similar attitude toward unintentional sins, see my commentary on Lev. 4:1–2). The Nazirite is thus guilty; he has defiled (lit.) "the head of his consecration" (v. 9; cf. also v. 11). He has to start all over again, but only after the prescribed seven-day period of uncleanness that follows contact with a dead body (19:14ff.). Chapter 6 does not specifically mention this seven-day period, but it is implied in verse 9: "the day of his cleansing—the seventh day." He must begin by shaving his head, so that he appears before the Lord without *nezer* (see above) when on the following day, the eighth, he brings a sin offering for the removal of his defilement and a burnt offering to declare his renewed dedication. This burnt offering is the same as that of the poor (Lev. 5:7) and of the man who has been cleansed from a discharge (Lev. 15:13–15).

Only after this has been done and atonement has been made can he (i.e., the priest, who is the subject of v. 11) declare the shaven head of the Nazirite to be consecrated; he is now again a Nazirite and must live in accordance with the requirements of verses 2–8 like one who has consecrated himself to the Lord. But since he stands once again at the beginning

---

[9]See Publisher's Note.

of the time period to which he committed himself in his vow, he must bring a year-old male lamb as a guilt offering (cf. Lev. 14:12, 21) in order to cleanse himself of the unknown guilt (cf. Lev. 5:14ff.) that caused his defilement with the dead body.

The end of this section emphasizes the seriousness of this defilement. By his vow the man has placed himself as it were within the sphere of divine holiness. Any shortcoming is serious, so serious that not only the usual cleansing ceremony of Numbers 19 can not be applied, but that also the time spent as a Nazirite before the defilement does not count and a new beginning must be made.

C. *The end of the Nazirite vow* (6:13–21)

6:13–21 *" 'Now this is the law for the Nazirite when the period of his separation is over. He is to be brought to the entrance to the Tent of Meeting. There he is to present his offerings to the* Lord: *a year-old male lamb without defect for a burnt offering, a year-old ewe lamb without defect for a sin offering, a ram without defect for a fellowship offering, together with their grain offerings and drink offerings, and a basket of bread made without yeast—cakes made of fine flour mixed with oil, and wafers spread with oil.*

" 'The priest is to present them before the Lord *and make the sin offering and the burnt offering. He is to present the basket of unleavened bread and is to sacrifice the ram as a fellowship offering to the* Lord, *together with its grain offering and drink offering.*

" 'Then at the entrance to the Tent of Meeting, the Nazirite must shave off the hair that he dedicated. He is to take the hair and put it in the fire that is under the sacrifice of the fellowship offering.

" 'After the Nazirite has shaved off the hair of his dedication, the priest is to place in his hands a boiled shoulder of the ram, and a cake and a wafer from the basket, both made without yeast. The priest shall then wave them before the Lord *as a wave offering; they are holy and belong to the priest, together with the breast that was waved and the thigh that was presented. After that, the Nazirite may drink wine.*

" 'This is the law of the Nazirite who vows his offering to the Lord *in accordance with his separation, in addition to whatever else he can afford. He must fulfill the vow he has made, according to the law of the Nazirite.' "*

This section begins with a new superscription (cf. Lev. 6:9, 14; 7:1, 11; 14:2; Num. 5:29). It is addressed to the priest who finds here the regulations he must observe, in this case concerning the ceremony that marks the end of the Nazirite vow. This ceremony takes place at the sanctuary where the Nazirite is to be brought, probably by the priests on duty, or by at least one of them.

First, three offerings are brought that are reminiscent of those brought on the occasion of the consecration of the priests (Exod. 29:10–25; Lev. 8:14–21). Verse 14 lists the burnt offering, the sin offering, and the fellowship offering, but this is not the order in which they were actually brought. Because of its nature, the sin offering must be brought first (see v. 16). A year-old ewe lamb (cf. Lev. 4:32; 5:6; 14:10) must make atonement for any sins the Nazirite may have inadvertently committed. Then follows the burnt offering, which speaks of the complete surrender of one's life: a year-old male lamb without defect. Needless to say, the animals for the other two offerings were also to be without defect, as all sacrificial animals had to be (cf. Lev. 1:3, 10; 3:1, 6; etc.). The proceedings are concluded with the bringing of a ram as a fellowship offering (see my commentary on Lev. 3:1) and the accompanying meal that speaks of harmony between God and man. A drink offering and a basket with unleavened bread ("cakes made of fine flour mixed with oil, and wafers spread with oil") are also part of the fellowship offering (cf. Lev. 7:12). The burnt offering is accompanied by a drink offering and a grain offering (cf. 15:3ff.).

After these offerings are brought the hair of the Nazirite's head is shaved off and without further ceremony thrown into the fire under the fellowship offering. As noted above, this is not a hair offering; the hair was to be burned because it was holy to the Lord ("the *nezer* of his God," v. 7).

A large portion of the fellowship offering falls to the priest on duty: the shoulder, the "breast that was waved," and the "thigh that was presented" (vv. 19–20). In Exodus 29:26–28 and Leviticus 7:28–34 only the breast and thigh are mentioned, while Deuteronomy 18:3 speaks of "the shoulder, the jowls and the inner parts." This has given rise to the idea that verse 20a is a (clumsy!) attempt to harmonize the above references, an attempt that inadvertently made the priest's portion abnormally large. But there is no reasonable ground for this supposition. Deuteronomy 18:3 does not refer to the fellowship offering but rather emphasizes the sacrificial meal, while the offering itself is secondary. And the difference between verse 20 and Exodus 29 and Leviticus 7 can be readily explained from the lawgiver's efforts to maximize the importance of the Nazirite vow; Israel must realize its seriousness, and this is achieved in part by the high cost involved. It is therefore doubtful that the later custom of rich citizens assuming the cost of the vow for the poor (Josephus, *Antiquities,* XIX, 6. 1) was in agreement with the lawgiver's intent.

After this meal the Nazirite is allowed to drink wine again. The law concludes with a subscript (v. 21), which indicates that these offerings are a minimum requirement that may be exceeded.

D. *The Nazirite for life*

The temporary Nazirite vow was especially in vogue during the Maccabean wars (1 Macc. 3:49; Josephus, *Antiquities,* XIX, 6; *Jewish Wars,* II, 15. 1); the Talmud devotes an entire tract to it (*Nazir*). The Old Testament refers to Nazirites (probably temporary) in Amos 2:11f. But there are also two men who were Nazirites for life: Samson and Samuel. Judges 13:5 states that Samson was a "Nazirite, set apart to God from birth," and that no razor was to be used on his head. Samuel's mother vowed that the son she so fervently wanted would be given to the Lord "for all the days of his life" and that no razor would be used on his head (1 Sam. 1:11). And in the New Testament we hear of John the Baptist that "He is never to take wine or other fermented drink, and he will be filled with the Holy Spirit even from birth" (Luke 1:15), which makes him a Nazirite.

The currently accepted view is that the Nazirite vow was originally a life-long commitment, while the temporary vow of Numbers 6 came about "after a long period of development" (Edelkoort). But it appears to me that this view is incorrect, even apart from the fact that it is based on a conception of the origin of Israel's laws that is in my opinion contrary to the facts. The vows of the ancient Near Eastern world show a tendency toward expansion rather than reduction of content; this would indicate that the Nazirite vow in Israel was originally temporary in nature and was made for a definite period of time. Under the pressure of unusual circumstances this temporary vow could easily be expanded into a life-long vow. The unusual nature of Samson's and Samuel's Naziritism is underlined by the words "from birth" (Judg. 13:5) and "for all the days of his life" (1 Sam. 1:11).

Samson's lifestyle has given rise to the conjecture that the later lawgiver has made the requirements for the Nazirite more severe. But my impression of Samson as he is portrayed in the Book of Judges is that he was a man who misused the exceptional powers with which he was endowed, an abuse that led to his downfall; yet, his divine Sender accomplished His purpose with him, which was to make the Philistines feel the power of Israel's God. We must therefore not draw conclusions concerning the content of the Nazirite vow in Samson's time from his lifestyle.

5. *The Priestly Blessing* (6:22–27)

We would expect to find these verses, which seem to be out of place here, after Leviticus 9:22–23, where Moses and Aaron bless the people. Dillmann suggests this in his commentary, but he fails to explain why and how these verses strayed here. There are other sections in Numbers that would seem to fit better in Leviticus (9:1–14; 19:1–22).

6:22–23 *The L<small>ORD</small> said to Moses, "Tell Aaron and his sons, 'This is how you are to bless the Israelites. Say to them.'"*

The Hebrew verb *barak* is usually rendered "to bless," but this rendering does not convey the exact meaning of the Hebrew. To us, "blessing" someone means that we wish that things may go well with that person, that he or she may receive help and assistance. To understand the meaning of *barak* we must remember that in the ancient Near East words were considered to be more than merely sounds: they were "word-things" that came from the "heart," i.e., from the "workshop" where man's actions are born. *Barak* thus contains the idea that by means of a formal series of words something is actually introduced into a person's life-center, which can either hinder or promote the unfolding of life. *Barak* is thus the act of imparting the *baraka,* the force from which the fullness of life springs and which enables one to perform a wide variety of life-tasks.

Strictly speaking, only the Lord has the ability to *barak* because only He is "the living One"; in the fullness of His Being lies the inexhaustible source of "life-deeds." But He has given the power to "bless" to His servants, who do not, however, have this power at their disposal like magic: they are limited by the parameters the Lord Himself has established. Those parameters are indicated here in a form that shows an unusual rhythmic conception, a form that in turn is based on the desire to make the content of the *baraka* penetrate, by means of the majestic series of words, as deeply as possible the understanding of the one who is blessed and to allow it to sink as far as possible into the soul's consciousness, so that the *baraka* can unfold there and have its effect.

The priestly blessing consists of three parts, "three" being the basic form of harmonious development, the number of inner perfection (cf. 1 Sam. 3:8; Isa. 6:3). Each of these parts consists again of two halves, like the up-and-down movement of a wave, and in all three cases the first segment is longer than the second. In the Hebrew text the three parts consist of $2 + 1$, $3 + 2$, and $4 + 3$ words respectively, a total of $3 + 5 + 7$ words. If we count the letters of the words, we find that the first part contains 3×5, the second 4×5, and the third part 5×5 letters. It is therefore a steadily increasing flow of blessing that is poured over the people, consisting of fifteen words or, when we omit the name Jahweh that is used three times, twelve words in accordance with the twelve tribes of Israel. This "torrent" of blessing is directed to the whole people of Israel rather than to the individual; Israel is destined to be a spiritual unit, and is therefore addressed in the singular. This blessing occupied an important position in the consciousness of Israel's faithful, as shown not only by Psalm 67, but also by other statements such as Psalms 4:6; 31:16; 44:3; 80:3, 7, 19; 89:15; 119:35.

6:24 '''*The* Lord *bless you and keep you:*''''

The first part refers to the descending of the *baraka* of Him who made a covenant with Israel and who, at the beginning of Israel's existence as a nation, set Himself the goal: I will be your God and you will be My people (Exod. 6:7). In that *baraka* lies the driving force Israel needs to live as the Lord's people. It is also the basis for Israel's certainty that the Lord will give it that which every nation of the ancient Near East expected from its god: effectual protection and material wealth (cf. Abraham, Gen. 24:1), i.e., prosperity, many children, bountiful harvests, etc.

"And keep you" or, protect you; from what Israel is to be protected is not specified. Judaism (which lived in constant fear of the *mazziqin,* i.e., the demons that can bring all kinds of disasters and evil; cf. S. Krauss, *Talmudische Archaeologie,* I, p. 261) understood these verses to refer to protection from evil forces (F. W. Weber, *Jüdische Theologie,* 1897, §54, 3). But this is certainly too limited an interpretation. Rather, "and keep you" refers to anything that could oppose the fullness of life that is contained in the *baraka,* i.e., poor harvests, poverty, disease, war, etc.

6:25 '''*The* Lord *make his face shine upon you and be gracious to you;*''''

The second part of the blessing goes beyond the first one in that it focuses on the ethical side of the Lord's being, which is revealed in His favor and grace. He wants to "make his face shine upon" Israel. This is the opposite of "hiding one's face" (Isa. 57:17) and "showing one's back" (Jer. 18:17) or "to be hostile" (Lev. 26:23, 28). The shining of one's face indicates pleasure and is the opposite of anger (see Prov. 16:14f.; 15:30 KJV). When the Lord is angry He turns His back toward man; when He is gracious man sees His shining (radiant) face (cf. Pss. 4:6; 31:16; 44:3; etc.). "Grace" reflects guilt on the part of the receiver, condescending love and mercy on the part of the giver.

6:26 '''*The* Lord *turn his face toward you and give you peace.*''''

The third and final part of the blessing goes beyond the first two, since "to lift up one's face" (cf. KJV; this expression is also found in Assyrian with the same meaning; cf. Fr. Delitzsch, *Assyrisches Handwörterbuch,* p. 484a) means to love, to give in love with all the riches of one's being (cf. Pss. 33:18; 34:17). The result is "peace." But *šalom* in the Old Testament does not have the same negative content as our "peace," which means "not being in a state of war." *Šalom* is the state of being *šalem,* of being complete so that nothing is missing. "Peace" thus speaks of harmony, and therefore of happiness and the free and full development of life, and thus of unhindered strength (Ps. 29:11) and "joie de vivre" (Isa. 55:12). "Peace" includes everything an individual or community needs for well-being and prosperity (cf. Mal. 2:5). The opposite of "peace," therefore, is not war but evil (Isa. 45:7 KJV, cf. NIV; Jer. 29:11 KJV). Peace is the most important thing in life; it is what makes life truly "life." So we have a question as in Genesis 29:6 (lit. "is *šalom* to him") and 2 Kings 4:26 (lit. "is *šalom* to you, etc.") and a command as in Genesis 37:14 (lit. "see the *šalom* of your brothers").

We can compare this priestly blessing with a Babylonian blessing: "May Ea rejoice over you Damkina, may her face enlighten you, may Marduk raise up his head." While there is some similarity in the form, the Babylonian blessing was born out of polytheism, was addressed to one of the leaders, and remains vague, because the second part of the formula was always missing. And this is the shortest example: the Babylonians generally prefered long blessing formulas with many names of deities, since in their view the effectiveness of the blessing depended on its length (cf. Matt. 6:7).

6:27 *"So they will put my name on the Israelites, and I will bless them."*

This verse gives Israel the assurance that, as often as the priest with uplifted hands (Lev. 9:22) places the name of the Lord on the congregation three times, the blessing contained in these words shall indeed come on the people and make its effect felt. "And I will bless them," i.e., then the *baraka* that indwells Me shall descend on Israel from the fullness of My being and accomplish what I desire (Isa. 55:11). Is the blessing of the Lord here magically linked with the words of the priests so that the priests actually have the *baraka* at their disposal? This seems to be the case—but only like a stream runs through the channel it has made for itself!

One more comment: in Israel only the priests had the right to bless (cf. Lev. 9:22f.; Deut. 10:8; 27:14). In the ancient Near East, kings who, as sons of the deity, were also chief priests, had this right as well. It is to be expected that this commonly held royal prerogative also influenced the thinking of Israel's kings. Thus, after the spiritual degeneration and confusion of the period of the judges, David (2 Sam. 6:18; 1 Chron. 16:2) and Solomon !1 Kings 8:55) both assume this prerogative (see my commentary on 2 Chronicles 8:1–6). The view that also in Israel the king originally had certain priestly rights that were surrendered to the priests only after Uz-ziah's experience (2 Chron. 26:16-18), seems to me to be contrary to the facts (cf. Edelkoort, *Numeri*, p. 107; see my commentary on 2 Chron. 26:16-18).

Offerings at the Dedication of the Tabernacle
(7:1-8:4)

7:1-2 *When Moses finished setting up the tabernacle, he anointed it and conse-crated it and all its furnishings. He also anointed and consecrated the altar and all its utensils. Then the leaders of Israel, the heads of families who were the tribal leaders in charge of those who were counted, made offerings.*

This chapter takes us back to one month before the date given in 1:1, the first day of the second month of the second year, since according to Exodus 40:17 the tabernacle was set up on the first day of the *first* month of the second year after the Exodus. Chapter 9 (vv. 1, 15) takes us back to the time when the tabernacle was set up, while 10:11 takes place nineteen days after the date given in 1:1 ("the twentieth day of the second month of the second year"). This shows that the material in Numbers is arranged in a manner that does not follow the chronological sequence of events.

Although this chapter comes after chapter 1, where the same names of the leaders of Israel were listed (1:6-16), the author nevertheless deems it necessary to point out that the leaders referred to in this chapter are "the heads of families who were the tribal leaders." This indicates that chapter 1 originally had a different setting that did not include chapter 7. The order of the names in chapter 7 is the same as in chapter 2.

1. Offerings for the Transportation of the Tabernacle (7:3-9)

7:3-9 *They brought as their gifts before the Lord six covered carts and twelve oxen—an ox from each leader and a cart from every two. These they presented before the tabernacle.*

The Lord said to Moses, "Accept these from them, that they may be used in the work at the Tent of Meeting. Give them to the Levites as each man's work requires."

So Moses took the carts and oxen and gave them to the Levites. He gave two carts and four oxen to the Gershonites, as their work required, and he gave four carts and eight oxen to the Merarites, as their work required. They were all under the direction of Ithamar son of Aaron, the priest. But Moses did not give any to the Kohathites, because they were to carry on their shoulders the holy things, for which they were responsible.

First, we hear of the offerings that were brought when the tabernacle was set up. Under the circumstances these offerings were eminently practical: one cart from every two leaders. These carts were probably two-wheeled, covered vehicles, pulled by two oxen each (see H. Gressmann, *Altorientalische Bilder zum Alten Testament*, 2nd ed., no. 111; A. Jeremias, *Das Alte Testament und die alte Orient*, 4th ed., p. 520). The tabernacle and its accessories could be transported on these carts. Four of these six carts were entrusted to the Merarites, who were responsible for the transportation of the wooden frames, posts, etc. (4:29–33); the other two were used by the Gershonites, who were in charge of the various curtains (4:21–28). However, the Kohathites did not need any carts, since they were responsible for the "most holy things" (4:4ff.) that were to be carried on the shoulders. Under the influence of the custom of their Philistine neighbors (see 1 Sam. 6:7) the requirement that these "most holy things" were to be carried was later forgotten (2 Sam. 6:3; 1 Chron. 13:7), but reinstated after Uzzah's experience (2 Sam. 6; 1 Chron. 15:15). The use of carts by the Gershonites and Merarites does not contradict 4:25, 31, where the verb rendered "to carry" (*nasa'*) means in the first place "to lift up."

2. Offerings at the Dedication of the Altar (7:10–83)

7:10–83 *When the altar was anointed, the leaders brought their offerings for its dedication and presented them before the altar. For the* Lord *had said to Moses, "Each day one leader is to bring his offering for the dedication of the altar."*

The one who brought his offering on the first day was Nahshon son of Amminadab of the tribe of Judah.

His offering was one silver plate weighing a hundred and thirty shekels, and one silver sprinkling bowl weighing seventy shekels, both according to the sanctuary shekel, each filled with fine flour mixed with oil as a grain offering; one gold ladle weighing ten shekels, filled with incense; one young bull, one ram and one male lamb a year old, for a burnt offering; one male goat for a sin offering; and two oxen, five rams, five male goats and five male lambs a year old, to be sacrificed as a fellowship offering. This was the offering of Nahshon son of Amminadab.

On the second day Nethanel son of Zuar, the leader of Issachar, brought his offering.

The offering he brought was one silver plate weighing a hundred and thirty shekels, and one silver sprinkling bowl weighing seventy shekels, both according to the sanctuary shekel, each filled with fine flour mixed with oil as a grain offering; one gold ladle weighing ten shekels, filled with incense; one young bull, one ram and one male lamb a year old, for a burnt offering; one male goat for a sin offering; and two oxen, five rams, five male goats and five male lambs a year old, to be sacrificed as a fellowship offering. This was the offering of Nethanel son of Zuar.

On the third day Eliab son of Helon, the leader of the people of Zebulun, brought his offering.

His offering was one silver plate weighing a hundred and thirty shekels, and one silver spinkling bowl weighing seventy shekels, both according to the sanctuary shekel, each filled with fine fiour mixed with oil as a grain offering; one gold ladle weighing ten shekels, filled with incense; one young bull, one ram and one male lamb a year old, for a burnt offering; one male goat for a sin offering; and two oxen, five rams, five male goats and five male lambs a year old, to be sacrificed as a fellowship offering. This was the offering of Eliab son of Helon.

On the fourth day Elizur son of Shedeur, the leader of the people of Reuben, brought his offering.

His offering was one silver plate weighing a hundred and thirty shekels, and one silver sprinkling bowl weighing seventy shekels, both according to the sanctuary shekel, each filled with fine flour mixed with oil as a grain offering; one gold ladle weighing ten shekels, filled with incense; one young bull, one ram and one male lamb a year old, for a burnt offering; one male goat for a sin offering; and two oxen, five rams, five male goats and five male lambs a year old, to be sacrificed as a fellowship offering. This was the offering of Elizur son of Shedeur.

On the fifth day Shelumiel son of Zurishaddai, the leader of the people of Simeon, brought his offering.

His offering was one silver plate weighing a hundred and thirty shekels, and one silver sprinkling bowl weighing seventy shekels, both according to the sanctuary shekel, each filled with fine flour mixed with oil as a grain offering; one gold ladle weighing ten shekels, filled with incense; one young bull, one ram and one male lamb a year old, for a burnt offering; one male goat for a sin offering; and two oxen, five rams, five male goats and five male lambs a year old, to be sacrificed as a fellowship offering. This was the offering of Shelumiel son of Zurishaddai.

On the sixth day Eliasaph son of Deuel, the leader of the people of Gad, brought his offering.

His offering was one silver plate weighing a hundred and thirty shekels, and one silver sprinkling bowl weighing seventy shekels, both according to the sanctuary shekel, each filled with fine flour mixed with oil as a grain offering; one gold ladle weighing ten shekels, filled with incense; one young bull, one ram and one male lamb a year old, for a burnt offering; one male goat for a sin offering; and two oxen, five rams, five male goats and five male lambs a year old, to be sacrificed as a fellowship offering. This was the offering of Eliasaph son of Deuel.

On the seventh day Elishama son of Ammihud, the leader of the people of Ephraim, brought his offering.

His offering was one silver plate weighing a hundred and thirty shekels, and one silver sprinkling bowl weighing seventy shekels, both according to the sanctuary shekel, each filled with fine flour mixed with oil as a grain offering; one gold *ladle weighing ten shekels, filled with incense; one young bull, one ram and one male lamb a year old, for a burnt offering; one male goat for a sin offering; and two oxen, five rams, five male goats and five male lambs a year old, to be sacrificed as a fellowship offering. This was the offering of Elishama son of Ammihud.*

On the eighth day Gamaliel son of Pedahzur, the leader of the people of Manasseh, brought his offering.

His offering was one silver plate weighing a hundred and thirty shekels, and one silver sprinkling bowl weighing seventy shekels, both according to the sanctuary shekel, each filled with fine flour mixed with oil as a grain offering; one gold ladle weighing ten shekels, filled with incense; one young bull, one ram and one male lamb a year old, for a burnt offering; one male goat for a sin offering; and two oxen, five rams, five male goats and five male lambs a year old, to be sacrificed as a fellowship offering. This was the offering of Gamaliel son of Pedahzur.

On the ninth day Abidan son of Gideoni, the leader of the people of Benjamin, brought his offering.

His offering was one silver plate weighing a hundred and thirty shekels, and one silver sprinkling bowl weighing seventy shekels, both according to the sanctuary shekel, each filled with fine flour mixed with oil as a grain offering; one gold ladle weighing ten shekels, filled with incense; one young bull, one ram and one male lamb a year old, for a burnt offering; one male goat for a sin offering; and two oxen, five rams, five male goats and five male lambs a year old, to be sacrificed as a fellowship offering. This was the offering of Abidan son of Gideoni.

On the tenth day Ahiezer son of Ammishaddai, the leader of the people of Dan, brought his offering.

His offering was one silver plate weighing a hundred and thirty shekels, and one silver sprinkling bowl weighing seventy shekels, both according to the sanctuary shekel, each filled with fine flour mixed with oil as a grain offering; one gold ladle weighing ten shekels, filled with incense; one young bull, one ram and one male lamb a year old, for a burnt offering; one male goat for a sin offering; and two oxen, five rams, five male goats and five male lambs a year old, to be sacrificed as a fellowship offering. This was the offering of Ahiezer son of Ammishaddai.

On the eleventh day Pagiel son of Ocran, the leader of the people of Asher, brought his offering.

His offering was one silver plate weighing a hundred and thirty shekels, and one silver sprinkling bowl weighing seventy shekels, both according to the sanctuary shekel, each filled with fine flour mixed with oil as a grain offering; one gold ladle weighing ten shekels, filled with incense; one young bull, one ram and one male lamb a year old, for a burnt offering; one male goat for a sin offering; and two oxen, five rams, five male goats and five male lambs a year old, to be sacrificed as a fellowship offering. This was the offering of Pagiel son of Ocran.

On the twelfth day Ahira son of Enan, the leader of the people of Naphtali, brought his offering.

His offering was one silver plate weighing a hundred and thirty shekels, and one silver sprinkling bowl weighing seventy shekels, both according to the sanctuary shekel, each filled with fine flour mixed with oil as a grain offering; one gold ladle weighing ten shekels, filled with incense; one young bull, one ram and one male lamb a year old, for a burnt offering; one male goat for a sin offering; and two oxen, five rams, five male goats and five male lambs a year old, to be sacrificed as a fellowship offering. This was the offering of Ahira son of Enan.

Following the offerings of the leaders come the offerings of the tribes. All the gifts are identical, apparently to avoid any unholy competition and jealousy. These gifts concern the altar of burnt offering, which is now ceremoniously dedicated with a large offering followed, of course, by a sacrificial meal. The word used for "dedicate" (*chanak*) is also found in Egyptian, where it means "to give to the deity." The Hebrew verb is also used to refer to the "dedication" of a new house, which involved all kinds of ceremonies to ward off evil forces. Later we hear of the "dedication" of the temple (1 Kings 8:63; 2 Chron. 7:5), of the altar (2 Chron. 7:9), and of the wall of Jerusalem (Neh. 12:27). In each case the purpose was the same: to ward off demonic forces.[10]

Although the offerings are all identical, each is nevertheless listed in detail; this corresponds to a custom still found in the East, whereby at the wedding feast the friend of the groom calls out the name of each guest, followed by his or her gift (de Groot, *Palestijnsche achtergrond*, pp. 8f.). We know from Egyptian documents that Near Eastern antiquity valued preciseness and was not afraid of long lists. It is this constant repetition that makes a festive impression on the Israelite reader; we feel rather differently.

As stated before, the tribes are listed here in the same order as in chapter 2. Through its leader each tribe gives a silver plate weighing a hundred and thirty shekels (about 3.25 pounds) and a silver sprinkling bowl weighing seventy shekels (about 1.75 pounds), both filled with fine flour mixed with oil for the grain offering; also a gold ladle weighing ten shekels (about four ounces), filled with incense for the incense offering. In addition, each tribe gives one young bull, one ram, and one male lamb a year old for the burnt offering; one male goat for the sin offering; and finally, two oxen, five rams, five male goats, and five male lambs a year old for the fellowship offering and for the meal that followed. A different term is used for the male goat for the sin offering (*se'ir 'izzim*) than for the male goat for the

---

[10]See Publisher's Note.

fellowship offering; this distinction is, of course, intentional. This is the term that is always used for the goat for the sin offering (Lev. 4:23f., 28; 5:6; 9:3; 16:5–27; 23:19; Num. 15:24; 28:15, 22, 30; 29:5–38; Ezek. 43:22; 45:23; see also Lev. 9:15; 10:16; 16:15, 27; Ezek. 43:25; 2 Chron. 29:23). This may be related to the fact that the word for "goat" (*sa'ir*) and the word for "demon" (*sa'ir*) both mean "the hairy one"; the latter is frequently represented in the shape of the former.

3. *Totals* (7:84–89)

7:84–88 *These were the offerings of the Israelite leaders for the dedication of the altar when it was anointed: twelve silver plates, twelve silver sprinkling bowls and twelve gold ladles. Each silver plate weighed a hundred and thirty shekels, and each sprinkling bowl seventy shekels. Altogether, the silver dishes weighed two thousand four hundred shekels, according to the sanctuary shekel. The twelve gold ladles filled with incense weighed ten shekels each, according to the sanctuary shekel. Altogether, the gold ladles weighed a hundred and twenty shekels. The total number of animals for the burnt offering came to twelve bulls, twelve rams and twelve male lambs a year old, together with their grain offering. Twelve male goats were used for the sin offering. The total number of animals for the sacrifice of the fellowship offering came to twenty-four bulls, sixty rams, sixty male goats and sixty male lambs a year old. These were the offerings for the dedication of the altar after it was anointed.*

After the same list of gifts is repeated twelve times in identical words, the totals of each of the parts are given with the preciseness characteristic of the ancient Near East. The total amount of silver in the bowls and plates was about sixty pounds, the total amount of gold in the ladles about three pounds.[11]

7:89 *When Moses entered the Tent of Meeting to speak with the LORD, he heard the voice speaking to him from between the two cherubim above the atonement cover on the ark of the Testimony. And he spoke with him.*

This verse points out that the promise of Exodus 25:22 is fulfilled immediately after the tabernacle and the altar have been dedicated. This verse has been inserted here from a different context, as indicated by the statement that Moses entered the Tent of Meeting to speak "with him" (cf. KJV; NIV: "the LORD"), while no mention is made of "him" in the rest of the chapter.

---

[11]It is misleading to express the value of these offerings in terms of today's market prices. which reflect purchasing power rather than intrinsic value. The question as to the value of silver and gold to the Israelites (purchasing power) is impossible to determine with any degree of certainty (tr).

Whenever Moses entered the Tent of Meeting (which he did only when he needed the special guidance of the Lord in the carrying out of his official duties), he heard a voice speak to him "from between the two cherubim above the atonement cover on the ark of the Testimony." The terminology leaves no doubt that this refers to an audible voice (cf. 12:7f.) with which God spoke to Moses. The prophets no longer hear this audible voice, but hear "inwardly," even as the "seeing of God" later became an inward experience in Israel.

4. *Setting Up the Lamps* (8:1–4)

8:1–4 *The Lord said to Moses, "Speak to Aaron and say to him, 'When you set up the seven lamps, they are to light the area in front of the lampstand.'"*

Aaron did so; he set up the lamps so that they faced forward on the lampstand, just as the Lord commanded Moses. This is how the lampstand was made: It was made of hammered gold—from its base to its blossoms. The lampstand was made exactly like the pattern the Lord had shown Moses.

These verses contain instructions, primarily directed to Aaron, concerning the manner in which the gold lampstand, which, according to Exodus 40:24, stood "opposite the table on the south side of the tabernacle," is to provide light. The lampstand with its seven lamps looked like a stylized almond tree with seven branches (the almond tree blooms in January and thus speaks of awakening life, hence Jer. 1:11). According to Exodus 25:37, the lamps were to be placed on the lampstand in such a manner that they lighted the area in front of it; therefore, if the lampstand was to serve its intended function, care had to be taken as to its placement. The lampstand was to illuminate the dark area of the Most Holy Place, and was thus turned toward the open area of the Holy Place. Leviticus 24:1–4, which also speaks of the lampstand, does not make mention of this; there the only requirement is that the lamps be kept burning all night (cf. 1 Sam. 3:3).

Verse 4 describes how the lampstand (which weighed no less than seventy-five pounds according to Exod. 25:39) was made: of hammered gold, exactly like the pattern the Lord had shown Moses. A detailed description is found in Exodus 25:31–40 and 37:17–24; the fact that verse 4 is included here proves, in my opinion, that 8:1–4 did not originally belong to a document that also included these sections of Exodus 25 and 37. It found a place here because chapter 7 speaks of the implements of the tabernacle.

The Consecration of the Levites and the Length of Their Service (8:5–26)

This chapter, which speaks of the consecration of the Levites, is reminiscent of Leviticus 8, which describes the consecration of the priests. A comparison of the two chapters gives us an impression of the gap that separates the priests from the Levites. The various ceremonial acts are to make the priests "holy" (*qadoš*), the Levites "clean" (*tahor*). The priests thus acquire a "positive," the Levites a "negative" quality. This is also why the priests are anointed, which imbues them with life-force. The priests are washed, the Levites sprinkled; the priests are to put on new garments, the Levites must wash their clothes. The use of the blood of the offering is also different: the blood is to be put on the lobe of the right ear, on the right thumb, and on the big toe of the right foot of the priests; in the case of the Levites it is only "waved." These differences show how incorrect the view is (e.g., Edelkoort, *Numeri,* p. 14) that this chapter originally referred to the consecration of the priests and was later made into a ceremony concerning the consecration of the Levites in order to (*sic*) prevent two different rites from being prescribed for the same occasion. What we see here is the difference between the Lord's servants and their helpers.

1. *Preliminary Cleansings* (8:5–7)

8:5–7 *The LORD said to Moses: "Take the Levites from among the other Israelites and make them ceremonially clean. To purify them, do this: Sprinkle the water of cleansing on them; then have them shave their whole bodies and wash their clothes, and so purify themselves."*

The Levites are prepared for their consecration by being sprinkled with the "water of cleansing," by shaving their whole bodies, and by washing their clothes. The term "water of cleansing" (v. 7 NIV; KJV: "water of purifying"; RSV: "water of expiation") is literally "water of sin" and is found only here; it is more appropriately rendered "water for the removal of sin." It is not the same as the "water of cleansing" (NIV; KJV: "water of separation"; RSV: "water for impurity") in Numbers 19:9, 13, 20–21, which is literally "water of impurity." Thus, the purpose of the sin offering is propitiation (v. 8; cf. Lev. 4:3ff.), the "water of impurity" (Num. 19) removes uncleanness, while the "water for the removal of sin" here frees from sin. A different term is used in Leviticus 14:3–7, and the water there is prepared in a different manner. Some are of the opinion that the water in verse 7 is pure spring water, while others identify it with the "holy water" of 5:17. The former view finds support in Ezekiel 36:25 and Zechariah 13:1.

The concept behind this "water for the removal of sin" is purely dynamistic[12]; it stems from a material concept of sin, which is seen as impurity that clings to the person and to the clothing. Hence also a prayer such as in Psalm 51:2a, which implies the washing of one's clothing (cf. verse 7), and e.g., Genesis 49:11 and 2 Samuel 19:24. The same concept is found throughout the ancient Near Eastern world.

The same idea also underlies the shaving of the whole body (lit. "they shall cause a razor to pass over" their whole body). This is not "shaving" in our Western sense of the word, for which a different verb is used (*gillach*); the latter verb is used in the case of the cleansing of a leper (Lev. 14:8-9) and of the Nazirite who has touched a dead body (Num. 6:9; cf. also Deut. 21:12). I do not know exactly what the phrase used here implies. Hebrew also has a different verb for the "cutting" of hair (*kasam*, Ezek. 44:20). In Egypt, priests had to remove the hair from their whole body every other day (Herodotus, II. 37). All this is based on the concept that sin clings to hair.

The same is true of the washing of the clothes that sin penetrates. In order to become pure one must wash his or her clothes (Exod. 19:10). This is all the more necessary for the Levites, since they, unlike the priests, do not have official garments (see also my *Gods Woord,* pp. 88ff.; Edelkoort, *Zondebesef,* p. 131).

2. *The Offerings* (8:8-12)

8:8-12 *"Have them take a young bull with its grain offering of fine flour mixed with oil; then you are to take a second young bull for a sin offering. Bring the Levites to the front of the Tent of Meeting and assemble the whole Israelite community. You are to bring the Levites before the* LORD, *and the Israelites are to lay their hands on them. Aaron is to present the Levites before the* LORD *as a wave offering from the Israelites, so that they may be ready to do the work of the* LORD.

"After the Levites lay their hands on the heads of the bulls, use the one for a sin offering to the LORD *and the other for a burnt offering, to make atonement for the Levites."*

After the cleansing, which must be performed under Moses' direct supervision (vv. 6-7) since he must later (v. 13) present the Levites pure to the priests, follow the offerings. The animals to be offered must, of course, be provided by the Levites themselves: two young bulls, one for a sin offering, the other for a burnt offering (v. 12), the latter with its

---

[12]See Publisher's Note.

accompanying grain offering (15:9). But the offerings must be preceded by ceremonial acts. The Levites, who had been set apart (v. 6), must be taken to the front of the tabernacle along with the whole Israelite community (v. 9); the Israelites are then to lay their hands on the Levites and Aaron is to present the Levites to the Lord as a wave offering (vv. 10–11). The latter is a priestly act and must thus be performed by Aaron: the Levites are "turned over" to God.

The laying on of hands is clear: it is the *semika,* which expresses the bond between the offerer and the offering, whereby the latter takes the place of the former (see my commentary on Lev. 1:3–9). The "waving" is also clear (v. 11 reads literally, "and Aaron shall wave the Levites, a wave offering before the LORD"). It is a double movement made by the priest to consecrate the offering: first in the direction of the sanctuary to symbolize the presentation of the offering, and then in the direction of the offerer, indicating that the Lord places the offering at his or her disposal (see my commentary on Lev. 7:28–34).

But how can the whole community lay hands on 20 *'elef* Levites, and how can Aaron "wave" this large a group of people before the Lord? In 27:21 a clear distinction is made between "all the sons of Israel" and "the whole community" (KJV). The latter term probably refers to Israel's official representatives. The "waving" then may mean that Aaron made the prescribed motions in front of the Levites, while Israel's representatives did the same when they laid on hands. In verse 11 Aaron must do the waving, since it is the work of a priest; this is different from the waving in verse 13 (see below).

The offering required for the consecration of the Levites (see above) differs from that for the consecration of the priests. One bull and two rams are required for the latter (Lev. 8:14, 18, 22); here two young bulls are called for. This difference is related to the differences in the rites of consecration for the two groups (see my commentary on Lev. 8). The sin offering for an ordinary Israelite consists of a goat, but this is not sufficient for the Levite because of his special position in the cultus. For the Levite the sin offering is the same as for a priest who has sinned unintentionally: a bull (Lev. 4:3). But in this case the sin offering is not brought for sins already committed, since it would then have had to precede the cleansing rites; rather, it represents a reinforcement of those rites, since henceforth the Levite will be in close contact with the holy things and the Levite, like the priest must, so to speak, be safeguarded against the dangers that lie in contact with the holy (cf. Lev. 8:14–17).

The burnt offering follows the sin offering; as in 6:11, it has atoning power, as verse 12 explicitly states.

3. The Levites Are Presented to the Priests (8:13–19)

8:13–19 *"Have the Levites stand in front of Aaron and his sons and then present them as a wave offering to the LORD. In this way you are to set the Levites apart from the other Israelites, and the Levites will be mine.*

"After you have purified the Levites and presented them as a wave offering, they are to come to do their work at the Tent of Meeting. They are the Israelites who are to be given wholly to me. I have taken them as my own in place of the firstborn, the first male offspring from every Israelite woman. Every firstborn male in Israel, whether man or animal, is mine. When I struck down all the firstborn in Egypt, I set them apart for myself. And I have taken the Levites in place of all the firstborn sons in Israel. Of all the Israelites, I have given the Levites as gifts to Aaron and his sons to do the work at the Tent of Meeting on behalf of the Israelites and to make atonement for them so that no plague will strike the Israelites when they go near the sanctuary."

The cleansed Levites, for whom atonement has been made, are now to be "handed over" to the priests. They must be placed in front of "Aaron and his sons" and once again they must be "waved" as a wave offering. This time it is Moses who "waves" them and hands over the Lord's "gift" as the mediator. Here it is not a priestly act, as in verse 11, but a handing over in the name of the Lord. The following verses substantiate this; they are closely related to 3:11–13, 41 (see commentary on those verses) and contain the reminder that the Levites take the place of the firstborn of Israel. The firstborn are actually those who were called to serve under the priests, but they would be in danger of committing cultic errors (1:53; 18:22–23), in which case a "plague" would come over Israel because Israel's sins would kindle the Lord's wrath (cf. Exod. 12:13; 30:12; Num. 17:12–13; Josh. 22:17).

4. Summary (8:20–22)

8:20–22 *Moses, Aaron and the whole Israelite community did with the Levites just as the LORD commanded Moses. The Levites purified themselves and washed their clothes. Then Aaron presented them as a wave offering before the LORD and made atonement for them to purify them. After that, the Levites came to do their work at the Tent of Meeting under the supervision of Aaron and his sons. They did with the Levites just as the Lord commanded Moses.*

These verses, which are definitely not proof of a "double revision" as Wellhausen's school maintains, summarize the preceding. First, the prominent participants are mentioned (v. 20). Then is described how the Levites were prepared for their task through purification and atonement, after which Aaron performs the decisive act (v. 21). And finally, it is emphasized that only "after that" the Levites began their official duties under priestly supervision.

The lawgiver is thus primarily concerned with three things: 1) the Levites take the place of the firstborn of the Israelites; 2) the Levites are servants of the priests; and 3) their cooperation (v. 22) shows that they assume their duties willingly.

5. *Length of Service* (8:23–26)

8:23–26 *The L*ord *said to Moses, "This applies to the Levites: Men twenty-five years old or more shall come to take part in the work at the Tent of Meeting, but at the age of fifty, they must retire from their regular service and work no longer. They may assist their brothers in performing their duties at the Tent of Meeting, but they themselves must not do the work. This, then, is how you are to assign the responsibilities of the Levites."*

Every male Levite who does not have a physical handicap that would make him unfit (see commentary on Lev. 21:16–23) is to serve at the sanctuary from age twenty-five until age fifty. In 4:3, 23, 30 the age limits are thirty to fifty, while David set the lower age limit at twenty (1 Chron. 23:24, 27; cf. also 2 Chron. 31:17; Ezra 3:8). The latter change was undoubtedly due to the increased services needed in a royal sanctuary, and shows that the devout Israelite definitely did not consider the *torah* immutable (see my commentary on 2 Chron. 31:2–18; 35:7–15). The different age limits in 8:23 and 4:3, 23, 30 can be explained only on the basis of changes in circumstances. The rabbinical claim that the period between the twenty-fifth and thirtieth year was a time of training is of course nothing more than an exegetical contrivance. And 8:23ff. does not support the view of Hengstenberg and his school that these verses refer to the service of the Levites in general and 4:3 only to their service in the transportation of the tabernacle.

The upper age limit never changed. But there were always Levites who wanted to continue working after age fifty, perhaps in part because of the perquisites of the office. Their service is to be limited to "assisting their brothers," i.e., it must be entirely voluntary and only occasionally, e.g., during the annual festivals.

The Second Passover
(9:1–14)

These verses take us two weeks past the date of 1:1 (see v. 5), and thus seven weeks past the date of 7:1. They deal with the celebration of the

Passover (vv. 2–4) and the practical difficulties that prevented some from celebrating it (vv. 6–14).

1. *The Normal Celebration of the Passover* (9:1–5)

9:1–5 *The Lord spoke to Moses in the Desert of Sinai in the first month of the second year after they came out of Egypt. He said, "Have the Israelites celebrate the Passover at the appointed time. Celebrate it at the appointed time, at twilight on the fourteenth day of this month, in accordance with all its rules and regulations."*

So Moses told the Israelites to celebrate the Passover, and they did so in the Desert of Sinai at twilight on the fourteenth day of the first month. The Israelites did everything just as the Lord commanded Moses.

Verse 2 does not state what "the appointed time" is, nor does it explain how the Passover lamb is to be prepared. The regulations concerning these matters (Exod. 12) are presupposed and are here and in verses 12, 14 called "rules and regulations." Verses 11–12 point out only three things concerning the Passover (see commentary on v. 11), and verse 3 states that it is to be celebrated (lit. "prepared") "at twilight," a requirement that is repeated in verse 11; this was thus considered important (see also v. 5). "At twilight" is literally "between the two evenings," which some translate "by the light of the full moon" or "between the two settings" (i.e., of the sun and of the moon), or "toward evening." The intended meaning is probably "after sunset," before it is fully dark. According to Rashi it means "after the sixth hour." Strictly speaking, the Passover falls on the fifteenth day of the first month, since the Israelite day begins with the evening rather than the morning. The feast is thus celebrated under a full moon (*chodeš*), since the month (*chodeš*) begins with the new moon (*chadaš*). Concerning the Passover, see my commentary on Leviticus 23:5–8.

In verse 5 I translate *bari'šon* "in the first month" on the basis of Genesis 8:13; Exodus 12:2, 18; Ezekiel 29:17; cf. Exodus 40:2, 17; Leviticus 23:5; Ezra 6:19, as do the English versions. Others prefer the rendering "for the first time," which is also possible (cf. Gen. 13:4; Josh. 8:5–6 KJV). This would then express the thought that the celebration of the Passover referred to in Exodus 12 was more a celebration at home, while from now on the Passover acquires a ceremonial character. But this did not happen until it was celebrated at the sanctuary (see Deut. 16:6; 2 Kings 23:23).

2. *Special Provisions for the Ceremonially Unclean* (9:6–14)

9:6–9 *But some of them could not celebrate the Passover on that day because they were ceremonially unclean on account of a dead body. So they came to Moses and Aaron that same day and said to Moses, "We have become unclean because of a dead*

---

body, but why should we be kept from presenting the LORD's offering with the other Israelites at the appointed time?"

Moses answered them, "Wait until I find out what the LORD commands concerning you."

Several men, however, could not celebrate this Passover: they had been in contact with a dead body and were thus ceremonially unclean. This implies two things: 1) contact with a dead body results in ceremonial uncleanness, which is not explicitly stated anywhere in the law, but is assumed to be generally known (see 6:7); and 2) the ceremonially unclean individual cannot participate in the Passover celebration; this also is not stated explicitly in Exodus 12 nor in Leviticus 23:5-8, but is self-evident, since in the dynamistic perspective[13] that Israel shared with the rest of the ancient Near East ceremonial uncleanness bars an individual from participation in any cultic act.

These men approach Moses with a question to which he does not have an immediate answer: Why are they not allowed to participate in the Passover celebration? This practically excludes them from their own people, since the Passover is for Israel the celebration of their redemption from Egypt, of the new beginning of Israel's life as a nation (see my commentary on Lev. 23:4-8). Should the consequences of their ceremonial uncleanness be this severe? Moses does not have the answer, as in the case of the blasphemer (Lev. 24:13-14) and of the man gathering wood on the Sabbath (Num. 15:32-36). He therefore turns to the Lord.

9:9-12 *Then the LORD said to Moses, "Tell the Israelites: 'When any of you or your descendants are unclean because of a dead body or are away on a journey, they may still celebrate the LORD's Passover. They are to celebrate it on the fourteenth day of the second month at twilight. They are to eat the lamb, together with unleavened bread and bitter herbs. They must not leave any of it till morning or break any of its bones. When they celebrate the Passover, they must follow all the regulations.'"*

The answer we find here covers more than Moses' question: it deals not only with possible ceremonial uncleanness, but also with potential absence due to a long journey, apparently a journey of such length that it was impossible to return in time for the Passover ("away on a journey," lit. "on a distant journey"). The words "on a distant journey" (v. 10) and "is not on a journey" (v. 13) must be later additions. The wilderness period precludes the possibility of distant commercial travel for the Israelite; this

---

[13]See Publisher's Note.

became possible only when Israel began to participate in international commerce in the time after Solomon (1 Kings 10:22ff.). The rabbis made any kind of uncleanness, not only that caused by contact with a dead body, a legal obstacle to participation in the celebration of the Passover in the night of the fourteenth of Abib (later Nisan, approximately April; *Pesachim* 9. 2).

In the case of ceremonial uncleanness or absence the opportunity is given to celebrate the Passover later, in the night of the fourteenth of Ziv (later Iyyar), i.e., the month after Nisan, approximately our month of May. But it is made very clear that this second Passover must not differ in any way from the first: the Passover lamb must be eaten that very night with the unleavened loaves (*mazzoth*) and the bitter herbs (according to *Pesachim* 2.6 five plants are suitable, among them lettuce and endive); furthermore, none of the bones of the lamb must be broken, i.e., the lamb must not be treated as ordinary food and cut in pieces—it must be roasted over the fire (Exod. 12:9, 46). No mention is made of the application of the blood to the sides and tops of the door frames, which is understandable, since in the wilderness the Israelites lived in tents. This law reflects the wilderness period in yet another respect: the Passover still retains its domestic character (Exod. 12:3–4). Later the meat of the Passover lamb is treated like the meat of an offering and is thus boiled (cf. Exod. 29:31 RSV; Lev. 8:31 RSV; Deut. 16:7 RSV; 1 Sam. 2:13; cf. my commentary on 2 Chron. 35:13–14).

9:13 *"'But if a man who is ceremonially clean and not on a journey fails to celebrate the Passover, that person must be cut off from his people because he did not present the LORD's offering at the appointed time. That man will bear the consequences of his sin.'"*

This verse states explicitly that anyone who deliberately fails to celebrate the Passover removes himself from the community and severs all ties with his own people and thus also with the Lord, Israel's God. For such an individual there is no place left in Israel: he must be "cut off from his people," a phrase that is also found elsewhere (Gen. 17:14; Exod. 12:15, 19; 31:14; Lev. 7:20f., 25, 27; 17:9f., 14; 18:29; 19:8; 23:29; Num. 15:30f.; 19:13, 20). This phrase generally refers to the death penalty, but Leviticus 17:10; 20:3, 6 show that it can also involve an act on the part of God Himself (cf. Num. 15:35 and my commentary on Lev. 17:10 and 20:1–6).

9:14 *"'An alien living among you who wants to celebrate the LORD's Passover must do so in accordance with its rules and regulations. You must have the same regulations for the alien and the native-born.'"*

Here the possibility is raised that an alien (*ger*) expresses the desire to participate in the Passover celebration. The *ger* is a non-Israelite who lives under the protection of a smaller or larger Israelite community and derives certain privileges from this arrangement (cf. Abraham in Hebron, Gen. 23:4). Assumed is that his eyes have been opened to the riches of Israel's religion and that he wishes to live in accordance with this religion. The *ger* then must observe all the rules and regulations of the Passover like a native-born Israelite. This is, of course, a later addition from the time when an Israelite could call himself "native-born" in Canaan (see my commentary on Lev. 16:29–34). Exodus 12:48 requires that the alien and the males in his household be circumcised before participating. This is not mentioned here, but clearly included in the statement "You must have the same regulations."

We hear of such a second Passover in 2 Chronicles 30 when the Passover had to be postponed for a month in the days of Hezekiah. In that situation the law of Numbers 9:6–14 was applied, even though the case was entirely different. This is another proof that at that time the law was not considered an immutable entity as it was in later Judaism (cf. commentary on 8:23–26).

The Signs for Setting Out and Setting Up Camp (9:15–10:10)

1. *The Pillar of Cloud and Fire* (9:15–23)

9:15–23 *On the day the tabernacle, the Tent of the Testimony, was set up, the cloud covered it. From evening till morning the cloud above the tabernacle looked like fire. That is how it continued to be; the cloud covered it, and at night it looked like fire. Whenever the cloud lifted from above the Tent, the Israelites set out; wherever the cloud settled, the Israelites encamped. At the LORD's command the Israelites set out, and at his command they encamped. As long as the cloud stayed over the tabernacle, they remained in camp. When the cloud remained over the tabernacle a long time, the Israelites obeyed the LORD's order and did not set out. Sometimes the cloud was over the tabernacle only a few days; at the LORD's command they would encamp, and then at his command they would set out. Sometimes the cloud stayed only from evening till morning, and when it lifted in the morning, they set out. Whether by day or by night, whenever the cloud lifted, they set out. Whether the cloud stayed over the tabernacle for two days or a month or a year, the Israelites would remain in camp and not set out; but when it lifted, they would set out. At the LORD's command they encamped, and at the LORD's command they set out. They obeyed the LORD's order, in accordance with his command through Moses.*

This section, which must prepare the reader for the departure from Sinai, takes us to the first day of the second year after the Exodus (cf. 7:1; 9:1). The purpose of these verses is to give us an impression of Israel's complete obedience to the Lord's signs as to the breaking up and setting up of the camp. Hence the repeated phrase "at the LORD's command," which occurs no fewer than eight times, and "the LORD's order," which is found twice. Attention is drawn to the fact that the length of Israel's stay in a given place and the time of their arrival and departure are in no way determined by Israel. It is always the "cloud" that determines Israel's actions as these verses state no fewer than ten times. The cloud is Israel's guide during the day, while at night there is (literally) "on the tabernacle as the appearance of fire" (cf. Ezek. 1). Both the cloud and the fire are closely connected with the tabernacle; both always hover immediately above it. There can be no reasonable doubt that this "cloud" (cf. Exod. 16:10; Num. 10:12; etc.) and this "appearance of fire" are the same as the "pillar of cloud" and the "pillar of fire" in e.g., Exodus 13:21–22; 14:19, 24; 33:9–10; Numbers 12:5; 14:14. In Exodus 13:21–22 the pillar of cloud is Israel's guide, while in Exodus 14:19, 24, the pillar of cloud and the pillar of fire are Israel's protectors. Both are always described as a manifestation of the Lord that speaks of His presence (cf. Exod. 40:36–38); the preposition "in" (Exod. 13:21) should therefore not be understood in a spatial sense. Thus, when 10:33 states that the ark served as Israel's guide it is essentially the same as saying that the cloud served that function, since the ark is the portable sanctuary of the invisible God (see commentary on 10:33).

The view that the cloud was a one-time phenomenon (e.g., Edelkoort, *Numeri,* p. 114) contradicts the Old Testament data. The concept that "the cloud" was the result of the volcanic activity of Mount Sinai does justice neither to the description of Exodus 13:21; 14:19, nor to Exodus 19:16, apart even from the fact that there are no traces of volcanic activity on the Sinai peninsula (cf. also Böhl, *Exodus,* p. 125; Edelkoort, *Uittocht en Intocht,* pp. 83f.). The suggestion that we must think here of smoke and fire signals does not merit rebuttal.

We are not informed what happened to the tabernacle during a one-day stay; it was probably not set up, since this would have required too much time. Verse 22 indicates that in all other cases a beginning was made with setting up the tabernacle.

2. The Trumpets (10:1–10)

10:1–2 *The LORD said to Moses: "Make two trumpets of hammered silver, and use them for calling the community together and for having the camps set out."*

This section, like the previous one, prepares the reader for the departure from Sinai. It regulates the use of the two trumpets that were made of hammered silver specifically for use on the occasions listed. The trumpets served to call together the whole Israelite community or its leaders (vv. 3–4), to give the sign for the breaking up of the camp (vv. 5–6), or to signal the going into battle (v. 9), and were used at the feasts (v. 10).

No description of the trumpets is given here. Josephus (*Antiquities,* III, 12. 6) relates that they consisted of narrow tubes approximately one cubit long, widening at the end into a bell-shaped opening; this description matches the trumpets depicted on the Arch of Titus in Rome. The model was probably provided by the Egyptian trumpet. Silver trumpets are also depicted on coins of Bar Kochba, but these are much shorter and appear to be much less artistic in design; the mouthpiece shows a spherical enlargement, perhaps to increase the volume.

10:3–4 *"When both are sounded, the whole community is to assemble before you at the entrance to the Tent of Meeting. If only one is sounded, the leaders—the heads of the clans of Israel—are to assemble before you."*

When both trumpets are sounded it is the sign for "the whole community," i.e., Israel's lawful representatives, to assemble at the entrance to the tabernacle to receive Moses' instructions or to confer with him. When just one trumpet is sounded "the leaders" (see 1:16) are to come.

10:5–7 *"When a trumpet blast is sounded, the tribes camping on the east are to set out. At the sounding of a second blast, the camps on the south are to set out. The blast will be the signal for setting out. To gather the assembly, blow the trumpets, but not with the same signal."*

A different signal, the *terua',* is used when Israel is to break up camp and set out. It is not exactly clear what this word means in this context. The Dutch AV thinks of a "broken sound," the KJV renders it "alarm," while the NIV translates it "trumpet blast." The *terua'* is in any case longer than the "sounding" of the trumpet in verses 3–4, since the same word is used also for the jubilation with which someone is welcomed (e.g., Num. 23:21). With Edelkoort I prefer the rendering "signal," a fixed sequence of sounds that is the sign that something is to be done, in this case the breaking up of the camp. I suspect that the four signals in verses 5–6[14] each

---

[15]With the LXX I emend the text of verse 6 to read: "At the sounding of the second signal, the camps on the south are to set out. At the sounding of the third signal, the camps on the west are to set out. At the sounding of the fourth signal, the camps on the north are to set out. The signal will be the sign for setting out."

consisted of a different sequence of tones to avoid confusion as to the order in which the four camps were to be set out.

10:8 *"The sons of Aaron, the priests, are to blow the trumpets. This is to be a lasting ordinance for you and the generations to come."*

The sounding of the trumpets is the task of the priests, because Israel is seen as a primarily religious, rather than national, entity (otherwise the "leaders" would have been a more logical choice for this task). Israel is the Lord's people and the sounding of the trumpet is thus a cultic task (see also 1 Chron. 15:24; 16:6, 42; 2 Chron. 5:12f.; 7:6; 13:12; 15:14; 29:26–28; Ezra 3:10; Neh. 12:35, 41). This cultic sounding of the trumpets is also found in other religions to add luster to the cultus and perhaps also to ward off evil spirits.[15]

This sounding of the two trumpets is to be distinguished from the blowing of the trumpets mentioned in 2 Kings 11:14; 1 Chronicles 13:8; 15:28; 2 Chronicles 15:14; 20:28; 23:13, which is purely an expression of joy (see my commentary on these references in 2 Chron.).

10:9 *"When you go into battle in your own land against an enemy who is oppressing you, sound a blast on the trumpets. Then you will be remembered by the L*ORD *your God and rescued from your enemies."*

This verse speaks of calling the people to armed resistance against invaders. It dates, as the addition "in your land" indicates, from the time after the settling in Canaan when Israel was indeed in possession of a land. The attempt to make this verse refer to enemies on the wilderness journey negates the force of "in your land." In case of an invasion the priests are again to sound the trumpets; the signal to go into battle thus comes from the sanctuary. The trumpet signal must "remind" the Lord of Israel's existence; as a result, the Lord will make the enemies feel His power, so that Israel will be rescued. Hosea 5:8 also speaks of such a call to war and mentions both the "trumpet" and the "horn" (*šofar,* a curved horn with a deep, penetrating sound), while in Judges 3:27; 6:34 only the horn is used (the English versions render *šofar* "trumpet" in these verses). This "reminding" of the Lord is also mentioned in Exodus 28:12, 29; 39:7 in connection with the ephod of the high priest. The thought behind this is parallel to the "seeing" of Genesis 11:5 and was also common among Eli's contemporaries (1 Sam. 4:3). It is highly anthropomorphic and is the opposite of "forgetting" (1 Sam. 1:11; Isa. 49:14f.; Hos. 4:6 KJV) or "sleep-

---

[15] See Publisher's Note.

ing'' (Pss. 44:23; 121:4). Later, more frequent reference is made to the "remembering" of iniquities (Ps. 35:23). But this thought also implies that Israel can be assured of the Lord's help—He will help His people if He is "reminded." In Canaan, Israel will find that certain conditions are attached to this help, e.g., at Ai and during the period of the later kings when the captivity looms.

10:10 *"Also at your times of rejoicing—your appointed feasts and New Moon festivals—you are to sound the trumpets over your burnt offerings and fellowship offerings, and they will be a memorial for you before your God. I am the Lord your God."*

The trumpets must also sound at times of rejoicing (after a victory?) and at the annual feasts (Passover, Pentecost, Day of Atonement, Feast of Tabernacles). They must also sound at the New Moon festivals, which the *torah* mentions only here and in Numbers 28:11, 14, but which later assumed an important place in Israel. But the trumpets must sound only when burnt and fellowship offerings are brought; then the Lord must be "reminded" of Israel, so that He will accept Israel's offerings and bless His people. This sounding of the trumpets over the festival offerings is curious and involuntarily raises the question whether the offerings were not in themselves sufficient to "remind" the Lord of Israel's existence. The question implies the answer, and we must conclude that this reflects an ancient custom from the time when the "forefathers . . . lived beyond the River" (Josh. 24:2) and, in keeping with the ancient Near Eastern custom, sounded the trumpet when bringing sacrifices in order to keep the demonic forces away from the offerings.[16] Another reminder of that time is the fact that the trumpets are silent when the sin offering is brought: the sin offering is already connected with these demonic forces. This is the only reference to the sounding of the trumpet over burnt and fellowship offerings.

---

[16]See Publisher's Note.

Part Two

From Sinai to Kadesh
(10:11–20:13)

The Departure From Sinai
(10:11–36)

1. The Order in Which Israel Set Out (10:11–28)

10:11–28 *On the twentieth day of the second month of the second year, the cloud lifted from above the tabernacle of the Testimony. Then the Israelites set out from the Desert of Sinai and traveled from place to place until the cloud came to rest in the Desert of Paran. They set out, this first time, at the* Lord's *command through Moses.*

The divisions of the camp of Judah went first, under their standard. Nahshon son of Amminadab was in command. Nethanel son of Zuar was over the division of the tribe of Issachar, and Eliab son of Helon was over the division of the tribe of Zebulun. Then the tabernacle was taken down, and the Gershonites and Merarites, who carried it, set out.

The divisions of the camp of Reuben went next, under their standard. Elizur son of Shedeur was in command. Shelumiel son of Zurishaddai was over the division of the tribe of Simeon, and Eliasaph son of Deuel was over the division of the tribe of Gad. Then the Kohathites set out, carrying the holy things. The tabernacle was to be set up before they arrived.

The divisions of the camp of Ephraim went next, under their standard. Elishama son of Ammihud was in command. Gamaliel son of Pedahzur was over the division of the tribe of Manasseh, and Abidan son of Gideoni was over the division of the tribe of Benjamin.

Finally, as the rear guard for all the units, the divisions of the camp of Dan set out, under their standard. Ahiezer son of Ammishaddai was in command. Pagiel son of Ocran was over the division of the tribe of Asher, and Ahira son of Enan was over the division of the tribe of Naphtali. This was the order of march for the Israelite divisions as they set out.

Exodus 19:1 states that Israel arrived at Sinai three months after the Exodus. According to verse 11, the journey is resumed about one year later. During that one-year period Moses applied himself to the organization of Israel as the Lord's people. A variety of laws and regulations, covering both the social and the religious life, were issued; Israel was to implement these if it wanted to do its part in the realization of the Lord's purpose, revealed earlier to Moses at Sinai: "I will take you as my own people, and I will be your God" (Exod. 6:7).

And now the time has come for Israel to continue its journey to Canaan where it is to occupy the position among the nations of the ancient Near East to which it is entitled, and where it is to show by the way it lives what it means to be the Lord's people. The signal for the departure is given by "the cloud" (cf. 9:15ff.), the visible sign of the Lord's command. The cloud lifts and does not come to rest until it reaches the Desert of Paran. The stops along the way are reported in chapter 11 (vv. 3, 34–35); the arrival in Paran is not mentioned until 12:16.

The first mention of Paran is in the story of Hagar (Gen. 21:21); Deuteronomy 33:2 and Habakkuk 3:3 speak of "Mount Paran" (the present Gebel el-Maqrah south of Kadesh?), which is usually identified with Elath near the present Tell el-Kheleifeh, the well-known harbor on the Gulf of Aqaba, at the north-eastern tip of the Red Sea. But there are no convincing arguments to support this identification (cf. J. H. Kroeze, *Genesis XIV*, 1937, pp. 60–61; concerning the excavations at that location, see *Jaarbericht van het Gezelschap Ex Oriente Lux*, No. 7, 1940, p. 427). Since Kadesh (or Kadesh Barnea as it is called elsewhere, e.g., 32:8; 34:4; Gen. 14:7: En Mishpat) is probably the present Ain Qadeis, located about forty-five miles south of Beersheba (see commentary on 13:1), the Desert of Paran must be sought north of Mount Sinai. This means that this desert, of which the northernmost part must have been called the Desert of Zin (cf. 20:1 and 33:36 with 13:26), is to be identified with the limestone tableland that is now called et-Tih and covers the northern half of the Sinai peninsula. As the Hebrew *midbar* (which we usually, but not accurately, translate "desert") expresses, it is a steppe; it contains a few mountain ranges and numerous wadis. It is possible to graze cattle on the steppe until shortly after the rainy season (cf. 1:1). David sought refuge in this region (1 Sam. 25:1 NIV margin). Israel thus takes the shortest route to Canaan.

Kadesh could not, of course, be reached in a single day; hence the phrase "from place to place" in verse 12 (cf. 11:3, 34-35). Whenever Israel resumes its journey it is in the order of march given in chapter 2, but with one exception. According to 2:17, the Levites with the tabernacle were to travel between the Reubenites and the Ephraimites. But 10:17 states that the Gershonites and the Merarites followed Judah, while the Kohathites traveled between Reuben and Ephraim (v. 21). The reason for this arrangement is also given in verses 17 and 21: the Gershonites and Merarites take down the tabernacle and set it up again before the Kohathites arrive. The "holy things"—the ark, the table, the altars, etc.—must not be exposed to unauthorized eyes (4:20). It is thus logical to assume that the "taking down" of the tabernacle (10:17) included everything mentioned in chapter 4 concerning the "holy things." It is thus out of practical necessity that the Gershonites and Merarites leave first, while only the Kohathites with the "holy things" occupy the central position in the marching column. Only thus could the holy things be safeguarded against losing something of their exceptional character.

2. *Moses Is Joined by His Brother-in-law* (10:29-34)

Now that Israel is breaking camp at Sinai, Moses tells Hobab (the name is found in Akkadian as Hababa) where Israel will be going, and he tries to convince Hobab to come along. The MT calls Hobab Moses' father-in-law (*choten*). This has led to the view that Hobab is an abbreviation of Hobab-el; Hobab is then assumed to be related to the Arabic verb *chabba,* which means "to love," so that Hobab-el would mean "Beloved of God." And since Reuel (Exod. 2:18) means "friend of God," Hobab and Reuel would be synonymous. This would mean that we have here a man with two names, which is highly unlikely. In Exodus 3:1; 4:18b; 18:1-2, 5-6, 12 Moses' father-in-law is called Jethro, while in Exodus 4:18a he is called Jether[1] without the old nominative ending -*o*. Jethro, however, is a title rather than a proper noun, indicating his official position as priest, something like our "eminence" (cf. Böhl, *Exodus,* p. 99; Gispen on Exod. 3:1 in this commentary series). In Exodus 2:16 and 18:1 he is called "priest of Midian," while in Judges 1:16 his people are said to belong to the Kenites; there is no real difference, however, since the Kenites are part of the Midianites.

But Hobab is mentioned only here and in Judges 4:11. In both places he is called the *chtn* of Moses. If we vocalize this with the MT as *choten,* then not only must verses 29-34 be a pendant of Exodus 18:27, but we are also

---

[1]Cf. ASV margin; the English versions treat Jether as a variant spelling and render it "Jethro" (tr).

faced with the problem that, while according to Exodus 18:27 Moses' father-in-law returned to his own country after a brief visit, according to Numbers 10:29 he stayed with Moses for almost a full year. I therefore prefer (as do other exegetes, e.g., Baentsch, *Numeri;* Gesenius, *Wörterbuch*) to vocalize *chatun,* "brother-in-law." The LXX uses a word (*gambros*) that can mean both "father-in-law" and "brother-in-law," while the Latin speaks of *cognatus,* "relative." I believe that the vocalization of the MT is based on a desire to make the link between the Kenites and Israel as strong as possible, since the Kenites were later absorbed into Israel.

10:29–32 *Now Moses said to Hobab son of Reuel the Midianite, Moses' father-in-law, "We are setting out for the place about which the Lord said, 'I will give it to you.' Come with us and we will treat you well, for the Lord has promised good things to Israel."*

He answered, "No, I will not go; I am going back to my own land and my own people."

But Moses said, "Please do not leave us. You know where we should camp in the desert, and you can be our eyes. If you come with us, we will share with you whatever good things the Lord gives us."

Moses asks his brother-in-law to go with Israel to "the place about which the Lord said, 'I will give it to you.'" This description is reminiscent of Exodus 23:20. Moses probably used it to assure Hobab of the success of Israel's journey to the civilized country of Canaan, the desire of all Bedouins. The second part of Moses' speech refers to the promising future that awaits Hobab there. But Hobab declines Moses' invitation. His words imply two things: first, that Mount Sinai does not lie in Midian, since after his departure from Israel Hobab plans to return to Midian; and second, that the road from Sinai to the southern part of Canaan does not go through Midian. The decisive factor in Hobab's decision is the tie with his own people (cf. Gen. 31:13f.; Ruth 2:11; Jer. 46:16). But Moses insists and points out the important role Hobab can play in Israel and the reward that awaits him: with his extensive knowledge of the desert Hobab can be Israel's "eyes" (cf. Job 29:15). This last statement has led some to conclude that this narrative knows nothing of the pillar of cloud and fire that guided Israel, nor of the ark being its guide. I would draw a different conclusion: even Moses remains human. Hobab's knowledge of the areas where cattle can graze and of the wells along the way seems to him to be a desirable source of help. And the sacred author does not fail to mention also this weakness on Moses' part; he paints a realistic picture without flattery. It is typical of the spirit of later Judaism that the Targums and the LXX have changed Hobab into a messenger of Moses, rather than a guide.

Hobab's answer to the second invitation is not recorded. Some (e.g., Edelkoort) believe that it was again negative and was deleted for some reason. But, apart from the fact that it would be difficult to give a reason for this omission, two considerations would tend to lead me to the opposite conclusion: first, we find these Kenites among Israel when it enters Canaan (Judg. 1:16; 4:11; 1 Sam. 15:6); and second, it is customary in the Near East to accede to a request only after it has been repeated.

10:33–34 *So they set out from the mountain of the LORD and traveled for three days. The ark of the covenant of the LORD went before them during those three days to find them a place to rest. The cloud of the LORD was over them by day when they set out from the camp.*

Verse 33 refers back to verse 12 to emphasize two things: the ark leads, and only after three days does Israel encamp again—not until then does Israel find "a place to rest." The fact that verse 33 speaks of the ark as Israel's guide rather than the cloud does not contradict 9:15ff. and Deuteronomy 1:33, but if differs from verse 21 and 2:17, which state that the ark's position was in the center of Israel's column. I suspect that the ark went ahead of Israel only during the journey from Sinai to Paran (i.e., Kadesh) in order to show Israel (which was going north to attack Canaan from the south) clearly that the Lord Himself guided them. Furthermore, the "cloud of the LORD was over them" as a sign of protection. Apparently Israel needed to have any fear removed, especially at the beginning of its journey.

I omit "during those three days" in verse 33b (Heb.: "the ark . . . set out before them, three days' journey"), since it appears to be an inadvertent repetition (the same phrase is used in v. 33a). If we retain the phrase we must assume (based on the literal meaning) that the ark went three days ahead and waited for Israel in Paran when it had found a place to rest (cf. RSV, ASV), or the phrase must be taken to mean "during the three days' journey" (cf. KJV, NIV). Only here is Mount Sinai called "the mountain of the LORD," quite understandably so after all that has taken place here. Later Mount Zion will be called by that name (Ps. 24:3; Isa. 2:3; 30:29; Mic. 4:2). Elsewhere Mount Sinai is always called "the mountain of God" (Exod. 3:1; 4:27; 18:5; 24:13; 1 Kings 19:8).

3. *The Formulas for Setting Out and Stopping* (10:35–36)

10:35–36 *Whenever the ark set out, Moses said,*
  "Rise up, O LORD!
    May your enemies be scattered;
    may your foes flee before you."

Whenever it came to rest, he said,
  "Return, O Lᴏʀᴅ,
    to the countless thousands of Israel."

The wording of these verses (*wayyehi binsoa*) indicates that they do not refer to a unique event, but rather to what was said "whenever the ark set out" (the ᴋᴊᴠ and ᴀsᴠ obscure this by a literal rendering). These verses thus do not follow the preceding in a strictly chronological sense. The impression has been given that Moses here gives the sign to set out, and that these verses thus represent a different perspective than the rest of the Pentateuch, where the Lord Himself gives the sign by means of the cloud or the ark; the Hebrew text is then inaccurately paraphrased "whenever the ark was to set out," or something similar. But the text clearly states that the setting out of the ark always preceded Moses' speaking. What happened "whenever the ark set out" is assumed to be known here, since it has been mentioned frequently in 9:15–23 and 10:11–13, 33–34. The idea that Moses could command the Lord as to whether and when He was to set out is in direct contradiction to Israel's knowledge concerning man's position relative to God.

There are two formulas; the first one is pronounced when the ark sets out (v. 35), the second one when the ark comes to rest (v. 36). The first formula has a distinctly military character: it speaks of the scattering of the Lord's "enemies," and of the fleeing of His "foes" (lit. "those hating you," cf. ᴋᴊᴠ) because the Lord "rises up." The purpose of this rising up is to help Israel (Ps. 35:2; 44:26), to save (Jer. 2:27 ᴋᴊᴠ; 46:16), to destroy His enemies (Isa. 14:22; Ps. 33:10). This formula is quoted almost verbatim in Psalm 68:1 (cf. also Ps. 132:8). It is not surprising that the destruction of the enemies is asked for at this point; the enemies would not necessarily stage a direct attack on Israel, but they might gain control over that which Israel needs most at this point: pastures and springs. There is no reason, therefore, to see these verses as "war formulas" from the time immediately after the conquest.

It is not surprising that the enemies of Israel are called the Lord's enemies. In the ancient Near Eastern perspective a nation and its god are one. Hence, the defeat of a nation involves the defeat of its national god, whose image is carried away as a prisoner to the temple of the national god of the victors (cf. 1 Sam. 5:1; also 2 Kings 24:13; 25:14–15). A nation's god is therefore also thought of as marching at the head of the army. Thus, one of the Assyrian kings says, "With the exalted help of (god) Negal, who went ahead of me, I did battle with them." This verse, as well as e.g., Joshua 3:10–11 and 1 Samuel 4:3, shows that the same concept was also present in Israel.

In the MT the second formula reads literally "Return (*šbh*), Lord, the myriads (*rbbt*) of the thousands of Israel." But the verb "to return" can lack the preposition of direction only if it is followed by a place name, which is not the case here. I therefore prefer with many other interpreters to vocalize *šbh* "shebah" ("descend") rather than *shubah* ("return"), which also provides a contrast to the immediately preceding "came to rest." Instead of *rbbt* we should read *wbrkt* ("and bless"), since otherwise the second part of the formula is suspended and no indication is given as to the effect of this descending, as in the first formula it is made clear what the result of the rising up will be. After the destruction of the enemies, Israel thus asks its God for His "blessing," i.e., His life-supporting power that alone is capable of bringing happiness and prosperity (see commentary on 6:24).

Events on the Journey to Kadesh
(11:1–14:45)

1. *The Disaster at Taberah* (11:1–3)

11:1–3 *Now the people complained about their hardships in the hearing of the* LORD, *and when he heard them his anger was aroused. Then fire from the* LORD *burned among them and consumed some of the outskirts of the camp. When the people cried out to Moses, he prayed to the* LORD *and the fire died down. So that place was called Taberah, because fire from the* LORD *had burned among them.*

The people have barely departed when they experience the kinds of problems that are natural on a journey through an inhospitable region such as the Sinai peninsula—and they fall back into their old sin. They once again begin to grumble and complain (cf. Exod. 15:24; 16:2; 17:3; also Num. 11:4; 14:2; 16:3; 20:3; 21:5). Verse 1 literally says, "the people (is) as those who complain about evil." This time we are not told what the nature of their hardships was, but the author points out that the people complain audibly: there is thus no longer any reticence. They intend the Lord to hear them, since it is His fault! The Lord does indeed hear, and "his anger is aroused," an anthropomorphism that is found in numerous places and speaks of impending punishment. This time the punishment is "the fire from the LORD" (see also 16:35; Lev. 10:2; Job 1:16; "fire from heaven," Exod. 9:23 RSV; 2 Kings 1:10). In other words, a tremendous thunderstorm is unleashed over Israel. Yet the Lord's mercy is evident in His judgment: only the outskirts of the camp are destroyed. But there the fire burns, a serious danger to a tent camp, and also a warning that the Lord's anger does not spare even His own people.

The loud calling, the crying in dismay, begins. The revelation of the Lord's power makes a deep impression. The people know that Moses lives close to the Lord and they are familiar with his willingness to intercede for them (Exod. 14:15; 17:4); Moses now must provide relief through his prayer. And again Moses is willing (cf. Exod. 15:25; 32:11–14, 31–33; see also Num. 14:5, 13ff.; 21:7) to implore the Lord to be merciful and to forgive His sinful people. The fire dies down, and Israel's camp is saved. But the fire made a deep impression on the people; this stopping place is from that time on called Taberah, "Place of Burning" (cf. Deut. 9:22). It is not mentioned in Numbers 33, and we do not know its location.

2. *The Dissatisfaction With the Manna* (11:4–6)

11:4–6 *The rabble with them began to crave other food, and again the Israelites started wailing and said, "If only we had meat to eat! We remember the fish we ate in Egypt at no cost—also the cucumbers, melons, leeks, onions and garlic. But now we have lost our appetite; we never see anything but this manna!"*

These verses have only a loose connection with the preceding; no mention is made of the departure from Taberah and the arrival at Kibroth Hattaavah (cf. 11:35; 12:16). Also, "with them" (lit. "among them") in verse 4 lacks an antecedent and shows that this pericope is taken from a different source than verses 1–3. The fact that "the rabble" (KJV: "mixed multitude") rather than the Israelites themselves instigates the complaining also points in that direction. "The rabble" refers, of course, to the "many other people" who joined Israel in the Exodus (Exod. 12:38) and who were perhaps reinforced by others who had joined later. They are the ones who begin to complain and who stir up Israel.

The complaint concerns the lack of meat. Israel did have "large droves of livestock, both flocks and herds "when they left Egypt (Exod. 12:38; also 17:3; 34:3; Num 14:33; 32:1), but a stockman is naturally protective of his flock and slaughters only those animals that are no longer useful to him. Hence the lack of meat in spite of the large herds and flocks. And now the past takes on a new luster. The miseries of the past have gradually been forgotten and what they lack in the present is perceived as the lost riches of the past. The pressures that led to their departure have lost their immediacy and the stark realities of life in the wilderness make the freedom for which they once yearned seem of little value. The "house of slavery" has become a land of idleness and luxury. There they had everything in abundance: fish—the canals, ponds, and lakes were full of fish (cf. Isa. 19:8), a favorite food of the poorer classes, handed out at no cost to those who were engaged in forced labor; cucumbers and watermelons, which are still grown in abundance in Egypt; leeks, onions, and garlic, a delicacy in the Near East (which caused the Romans to scoff about the evil-smelling Jews, and not entirely without reason). As Esau sold his birthright for "some of that red stew" (Gen. 25:30), so their freedom seems of little value without meat. What do they see other than "this manna"? That which was at first so valuable to them that they did not even obey Moses' instructions (Exod. 16:20) is now contemptuously called "this manna."

Israel has thus enjoyed this "bread of angels" (Ps. 78:25) for some time, which proves that Numbers 11 is not a parallel of Exod. 16, although there we also hear of manna and quail. In Exodus 16 Israel was pleased with the manna, while here they have developed an aversion for it. Israel apparently has known this manna for some time in these verses, since they know exactly how it can be ground and made into a type of bread.

3. *The Preparation of the Manna* (11:7–9)

11:7–9 *The manna was like coriander seed and looked like resin. The people went around gathering it, and then ground it in a handmill or crushed it in a mortar. They cooked it in a pot or made it into cakes. And it tasted like something made with olive oil. When the dew settled on the camp at night, the manna also came down.*

The author of this section felt the need to give his readers some information about the manna, although he assumes that the history of the manna is known. He wants to make clear how unjustified the complaints about "this manna" are. These verses are thus definitely not from the hand of the author of Exodus 16. The manna is here (as in Exod. 16:31) said to be like coriander seed; it also looks like resin. The manna is probably the sap that drips from the *Tamarix mannifera* after a spring rain as the result of the sting of a type of coccus; this sap, which is still found on the Sinai peninsula, melts in the sun and covers the ground like hoarfrost.[2] The manna tasted like the strong-smelling coriander seed (still used today in food preparation) and looked very similar to the *bedolach* (see also Gen. 2:12), which was not a gem, as the Jewish exegete Rashi suggested, but a fragrant balsamic resin derived from the wine palm that has a consistency like wax. The white manna flour (Exod. 16:31) can be made into a sweet food, reminiscent of the Jewish Passover bread. It was perhaps this sweet flavor, also mentioned in Exodus 16:31, that the people finally began to dislike.

While Exodus 16:23 says only that the manna could be baked or boiled,

---

[2]See Gispen in his commentary on Exodus 16:4–5 for a rather different view of what constituted manna.

here the preparation is described in more detail. It could be ground in a handmill; such a mill, found at Gezer, shows that it consisted of a round stone with a flat top and a depression in the center, in which another stone (the "upper millstone," Judg. 9:53; 2 Sam. 11:21) was turned by hand (see also Deut. 24:6). The manna could also be crushed in a mortar, a large, hard piece of basalt with a semi-spherical depression; the mortar, which produced only coarse flour, was used especially for young seed that was too tender for the handmill. The grains were boiled briefly, then dried in the sun, and finally crushed in the mortar. When the manna was made into cakes its sweet flavor was reminiscent of "something made with olive oil."

4. *Moses' Complaint* (11:10–15)

11:10–15 *Moses heard the people of every family wailing, each at the entrance to his tent. The Lord became exceedingly angry, and Moses was troubled. He asked the Lord, "Why have you brought this trouble on your servant? What have I done to displease you that you put the burden of all these people on me? Did I conceive all these people? Did I give them birth? Why do you tell me to carry them in my arms, as a nurse carries an infant, to the land you promised on oath to their forefathers? Where can I get meat for all these people? They keep wailing to me, 'Give us meat to eat!' I cannot carry all these people by myself; the burden is too heavy for me. If this is how you are going to treat me, put me to death right now—if I have found favor in your eyes—and do not let me face my own ruin."*

Verse 10, which summarizes verses 4–6, also brings out a new element: the wailing is general and can be heard in every tent, and therefore Moses also hears the wailing. We would expect to read in verse 11 of the impression this made on Moses; but instead we hear first that the Lord becomes "exceedingly angry." This has led some to assume that verse 10b originally belonged after verse 6, while others place it after verse 15, so that the Lord's anger was not the result of the people's wailing, but rather of Moses' inappropriate words (vv. 11–15). Out of respect for Moses verse 10b then would have been transferred to its present position. But verse 10b fits better after verse 6 than after verse 10a, so that it would be easier to understand if a later copyist had placed it there, assuming that a copyist would be inclined to make such a textual change. But these attempts also overlook the fact that it was precisely this manifestation of the Lord's anger that caused what I would call "Moses' tantrum." Had the Lord's anger been directed against the people, it would have manifested itself in a destructive act; but this is not the case here. It appears to me that the Lord's anger is rather directed against Moses, because he provides inadequate leadership for the people and because he dares to bother his God with the complaints of the people (cf. v. 24). And Moses feels that the Lord treats him unfairly—hence his repeated ''why?'' in verse 11. He presumes to reproach the Lord about a number of things. He asks the Lord three questions, followed by the request that the Lord put him to death if the situation remains unchanged. Here we suddenly come face to face again with the Moses who gets carried away by his temper, as had happened in the past. Then it led to manslaughter (Exod. 2:11-15), now it brings him on the verge of blasphemy. He blames God: the Lord did not have the right to place the burden of the entire people on Moses' shoulders (v. 11). The Lord has forgotten that He Himself ''gave birth'' to Israel, which makes Him, rather than Moses, responsible for what Israel does (v. 12; cf. Exod. 4:22f.; Hos. 11:1). The Lord had better tell Moses where he can find meat for this many people (v. 13). Moses cannot carry on this way! The Lord had better put him to death; Moses is headed for ruin (or, Moses' experiences with this people amount to ''wretchedness''—v. 15 KJV).

What a moving insight into the depths of the sinful human heart! It can be compared to the double complaint of Jeremiah when he dares to tell the Lord, ''Will you be to me like a deceptive brook, like a spring that fails?'' (Jer. 15:18), and claims that the Lord has taken advantage of his youthful inexperience to entice him to assume the prophetic ministry that has brought Jeremiah so much misery (20:7). We must also remember that the Near Eastern temperament is more excitable than the occidental temperament (cf. also 1 Kings 19:4).

5. *The Lord's Mercy* (11:16-20)

11:16-20 *The LORD said to Moses: ''Bring me seventy of Israel's elders who are known to you as leaders and officials among the people. Have them come to the Tent of Meeting, that they may stand there with you. I will come down and speak with you there, and I will take of the Spirit that is on you and put the Spirit on them. They will help you carry the burden of the people so that you will not have to carry it alone.*

''Tell the people: 'Consecrate yourselves in preparation for tomorrow, when you will eat meat. The LORD heard you when you wailed, ''If only we had meat to eat! We were better off in Egypt!'' Now the LORD will give you meat, and you will eat it. You will not eat it for just one day, or two days, or five, ten or twenty days, but for a whole month—until it comes out of your nostrils and you loathe it—because you have rejected the LORD, who is among you, and have wailed before him, saying, ''Why did we ever leave Egypt?'''''

Moses now experiences the profound meaning of what he once heard about the Lord's divine Being on Mount Sinai: "the compassionate and gracious God, slow to anger, abounding in love and faithfulness" (Exod. 34:6). The Lord's response is not a destructive judgment, but a granting of Moses' wish: seventy elders (the number of completeness or totality) will now share with Moses the burden of the people. But this Moses will no longer be the old Moses: part of the Lord's Spirit will be taken from him and divided among the seventy. The reason for this will be made clear to Moses when the Lord will speak with him (v. 17). We are not told what is communicated; but the Lord probably makes it clear that the measure of the Spirit that rested on Moses would be as sufficient after it has been divided among Moses and the seventy as it was when it rested on Moses alone.

But the people do not go scot-free. They wailed as if the Lord did not take care of them as He ought to, and their nostalgic harking back to Egypt made the Lord's deliverance into something of little or no value, the very act of God on which they are to focus over and over again (Judg. 6:8; 1 Kings 8:16; 9:9; Jer. 7:22; 11:4; 31:32; 32:21; 34:13; Ezek. 20:4–22). They ask for meat, and meat they shall have, so much and for so long that they will come to loathe it. The command "consecrate yourselves" (cf. Josh. 3:5) shows Israel that this provision of meat will be miraculous, the result of a special revelation of the Lord's power. The command to consecrate themselves (which in Exod. 19:22 was given to the priests) includes the requirements that they wash their bodies and abstain from sexual relations (Exod. 19:10f.). At the same time, the Lord points out that their loathing of the meat they so fervently desired will be much more severe than their aversion for the manna they had despised—they will be sick even of the smell. The miracle is therefore at the same time punishment because they "rejected the Lord" by their failure to appreciate what He had done in Egypt to deliver them. All this will happen "tomorrow" (cf. Exod. 8:23, 29; 9:5, 18; 10:4; Num. 14:25; et al.).

6. *Moses' Lack of Faith* (11:21–23)

11:21–23 *But Moses said, "Here I am among six hundred thousand men on foot, and you say, 'I will give them meat to eat for a whole month!' Would they have enough if flocks and herds were slaughtered for them? Would they have enough if all the fish in the sea were caught for them?"*

The LORD answered Moses, "Is the LORD's arm too short? You will now see whether or not what I say will come true for you."

Moses has heard what the Lord said, but his mood, which was reflected in his reproach (see above), has not changed. Meat for "six *'elef* men on foot'' (see commentary on ch. 1), and that for a whole month! There simply are not enough flocks or fish. We see in Moses something of the spirit of the officer of Samaria (2 Kings 7:2). Moses takes into consideration only what he sees here and now, not what he *has* seen of the Lord's power. Nevertheless, he again experiences the Lord's mercy: the Lord does not become angry. The rabbis assigned a reason to this that shows a total lack of spiritual insight: God's anger does not burn because Moses did not express his unbelief in the hearing of the people; as if this would nullify the sin of such lack of faith! Rather, we see here the mercy of a father: the Lord merely reminds Moses of His power (cf. Isa. 50:2; 59:1). And this is the same Moses who was the Lord's spokesman when He demonstrated His power in Egypt! But the Lord does not even remind Moses of that—Moses ''will see.'' With these words Moses is dismissed. At the appropriate time he will experience the truth that the Lord's word never returns ''empty'' (Isa. 55:11).

7. *Eldad and Medad Prophesy* (11:24–30)

11:24–30 *So Moses went out and told the people what the LORD had said. He brought together seventy of their elders and had them stand around the tent. Then the LORD came down in the cloud and spoke with him, and he took of the Spirit that was on him and put the Spirit on the seventy elders. When the Spirit rested on them, they prophesied, but they did not do so again.*

However, two men, whose names were Eldad and Medad, had remained in the camp. They were listed among the elders, but did not go out to the tent. Yet the Spirit also rested on them, and they prophesied in the camp. A young man ran and told Moses, ''Eldad and Medad are prophesying in the camp.''

Joshua son of Nun, who had been Moses' aide since youth, spoke up and said, ''Moses, my lord, stop them!''

But Moses replied, ''Are you jealous for my sake? I wish that all the LORD's people were prophets and that the LORD would put his Spirit on them!'' Then Moses and the elders of Israel returned to the camp.

The Lord has finished speaking with Moses, who ''goes out'' from the Lord's presence to tell Israel that its desire for meat will be satisfied so completely that the gift will become punishment, and also to explain to them that the unique position he has occupied among them until now has come to an end: henceforth seventy elders will assist him in providing leadership for the people.

We are not told how Israel received the Lord's message; perhaps with skepticism and mockery. The narrative focuses only on the seventy elders who are now made to stand around the tabernacle, as the royal court stands around the king when he makes an announcement. We probably must understand this in the sense of standing before the entrance to the tent as in 12:5 and Exodus 33:9. Then, as promised in verse 17, the Lord descends in the cloud. And then something is taken from Moses, something that until now he has had in its fullness: from now on he must share his "having-of-the-Spirit" with the seventy, although Moses retains a larger measure than they receive. And this act of the Lord immediately manifests itself: the seventy men prophesy, something they had not been able to do before. It is not entirely clear what this entailed (the same verb is also used in 1 Sam. 10; 19:20–24; 1 Kings 22:10; Jer. 29:26). This is not a prophetic activity such as that of e.g., Amos, Hosea, Isaiah, and Jeremiah, but a form of ecstasy such as Saul experienced, accompanied by various utterances. It is therefore a visible demonstration of their being controlled by a mighty Spirit who did not rest on them before. It seems to me that we must understand the prophesying of the seventy in this sense, and that this demonstration was necessary so that Israel might see that a divine power was active in these men who therefore had the right to be obeyed by the people.

In the Hebrew text the consonants *wl' jsfw* follow. There is no question about the first three: they are to be vocalized *w$_e$lo'*, "and not." The MT vocalizes the second group *jasefu,* "they added to it," so that the whole phrase then reads "and they did not add to it" or, "they did not prophesy again." This is also the view of the ancient Jewish commentary *Sifre,* the oldest Midrash on Numbers and Deuteronomy. But the vocalization *jasufu* is equally possible, which gives the opposite meaning: "and they did not cease." This is the reading accepted by the Vulgate and the Targums Onkelos and Jonathan, and also by Luther. Both readings are defensible, but I prefer the former, since this form of prophesying was no longer needed for the carrying out of their duties afterward, and we never hear of Moses prophesying.

Two of the seventy elders summoned by Moses did not consider it necessary to respond; the reason for their absence is not stated, only the fact. These two men, Eldad and Medad (it is perhaps more correct to read with the LXX and the Syriac "Modad," "Beloved"; on ancient Babylonian contract tablets a similar name is found, Mudadi), are not mentioned anywhere else, unless Eldad ("God loves") is the same as Elidad, the leader from Benjamin (34:21; cf. the Akkadian name Abu-dadi). Jewish tradition has many things to say about them, and even claims that they are the authors of a prophetic work, mentioned in the *Shepherd of Hermas,* a writing from the first period of the Christian church (II, 3. 4).

The power of the Lord's Spirit is revealed to them also. They begin to prophesy in spite of the fact that they did not come to the tabernacle and are thus outside the immediate sphere of influence of the Spirit who reveals Himself here. "In the camp" rather than "in the holy place"—but this does not mean that the tabernacle stood outside the camp as a whole, as some have suggested. Israel learns here that the working of the Lord's Spirit is not limited to the sanctuary, even as it is not limited by regional boundaries. Even a man like Ezekiel will have to learn this many centuries later (see my commentary on Ezekiel, Introduction). Israel also sees here that the Lord gives His Spirit to whomever He wills; He Himself provides the enablement for the task to which He calls.

But there is a young man in the camp who does not know this yet. He is surprised by what he sees and hears happening so far from the sanctuary and he considers it his duty to inform Moses so that Moses can put a stop to it. The Ephraimite Joshua, the son of Nun, "who had been Moses' aide since youth" (Exod. 17:9ff.; 24:13; 32:17; 33:11) says to Moses: "Moses, my lord, stop them!" He feels that Moses' prestige will suffer because of this. But Moses sees in an entirely different light what is happening. He sharply rejects Joshua's intervention; Moses can look after his own prestige and his own rights; he does not need Joshua's help in this. Actually, far from being a threat to Moses, what happens is the fulfillment of his most fervent wish. Joshua wants to keep the number of those who by the working of God's Spirit are driven to great things as small as possible, so that Moses may be the more prominent. But Moses' wish is that all Israelites without a single exception be controlled by the Spirit that has filled him since his calling (Exod. 3:12; 4:12, 15), that they would all be the Lord's prophets, filled by Him with a common desire to do the Lord's will and to be His servants, both inside and outside the sanctuary. It is not Moses who is indispensable for Israel, but the Lord's Spirit (cf. Jer. 31:33–34; Ezek. 11:19; 36:27; Joel 2:28).

The Lord's communication of His Spirit to the seventy elders is now complete and they can all leave the sanctuary. Moses and his new assistants return to their tents: a prophet is not a priest, his duty lies in the camp. We are not told in what way the seventy elders assisted Moses after this. The focus in these verses is on the Lord's sovereign power rather than on the seventy and their work.

8. *The Quail* (11:31–35)

11:31–35 *Now a wind went out from the L*ord *and drove quail in from the sea. It brought them down all around the camp to about three feet above the ground, as far as a day's walk in any direction. All that day and night and all the next day the* *people went out and gathered quail. No one gathered less than ten homers. Then they spread them out all around the camp. But while the meat was still between their teeth and before it could be consumed, the anger of the L*ORD *burned against the people, and he struck them with a severe plague. Therefore the place was named Kibroth Hattaavah, because there they buried the people who had craved other food.*

From Kibroth Hattaavah the people traveled to Hazeroth and stayed there.

Moses' request has been granted. And now the promised miracle (v. 18), the response to the people's desire for meat, takes place, but not on the same day as the events recorded in the preceding verses; had the author wanted to state that it did happen on the same day, he would have expressed himself differently (*wayyissa‘*). It happens on the day indicated in verse 18, "tomorrow." The quail (*selaw;* it is still called *salwa* in Egypt and Syria) come to the camp in exceptionally large numbers. Large flocks of these birds still fly north from central Africa in the spring (cf. 13:20). These fat animals, whose meat is such a delicacy, are then frequently tired from flying and land on the ground where they can be easily caught or killed with sticks. But the miracle lies in the fact that they arrive at this precise moment and in such large numbers, driven to Israel's camp by a wind unleashed by the Lord (cf. Exod. 14:21): "He makes winds his messengers" (Ps. 104:4). It is also miraculous that the birds descend "as far as a day's walk in any direction" around the camp. They are not "two cubits high upon the face of the earth" (KJV), i.e., they did not cover the ground to a depth of two cubits (three feet), but, as the Vulgate, the Targums, and Rashi agree, they kept flying around the camp at a height of about three feet. They are "brought down" in the sense that the wind keeps them from flying any higher, and they can thus be captured easily. The people were busy gathering the quail for two days and a night, and in such large quantities that no one had less than ten homers, approximately sixty bushels (per family?). They were, of course, not all consumed immediately, but after the Egyptian manner (Herodotus II, 77) dried in the sun, after which they could be eaten without cooking.

But Israel "gratifies the desires of the sinful nature" against which Paul warns (Gal. 5:16). They throw themselves on the quail as if they were starving, as if the manna had no nutritional value at all. The people do not even take time to chew the meat. They show contempt for the Lord's gift. And after two days the feast comes to a sad end. The Lord's anger burns against the people and a large number of them die. Verses 18ff. do not mention, of course, that this might happen; they state only the Lord's intention, contingent on Israel's consecration, which also includes behaving in a consecrated manner. But since the latter is ignored, punishment follows. We are not told what the nature of the punishment was—the focus is on its suddenness: many died with the meat still between their teeth. Rationalists, who can explain anything, say that death was the result of poisonous food eaten by the quail!

The memory of this event is kept alive in Israel's history by the name given to this place: Kibroth Hattaavah, "Graves of Craving." The craving is stilled in accordance with the Lord's promise, but Israel's sin turns it into the stillness of the grave. Israel cannot stay here, so it travels to Hazeroth. The location of both these camps is unknown. The first one is sought in the oasis Erweis el-Ebeirig; this identification is then supported by the fact that a large number of ancient graves are found here; but this is not surprising in any oasis. The second place is sought in Ain el-Chadra, two days' journey from Sinai toward the Gulf of Aqaba. But this is based on the questionable assumption that only a two-day journey separates 11:35 from 10:11.

9. *Miriam Punished With Leprosy* (12:1–16)

This chapter gives us an insight into shameful family jealousy, brotherly gentleness, and the Lord's faithfulness toward His servant. Verse 16 indicates that these events take place during Israel's stay at Hazeroth.

A. *Miriam and Aaron reproach Moses* (12:1–3)

12:1–3 *Miriam and Aaron began to talk against Moses because of his Cushite wife, for he had married a Cushite. "Has the Lord spoken only through Moses?" they asked. "Hasn't he also spoken through us?" And the Lord heard this.*

(Now Moses was a very humble man, more humble than anyone else on the face of the earth.)

Moses has married a Cushite woman. The rabbinical tradition has changed this into "a beautiful wife" to clear Moses of marriage to an Ethiopian (Onkelos, Rashi). Calvin and others believed that this refers to Zipporah (e.g., P. Heinisch, *Numeri*, p. 52; H. M. Wiener, *Monatsschrift für Geschichte und Wissenschaft des Judentums,* 1928, p. 309). But neither solution is possible. "Cush" is the Hebraization of the Egyptian *Kosh,* the name of the region between Assuan and Meru, north of what we call Ethiopia; this region has been inhabited by Nubian tribes with an African culture since 2200 B.C. It is indeed true that in the Old Testament a portion of southern Arabia is called Cush (see 2 Chron. 14:9; 21:16); but the Midianite woman Zipporah came from the northern region of the Sinai peninsula (Exod. 3:1; 18:1), and according to 1 Kings 11:18; Habakkuk 3:7 from near Paran. Moses has thus married a second time, probably a woman who belonged to the "many other people" of Exodus 12:38 (Rashi claims that Moses first divorced Zipporah). The Midrash states that the Cushite woman was Tharbis, daughter of the king of Ethiopia, from Meru (Josephus, *Antiquities,* II, 10. 2).

Miriam and Aaron complain to Moses about this marriage (both, in spite of the singular verb; cf. Jer. 12:4b; Esth. 7:3b; 9:29a). But apparently Miriam was the instigator, while Aaron once again gives evidence of a weak character (cf. Exod. 32:2ff., 22ff.; Num. 16:11). Miriam cannot have been upset because Moses married a non-Israelite woman, since Zipporah was also an "alien." Nor can she have been hurt in her national pride, since such marriages were not at all uncommon in Israel (see 1 Chron. 2:34). I conclude from verse 2 that Moses' marriage to the Cushite woman was nothing more than an excuse. This is why Aaron, who probably thought differently about such a marriage than Miriam, goes along with her. Both take offense at Moses' unique position. Miriam is Moses' elder sister (who once saved him, Exod. 2:4, 7–8) and as a woman she does not consider herself in any way inferior to Moses. She certainly has not forgotten that after the crossing of the Red Sea the Lord had chosen her to lead the chorus of Israel's women in singing His praises (Exod. 15:20). And Aaron has not forgotten that the Lord appointed him to be Moses' spokesman and told him to meet Moses on his return from Midian (Exod. 4:16, 27). Nor does he consider it a small matter that in the Urim and Thummim he always bears "the means of making decisions for the Israelites over his heart before the Lord" (Exod. 28:30). Both Miriam and Aaron thus feel fully justified in disputing Moses' right to be the exclusive interpreter of the Lord's revelations; later others will follow their example (16:3f.).

Moses does not defend himself and his position, nor could he do so. If he were to defend himself he would fall into the same sin as Miriam and Aaron: trying to control the Lord's sovereign power. Later Jeremiah will follow his example when Hananiah claims that the Lord also speaks through him (Jer. 28:1–4). Both Moses and Jeremiah surrender the issue to the Lord. Moses clearly has not forgotten the lesson of Kibroth Hattaavah (11:10ff.)! He has become the most humble (kjv: "meek") of all men.

B. *The Lord defends His servant* (12:4–8)

12:4–8 *At once the Lord said to Moses, Aaron and Miriam, "Come out to the Tent of Meeting, all three of you." So the three of them came out. Then the Lord came down in a pillar of cloud; he stood at the entrance to the Tent and summoned Aaron and Miriam. When both of them stepped forward, he said, "Listen to my words:*

107

> *"When a prophet of the L*ORD* is among you,*
>   *I reveal myself to him in visions,*
>   *I speak to him in dreams.*
> *But this is not true of my servant Moses;*
>   *he is faithful in all my house.*
> *With him I speak face to face,*
>   *clearly and not in riddles;*
>   *he sees the form of the L*ORD*.*
> *Why then were you not afraid*
>   *to speak against my servant Moses?"*

Although the attack is directed against Moses, it also involves the Lord. Miriam and Aaron have done no less than to dictate to the Lord through whom He must speak. The Lord has heard what they said, and He will make clear to Miriam and Aaron that "I will not give my glory to another" (Isa. 42:8). And this must happen in Moses' presence, since now more than ever before Moses needs to know what his Sender thinks about his work.

Miriam and Aaron must go with Moses to the Tent of Meeting. "Come out" (v. 4) does not imply that the Tent stood somewhere outside the camp; here, as in 11:26, a distinction is made between "the camp" and "the Tent," because the latter is the holy place, the Lord's "dwelling place." This is the only instance where we hear that the Lord speaks "at once" (KJV: "suddenly"), i.e., immediately following Miriam and Aaron's complaint. We are not told from where this "speaking" came. A number of exegetes feel that verse 5 is a doublet of verse 4, proof that this is a conflation of two narratives, since verse 5 speaks of a descending of the Lord in a pillar of cloud, followed by the summoning of Miriam and Aaron. I do not believe that this is correct. Verse 4b shows that Miriam and Aaron speak to Moses in the camp, since they must "come out to the Tent of Meeting." And verse 5 states that, when they are at the Tent, the cloud, the visible proof of the Lord's presence, places itself in front of the Tent; the Lord summons Miriam and Aaron and they step forward. It is now that all three must see the cloud, since what is about to take place will make a lasting impression: hearing and seeing must go together.

"If [cf. KJV, ASV, RSV] a prophet of the LORD is among you": the opening words immediately call into question what Miriam and Aaron have assumed to be a certainty. It is a statement of possibility, since the Lord's will is not dependent on anyone. But even if this possibility were to become a reality, it would not give Miriam and Aaron any reason to put themselves on a level with Moses. The Lord would communicate with them by means of "visions" and "dreams," as he did with the ordinary prophets (cf. Gen. 15:1; 20:3; 28:11f.; 31:11, 24; et al.; Ezek. 1:1; 8:3;

40:2). Both forms of revelation take the prophet outside the framework of space and time, so that the prophet sees what will happen as already having taken place (2 Kings 8:13; Jer. 4:20; 38:22; et al.) and his spirit is elsewhere (see my commentary on Ezek. 8:1–18).

It strikes us that in verse 6 visions and dreams are considered the normal means by which the Lord makes His will known to a prophet; yet, in the case of Isaiah we hear of a vision only once (6:1), in Amos five times (chs. 7–9). In Ezekiel the receiving of visions is related to the fact that he must convey to his fellow captives what is happening in Jerusalem. In Daniel we hear of one dream (7:1) and one vision (10:5), and the eight night visions of Zechariah are well-known. It is thus clear that in what I would call the flowering period of Israel's prophetism the Lord's prophets received their revelations while they were awake, and had no respect for those who appealed to dreams (Jer. 23:25ff.; 27:9; Zech. 10:2). This indicates that a statement such as we find in verse 6 could not possibly date from later times, when most likely almost the opposite would have been said. Israel's prophetism underwent a significant development in this respect.

"But this is not true of my servant Moses" (v. 7). The exceptional position of Moses among his contemporaries is clearly expressed here. In Moses' case the Lord uses neither visions nor dreams; the latter are here called "riddles," since they are purposely given in unclear terms and require further interpretation. With Moses the Lord speaks "mouth to mouth" (cf. kjv; Jer. 32:4 kjv) as in a normal conversation between two people; this is synonymous with "face to face" in Exodus 33:11; Deut. 34:10; cf. Numbers 7:89. Furthermore, Moses saw the Lord's "form," which Israel did not see at Sinai (Deut. 4:12, 15), which Job saw only in a dream (Job 4:16), and the author of Psalm 17 perceived as a joy to be experienced in the future (v. 15). That which the elders of Israel saw only once (Exod. 24:10) Moses sees as often as the "mouth to mouth" communication takes place. Between the Lord and Moses there is, so to speak, direct communication. And, like all direct verbal communication, it is clear and unambiguous, unlike dreams and visions. The reason for this is that Moses is "my servant." Moses is called the Lord's servant elsewhere (Exod. 14:31; Deut. 34:5; and frequently in Joshua), but only here does the Lord speak of him as "my servant." This is a very special distinction that Moses shares only with Abraham (Gen. 26:24), Caleb (Num. 14:24), with Israel as a whole (Isa. 43:10; 44:21; et al.), and with the coming Son of David (Isa. 42:1; 53:11). And this title is bestowed on Moses because "he is faithful in all my house"—faithful, i.e., the Lord can depend on him; in all my house, i.e., in taking care of everything connected with the Lord's counsel for Israel. The relationship between the Lord and Moses is therefore the same as that between Abraham and Eliezer (Gen. 15:2; 24:2) and between Pharaoh and Joseph (Gen. 39:4). Here we have striking proof of the Lord's humbling grace, after Moses' question "why?" (11:11ff.).

After this delineation of the immense distance that separates Moses from Miriam and Aaron, the Lord asks His own "why?" in order to make it clear to Miriam and Aaron that in attacking Moses they have attacked the Lord's honor and have challenged the sovereignty of His grace.

C. *Miriam's punishment* (12:9–12)

12:9–12 *The anger of the LORD burned against them, and he left them.*
When the cloud lifted from above the Tent, there stood Miriam—leprous, like snow. Aaron turned toward her and saw that she had leprosy; and he said to Moses, "Please, my lord, do not hold against us the sin we have so foolishly committed. Do not let her be like a stillborn infant coming from its mother's womb with its flesh half eaten away."

The Lord "left them," but not like He left after speaking with Abraham (Gen. 18:33): He now leaves in burning anger, of which the preceding verses were already an expression. This leaving manifests itself in the departure of the cloud; when it lifts, the result of His anger becomes evident: Miriam is "leprous, like snow." Only Miriam is punished; Aaron gets off with a fright, as is reflected in the unusual Hebrew sentence structure. We are not told why Aaron is not punished, which leaves room for various speculations. The usual explanation that Aaron was not punished because he was persuaded by Miriam seems to me unsatisfactory. In any case, Miriam was "leprous, like snow," not only her hand as in the case of Moses (Exod. 4:6), but her entire body. The word *sara'at,* which we usually render "leprosy," refers to a number of skin diseases, several of which are unrelated to our "leprosy" (see my commentary on Lev. 13:1–59). The *nega',* the "stroke" or "plague" the Lord has sent, is in this case leukodermia, caused by the cessation of the normal pigmentation of the skin; the skin is finally entirely covered with white flakes that gradually fall off, which marks the end of the disease. This disease is thus not incurable. Aaron sees, of course, only the whiteness of Miriam's skin, while the true nature of the disease escapes him. He does not know whether Miriam is ceremonially clean or unclean (see Lev. 13:13f.). He sees the *sara'at* and is frightened by the consequences of their action; this is why he turns to Moses: "Please, my lord."

In spite of the fact that he is the high priest, he also gives evidence of not having a very exalted concept of God when he interprets Miriam's "leprosy" as the result of Moses' influence on the Lord's will (v. 11). He thinks that Moses wanted revenge and misused his influence (!) with the Lord to punish her. He says literally, "do not lay a sin upon us by which we have done foolishly and by which we have sinned," i.e., "do not make us bear the consequences of this sin" (cf. Exod. 15:26), as if this were up to Moses. It is a typically ancient Near Eastern perspective that ascribes to certain people the power to determine the will of the deity (cf. Job 42:7f.; also Num. 16:41). Aaron's thinking here is again entirely in line with his behavior in connection with the golden calf (Exod. 32:1–6).

In verse 12 Aaron compares Miriam to a child that already suffers from a fatal disease when it is born and slowly sinks into death—no minor exaggeration of Miriam's leukodermia, apparently designed to stir Moses' brotherly love. Jewish exegesis (which found its way into the Syriac version and is even defended by someone like Geiger, *Urschrift,* pp. 384f.) claims, on the basis of the phrase "half eaten away," that the original reading of verse 12a was "Do not let *us* be . . ."; Aaron then would be the healthy half, Miriam the half with the fatal disease. Later "our mother" and "our flesh" then were supposedly changed to "its mother" and "its flesh." But the sense of verse 12 is perfectly clear: a leper is as certain to die as a fetus that is born without the normal ability to sustain life.

D. *Moses' intercession* (12:13–16)

12:13 *So Moses cried out to the LORD, "O God, please heal her!"*

Moses' action proves that the description of him in verse 3 is fully justified: not for a moment does he consider ignoring Aaron's humble request ("Please, my lord"). But he also shows that his understanding of God is far superior to that of the high priest. He knows that what has happened to Miriam is not the result of his own will or power, but that he is faced with a *nega'* (stroke), the result of the Lord's omnipotence. This is why he cries out to the Lord (Israel's physician! Exod. 15:26), a loud cry as can only come from a soul in distress, and brief, as only extreme distress can teach us to pray.

12:14–16 *The LORD replied to Moses, "If her father had spit in her face, would she not have been in disgrace for seven days? Confine her outside the camp for seven days; after that she can be brought back." So Miriam was confined outside the camp for seven days, and the people did not move on till she was brought back. After that, the people left Hazeroth and encamped in the Desert of Paran.*

Moses' prayer is answered, but not without Miriam's pride having heen taught a painful lesson. What happened to her was to become a permanent part of Israel's memory (Deut. 24:9). Israel must not consider the kind of *sara'at* that afflicted Miriam of little significance. It is comparable to the act of a father who spits in his child's face after the child has misbehaved, the most serious indignity imaginable to the Near Eastern mind (Deut. 25:9). A child to whom this happened would not dare show itself for a week. And in the same way the proud Miriam, who misbehaved against the Lord, must bear the shame of her action for seven days. She is expelled from the camp for a week, which means that she could not participate in the Lord's service during that time. The phrase "confined outside the camp" (KJV: "shut out from the camp") is used only here; it probably means something more than "living outside the camp" (Lev. 13:46). So that everyone in Israel may know what has happened to her, the people must wait for Miriam. They must wait for seven days while the Promised Land beckons. Only then are they allowed to proceed northward.

10. *The Twelve Spies* (13:1–14:38)

A. *The names of the spies* (13:1–16)

13:1–16 *The LORD said to Moses, "Send some men to explore the land of Canaan, which I am giving to the Israelites. From each ancestral tribe send one of its leaders."*

So at the LORD's command Moses sent them out from the Desert of Paran. All of them were leaders of the Israelites. These are their names:

from the tribe of Reuben, Shammua son of Zaccur;
from the tribe of Simeon, Shaphat son of Hori;
from the tribe of Judah, Caleb son of Jephunneh;
from the tribe of Issachar, Igal son of Joseph;
from the tribe of Ephraim, Hoshea son of Nun;
from the tribe of Benjamin, Palti son of Raphu;
from the tribe of Zebulun, Gaddiel son of Sodi;
from the tribe of Manasseh (a tribe of Joseph), Gaddi son of Susi;
from the tribe of Dan, Ammiel son of Gemalli;
from the tribe of Asher, Sethur son of Michael;
from the tribe of Naphtali, Nahbi son of Vophsi;
from the tribe of Gad, Geuel son of Maki.

These are the names of the men Moses sent to explore the land. (Moses gave Hoshea son of Nun the name Joshua.)

This section takes us, as is mentioned in passing in verse 26, to Kadesh, where Israel had encamped after entering the Desert of Paran (12:16). According to 20:1 the oasis of Kadesh lies in the Desert of Zin, not to be confused with the strip of desert called Sin (Exod. 16:1; 17:1; Num.

33:11–12), which lies between the oasis of Elim (Exod. 15:27; perhaps the present Ain Musa, eight miles southeast of Suez?) and the Sinai range. The Desert of Zin (Num. 20:1) is the northern part of the Desert of Paran. Kadesh itself must probably be sought in the vicinity of the present oasis Ain Qadeis, approximately sixty miles southwest of the southern tip of the Dead Sea (see also commentary on 10:12). Kadesh was well-known since ancient times; wandering tribes favored settling their judicial disputes at the sanctuary at Kadesh. Hence the name En Mishpat, "Fountain of Judgment," for Kadesh in Genesis 14:7.

At Kadesh the event takes place that turns Israel's wilderness journey into a tragedy, and that makes Canaan an unreachable goal for many years. Israel has come close to the southern border of the Promised Land, and twelve men are sent out from Kadesh "to explore the land of Canaan" (v. 2) at the Lord's command. In Deuteronomy 1:19ff. we are told that Moses, upon arrival at Kadesh, instructs Israel to enter and "take possession" of the land the Lord had given to Israel (vv. 20–21); the idea to send spies first to gather information about the towns and the route to be taken comes from the people (v. 22), and Moses goes along with the suggestion. A number of scholars have declared this to be a variant narrative; but the difference between Numbers 13:2 and Deuteronomy 1:19ff. lies in this, that Numbers focuses on the "first cause," while Deuteronomy describes the secondary cause, except in verse 26. Both narratives speak of twelve spies, one from each tribe. But Numbers adds that "every one must be a ruler among them" (v. 2; cf. KJV). Their names are given in verses 4–16a; the name of the leader from Manasseh (v. 11) is out of its proper place, due to some copyist's error, as is probably true of Zebulon (v. 20), which is always listed together with Issachar.

These are entirely different names than those of the leaders in 1:6–15. This proves that each tribe had more than one "leader," which is also supported by 3:32, where Eleazar is called the "leader of the leaders of the Levites." We must therefore probably think of clan leaders rather than of leaders of the tribe as a whole in both cases. None of the names in chapter 13 contain the name Jahweh, as is also true of the names in chapter 1. This indicates that these names must be very ancient (cf. F. Hommel, *Die altisraelitische Ueberlieferung,* pp. 298ff.). It is also striking that eleven of the twenty-three names given here are not found elsewhere. This argues against a later fabrication such as Wellhausen suggested. We can no longer determine whether each of these names has been transmitted accurately; thus, we find in the Syriac version Haddi instead of Hori (v. 5), and Suri instead of Sodi (v. 10); in both cases *daleth* has been substituted for *resh.* It is also curious that we find the name Hoshea, rather than the usual name

Joshua, for Moses' servant (Exod. 17:9, 13; 24:13; 32:17; 33:11; Num. 11:28; Deut. 32:44). Verse 16b indicates that Moses changed the name of the son of Nun: the relatively neutral name Hoshea ("He has saved") becomes Joshua ("The Lord is salvation"). Moses must not have done this lightly—this name change expresses Moses' conviction that Israel's salvation depends only on the Lord and not on some other god. It was thus a confession of faith on Moses' part, of which his servant is, so to speak, the personification (cf. e.g., Abram–Abraham; Jacob–Israel; Gideon–Jerub-Baal).

Among the twelve spies is another whose name we also find elsewhere: Caleb, the son of Jephunneh. Two things strike us here: first, that he is called the son of Jephunneh, while in 1 Chronicles 2:9, 18 he is called the son of Hezron; and second, that he is here a "leader" of Judah, while in 32:12; Josh. 14:6, 14 he is a Kenizzite, i.e., a member of a clan closely related to Edom (Gen. 36:11, 15, 42) that is listed in Genesis 15:19 among the tribes that inhabit Canaan. These two apparent discrepancies are related. According to Joshua 14:6ff.; Judges 1:13f., 20 (Caleb), and Joshua 15:17; Judges 1:13 (Othniel), the Kenizzites were completely absorbed into the tribe of Judah, where they found a place in the clan of Hezron; consequently, Caleb can be called Hezron's "son" in terms of the structure of the tribe of Judah (1 Chron. 2:9, 18) and can also be listed as a "leader" of Judah here.

During the period when totemism was in vogue (see e.g., Stade, *Biblische Theologie des Alten Testaments I,* 1905, §15, 2) the name Caleb ("dog") was taken to reflect this concept. But in the Cassite period we find (as Jirku observes, *Altorientalischer Kommentar zum Alten Testament,* 1923, p. 111) a number of Akkadian names that are composites of Kalbu (=Caleb), followed by the name of a god, meaning "dog [=priest?] of god X." It is possible that Caleb's name was originally longer; we find the elimination of the name of the deity in other cases as well (e.g., Palti–Paltiel, Micah–Micajehu, Ezra–Azariah, Pekah–Pekahja, and the well-known case of King Ahaz, whom the Assyrians always call Jauchazi=Joahaz).

B. *Their assignment* (13:17–20)

13:17–20 *When Moses sent them to explore Canaan, he said, "Go up through the Negev and on into the hill country. See what the land is like and whether the people who live there are strong or weak, few or many. What kind of land do they live in? Is it good or bad? What kind of towns do they live in? Are they unwalled or fortified? How is the soil? Is it fertile or poor? Are there trees on it or not? Do your best to bring back some of the fruit of the land." (It was the season for the first ripe grapes.)*

These twelve men, who have been especially selected for this mission (they are men who have the respect of the people), receive detailed instructions. They are to bring back information about Canaan's inhabitants, its cities, ar·d the fertility of the soil; as proof of the latter they must bring back "some of the fruit of the land." By way of introduction to what follows in verses 21–24 the author points out that "it was the season for the first ripe grapes," i.e., July-August. This means that three months have passed since the events of chapter 11 (see commentary on 11:31).

They must first go through the Negev. The KJV renders this "southward," which is confusing, since they are actually going north. The Negev (which probably means "dry, parched land," hence Ps. 126:4) lies largely south of the territory of Judah and Simeon, and begins halfway between Hebron and Beersheba. It consists of a virtually inaccessible (cf. Isa. 21:1; 30:6) mountainous wilderness where semi-nomadic tribes wander with their livestock (1 Sam. 27:10; 30:14). Joshua 15:21–32 gives a list of towns in the Negev. Since the Negev was south of Canaan proper, it came to be used to mean "south," just as "the sea" came to mean "west" (cf. e.g., 35:5; Josh. 11:2).

After the Negev the spies will reach the "hill country"; according to Joshua 15:48ff. this is later to become the tribal territory of Judah. Its highest point is at Hebron, where it reaches an elevation of 2953 feet. On the west it slopes down to the "low country" (NIV: "foothills"), which borders on the plains of Philistia (Josh. 15:33ff.), and on the east to the "desert" above the Dead Sea (Josh. 15:61f.); the northern part of this hill country will later be called "mountains of Ephraim."

C. *Their exploration* (13:21–24)

13:21–24 *So they went up and explored the land from the Desert of Zin as far as Rehob, toward Lebo Hamath. They went up through the Negev and came to Hebron, where Ahiman, Sheshai and Talmai, the descendants of Anak, lived. (Hebron had been built seven years before Zoan in Egypt.) When they reached the Valley of Eshcol, they cut off a branch bearing a single cluster of grapes. Two of them carried it on a pole between them, along with some pomegranates and figs. That place was called the Valley of Eshcol because of the cluster of grapes the Israelites cut off there.*

The journey of the spies is of course not described in full detail; the author limits himself to an indication of the northernmost point (v. 21) and adds in verses 22–24 a vignette which, more than any other, could give the Israelite reader a vivid picture of the exceptional fertility of the soil. It is incorrect to see in verses 21–24 proof for the assumption that this chapter is a composite of two interwoven narratives.

They travel from south to north, from the Desert of Zin to Rehob, toward the entrance of Hamath (v. 21 NIV margin). The Desert of Zin is the northern part of the Desert of Paran, so that Kadesh is sometimes said to be located in the Desert of Zin (20:1; 27:14; 33:36; Deut. 32:51), sometimes in the Desert of Paran (13:26). Geographical preciseness is something that was not practiced until much later!

We run into problems when it comes to the location of Rehob and Hamath. Joshua 19:28, 30 mentions twice a Rehob in the territory of Asher, which included the three-to-four-hour-wide strip along the Mediterranean north of the Carmel. In Judges 18:28 and 2 Samuel 10:6, 8 we hear of Beth Rehob, which was apparently situated north of Lake Hule in the plains where Dan had its territory. In David's time it was under Aramaean control. Which of these two is the Rehob of Numbers 13?

The "entrance to Hamath" is also mentioned in e.g., 34:8; Joshua 13:5; Judges 3:3; 2 Kings 14:25; Amos 6:14. Again, we know of two Hamaths. One is the "great Hamath" (Amos 6:2), which the Assyrians called by the same name and was later called Epiphania, the present Hama; it is situated on the Orontes in the valley between the Lebanon and the Antilebanon. The other is Hamath Zobah (1 Chron. 18:3; 2 Chron. 8:3), which must have been in the vicinity of Mount Hermon, southeast of Damascus, and was under Aramaean control in the days of David. Which of these two is the Hamath of Numbers 13? According to M. Noth (*"Das Reich von Hamath als Grenznachbar des Reiches Israels,"* *Palästina-Jahrbuch,* 1937, pp. 36–51) we should seek the Hamath of Numbers 13 in the northeastern Jordan region. But the debate over Rehob and Hamath continues; we can only say with certainty that Rehob and Hamath lie approximately on the northern border of what will later be Israel's territory.

The only episode of the wanderings of the spies recorded in Numbers takes place in the vicinity of Hebron, which will later be under the control of Caleb and his clan (Josh. 14:13; 15:13; Judg. 1:20). The author adds a footnote stating that Hebron was built seven years before the Egyptian city of Zoan, the Greek Tanis, which lay close to the Tanite arm of the Nile on the east bank; it was for many years the residence of the Hyksos rulers (see my *Gods Woord,* pp. 275ff.). We do not know exactly when Zoan was founded; we only know that this city played an important role in Egypt as early as the twelfth dynasty (2000-1788 B.C.) and was even then a relatively old city (sixth dynasty? 2625-2475 B.C.). An Egyptian inscription from ca. 1290 B.C. indicates that a system for numbering years existed that was connected with Zoan; according to this inscription, which dates from the four-hundredth year of that era, the numbering began around 1690 B.C. (see e.g., Jirku, *Altorientalischer Kommentar zum Alten Testament,* p. 111).

Hebron ("league, confederacy, center"), the natural capital of southern Judah and therefore sought by both David (2 Sam. 2:11; 5:5) and Absalom (2 Sam. 15:9–10), originally had a different name: Kiriath Arba. Israel understood this name to mean "City of Arba," the father of the Enakites (Josh. 14:15; 15:13; 21:11). However, it can also mean "city of four": four quarters (tetrapolis), or four deities, or four famous men. According to Jerome these four famous men were Adam, Abraham, Isaac, and Jacob, according to others Abraham, Aner, Eshcol, and Mamre (Gen. 14:13).

"Where Ahiman, Sheshai and Talmai, the descendants of Anak, lived" (v. 22). These names refer not to persons, but rather to three clans (Josh. 15:14; Judg. 1:20), belonging to a tribe that lived in and around Hebron prior to Israel's arrival, which was entirely destroyed except for a few small remnants in Gaza, Gad, and Ashdod. They are sometimes called "Anakites" (Josh. 11:21–22; 14:12, 15; Deut. 2:10–11, 21), or "the sons of the Anakim" (Deut. 1:28 KJV; 9:2 KJV), or "the sons of Anak" (Josh. 15:14), who is called the son of Arba in Joshua 21:11; this Arba is called "the greatest man among the Anakites" in Joshua 14:15. It is possible that the gigantic structures that have been found in Palestine were made in part by the "sons of Anak," who are called a "strong, numerous and tall people" in Deuteronomy 2:21 (see my *Gods Woord,* p. 256). If F. Schwally's explanation that *Anakim* means "the tall ones" is correct (*Zeitschrift für die alttestamentliche Wissenschaft,* 1898, p. 139), then the name was originally a generic rather than a proper noun. In verse 33 the descendants of Anak are said to belong to the Nephilim, who are also mentioned in Genesis 6:4 and in Ezekiel 32:27 (with a change in vocalization); the word is usually translated "giants" after the LXX. The name Talmai is also found elsewhere in the Old Testament and on Nabatean inscriptions. In 1 Chronicles 2:31 we find a Judahite clan (Sheshan), whose name is strongly reminiscent of Sheshai.

In a valley, some of the spies find vineyards with enormous clusters of grapes. One of these clusters is cut off and carried along on a pole; it takes two men to carry the cluster. To commemorate this find the valley was later known as the Valley of Eshcol ("Valley of the Cluster"; cf. also 32:9; Deut. 1:24). This is usually thought to be somewhere near Hebron, and is frequently identified with the Wadi bit-Ishkahil, northwest of Hebron; but this is not entirely certain, since neither 32:9 nor Deuteronomy 1:24 connects it with Hebron, and it is not at all certain that verse 23 intends to do so. The identification is supported, however, by the fact that the viniculture around Hebron still has a good reputation, while pomegranates and figs are also still found there.

D. *The report of the spies* (13:25–29)

13:25–26 *At the end of forty days they returned from exploring the land. They came back to Moses and Aaron and the whole Israelite community at Kadesh in the Desert of Paran. There they reported to them and to the whole assembly and showed them the fruit of the land.*

After these verses, which are intended to give an impression of both the size of the explored territory and its fertility, the report brought back by the spies is presented. It opens with the statement that they did not return until after forty days (v. 25). The purpose of this statement is clear: the report of the spies is based on careful investigation and will therefore impress those to whom it is made.

13:27 *They gave Moses this account: "We went into the land to which you sent us, and it does flow with milk and honey! Here is its fruit."*

The fertility of the soil is emphasized: "it does flow with milk and honey" (v. 27). This expression is found repeatedly in the Pentateuch (Exod. 3:8, 17; 13:5; 33:3; Lev. 20:24; Num. 14:8; 16:14; Deut. 6:3; 11:9; 26:9, 15; 27:3; 31:20) and five times outside the Pentateuch (Josh. 5:6; Jer. 11:5; 32:22; Ezek. 20:6, 15); its meaning is not entirely clear. It is usually understood to refer to the cattle-raising and viniculture in Canaan; the honey is then the "honey" from grapes, rather than from bees. But it can also be understood in a different sense: to the Oriental, milk and (bee) honey are the drink and food of the gods; they speak of the garden of the gods, where both are found in abundance. The expression then compares Canaan to a kind of paradise (cf. 16:13, where Egypt is said to be "a land flowing with milk and honey"). Whichever interpretation is correct, Canaan at that time was certainly a richly endowed land. This is also attested to in the description of Canaan by the Egyptian Sinuhe (ca. 1780 B.C.), set in the time of King Sesostris I (ca. 1980-1935 B.C.). He says of Canaan, "A beautiful land called Yaa. There were figs and grapes, and more wine than water. Honey was there in abundance and its olive trees were numerous, and all kinds of fruits hung on the trees. There was barley and wheat, and various herds without number. . . . I had bread as my daily food and wine as my daily drink, boiled meat and roasted geese; and also game from the desert" (H. Gressmann, *Altorientalische Texte und Bilder,* 2nd ed., 1926, pp. 55–61).

13:28–29 *"But the people who live there are powerful, and the cities are fortified and very large. We even saw descendants of Anak there. The Amalekites live in the*

Negev; the Hittites, Jebusites and Amorites live in the hill country; and the Canaanites live near the sea and along the Jordan.''

But then follows the report on the inhabitants. The description is introduced by *'efes ki,* which is always restrictive (cf. Judg. 4:9) and prefaces the negative side. The people are powerful, the cities are fortified. And to top it all off, "we even saw descendants of Anak there"! This is, of course, a later description—since they were strangers to Canaan, the Israelites could not have understood this statement. But the description of what the spies had seen undoubtedly did not lack in clarity. The author explains to his readers what this meant by a further portrayal of the inhabitants of Canaan. First of all, the Amalekites live in the Negev; the Israelites had already encountered them near Sinai (Rephidim, Exod. 17). Here the term is a collective name for the nomadic inhabitants of the Sinai peninsula. Further north are the Hitties, the Jebusites, and the Amorites. The Hittites were, according to Genesis 23:3, the rulers of Hebron at that time, apparently the vanguard of the Indo-Germanic complex of tribes that had established a great empire in Asia Minor and Syria and for some time constituted a threat to Egypt (see A. A. Kampman, "Schets der Hetietische Geschiedenis en Beschauing,'' *Jaarbericht van het Gezelschap Ex Oriente Lux,* No. 6, 1939). The Jebusites controlled Jerusalem: Putiheba, known from the Amarna letters, belonged to them, as did Uriah (2 Sam. 11) and Araunah (2 Sam. 24). The latter name clearly points to Cappadocia, and the Jebusites therefore probably belonged to the Hittites (see my *Gods Woord,* pp. 252f.). The Amorites entered Canaan in 2700 B.C. and ruled it for many centuries, until the Canaanites forced them out of the rich coastal plains and out of the Jordan Valley into the mountains (see my *Gods Woord,* pp. 257ff.).

Excavations in Palestine have shown the report of the spies to have been in full agreement with the facts. At that time Canaan was densely populated and, as it were, covered with well-fortified cities (see my *Gods Woord,* pp. 343ff.). Anyone contemplating conquering it would have to expect forceful resistance. The spies clearly perceive this. Their problem is that they take into consideration only what they have seen in Canaan with a total disregard for that which since the beginning of Moses' work had manifested itself among them as a no less actual reality: the unlimited power of Israel's God, which not even Egypt's power could oppose.

E. *The response to their report* (13:30–33)

13:30–33 *Then Caleb silenced the people before Moses and said, "We should go up and take possession of the land, for we can certainly do it."*

> *But the men who had gone up with him said, "We can't attack those people; they are stronger than we are." And they spread among the Israelites a bad report about the land they had explored. They said, "The land we explored devours those living in it. All the people we saw there are of great size. We saw the Nephilim there (the descendants of Anak come from the Nephilim). We seemed like grasshoppers in our own eyes, and we looked the same to them."*

The author does not say in so many words what impression the report of the spies makes on the people, but after what was said about their mentality in chapter 11 it is clear to his readers how fatal this impression must have been. He only says in passing (v. 30) that Caleb deemed it necessary "to silence the people before Moses"; the Kenizzite Caleb, rather than Moses' servant Joshua, who does not stand with Caleb until later, when the grumbling is no longer directed against Moses but against the Lord (14:6). "Silenced": the opposition is just beginning, and the people are not yet raising their voices and weeping (14:1). Caleb's words do not constitute a "minority report" (as Wellhausen's school claims). He does not deny that what the others have reported is true. But Caleb states his conclusion "we should go up" over against the conclusion (not explicitly stated, but suggested by their report) of the other spies, "we should not go up." Caleb does not explain why he believes that "we certainly can do it," at least, it is not reported here.

Now the other spies go one step further. What they initially implied is now stated explicitly: "we can't attack those people." And, of course, they now have to play down somewhat the first part of their report, which spoke of the exceptional fertility of the land. They now spread *dibba* ("defamation, evil report," from *dabad,* "to whisper"). These "whisperings" concern first of all the land itself: it "devours those living in it." This does not mean (cf. Ezek. 36:13–14) that the land cannot support its inhabitants, as has been suggested. This meaning can be read into the text only when we start with the assumption that the text is composed of several mutually incompatible elements. What is meant by this statement is that Canaan has never been the uncontested property of its inhabitants. This "bridge of the nations" is also the "battleground of the nations" (see my commentary on Ezek. 36:1–15).

In the second place, they spread an "evil report" about the inhabitants of the land, Israel's future enemies. Suddenly *all* the people there "are of great size" (cf. v. 28). And they add emphasis by bringing up the Nephilim from the hoary past (cf. Gen. 6:4) who, according to legend, were people of great size and awesome ability. In their zeal they overlook the fact that if Canaan were indeed inhabited by such people it could hardly be said that "it devours those living in it"; such Nephilim could undoubtedly defend themselves adequately! (Concerning the Nephilim, see P. Karge, *Rephaïm, die vorgeschichtliche Kultur Palästina's und Phöniziens,* 2nd ed., 1926.)

F. *The people weep and rebel* (14:1–4)

14:1–4 *That night all the people of the community raised their voices and wept aloud. All the Israelites grumbled against Moses and Aaron, and the whole assembly said to them, "If only we had died in Egypt! Or in this desert! Why is the LORD bringing us to this land only to let us fall by the sword? Our wives and children will be taken as plunder. Wouldn't it be better for us to go back to Egypt?" And they said to each other, "We should choose a leader and go back to Egypt."*

One can hardly expect logical thinking from a crowd that is already dissatisfied and inclined to grumble. The inner contradiction of the "evil report" of the spies completely escapes them. Their dissatisfaction now turns into crying and wailing, constantly throughout the night. And when Moses and Aaron attempt to use their personal influence to counteract this, the wailing turns into grumbling. Barely suppressed emotions erupt again (cf. 11:5) and they are gripped by a sense of fear. *All* are involved, "all the people of the community" (v. 1), "all the Israelites," "the whole assembly" (v. 2). Their reaction progresses from "raising their voices" to "weeping" to "grumbling." They would rather do anything than go up and attack those "giants"! The misery of the slavery in Egypt recedes into insignificance in the face of this. It would be better to die in this desert! And then, from the depths of their soul, the old "why?" suddenly comes to the surface (cf. 11:20) and they accuse the Lord of all kinds of sinister plans to kill them. He brought them to Canaan to make all the more sure that they would die, so that their wives and children would be "taken as plunder" (v. 3); this would mean degradation for the wives and daughters, brutal forced labor for the sons, and unbearable slavery for all. How can Israel escape these sinister intentions? By returning to Egypt! And because they know that Moses is certainly not prepared to go along with this, they decide that they should choose another leader. As if they had chosen Moses! Thus the grumbling against Moses and Aaron turns into nothing less than rebellion against the Lord. He and He *alone* is to blame for all their misery!

G. *The futile attempt of Joshua and Caleb* (14:5–9)

14:5–9 *Then Moses and Aaron fell facedown in front of the whole Israelite assembly gathered there. Joshua son of Nun and Caleb son of Jephunneh, who were*

121

among those who had explored the land, tore their clothes and said to the entire Israelite assembly, "The land we passed through and explored is exceedingly good. If the Lᴏʀᴅ is pleased with us, he will lead us into that land, a land flowing with milk and honey, and will give it to us. Only do not rebel against the Lᴏʀᴅ. And do not be afraid of the people of the land, because we will swallow them up. Their protection is gone, but the Lᴏʀᴅ is with us. Do not be afraid of them."

What can Moses and Aaron do when faced with such godlessness? They fall "facedown"; this can be a sign of prayer (Num. 16:22, 45; Josh. 7:6), of worship (Gen. 17:3; Lev. 9:24; Josh. 5:14), or of surrendering something entirely to the Lord (16:4; 20:6). The latter is probably intended here. They are in a situation where they can no longer defend themselves, nor justify the actions of their Sender. The only thing to do here is to wait for what the Lord will do in an attitude of prayer, which also speaks of deep humility and unspeakable anguish.

But it is different for Joshua and Caleb. They are part of the group of men who have unleashed these emotions by their *dibba* (see above). They would share in their guilt if they were to remain silent. Joshua now also speaks out, in contrast to 13:30; this does not indicate that this is a different narrative, but rather that the situation now does not concern just Moses, his master, but ultimately the honor of the Lord, Israel's God.

Both Caleb and Joshua tear their clothes as a sign of mourning for the godlessness of their people (cf. Lev. 21:10; Josh. 7:6; Judg. 11:35; et al.) and put their lives on the line (cf. v. 10) in their attempt to counteract the effect of the *dibba* of their fellow spies and to return their people to a child-like trust in the Lord's omnipotence. They begin by reminding the people of what the other spies had also said: Canaan is "exceedingly good," it flows with milk and honey. But then they immediately turn to what the others had completely lost sight of: the Lord's being pleased with them was the only, but also the quite sufficient, means of giving this beautiful land into Israel's possession. His "pleasure" or "delight," i.e., the disposition that impels His Being to act in accordance with Israel's desire, places the effective power of the Lord's will behind Israel's actions, so that any human resistance is rendered completely ineffective. Israel's victory then becomes the fruit of His "giving." Their next statement (v. 9) goes counter to the ancient Near Eastern way of thinking, which played an important role in Israel's thought: the tie between a nation and its god was a necessary one, anchored in the nature of things; they are mutually dependent without moral or religious conditions. The people worship their god and the god in turn helps his people. But Israel must not think like this. The "only" must open Israel's eyes to the moral and religious condition that they must fulfill if the Lord's delight or pleasure is to go into action.

This condition is expressed by means of two negatives that apply to the present situation: "do not rebel" (against the Lord) and "do not be afraid" (of the people of Canaan). "Do not rebel," i.e., do not give up obedience, do not withdraw from your obligation to be submissive; this would be wrong even in the case of an earthly king. Thus, when Moses at the Lord's command assures Israel that He will give them the land, then Israel must also obey without reservation the command, implicit in the promise, to enter the land after Canaan has been explored. "Do not rebel" also implies "do not be afraid" (see 1 John 4:18); they must act on the conviction that the Lord's omnipotence will go with them when He commands them to enter Canaan. Joshua and Caleb vividly express this conviction when they say, "we will swallow them up" (lit. "they are our bread," cf. kjv). Israel will conquer the large and small inhabitants of Canaan as easily as they eat a piece of bread (cf. Ps. 14:4; Jer. 10:25). The explanation for this miraculous fact is that "their protection [lit. 'shadow'] is gone," they are exposed to the burning rays that sap their strength (cf. Isa. 25:4; 32:2; Pss. 91:1; 121:5; Jer. 48:45). They are no match for Israel because, while the Lord is with Israel and His omnipotence accompanies them, their enemies have no one who will use his power to protect them. This expression also implies that the people of Canaan cannot count on the help of their gods; the Lord's omnipotence renders these gods ineffectual.

H. *The Lord's judgment and Moses' plea* (14:10–25)

14:10–19 *But the whole assembly talked about stoning them. Then the glory of the Lord appeared at the Tent of Meeting to all the Israelites. The Lord said to Moses, "How long will these people treat me with contempt? How long will they refuse to believe in me, in spite of all the miraculous signs I have performed among them? I will strike them down with a plague and destroy them, but I will make you into a nation greater and stronger than they."*

Moses said to the Lord, "Then the Egyptians will hear about it! By your power you brought these people up from among them. And they will tell the inhabitants of this land about it. They have already heard that you, O Lord, are with these people and that you, O Lord, have been seen face to face, that your cloud stays over them, and that you go before them in a pillar of cloud by day and a pillar of fire by night. If you put these people to death all at one time, the nations who have heard this report about you will say, 'The Lord was not able to bring these people into the land he promised them on oath; so he slaughtered them in the desert.'

"Now may the Lord's strength be displayed, just as you have declared: 'The Lord is slow to anger, abounding in love and forgiving sin and rebellion. Yet he does not leave the guilty unpunished; he punishes the children for the sin of the fathers to the third and fourth generation.' In accordance with your great love,

forgive the sin of these people, just as you have pardoned them from the time they left Egypt until now.''

But Israel does not understand this seeing of the Invisible, this living out of the only true reality. All they hear in Joshua and Caleb's words is an attempt to draw them into a hopeless battle with the inhabitants of Canaan. And this they want to avoid at any cost. Both men must therefore go! But before they can pick up stones to carry out their plan against Joshua and Caleb, the ''glory of the LORD'' intervenes, the visible revelation of the Lord's *kabod,* His weight, the fullness of His power; Israel saw this *kabod* for the first time at Sinai where it looked ''like a consuming fire'' (Exod. 24:17); its reflection showed in Moses' radiant face (Exod. 34:29–35). That glory appears ''on [lit. 'in'] the Tent of Meeting.'' The LXX and the Syriac change this into ''in the cloud over the Tent of Meeting,'' a reading that has been adopted by those who forget that ''the glory of the LORD'' did not always appear ''in the cloud'' (Lev. 9:6, 23; Num. 16:19; 20:6). The ''consuming fire'' radiates out from the tent and speaks to all those present of the imminent revelation of the Lord's power.

The Lord addresses Moses, and that for two reasons: he is the mediator between the Lord and His people, and he is directly involved in what the Lord is going to say. The Lord begins with ''How long?'' This is an expression of His burning anger (cf. Exod. 10:3; 16:28; Jer. 23:26; Hos. 8:5). And then follows a reminder of ''all the miraculous signs'' that have been performed in Israel's midst since Moses came to Israel with the Lord's message, of all those revelations of His power that addressed Israel's reason and consciousness and were intended to make them acknowledge what the Lord did for them. What Israel does now is show contempt; they do not consider it worth the trouble to look to Him or listen to Him (cf. 1 Sam. 2:17). It is a not-believing in Him, i.e., a failure to see Him as the Reliable One on whom man can always depend under all circumstances.

But in doing this Israel has lost its right to exist. What Israel is, it owes to the Lord. If it severs every tie with Him, then it turns toward its own ruin. Hence the Lord's ''I will.'' When the Lord ''strikes'' it is always something tremendous (cf. Exod. 9:15; Lev. 26:25; Deut. 28:21; 2 Sam. 24:13; Hab. 3:5). This time it is the plague, which especially in those days was the most terrible means to destroy an entire people. But what then about the promise to Abraham and his seed? It remains in force, because it is the Lord's program for the future; even Israel's sin cannot prevent its realization. A new people will replace the present Israel, again from one man, this time Moses, who is ''faithful in all my house'' (12:7). The threat of Exodus 32:9f. is thus repeated.

But Moses, who no longer feels the burden of the people as in 11:11ff., pleads again for mercy and forgiveness as he did at Sinai—not in the first place for the sake of his people, with whose ingratitude he is all too familiar, but, as in the past, for the sake of the honor of his God. What will the Egyptians and Canaanites say when they hear that Israel has perished in the wilderness? This is a typically ancient Near Eastern thought: god and people are one to the extent that the weakness of the one is the weakness of the other. If Israel perishes it proves that Israel's God was not able to keep them from destruction (see my commentary on Ezek. 36:1–15). The Lord is thus obligated to His own honor to keep Israel from perishing—this is why He *must* not send the plague. He *must* keep His promise to take *this* people into Canaan! (Cf. also Josh. 7:8ff.)

Moses adds a second argument, which to us may carry more force than the first. He reminds the Lord of what He Himself revealed concerning His divine Being: "The LORD, the compassionate and gracious God, slow to anger, abounding in love and faithfulness, maintaining love to thousands, and forgiving wickedness, rebellion and sin" (Exod. 34:6–7). This is how the Lord has proven Himself to be "from the time they left Egypt until now." May the Lord also now let mercy outweigh justice and forgive these people again! Because the sin is relatively minor? Not at all—it is "iniquity," the "crooked line" that always crosses the Lord's "straight line." But rather so that "the LORD's strength be displayed" (v. 17), i.e., that the Lord may show His power in such a way that both the nations and Israel may be deeply impressed by His divine power.

14:20–24 *The LORD replied, "I have forgiven them, as you asked. Nevertheless, as surely as I live and as surely as the glory of the LORD fills the whole earth, not one of the men who saw my glory and the miraculous signs I performed in Egypt and in the desert but who disobeyed me and tested me ten times—not one of them will ever see the land I promised on oath to their forefathers. No one who has treated me with contempt will ever see it. But because my servant Caleb has a different spirit and follows me wholeheartedly, I will bring him into the land he went to, and his descendants will inherit it."*

How long does Moses, who acknowledges that Israel deserves to be punished (v. 18b) and will be punished (but not in this manner), wrestle in prayer? In Deuteronomy 9:23–29 Moses says that he prayed forty days and forty nights, even as he had done before at Sinai. And only then does Moses' prayer, "please forgive," receive an answer: "I have forgiven." But not on the basis of Moses' first argument. To the Lord only the second argument is valid: the appeal to His mercy. That appeal is never in vain, even now! But the Lord's forgiveness does not negate His demand for obedience and faith. The riches of the covenant cannot be obtained without these two. This is why Israel as it shows itself at Kadesh is and remains totally unfit; it has shown all too clearly the spirit that motivates it. "Ten times" (v. 22), like our "dozen," is not an arithmetical statement; the Talmud tract *Arachin* 15a, b forgets this and lists ten instances of Israel's rebellion (Exod. 14:11f.; 15:23f.; 16:2, 20, 26–28; 17:2; 32:1ff.; Num. 11:1, 4ff.; 13–14). *This* Israel cannot, therefore, enter Canaan; it *must* die in the desert, whatever the Egyptians and Canaanites may say. And as proof of the immutability of His decision the Lord's answer begins with "as surely as I live." People swear by the Lord (cf. e.g., Judg. 8:19; 1 Sam. 14:39), although not always (cf. Gen. 42:15f.; 2 Sam. 15:21; 2 Kings 2:2). But the Lord (cf. Heb. 6:13) can only swear by Himself (see Gen. 22:16). This is followed by "as surely as the glory of the LORD fills the whole earth." This is not an underlining of the oath of verse 23, as the margin of the Dutch AV claims; rather, verse 22b goes back to Moses' first argument that only nonpunishment will leave the Lord's *kabod,* His "weight," the fullness of His power, unimpaired (v. 16). The response is that the Lord's *kabod* is inviolable; in order to destroy it, "the whole earth" would have to be destroyed. The Lord's *kabod* fills the whole earth, so that there is no room for anyone else, neither god nor man. A striking statement in an era of polytheism!

Hebrews 3:8–4:11 clearly refers to this dramatic event in Israel's history and draws a serious lesson from it for us, who know the fullness of the Lord's mercy in Christ, a lesson we forget all too easily: no "rest" without an unmoveable faith!

There is to be only one exception to the awesome verdict that has been pronounced over Israel: Caleb, who had immediately tried to counteract the disastrous impact of the report of the spies (13:30). In him is "a different spirit," i.e., a different motivating force, which was evidenced by his action that differed from that of the people as a whole. He "follows me wholeheartedly," literally, "he made (the being or going) after me full." This same testimony is stated in Deuteronomy 1:36; Joshua 14:8f., its negative form in 32:11–12; 1 Kings 11:6. Therefore, the way to Canaan remains open to Caleb, and his descendants are promised an inheritance in the land. This was fulfilled forty-five years later (Josh. 14:10, 13–14; 15:13; Judg. 1:20).

Only Caleb is mentioned in verse 24, while both Caleb and Joshua are mentioned in verse 30. The school of Wellhausen, which is always inclined to look for two or more "traditions," has concluded that 14:10–25 stems from a different tradition than 14:30. But this overlooks the fact that according to Deuteronomy 1:38 Joshua as Moses' servant and future leader of Israel occupied a unique position; Caleb is mentioned before Joshua in Deuteronomy 1:36 as well.

14:25a *"Since the Amalekites and Canaanites are living in the valleys."*

Verse 25a is usually considered to be a historical note concerning the fact that the Amalekites and Canaanites lived "in the valley" (Heb. singular, cf. KJV). But this would be a curious place to insert such a note: in the middle of the Lord's words. It appears to me that it is better to connect these words with verse 24 and to translate ". . . even though the Amalekites and Canaanites live in the valley." Their presence in this valley, which was eminently suitable for a display of military skill, cannot be a hindrance to the Lord's fulfillment of His promise, even though all Israel believes that these people are too powerful. This "valley," which unfortunately is not further specified, is of course situated in the southern part of Canaan where Israel was planning to invade. The Amalekites and Canaanites are mentioned in the same breath, which prepares us for 14:45.

14:25b *"Turn back tomorrow and set out toward the desert along the route to the Red Sea."*

The Lord's word to Moses ends with the command to stop the northward journey and to go back south into the wilderness, "in the direction of the Sea of Reeds (NIV margin). The designation "Sea of Reeds" is not entirely clear to us, since *both* arms of the Red Sea on either side of the Sinai peninsula are called "Sea of Reeds" in the Old Testament (cf. e.g., 21:4, which refers to the present Gulf of Aqaba, and 33:10–11, which refers to the Gulf of Suez). Here the Gulf of Suez is probably meant. Israel wants to go back (14:4)? Then so be it! Israel must turn its back on Canaan.

They must turn back "tomorrow," a term not to be taken here in our usual literal sense (cf. Exod. 13:14; Deut. 6:20; Josh. 4:6, 21; 22:24, 27f. KJV—"in time to come"; also Gen. 30:33; Isa. 22:13). Elsewhere we find indications that the stay at Kadesh lasted a long time. This is not only proven by the failed invasion (vv. 39–45), but is also stated explicitly in Deuteronomy 1:46: "and so you stayed in Kadesh many days—all the time you spent there"; the latter expression points to a prolonged but unspecified period of time (cf. Deut. 9:25; 1 Sam. 23:13; 2 Sam. 15:20). This period appears to have lasted for thirty-eight years (Deut. 2:14). But this, in turn, must be understood in the light of Deuteronomy 2:1, which speaks of traveling around the hill country of Seir "for a long time." Kadesh thus remained the central point where the tabernacle stayed, while the tribes looked for food for man and beast in different directions. Israel thus stayed in the desert.

I. *Further elucidation* (14:26–35)

14:26–35 *The Lᴏʀᴅ said to Moses and Aaron: "How long will this wicked community grumble against me? I have heard the complaints of these grumbling Israelites. So tell them, 'As surely as I live, declares the Lᴏʀᴅ, I will do to you the very things I heard you say: In this desert your bodies will fall—every one of you twenty years old or more who was counted in the census and who has grumbled against me. Not one of you will enter the land I swore with uplifted hand to make your home, except Caleb son of Jephunneh and Joshua son of Nun. As for your children that you said would be taken as plunder, I will bring them in to enjoy the land you have rejected. But you—your bodies will fall in the desert. Your children will be shepherds here for forty years, suffering for your unfaithfulness, until the last of your bodies lies in the desert. For forty years—one year for each of the forty days you explored the land—you will suffer for your sins and know what it is like to have me against you.' I, the Lᴏʀᴅ, have spoken, and I will surely do these things to this whole wicked community, which has banded together against me. They will meet their end in this desert; here they will die."*

These verses complement verses 10–25. They are addressed to Moses, as the singular in verses 28, 39 indicates. Aaron's name is mentioned in verse 26, but this is apparently a later addition, based on 13:6 and 14:2, 5. This elucidation was necessary because verse 23 stated only briefly that none of those who treated the Lord with contempt would ever see Canaan. But nothing was said about the manner in which, and the circumstances under which, God's judgment would be executed, nor about the duration of the wanderings that were to follow. The "treating with contempt" of verse 11 is here called "grumbling"; "these people" (lit. "this people"; cf. ᴋᴊᴠ) are here called "this wicked community." The tone of these verses is very sarcastic, just as in 11:18–20. The wish of the people to die in the desert (v. 2) will be granted (vv. 29–30); their fear for the children (14:3; nothing is said here about the women!) will turn out to be unfounded (v. 31), although they will have to wander along in the wilderness because of their fathers (v. 33).

Note that the punishment is limited specifically to "every one of you twenty years old or more who was counted in the census" of chapter 1. This means that the coming judgment will concern only the men able to bear arms, and not the priests and Levites, who were not counted in the census (1:47ff.), since they were charged with the service of the tabernacle. This has been construed as being in conflict with the seemingly all-inclusive "no one who has treated me with contempt" of verse 23, since the rebellion included all Israelites: "this people" (v. 11 KJV). But any attempt to see a contrast or contradiction here overlooks 1:52f., where "the Israelites" and "the Levites" are two distinct groups. Verse 29, therefore, does not limit verses 11 and 23, but is rather a clarification. It is clear from 20:22–26 that the judgment of 14:20–25 does not include the priests and Levites: there Eleazar, Aaron's son, succeeds Aaron as high priest. But Eleazar already functioned as a priest in the second year after the Exodus (Exod. 28:1; Num. 3:3–4), and must thus have been at least twenty years old at that time (perhaps even thirty, see 4:1–2). In Joshua 14:1 and 21:1 Eleazar works with Joshua, and his death is not recorded until Joshua 24:33. Moses and Aaron are, of course, not mentioned in verse 30, since, as Israel's leader and high priest, they were not counted (see 1:3). Only Caleb and Joshua are singled out as being exempt from the judgment of verse 30, since they belonged to "the people" and had been counted. Verse 30, unlike verse 6 and verse 38, lists Caleb first. I do not know the reason for this, unless it is related to the Judahite origin of this pericope. While verse 3 mentions the women along with the children, here nothing is said about the women's fate; this points once again to the position of unimportance women occupied in Israel's thinking.

As for the children, they will not bear the full impact of the punishment, although they will have to suffer under it. They must wander in the wilderness "until the last of your bodies lies in the desert." Thus the children must "suffer for your unfaithfulness" (v. 33). The word rendered "unfaithfulness" (*zenut*; KJV: "whoredoms") is found seven times in the prophets (Jer. 3:2, 9; 13:27; Ezek. 23:27; 43:7, 9; Hos. 6:10) and expresses Israel's "following after other gods" (Jer. 2:8; Hos. 5:11). Behind this word lies the thought that the covenant the Lord made with Israel has the character of a marriage, a thought emphasized especially by Hosea and later also taken up by Jeremiah and Ezekiel. Although the concept reflected in this word is found in the Pentateuch (Exod. 34:15f.; Lev. 17:7; 20:5; Deut. 31:16), the word itself is used only here, albeit in the more general sense of "unfaithfulness." But we must remember that to the ancient Near Eastern mind turning away from one god involved turning toward another god. Rebellion against the Lord (v. 9) was therefore also apostasy and implied of necessity a "following after other gods"; the later specific meaning of *zenut* is therefore already implicit here.

In verses 33–34 the duration of Israel's wanderings is determined: forty years; this is related to the death of all those who rebelled (v. 33) and the number of days the land was explored (v. 34). Verse 33 reflects Israel's custom to set the average length of one generation at forty years (hence

26:64; Deut. 2:14b; Josh. 5:6a). This "forty" is, of course, again a round number; Deuteronomy 2:14 speaks of thirty-eight years. A final note: in spite of the list in Numbers 33, we must not think that Israel did nothing but wander around in the desert. The laws of both Exodus and Numbers always presuppose some agriculture and indicate that smaller or larger segments of Israel must have spent considerable periods of time in one location, especially at Kadesh, which we must probably consider to have been the "base camp."

J. *The judgment begins* (14:36–38)

14:36–38 *So the men Moses had sent to explore the land, who returned and made the whole community grumble against him by spreading a bad report about it— these men responsible for spreading the bad report about the land were struck down and died of a plague before the Lord. Of the men who went to explore the land, only Joshua son of Nun and Caleb son of Jephunneh survived.*

Thus far the Lord has only spoken of the gradual dying off of the present adult generation (v. 29b). But now it must be made clear to Israel that the Lord's decision is immutable and that the announced judgment will indeed come. And this is done "before the Lord" by means of a "plague" (lit. "blow"), a disaster that strikes suddenly and can be explained only as an act of God (cf. 16:48–50; Ezek. 24:16). The plague strikes the spies whose bad report had stirred the negative emotions of the people, and who were thus the instigators of this drama; Joshua and Caleb are excluded. While they stand "before the Lord" the plague strikes them, because they "made the whole community grumble against him," i.e., in my opinion, against Moses (see 13:30; 14:2), since he is mentioned by name in verse 36. If "against him" referred to the Lord, the author would undoubtedly have made this clear.

K. *The failed invasion* (14:39–45)

14:39–45 *When Moses reported this to all the Israelites, they mourned bitterly. Early the next morning they went up toward the high hill country. "We have sinned," they said. "We will go up to the place the Lord promised."*

But Moses said, "Why are you disobeying the Lord's command? This will not succeed! Do not go up, because the Lord is not with you. You will be defeated by your enemies, for the Amalekites and Canaanites will face you there. Because you have turned away from the Lord, he will not be with you and you will fall by the sword."

Nevertheless, in their presumption they went up toward the high hill country, though neither Moses nor the ark of the Lord's covenant moved from the camp.

Then the Amalekites and Canaanites who lived in that hill country came down and attacked them and beat them down all the way to Hormah.

Moses has received a message of deep emotional impact from the Lord for his people: he must tell them to return to the wilderness, which will become the grave of every adult of "the people" (see commentary on 14:27–35). The impression this message makes on the people is as profound as that made by the one that followed the sin with the golden calf, , when Moses had to tell the people that the Lord would no longer go with them (cf. Gen. 37:34). They mourn, which includes the removal of all ornaments (Exod. 33:4).

But instead of obeying the Lord's command by turning south and abandoning any attempt to conquer Canaan, Israel still wants to try it. They assume the appearance of the obedience of faith ("see, we are here"; KJV, RSV, omitted in NIV) and of unconditional trust in the Lord's promise ("the place the LORD promised"). They believe that by an admission of guilt ("we have sinned") they can undo the events of Kadesh; but they forget that what has happened here is not an isolated event (14:22, "ten times") and that the Lord's judgment thus should be perceived in the light of a broader context. As soon as possible ("early the next morning") they want to go into "the high hill country"; the Hebrew reads literally "the top of the mountain" (cf. KJV), but Deuteronomy 1:41–45, where Moses relates this event, indicates that this refers to the hill country of Judah, which rises up to the north from Kadesh and which does indeed look like a "mountain top" from the south.

Moses tries to keep them from going, but without success. Their action is a new sin and as such is doomed to fail. No matter how much they believe that as long as *they* are willing the Lord is also willing, Moses, who knows the Lord better than they, keeps warning them and telling them that they must not count on the Lord's help: "the LORD is *not* with you." Their statement "we are here" (KJV, RSV) implies essentially another "turning away from the LORD." Without doubt they go toward their ruin and bring on themselves (but against the Lord's will) precisely that which they were afraid of when the Lord told them to enter the land (14:3). Moses points out that they will soon face the Amalekites and the Canaanites without the Lord. The Amalekites were already named as inhabitants of the hill country of Judah in 13:29. The mention of the Canaanites here, after 13:29, might be somewhat surprising. But the term "Canaanites" can sometimes be used in a geographical, rather than ethnological, sense to indicate the inhabitants of Canaan (see Gen. 12:6; 24:3; Exod. 13:11; Ezek. 16:3). In Deuteronomy 1:44 the Amorites are given as Israel's opponents instead;

this name must also be understood in a geographical sense (cf. Gen. 48:22; Josh. 24:15).

Moses' serious warning is brushed aside, even when the warning is followed by a concrete step: neither the ark nor the priests accompanying the ark will go with Israel, as they normally would when Israel went into battle (10:35f.; cf. also 1 Sam. 4:3). Israel believes that it can get along without the visible sign of the Lord's presence and that it can ignore Moses' warning, "the LORD is not with you." They go "in their presumption" (v. 44; lit. "they were swollen, puffed up"?). The result is a crushing defeat—the enemy meets them before they have even reached the top of the hills. They "attacked them" and "beat them" (a play on words in Hebrew: *wayyakum* and *wayyaketum*). Deuteronomy 1:44 says, "they chased you like a swarm of bees and beat you down from Seir all the way to Hormah." Here the Hebrew says literally, "all the way to *the* Hormah." If this reading is correct, then we have here a generic noun ("destruction"). But elsewhere (21:3; Deut. 1:44; Josh. 12:14; 15:30; 19:4; Judg. 1:17; 1 Chron. 4:30) "Hormah" is always used as a proper noun (as does the Sam. Pent. here). According to Judges 1:17 Hormah is a more recent name for Zephath, and according to Joshua 15:30; 19:4; 1 Chronicles 4:30 it belonged to the territory of Judah and Simeon. It is frequently identified with the present es-Sbeita between Beersheba and Gaza, but this is undoubtedly too far north. In any case, Hormah must have been centrally located, because it marks the end of a southward movement (Num. 14:45; Deut. 1:44; Judg. 1:17) as well as the end of a northward movement (Num. 21:3).

In the Samaritan Pentateuch, the LXX, and the old Latin Codex Lugdunensis we find the addition "and they returned to the camp." It is impossible to determine whether these verses were part of the original text.

Wiener ("The Exodus and the Southern Invasion," *Nieuwe Theologische Studiën,* 1927, pp. 71–81) has attempted to show that this victory of the Canaanites is the same as that mentioned on the victory stele of Pharaoh Merneptah (see my *Gods Woord,* p. 306). Merneptah claims to have utterly defeated Israel in the fifth year of his reign (1228 B.C.): "His seed no longer exists." This means that he claimed a victory of his Canaanite vassals as his own, which is in itself possible. But Wiener overlooks the fact that the Israel of which Merneptah speaks does not attempt to invade Canaan, but lives in Canaan in a region between Ashkelon and Jenoam near the Lebanon (see also e.g., Edelkoort, *Uittocht en Intocht,* pp. 54–56).

Ritual Laws
(15:1–41)

1. Supplementary Offerings (15:1–16)

The judgment of 14:29 ushers in the darkest period of the wilderness journey: the thirty-eight years of wandering in the wilderness, waiting for the "wicked community" (14:27, 36) to die; this would reopen the way to the Promised Land. Israel's experiences during this period are hidden in obscurity. Only one episode from that long span is recorded: the rebellion of Korah, Dathan, and Abiram (ch. 16), which is closely related to the story of the budding of Aaron's staff (ch. 17). Besides this, only a few ritual and cultic laws are given, which concern offerings (15:1–31), the relationship between priests and Levites and their respective incomes (18:1–32), and the water of cleansing (19:1–22), while 15:32–41 deals with gathering wood on the Sabbath (vv. 32–36) and the tassels on the garments (vv. 37–41).

The relative silence concerning such a long period has been explained by assuming that the wanderings are not historical, but rather the product of a "later expansion of Israel's tradition," that they have only "theoretical meaning," and constitute an attempt to fill an "empty space of forty years" (Baentsch). But further study has shown that the wanderings belong "definitely to the oldest tradition" (Edelkoort, p. 141). We cannot dispense with the Old Testament witness as easily as the school of Wellhausen once believed. Statements such as Exodus 16:35; Deuteronomy 1:3; 2:7, 14; 8:2, 4; 29:5; Joshua 5:6; Nehemiah 9:21, to name only a few, cannot be unceremoniously dismissed. I am convinced that since the Old Testament is the history of God's revelation, rather than the history of Israel, nothing happened during those long years of wandering that was of importance for our knowledge of the further progress of that revelation. They were years of dying, not years of progress. We can no longer determine where 15:1–20:13 fit in the chronology of the thirty-eight years. The only chronological reference is found in 20:1 (see commentary). I find it therefore surprising that Edelkoort (*Numeri*, p. 141) raises the question in connection with the fact that chapter 15 follows immediately after the judgment of 14:29. Was it not cruel to issue laws immediately after the punishment that were to be kept, and could only be kept, after entering Canaan? His use of "immediately after" is unsupported.

15:1–12 *The LORD said to Moses, "Speak to the Israelites and say to them: 'After you enter the land I am giving you as a home and present to the LORD offerings made by fire, from the herd or the flock, as an aroma pleasing to the LORD—whether burnt offerings or sacrifices, for special vows or freewill offerings or festival* *offerings—then the one who brings his offering shall present to the L*ORD *a grain offering of a tenth of an ephah of fine flour mixed with a fourth of a hin of oil. With each lamb for the burnt offering or the sacrifice, prepare a fourth of a hin of wine as a drink offering.*

*"'With a ram prepare a grain offering of two-tenths of an ephah of fine flour mixed with a third of a hin of oil, and a third of a hin of wine as a drink offering. Offer it as an aroma pleasing to the L*ORD*.*

*"'When you prepare a young bull as a burnt offering or sacrifice, for a special vow or a fellowship offering to the L*ORD*, bring with the bull a grain offering of three-tenths of an ephah of fine flour mixed with half a hin of oil. Also bring half a hin of wine as a drink offering. It will be an offering made by fire, an aroma pleasing to the L*ORD*. Each bull or ram, each lamb or young goat, is to be prepared in this manner. Do this for each one, for as many as you prepare.'"*

This law, which speaks of grain, wine, and oil is, like the law in verses 17–21 and a few others that relate to either agriculture (Lev. 19:23; 23:10; 25:2) or at least to life in Canaan (Lev. 14:34; Num. 34:2; Deut. 12:1; 18:9; 19:1), introduced by a statement as to when it is to go into effect: in Canaan, the land of grain, wine, and oil. This law specifies the quantities of these ingredients that are to be added as grain and drink offerings to the "burnt offerings and sacrifices" (i.e., fellowship offerings; here, as in Exod. 20:24; 32:6; Judg. 20:26, these two represent the offerings that involve animals), but *not* to the sin and guilt offerings (which consisted only of animals, unless they were part of the official offerings brought by Israel as a community, see ch. 28). Concerning the burnt offering, see Leviticus 1; concerning the fellowship offering, see Leviticus 3. We must remember that the "fellowship offering" *(šelem)* gives expression to the joy over life in, or a prayerfully reaching for, the state of being *šalem* ("perfect, complete") with God and man, i.e., of living in harmony and thus in peace *(šalom;* hence "peace offering," KJV). Also, the term "offering made by fire" is retained for lack of a better term; the *'isse* has nothing to do with fire *('eš),* but characterizes the offering as the means to reestablish the right relationship with God. And finally, the term "pleasing aroma" is not entirely correct, since it points to the stilling of God's anger (see my commentary on Lev. 1:9; 3:1).

The size of the grain and drink offerings that are to be added to the burnt offerings and fellowship offerings is determined by the size of the animal offered. Thus, when a lamb is offered a tenth of an ephah of fine flour (approximately two quarts) and one-fourth hin of wine (approximately one quart) and oil are added; when the offering is a young bull three-tenths of an ephah of fine flour (approximately six quarts) and half a hin of oil (approximately two quarts) and half a hin of wine. The increase is thus proportionately larger for the fine flour than for the wine and oil. Verse 10 states that the grain and drink offerings (which are a unit; the Torah does not know the drink offering as an offering by itself—it is always combined with the grain offering) are "an offering made by fire, an aroma pleasing to the LORD." This leads us to surmise that in ancient times the wine was poured over the animal on the altar, as was done by the Greeks and Romans. In the Temple of Herod two bowls stood at the southwest corner of the altar of burnt offering, one to pour the water at the Feast of Tabernacles, the other to pour the wine of the drink offering. From that bowl the wine flowed into an opening in the rock (cf. Mishna tract Zebachim 6. 2). Ecclesiasticus 50:17 says something similar: the wine is poured at the base of the altar, like the blood of certain kinds of sin offerings (Lev. 4:7, 18, 25, 30, 34.).

Verse 3 specifies on what occasions the grain and drink offerings are to be added to the burnt offering or sacrifice: "for special vows or freewill offerings or festival offerings." Concerning vows, see commentary on 30:3–10. Concerning the annual festivals, see my commentary on Leviticus 23.

It has been noted that the law hardly speaks of these supplementary grain and drink offerings, even when it deals with burnt offerings or fellowship offerings. The conclusion has been drawn that this pericope is therefore very recent. But this overlooks the fact that each section that deals with the burnt and fellowship offerings approached them from a specific perspective. Thus, Leviticus 7:11–21 is concerned with the meal that follows the fellowship offering; Exodus 29:15 and Leviticus 9:4 speak of the consecration offerings of the priests; Leviticus 23:19 focuses on the obligatory fellowship offering that Israel must bring as a community during the Feast of Weeks (Pentecost), while in Leviticus 22:21–25 the requirement that the animal for the offering be without defect, and in 1 Kings 18:34 the pouring of water over Elijah's altar are central. And finally, Leviticus 1 (burnt offering) and Leviticus 3 (fellowship offering) deal with the bringing of the animals for the offerings and the role of the individual bringing the offering.

15:13–16 *" 'Everyone who is native-born must do these things in this way when he brings an offering made by fire as an aroma pleasing to the LORD. For the generations to come, whenever an alien or anyone else living among you presents an offering made by fire as an aroma pleasing to the LORD, he must do exactly as you do. The community is to have the same rules for you and for the alien living among you; this is a lasting ordinance for the generations to come. You and the alien shall be the same before the LORD: The same laws and regulations will apply both to you and to the alien living among you.' "*

135

These verses stress that not only Israel is required to keep the instructions given here, but also the *ger* (alien), the person of non-Israelite descent who is part of Israel's community, as well as the alien who stays temporarily in Israel's midst. Whoever lives or stays in Canaan must live in full accord with the demands the Lord has made. There is no room for human arbitrariness or self-willed religion (cf. Exod. 12:19, 48f.; Lev. 16:29–31; 17:8, 10–16; 18:26; 20:2ff.; 22:18–20; 24:16; Num. 15:26, 30; 19:10–12; 35:15).

2. *The Cake From the First of the Ground Meal* (15:17–21)

15:17–21 *The* LORD *said to Moses, "Speak to the Israelites and say to them: 'When you enter the land to which I am taking you and you eat the food of the land, present a portion as an offering to the* LORD. *Present a cake from the first of your ground meal and present it as an offering from the threshing floor. Throughout the generations to come you are to give this offering to the* LORD *from the first of your ground meal.'"*

The law speaks in several places of the bringing of the firstfruits: the firstfruits of the soil in general (Exod. 23:19; 34:26; Deut. 26:2, 10), of the land (Num. 18:13), of the harvest (Lev. 23:10), or specifically of "grain, new wine and oil, and the first wool from the shearing of your sheep" (Deut. 18:4), of "your granaries, your vats, your sons, your cattle, and your sheep" (Exod. 22:29–30), and of "the crops you sow in your field" (Exod. 23:16). This requirement is presupposed in Leviticus 2:12. The firstfruits are the strongest and therefore the best (Gen. 49:3; Deut. 21:17). Hence the ancient Near Eastern custom (also found elsewhere) to dedicate the *rešit* (the "first," the *rešiti* of the Assyrians and Babylonians) to the deity (see also my commentary on Lev. 23:9–14). This is done "so that a blessing may rest on your household" (Ezek. 44:30). Verse 20 states that the firstfruits of the grain harvest ("the food of the land") must be presented in the form of a *challa*, a flat cake made of coarse flour. This is the only reference to this requirement; the Mishna devotes a separate tract to it *(Challa).* The word rendered "ground meal" (RSV: "coarse meal") is sometimes translated "dough" (KJV, ASV), a rendering that follows the LXX. In Romans 11:16 Paul alludes to this cake, and also follows the LXX when he speaks of "dough." But the word *'ariša* (found only here and in Neh. 10:37; Ezek. 44:30) means "hulled barley"(?)—the grain harvest began with the barley—or "coarse meal," which was not ground daily but only once a year and then of course in large quantities. Deuteronomy 26:1–11 proves that the firstfruits were originally an offering (see also Lev. 2:12), but became in Israel part of the priests' income (Lev. 23:10; Num. 18:13).

3. *Sin Offerings for the Community and for Individuals* (15:22–31)

15:22–31 *"'Now if you unintentionally fail to keep any of these commands the* LORD *gave Moses—any of the* LORD'*s commands to you through him, from the day the* LORD *gave them and continuing through the generations to come—and if this is done unintentionally without the community being aware of it, then the whole community is to offer a young bull for a burnt offering as an aroma pleasing to the* LORD, *along with its prescribed grain offering and drink offering, and a male goat for a sin offering. The priest is to make atonement for the whole Israelite community, and they will be forgiven, for it was not intentional and they have brought to the* LORD *for their wrong an offering made by fire and a sin offering. The whole Israelite community and the aliens living among them will be forgiven, because all the people were involved in the unintentional wrong.*

"'But if just one person sins unintentionally, he must bring a year-old female goat for a sin offering. The priest is to make atonement before the LORD *for the one who erred by sinning unintentionally, and when atonement has been made for him, he will be forgiven. One and the same law applies to everyone who sins unintentionally, whether he is a native-born Israelite or an alien.*

"'But anyone who sins defiantly, whether native-born or alien, blasphemes the LORD, *and that person must be cut off from his people. Because he has despised the* LORD'*s word and broken his commands, that person must surely be cut off; his guilt remains on him.'"*

This section deals with unintentional sin, whether on the part of the community as a whole (vv. 22–26), or on the part of the individual (vv. 27–31). This is reminiscent of Leviticus 4, which deals with four cases: the unintentional sin of the anointed priest (vv. 1–12; the sin offering is a young bull); of the whole community (vv. 13–21; also a young bull); of a leader (vv. 22–26; a male goat); and of a member of the community (vv. 27–35; a female goat or lamb). Leviticus 4 is more complete in other respects as well, since it also indicates what is to be done with the blood of the offering (vv. 6–7, 17–18, 25, 30, 34) and with the fat (vv. 8–10, 19–20, 26, 31, 35); in two cases it also specifies what is to be done with the remains (vv. 11–12, 21). None of these particulars are given here. Furthermore, Leviticus 4:13–21 speaks only of a young bull as the sin offering for the community (v. 14), while the requirement in this section consists of a young bull for a burnt offering as well as the supplementary grain and drink offerings and a male goat for a sin offering. And finally, the sin offering for a member of the community in Leviticus 4 is either a female goat (v. 28) or a lamb (v. 32), while here only a year-old female goat is required, and no separate burnt offering.

As I have observed in my commentary on Leviticus (on 4:1–2), the rabbis, in an effort to explain these discrepancies, maintained that

Leviticus 4 speaks of sins of commission, while Numbers 15:22–31 deals with sins of omission. But Numbers 15:24 says explicitly that something "is *done* unintentionally." Furthermore, the distinction, made only here, between sinning "unintentionally" and sinning "defiantly" (lit. "with a high hand," v. 30) makes it impossible to think of sins of omission here. I repeat what I wrote concerning this question in my commentary on Leviticus: "We must bear in mind that Israel's legal provisions were not immutable entities. This is why Israel's faithful approached them with a much greater degree of freedom than later Judaism, which distorted the Lord's 'instruction' *(tora)* into a complex of articles of law (see my *Gods Woord,* pp. 326ff., and my commentary on 2 Chron. 29:34; 30:17; 35:5–11; also the Introduction to my commentary on Leviticus, V)." The purpose of this law is to inculcate the distinction between unintentional and intentional sin, a distinction that also dominates Leviticus 4, although it is not expressed in the same manner. In the case of unintentional sin atonement is possible; in the second case, in which the Lord's will and man's will collide, only one punishment is possible: the offender must be "cut off," regardless of what kind of sin he committed. Whatever he has done, it constitutes a "blaspheming" (RSV: "reviling") of the Lord (*gadaf,* "to besmirch," to throw something at the Lord that is contrary to His Being); a "despising" of the Lord's word (*baza,* "to hold cheap"); a "breaking" of His commands (*parar,* "to break, render inoperative"). "His guilt remains on him," it clings to him, covers him, so that the removal of the sin requires total annihilation (cf. "his blood will be on his own head," Lev. 20:9, 11–13, 16, 27).

In conclusion, I point out that this section, even though the added "according to the ordinance" (NIV: "prescribed," v. 24c) connects it with the preceding, and it follows the preceding without any superscription, is not a continuation of it. Verse 23 proves this, which states explicitly that "any of these commands" in verse 22 (lit. "all these commands") must be understood to refer to the entire *tora.* It would therefore be incorrect to assume that the sin offerings prescribed in this section apply only in the case of transgression of one of the ordinances of verses 1–21.

4. *Gathering Wood on the Sabbath* (15:32–36)

15:32–36 *While the Israelites were in the desert, a man was found gathering wood on the Sabbath day. Those who found him gathering wood brought him to Moses and Aaron and the whole assembly, and they kept him in custody, because it was not clear what should be done to him. Then the LORD said to Moses, "The man must die. The whole assembly must stone him outside the camp." So the assembly took him outside the camp and stoned him to death, as the LORD commanded Moses.*

While these verses do not contain a legal precept, but rather record an event that took place "while the Israelites were in the desert" (this expression shows that these verses were written down when Israel no longer lived in the desert), they are included here because they illustrate what verse 30 said with regard to the intentional breaking of any of the Lord's commandments. The man who gathered wood on the Sabbath knew that he was breaking the Sabbath commandment of Exodus 31:12–17; 35:1–3, where those who do work on that day are threatened with the death penalty (31:15; 35:2), even if the work involves nothing more than lighting a fire (35:3).

"Those who found him gathering wood brought him to Moses" and his circle (see 32:2; 36:1), who do with him what they also did with the blasphemer of Leviticus 24:13–23: "they kept him in custody, because it was not clear what should be done to him" (v. 34). This can, of course, not mean that Moses and his circle were unclear as to the penalty this man should receive; the references in Exodus leave no room for doubt on this point. But Moses' problem is twofold: is gathering wood in the same category as lighting a fire? and did the man know this, so that his sin is intentional? Rashi believed that Moses and his circle did not know *which* death penalty should be applied. But this is unlikely: *the* death penalty in Israel was death by stoning, as is also reflected in the Lord's decision, which is that the assembly must stone the man. This implies (1) that gathering wood falls under the heading "work" and is thus forbidden on the Sabbath; and (2) that the man could know this and therefore did not sin out of ignorance. What he did was an intentional sin.

5. *Tassels on Garments* (15:37–41)

15:37–41 *The Lord said to Moses, "Speak to the Israelites and say to them: 'Throughout the generations to come you are to make tassels on the corners of your garments, with a blue cord on each tassel. You will have these tassels to look at and so you will remember all the commands of the Lord, that you may obey them and not prostitute yourselves by going after the lusts of your own hearts and eyes. Then you will remember to obey all my commands and will be consecrated to your God. I am the Lord your God, who brought you out of Egypt to be your God. I am the Lord your God.'"*

We might be surprised that a topic such as this has found its way into the Lord's "instruction" twice (here and in Deut. 22:12); but this was certainly not a "minor" matter in the context of that time. In the ancient Near Eastern world, which always battled demonic forces and tried to protect itself against them by various means, attaching tassels to under or outer garments for the purpose of warding off these demonic forces was customary; representations of Syro-Palestinian men found in Egyptian graves (W. M. Mueller, *Asien und Europa,* pp. 297–99) and in Persepolis (see e.g., Niebuhr, *Reisen,* II, plate 22) clearly show this. But in Israel there was, of course, no longer room for such amulets. This "ancestral custom" must therefore be cleared of any dynamistic concept. Thus, the garments of the high priest, which incorporated several elements from the time when the forefathers "lived beyond the River" (Josh. 24:2) and used all kinds of means to ward off the demonic powers, were "to give him dignity and honor" only. In the same way the tassels on the garments of the Israelites must no longer have reference to demons, but rather remind Israel of the Lord's commandments and exhort them to keep those.

The tassels are to be four in number and are attached to the four corners of the outer garment. This garment was basically nothing more than a large square piece of cloth that was wrapped around the body in such a manner that the right shoulder and the right arm were left free. The outer garment, today called the *tallith,* is still often called "the four corners" and is worn (in a smaller version) under the outer clothing by orthodox Jews, while a full-size *tallith* is put on during services in the synagogue. The tassels to be attached are called *zizit* in Numbers 15:38–39; this same word is used of the hairlock in Ezekiel 8:3, and is related to the Assyrian *sisu,* which means something woven or twisted. Today, the tassels are still made of twined and twisted strands. In Deuteronomy 22:12 *gadiel* is used, i.e., "twisted threads." Verse 38b indicates that a blue cord must be worked into the tassels (rather than that the tassels should be attached by means of a blue cord). The reason behind this blue cord is unclear. It was later claimed that the purpose of the blue cord was to help determine when the day began: as soon as the blue cord could be distinguished from the three other parts of the tassels, which were made of white wool. An ingenious explanation, but clearly one "made up" in the absence of any knowledge of the original reason. I believe that the blue cord reminded the Israelites of the time of their forefathers, when the color blue served to ward off demonic forces (see commentary on 4:6). The size of the tassels is not given; the Talmud *(Sisith)* defines the minimum, but not the maximum size. The New Testament refers to these tassels in several places (Matt. 9:20; 14:36; Mark 6:56; Luke 8:44; *kraspedos,* NIV: "edge," KJV: "hem, border," RSV: "fringe") which shows that the Jews of Christ's time assigned special power to them. Matthew 23:5 states that the Pharisees liked to wear especially long tassels; their extra length would give them increased power.

Verses 40–41 solemnly underline the importance of wearing the tassels. Verse 39 emphasizes again that they must serve to remind Israel of its obligation to keep the Lord's commands and to display in its entire way of life the holy character of Him who led them out of Egypt, solely because He wanted to be Israel's God. The purpose of this emphasis is clear: any thought of demonic powers must be banished.

Concerning the tassels and the *tallith,* see J. van Nes Czn, *Het Joden-dom,* pp. 24-25; also T. Stephens, ''The Ancient Significance of *ṣiṣṣith,*'' *Journal of Biblical Literature,* 1931, pp. 59–71.

The Rebellion of Korah, Dathan, and Abiram; the Budding of Aaron's Staff (16:1–17:13)

1. *The Rebellion* (16:1–50)

   A. *The leaders and their slogan* (16:1–3)

16:1–3 *Korah son of Izhar, the son of Kohath, the son of Levi, and certain Reubenites—Dathan and Abiram, sons of Eliab, and On son of Peleth—became insolent and rose up against Moses. With them were 250 Israelite men, well-known community leaders who had been appointed members of the council. They came as a group to oppose Moses and Aaron and said to them, "You have gone too far! The whole community is holy, every one of them, and the LORD is with them. Why then do you set yourselves above the LORD's assembly?"*

This chapter tells of the rebellion against Moses and Aaron, which involved 250 community leaders and 3 men whose names have gone down in Israel's history: Korah, Dathan, and Abiram. The first belonged to the tribe of Levi and was, through his father Izhar, a grandson of Kohath, after whom later one of the three Levite clans was named (cf. 1 Chron. 6:37–38; in 1 Chron. 6:22 he is called the son of Amminadab; see my commentary on those verses). The other two instigators are from the tribe of Reuben (see 26:5, 8; also Gen. 46:9; Exod. 6:14). The name Dathan is reminiscent of the Assyrian *datnu* (''strong''); the name Abiram is an alternate form of Abraham (see also 1 Kings 16:34) and means ''my father is exalted'' *(abi-ramu),* ''father'' referring to some deity. Their fellow rebels, no fewer than 250 of them, belong to the most prominent Israelite families and are leaders of the clans that make up the community (cf. 1:16; 13:2). As such they ''had been appointed members of the council,'' which probably means the small circle of Moses' assistants; this council is mentioned only here.

But, as often happens with such revolutionary movements that are directed against the universally accepted leaders of the people, not all three leaders have the same goal in mind. The two Reubenites are leaders of the tribe that could claim the birthright; they feel therefore that they have a claim to the priesthood over the tribe of Levi on the basis of Exodus 22:28; 24:5. They direct their rebellion basically only against Aaron. But because his much stronger brother Moses stands behind him (v. 11), they realize that they must first remove Moses before they can rob the tribe of Levi of its prerogatives. They present Moses with a twofold reproach, which they know will make an impression on the common people (vv. 12–15); thus they hope to effect Moses' ouster.

As for Korah, he seeks to put an end to the distinction between Aaron's family and the rest of the tribe of Levi, i.e., between priests and Levites (vv. 8–11). But he knows that the other tribes will see this as an internal matter of the tribe of Levi, so that he cannot count on their support. He therefore gives it the appearance that he wants to reinstate the ancient right of the firstborn to be priests (Exod. 24:5; Judg. 17). With this he hopes on the one hand to put an end to the unique position of Aaron's family, and on the other hand to prevent the tribe of Reuben from taking Levi's place. In this way he manages to gain the support of no fewer than 250 of the most outstanding leaders of Israel (see above; see also vv. 17, 35). In terms of shrewd tactics Korah is thus undoubtedly Dathan's and Abiram's superior.

Moses is therefore actually faced with two revolutionary movements, each pursuing its own goal, but seeking mutual support. This is why, although they are mentioned here together, they have each found their separate niche in Israel's memory. In Psalm 106:17–18 a clear distinction is made between Dathan and Abiram, who were buried alive, and their followers *('eda),* who were destroyed by fire. And in Numbers 27:3 the daughters of Zelophehad speak of Korah and his followers, but do not mention Dathan and Abiram.

The three leaders and their followers come to Moses as a group and present their slogan: "The whole community *('eda)* is holy, every one of them, and the LORD is with them"! "Holy" is here not an ethical but a cultic concept, which implies the right of every individual to approach the altar and to sacrifice on it. A shrewd slogan! The Lord is indeed with Israel (Exod. 25:8; 29:45; Lev. 26:12; Num. 5:3), as the ark and the atonement cover indicate. In that sense Israel can be called "the LORD's assembly," an expression also found in 20:4 and Deuteronomy 23:2–3, 8. But it does not follow that every Israelite has therefore the right to serve at the Lord's altar. Furthermore, the slogan reminds Israel of Exodus 19:6, "a kingdom of priests and a holy nation," and of the ideal expressed in Numbers 15:40, "consecrated to your God" (lit. "holy to your God"); it also seems to be in line with Moses' desire, "I wish that all the LORD's people were prophets!" (Num. 11:29). And thus each one hides his true motives behind beautiful words. They agree on one point only: Moses and Aaron should no longer stand above them; they have "exalted themselves above the LORD's assembly" (cf. RSV).

B. *Moses announces the ordeal* (16:4–7)

16:4–7 *When Moses heard this, he fell facedown. Then he said to Korah and all his followers: "In the morning the LORD will show who belongs to him and who is holy, and he will have that person come near him. The man he chooses he will cause to come near him. You, Korah, and all your followers are to do this: Take censers and tomorrow put fire and incense in them before the LORD. The man the LORD chooses will be the one who is holy. You Levites have gone too far!"*

The attack seems to focus primarily on Aaron, but Moses is the one who is hit most deeply, since he is the mediator between the Lord and his people. Any attack on his words implies a denial of the reality of his having been sent by the Lord. And thus he is the one who falls facedown, who bows in an attitude of prayer before his God (cf. 14:5; 17:10). Only after this does he know what he must do. We are not told how long Moses prayed. It has been suggested that Moses spoke immediately after he fell facedown; but comparison with 14:5 and Deuteronomy 9:25 should make us cautious. In any case, Moses knows what he must say to "Korah and all his followers" when he gets up. The word rendered "followers" *('eda)* can also mean "band," but only when a further designation as to its character is added (Pss. 22:16; 86:14; Job 15:34); here the word has a neutral meaning.

Moses knows that he has been sent to this people by the Lord (Exod. 3); he knows that the Lord speaks to him "face to face" (12:7–8); and he knows that Aaron's priesthood is based on the Lord's command (Exod. 28:1). Therefore, since seemingly Aaron's priesthood, but in reality his own leadership is at stake, the decision must rest with the Lord, as it did in the case of Miriam and Aaron (12:2–4) and of the spies (14:5). On this basis Moses announces the ordeal, which will take place "in the morning." Then the Lord will show who belongs to Him and is holy, and may therefore come "near him." The Lord will show this by means of making a "choice" (v. 5). Israel's priesthood is thus based solely on the Lord's election, on His divine and free choice, and not on descent or ordination, not even on the qualifications of the individual. The decision concerning Aaron's sole right to the priesthood, which Korah and his followers denied, is therefore placed in the Lord's hand. This is why "in the morning" Korah and his group must do what was heretofore the exclusive prerogative of Aaron and his family: they must burn incense before the Lord (Exod.

30:7), which is the privilege of those who have been chosen by the Lord and who are thus holy (Lev. 10:3). For whoever can burn incense before the Lord without being destroyed by the fire of the Lord's holiness has thereby proven that this privilege is not due to one's own choice but to the Lord's, who allows only those whom He chooses to approach Him. It is not the burning of the incense in itself that offers protection (dynamistic), but only the burning of incense by someone who is "authorized" (ethical). Therefore, if unauthorized individuals approach the Lord in this manner, their burning of incense will not protect them against the Lord's anger, as the death of Nadab and Abihu had proven earlier (Lev. 10). Only this exclusively priestly act of burning incense can therefore be the appropriate means for invoking the ordeal. The issue will appear to be Aaron's priestly function, but it is in fact Moses' position in Israel's midst. Korah's men must use the censers that they had apparently readied beforehand (cf. v. 17). The use of censers for the burning of incense here has led some to conclude that this author did not know of the golden altar of incense of Exodus 30:1–10; 37:25–29, but this is based on a misunderstanding. The altar was used for the daily burning of incense in order to close off, as it were, the Most Holy Place from the Holy Place by means of a cloud of incense, so that the proximity of the Lord who dwelled above the ark would not be dangerous to the priests. But the censer was used when the priest (in Israel this was only the high priest!) approached the ark itself (Lev. 16:12–13).

Moses then uses the very 'words of Korah and his followers: "You Levites have gone too far" (v. 7, cf. v. 3; the same expression is found in Deut. 1:6; 2:3; 3:26; 1 Kings 12:28) to indicate that he sees through Korah's pious slogan, but also that he wants their fifth-column activities stopped. And by adding "you Levites" he also lets him know that he sees Korah and his followers as the real instigators and that their slogan of a universal priesthood, which had convinced not only the Reubenites but also a large number of the most prominent men in Israel to follow him, was nothing more than an attempt to establish their own right to the priesthood. By specifically addressing the Levites, who constituted only a small part of the rebels, Moses tries to make the others aware of Korah's selfish intentions and to drive a wedge into the coalition.

C. *Moses' special warning to the Levites* (16:8–11)

16:8–11 *Moses also said to Korah, "Now listen, you Levites! Isn't it enough for you that the God of Israel has separated you from the rest of the Israelite community and brought you near himself to do the work at the Lᴏʀᴅ's tabernacle and to* *stand before the community and minister to them? He has brought you and all your fellow Levites near himself, but now you are trying to get the priesthood too. It is against the LORD that you and all your followers have banded together. Who is Aaron that you should grumble against him?''*

"Moses also said to Korah": those who see this narrative as a composite of two, or even three, entirely divergent traditions are convinced that these verses follow chronologically immediately after verses 3b–7. But this cannot be correct, since verses 1–3a state that the Reubenites were also present during the confrontation of verses 3b–7. But, according to verse 14, they were not present during Moses' speech of verses 8–11, nor during the burning of the incense (vv. 16, 25). Moses' purpose behind this separate meeting with the Levites is obvious: by emphasizing the special character of their assigned task he tries to sever their association with Korah and his non-Levite followers. He reminds them that they occupy a unique position in the Israelite community due to God's favor ("separated," see 8:14). They alone are the caretakers of the Lord's house, and they alone are allowed to take the place of all the other tribes with regard to the offerings (cf. 3:8). And would this choice on the Lord's part be so unimportant that without the priestly function it would be totally worthless? They have banded together, not against Moses and Aaron, but against the Lord Himself (cf. Exod. 16:7). Korah and his followers do essentially the same thing Israel did at Kadesh (14:35). Verse 11a is addressed to "you [Korah] and all your followers," rather than to "you Levites" (v. 8). This does not necessarily mean that all his followers are also present, but it is again an attempt on Moses' part to open the eyes of the Levites to the real motive behind Korah's efforts.

The conclusion of this speech to the Levites is characteristic of Moses, who basically did not have much respect for his brother Aaron. This is hardly surprising after Aaron's role in the sin with the golden calf (Exod. 32:22–24) and his going along with Miriam (Num. 12). Moses sees Aaron as an easily swayed, even weak man, who certainly did not deserve this from the Levites! Approximately the same words are found in Exodus 16:7–8, but there they concern the distance that separates the Lord from both Moses and Aaron.

D. *Dathan and Abiram refuse Moses' summons* (16:12–15)

16:12–15 *Then Moses summoned Dathan and Abiram, the sons of Eliab. But they said, "We will not come! Isn't it enough that you have brought us up out of a land flowing with milk and honey to kill us in the desert? And now you also want to lord it over us? Moreover, you haven't brought us into a land flowing with milk and* *honey or given us an inheritance of fields and vineyards. Will you gouge out the eyes of these men? No, we will not come!"*

Then Moses became very angry and said to the LORD, "Do not accept their offering. I have not taken so much as a donkey from them, nor have I wronged any of them."

The discussion with Korah and the Levites must, of course, be followed by a meeting with the leaders of the Reubenites, Dathan and Abiram. Once Moses has decided to lance the boil, he cannot limit himself to dealing with the goal of the Levites but must also address the motive of the Reubenites. He wants to keep them from any further action as well, and therefore summons them. Moses sees himself as Israel's leader and Dathan and Abiram must come to him. Only after they have refused to come does Moses go to them, but then in the company of the elders of Israel. Both Reubenites refuse to heed Moses' summons. They do not acknowledge Moses' right to command them—Moses' leadership has neither justification nor meaning, as far as they are concerned. They have two reasons for their attitude: Moses took them away from a "paradise" ("a land flowing with milk and honey," see commentary on 13:27), Egypt, and has not given them another (Canaan) to take in its place. Israel is poorer than ever before: they do not have fields nor vineyards, and all that is left for them is a miserable death in the desert. And such a man would "want to lord it" over them? They use a term that is found only here: "to make oneself a *sar.*" *Sar* is derived from the military organization of that time and has thus a military connotation. They gild Israel's past and make Egypt a paradise, as Israel also did at Kibroth Hattaavah (11:5) and at Kadesh (14:4), and as they had done before (Exod. 14:11–12; 16:3; 17:3). The Lord's deliverance from Egypt, from the land of slavery (Exod. 20:2) is thus turned into a deception. Dathan and Abiram also use the weapon of mockery. They intimate (v. 14) that the purpose of Moses' discussions with the rebels is only to "gouge out the eyes of these men," to blind them to the true state of affairs so that they will be prepared to continue to bear the yoke of Moses' leadership. But Dathan and Abiram will not be deceived; they will not come!

Even this "very humble man" (12:3) loses his patience at this answer, which surpasses in impudence anything Moses has experienced at the hands of Israel. He becomes *"very* angry," the only time this is said of him (cf. Exod. 32:19). And then there flows from his lips, in the form of a prayer to the Lord, a serious curse on Dathan and Abiram: may the Lord turn away from, and therefore not be pleased with, their offering, whatever form it may take (hence the use of *mincha,* which means here not "grain offering'' but "offering'' in general). If Moses' prayer is granted, then Dathan and Abiram will from that point on not be able to share in the blessing attached to the offerings the Lord had commanded; they will not be cleansed from sin and guilt, and they will therefore be cut off from the Lord's people. How did these men dare to blame Moses for the continued wanderings in the wilderness, which were solely the result of Israel's grumbling at Kadesh? "Lord it'' over them? But Moses has not enriched himself in any way; he has "not taken so much as a donkey from them'' and he has not wronged any of them. Samuel is the only other person who dared say this about himself (1 Sam. 12:3).

E. *The ordeal* (16:16–35)

Moses' efforts to break the opposition of the Levites and Reubenites have therefore failed. The ordeal must take place, but it will not be the same ordeal for all. Korah and his followers maintained their demand for a general priesthood and thus kept up the appearance that their opposition was directed against the prerogative of Aaron and his family, rather than against Moses. But Dathan and Abiram's rebellion has taken on an entirely different character than that of Korah and his followers by their blunt refusal to acknowledge Moses' leadership. The first ordeal takes place at the entrances to the tents of Dathan and Abiram; Moses, as the beleaguered leader, is prominent here (vv. 25–34); the second ordeal takes place at the Tent of Meeting, and the role of Moses and Aaron is limited to their plea for God's mercy on behalf of the whole *'eda* (vv. 16–24, 35).

But in this part of the narrative we run into some significant problems when we try to get a clear picture of exactly what took place. The first problem is the author's desire not to lose sight of the unity of the rebellious movement, in spite of the twofold ordeal. This is why he describes the ordeal of Dathan and Abiram as part of the ordeal to which Korah and his followers were subjected (vv. 25–34), and why he moves verse 35 to its present position, even though its content indicates that it should follow verse 24. But he does this in such a way that the grammatical form (nominal sentence) clearly indicates that chronologically verse 35 does not follow verses 25–34. The second problem lies in the repeated use of *'eda,* even though its meaning does not appear to be the same throughout. Its meaning is clear when we hear of "Korah and his whole *'eda''* (NIV: "Korah and all his followers''; vv. 5–6, cf. also vv. 16, 19); verses 2 and 17 indicate that Korah's *'eda* consists of the "250 Israelite men, well-known community leaders'' who had joined him and Dathan and Abiram in their rebellion against Moses. The daughters of Zelophehad refer to them as (lit.) "the *'eda* who met together against the Lord in the *'eda* of Korah" (27:3). This *'eda* undoubtedly means "circle of followers." But then there is also the *'eda* to which the glory of the Lord appears (v. 19b) and from which Moses and Aaron must separate themselves (v. 21), for whose salvation they both pray (v. 22), and which is later commanded to "move away from the tents" (v. 24). This cannot very well be Korah's *'eda,* although the latter is mentioned in verse 19a. This *'eda* must be the "assembly" of Israel, as the NIV translates. The third problem is that verses 24b, 27a speak of "the tents of Korah, Dathan and Abiram" (the Hebrew is singular, "tent"), while in the context of the destruction of Dathan and Abiram we hear of "all Korah's men" (v. 32). But it is clear that these must be later additions, the result of a desire to present the unity of the rebellion at any cost. This is supported by two things: (1) the Old Testament speaks of "tents" *(miškenot)* of people (e.g., Num. 24:5; Jer. 9:19; 30:18; 51:30), but whenever it speaks of "tent" it refers to the sanctuary, the Tent of the Lord (e.g., Exod. 25:9; Lev. 8:10; Num. 1:50). Thus, apart from all other considerations (such as the fact that according to v. 19 Korah and his followers have gathered in front of the Tent of Meeting, while v. 27b indicates that Dathan and Abiram stand "at the entrances to their tents" *without* Korah), a linguistic usage indicates that verses 24b and 27a cannot possibly speak of (lit.) "the tent *[miškan]* of Korah, Dathan and Abiram." (2) Verses 19–24, 27a and 35 already spoke of "Korah and all his followers"; this simple fact proves that "and all Korah's men" in verse 32 cannot have been part of the original text. Furthermore, verses 25–34 (without v. 27a, see below) speak only of Dathan and Abiram and their families. And finally, Korah's family was spared (26:11).

F. *The judgment on Korah and his followers* (16:16–24)

16:16–24 *Moses said to Korah, "You and all your followers are to appear before the LORD tomorrow—you and they and Aaron. Each man is to take his censer and put incense in it—250 censers in all—and present it before the LORD. You and Aaron are to present your censers also." So each man took his censer, put fire and incense in it, and stood with Moses and Aaron at the entrance to the Tent of Meeting. When Korah had gathered all his followers in opposition to them at the entrance to the Tent of Meeting, the glory of the LORD appeared to the entire assembly. The LORD said to Moses and Aaron, "Separate yourselves from this assembly so I can put an end to them at once."*

But Moses and Aaron fell facedown and cried out, "O God, God of the spirits of all mankind, will you be angry with the entire assembly when only one man sins?"

Then the LORD said to Moses, "Say to the assembly, 'Move away from the tents of Korah, Dathan and Abiram.'"[3]

These verses begin by adding further details to what was said in verse 6. Not only do they speak of Korah and all his followers, they also give the size of the group: no fewer than 250 censers will be needed. Furthermore, it is also stated here that Aaron must subject himself to the ordeal, which is not mentioned in verse 7, although his cooperation is implied in the words "the man the LORD chooses." A total of 252 censers was thus needed (not 253, as might be concluded from v. 18b; officially, Korah was concerned only with Aaron's priesthood, not with Moses' leadership). I believe that the words "Moses and" in verse 18 were added by a later redactor who drew an incorrect conclusion from the fact of Moses' presence in verse 20, forgetting that Moses never fulfilled a priestly function and was not authorized to burn incense.

Verse 18 moves on to the "tomorrow" of verse 16 (although this is not stated explicitly). The scene takes place before the Tent, at the entrance to the tabernacle (see vv. 24, 27). Aaron faces Korah and his clan; all have censers with burning incense. And then the Lord acts through a manifestation of His "glory." We are not told that this involved the cloud, as in 11:25 and 12:5; it is not likely that this was the case, since there the Lord is said to "come down," while here the Lord "appears." Rather, we have here the same manifestation as in 14:10: the presence of the Lord in "what looked like a consuming fire" (see commentary on 14:10). And here also the Lord expresses His intention to destroy, this time not the entire community, but the *'eda*, the assembly, which would deprive the people in one stroke of their representatives and leaders. Moses and Aaron are therefore enjoined to move away from the assembly, lest they are also struck by the consuming fire of the Lord. But again (see 14:13ff.), they both pray on behalf of Israel's leadership (v. 22). They first acknowledge the Lord's undisputed right to take back the life that He Himself gave: He is the "God of the spirits of all mankind." The same expression is also found in 27:16. And then follows the question that will determine the fate of all: if one man sins, should the entire assembly be destroyed? This has been interpreted incorrectly as an appeal to the Lord's justice. Rather, Moses appeals to His mercy, as he did in 14:17–20. These words have also been seen as proof

---

[3]For reasons explained in the commentary, Noordtzij emends the text in several places. In verse 18 "Moses and" is omitted. Verse 27a is placed between verses 24 and 25, and "of Korah, Dathan and Abiram" is omitted in both verse 24 and verse 27a; the text thus reads, [24]"Say to the assembly, 'Move away from the Tent.'" [27a]So they moved away from the Tent. [25]Moses got up. . . ." In verse 32 "and all Korah's men" is omitted. (tr.).

that the concept of individual retribution (everyone suffers the consequences of his or her own sins), which is central in our thinking, comes to the fore here. This is also incorrect, as proven by the fact that in the case of Dathan and Abiram their families, who were from our standpoint innocent, also die. We must not forget that the social concept of retribution as found in the ancient Near Eastern world was intertwined with the entire social structure of that time, and was no less in harmony with their sense of justice than the concept of individual retribution is with ours. The solidarity of guilt was paramount in Israel's thinking (Exod. 24:7b; Num. 14:18b; 2 Sam. 3:28; 21:6; see also Gen. 20:9; 26:10).

Again, their prayer is answered. But the assembly must show in deed that they do not want to associate with Korah and his followers. They must move away from the immediate vicinity of the Tent, i.e., of the tabernacle (see above). This they do, although it is not stated in so many words, at least not in our present MT. But it appears to me that verse 27a originally must have followed after verse 24, for two compelling reasons: (1) The judgment on Dathan and Abiram takes place near their tents (v. 27b), which must have stood behind the tents of the Kohathites south of the tabernacle (cf. 2:10; 3:29). Thus the command to move away from the tabernacle cannot have been given to those who were close to Dathan and Abiram. (2) In verse 26a they are told to "move back" *(suru na')*. If verse 27a reported that they obeyed this command, the Hebrew would read *wayyasuru*. But instead we read "and they moved away" *(wayye'alu)*, which can only refer back to a previous "move away" *(he'alu)*—which is found in verse 24b. Therefore, verse 27a must originally have followed after verse 24b, and must have been placed between verse 26 and verse 27b by the redactor who took the liberty to make a number of other changes (see above; cf. also H. Strack's commentary on Numbers). Here the description of the judgment on Korah and his followers suddenly breaks off; in verse 35 we hear only that Korah and his 250 followers were consumed because "fire came out from the LORD," i.e., from the tabernacle (see Lev. 10:2) while they were offering incense. "Offering" is not entirely correct; the purpose of burning incense was to provide protection against the deadly radiating out of the divine holiness by means of the incense smoke (Lev. 16:13, "so that he will not die").

G. *The judgment on Dathan and Abiram* (16:25–34)

16:25–34 *Moses got up and went to Dathan and Abiram, and the elders of Israel followed him. He warned the assembly, "Move back from the tents of these wicked men! Do not touch anything belonging to them, or you will be swept away because* *of all their sins." So they moved away from the tents of Korah, Dathan and Abiram. Dathan and Abiram had come out and were standing with their wives, children and little ones at the entrances to their tents.*

*Then Moses said, "This is how you will know that the L*ORD* has sent me to do all these things and that it was not my idea: If these men die a natural death and experience only what usually happens to men, then the L*ORD* has not sent me. But if the L*ORD* brings about something totally new, and the earth opens its mouth and swallows them, with everything that belongs to them, and they go down alive into the grave, then you will know that these men have treated the L*ORD* with contempt."*

As soon as he finished saying all this, the ground under them split apart and the earth opened its mouth and swallowed them, with their households and all Korah's men and all their possessions. They went down alive into the grave, with everything they owned; the earth closed over them, and they perished and were gone from the community. At their cries, all the Israelites around them fled, shouting, "The earth is going to swallow us too!"

Verses 12–15 report Moses' attempt to talk with Dathan and Abiram to turn them from their evil course. Not only was this attempt a complete failure, it also gave Dathan and Abiram the opportunity to formulate their complaints against Moses' leadership more precisely and to accuse him of wanting to "lord it" over them. Verses 25–34 (without v. 27a!) now describe the judgment that comes to them and their families.

Since Dathan and Abiram made an issue of Moses' leadership, and not of Aaron's priesthood, only Moses (accompanied by Israel's elders, cf. 11:30) goes to the camp of the Reubenites, south of the tabernacle, where once again he finds the *'eda*. This, of course, cannot be the same *'eda* as the one mentioned in connection with Korah (see above); rather, these are the people whom Moses also addresses in verses 28–30, and who are called "all the Israelites" in verse 34. Thus the "assembly" here refers to the followers of Dathan and Abiram. Moses addresses only them. First he advises them to no longer make common cause with "these wicked men," i.e., with Dathan and Abiram, and to move away from their tents. They must not even touch anything that belongs to them, since their sin clings to these things like "infectious matter" (see commentary on 8:5–7) and would "infect" anyone who touches these things, who would thus also become "sinful" and fall under the impending judgment. This reflects once again the concept of sin as something material that attaches itself to whomever comes in contact with it (see my *Gods Woord*, p. 89, and commentary on the Psalms, Vol. 1, page 156.). It is therefore better to translate "by all their sins" rather than "because of all their sins" in verse 26b.

Dathan and Abiram are determined to push their rebellion against Moses all the way. As soon as Moses approaches their tents they come out "with their wives, children and little ones" (v. 27) to show to all that they do not fear Moses, or perhaps in the hope that Moses had come for the meeting they had refused (v. 12). But Moses only announces to the bystanders the impending judgment of God, which will show whether he has made himself the leader (v. 13), as Dathan and Abiram claimed, or whether his leadership is based on God's will and choice (see Exod. 3:10ff.; 4:13, 28; et al.). But, Moses says, "It was not my idea" (lit. "that [it was] not from my own heart"; cf. Exod. 3:11). Like all of God's messengers he knows the "holy imperative," along with all the painful experiences this entails for the natural man. Even Balaam experienced something similar (24:13). Moses' work, including this event, must testify to his calling. So, Moses says, if these men die a natural death it will show that he has made himself Israel's leader. But if the Lord "brings about something totally new," i.e., if He causes something to happen that no one has ever seen before: if all these people lose their lives in one moment, all at the same time and in the same way, then. . . . On the basis of verse 29b we would expect Moses to say, "then the LORD has indeed sent me." But he does not say this; rather he says, "then you will know that these men have treated the LORD with contempt," i.e., they have treated Him as one whose will and choice can safely be ignored (cf. 14:11, 23). To Moses it is not his own calling, but the Lord's honor that is at issue. The stakes are high, but Moses is a man who not only knows that his God has called him, but also that he can rely on Him under all circumstances. Moses has barely finished speaking when "the earth opens its mouth" and they, together with their possessions, go "down alive into the grave" *(sheol)*. According to the MT of verse 32 "all Korah's men" are included in this, but this must be a later addition because (1) the judgment on Korah and his followers was of a different nature than that on Dathan and Abiram; and (2) because 26:11 clearly states that Korah's sons do not perish with their father. The later "Sons of Korah," mentioned in a number of superscriptions in the Psalms (42; 44–49; 84; 85; 87; 88) trace their descent to these sons of Korah.

Various explanations for this event have been suggested: Moses knew that there was a subterrane below their tents and announced a cave-in; or, both families were buried alive, after which the 250 men were slain and consumed by flames from the altar; or, a judicial verdict was rendered in front of the altar; or, what really took place was a lynching. All these explanations date, of course, from the heyday of rationalism, when one had to be satisfied with an "explanation" that did not explain anything in order to avoid having to take into account the possibility of a direct act of God. These verses do not say exactly what happened; they speak only of the destruction of both families and of the profound impression this makes on the bystanders.

16:35 *And fire came out from the* LORD *and consumed the 250 men who were offering the incense.*

As has been explained above, verse 35 speaks of the judgment on Korah and his followers; its form indicates that it does not follow chronologically after verses 25-34. It is thus a continuation of verses 19-24 and verse 27a. Korah and his 250 followers stand before the tabernacle with Aaron, burning incense. Like Nadab and Abihu (Lev. 10:2), Korah and his followers are instantaneously killed by fire that "came out from the LORD," while Aaron is spared. Thus his priesthood, as well as Moses' leadership, is vindicated beyond any doubt by the ordeal.

H. *The censers of the rebels* (16:36-40)

16:36-40 *The* LORD *said to Moses, "Tell Eleazar son of Aaron, the priest, to take the censers out of the smoldering remains and scatter the coals some distance away, for the censers are holy—the censers of the men who sinned at the cost of their lives. Hammer the censers into sheets to overlay the altar, for they were presented before the* LORD *and have become holy. Let them be a sign to the Israelites."*
So Eleazar the priest collected the bronze censers brought by those who had been burned up, and he had them hammered out to overlay the altar, as the LORD *directed him through Moses. This was to remind the Israelites that no one except a descendant of Aaron should come to burn incense before the* LORD, *or he would become like Korah and his followers.*

An element is presented here that is not mentioned in verse 35: the men who burned incense are killed, but their censers remain intact. According to Exodus 29:37; 30:29; Leviticus 6:18, 27 anything that has come in touch with the sanctuary in any way has thereby been withdrawn from the sphere of the profane and has become "holy." These censers may therefore no longer be used in everyday life, but neither may they be used in the sanctuary, since they have been used by unauthorized individuals. Eleazar must collect the censers and remove any fire that remains in them, because it was "unauthorized fire" (KJV: "strange fire"; cf. Lev. 10:1-2; Num. 3:4). It is striking that Eleazar, rather than Aaron, must do this. The reason for this has been sought in the fact that as high priest Aaron was not allowed to go among the corpses, since he would be defiled and therefore temporarily rendered unfit to carry out his duties (thus e.g., Heinisch, *Numeri*, p. 68; Strack and Dillmann). But verse 48 proves that this cannot have been the reason. Rather, a high priest must take care of the "clean holy things," and avoid any contact with "unclean holy things" (cf. Edelkoort, *Numeri,* p. 150). The censers belong in the latter category: they were "unclean" because they had been used by unauthorized persons and had held "unauthorized fire," but they were "holy" because they had been in touch with the sanctuary.

The question is now what to do with these censers. Moses orders them to be hammered into thin sheets "to overlay the altar," referring, of course, to the portable altar of burnt offering (see e.g., Exod. 27:1; 30:18; Num. 4:13). Exodus 27:2 and 38:2 state that the altar was to be overlaid with bronze sheets. The LXX has attempted to harmonize these two references with Numbers 16:38 by adding in Exodus 38:2 (LXX: 38:22), contrary to chronological possibility, that the censers of Korah and his followers were used for this. More recent exegetes are of the opinion that the author of Numbers 16 was wrong, since the altar was already covered with such sheets. I agree with Heinisch that the explanation must be sought in the fact that the bronze overlay of the altar had to be replaced periodically, as was probably also true of the coverings of the tabernacle.

The description of Korah and his followers is somewhat curious: "the men who sinned at the cost of their lives" (v. 38, lit. "these sinners against their own lives"); this can only mean that by their continued sinning they committed a sin against, and thus forfeited, their lives (cf. also Prov. 20:2; Hab. 2:10).

The purpose of this hammering out of the censers and of using them to overlay the altar is stated in verse 40: it "was to remind the Israelites," to be a warning. No one must henceforth doubt that an unauthorized individual may not assume the priestly prerogative of burning incense in the sanctuary; in this case (for another, see 1:51) "unauthorized" is anyone who does not belong to the descendants of Aaron (cf. 3:10), as Amaziah (Uzziah) of Judah personally experienced (2 Chron. 26:21).

I. *Renewed rebellion* (16:41–50)

16:41–50 *The next day the whole Israelite community grumbled against Moses and Aaron. "You have killed the LORD's people," they said.*

But when the assembly gathered in opposition to Moses and Aaron and turned toward the Tent of Meeting, suddenly the cloud covered it and the glory of the LORD appeared. Then Moses and Aaron went to the front of the Tent of Meeting, and the LORD said to Moses, "Get away from this assembly so I can put an end to them at once." And they fell facedown.

Then Moses said to Aaron, "Take your censer and put incense in it, along with fire from the altar, and hurry to the assembly to make atonement for them. Wrath has come out from the LORD; the plague has started." So Aaron did as Moses said, and ran into the midst of the assembly. The plague had already started among the people, but Aaron offered the incense and made atonement for them. He stood between the living and the dead, and the plague stopped.

But 14,700 people died from the plague, in addition to those who had died because of Korah. Then Aaron returned to Moses at the entrance to the Tent of Meeting, for the plague had stopped.

These verses refer back to the judgments of verses 19–35 and show how deeply the rebellion against Moses' leadership and Aaron's priesthood has penetrated all segments of the community, and how the people seize every opportunity to give vent to their rebellious feelings. In spite of the profound impression the recent events have made on the people (v. 34), they turn around and use them to level a fierce charge against Moses and Aaron: "You [emphatic] have killed the LORD's people," as if the Lord's choice and the resulting judgment had been the result of their personal influence on the deity (see also 12:11)! This accusation expresses the ancient Near Eastern way of thinking as well as any of Israel's neighbors could have. They call these men, who did not acknowledge any authority established by God (cf. Rom. 13:1) and who hid purely egocentric intentions behind pious slogans, "the LORD's people," the same words Moses had earlier used to refer to the entire community of Israel (11:29). And this is said by the people who had to thank Moses and Aaron for their lives (16:22)! Once again they all gather in opposition to both men (cf. v. 3). This renewed rebellion results in another manifestation of the Lord's glory, this time in its most visible form, "the cloud," which is the sign for Moses and Aaron to go to the tabernacle. They go to the front of the Tent but do not enter it, since "the cloud" covers it, which means that the glory of the Lord fills it entirely (cf. Exod. 40:35).

At the Tent of Meeting Moses hears that this renewed rebellion must lead to the annihilation of "this *'eda,*" also called the *kahal* (v. 47a), which, according to verse 47b, is the same as *'am,* "people." Since on the one hand we are not certain of the exact meaning of the words *'eda* and *kahal* (see my commentary on Lev. 4:13–21), and on the other hand *'am* does not always refer to the people as a whole (e.g., Judg. 5:18; Jer. 37:12), it is not quite clear whether the threat of Kadesh (14:11) is repeated here, or that of verse 21, where *'eda* referred to Israel's "assembly," i.e., its body of legal representatives. In my opinion the latter is more probable, since in both cases Moses and Aaron are told to get away from the *'eda.*

And again Moses and Aaron, always inclined to forgive, fall facedown before the Lord and pray that these people may be spared. Then Moses suddenly gives a command to Aaron. It is not stated that he received this command directly from the Lord, nor is it likely, since according to verse 46b Moses knows that the Lord's wrath has already begun and that "the plague" has started. Again, the nature of this "plague" (lit. "blow," see commentary on 14:37) is not stated. But Moses is certain that only one thing can help: the burning of incense. Hence the instruction to Aaron to "make atonement" (*kipper,* "covering") for the assembly *('eda).* Most exegetes are of the opinion that atoning power is ascribed to the incense offering here and is actually taken for granted, which then leads to the conclusion that this is a "recent" section, dating from a time when the burning of incense had come to be regarded as a true offering (see e.g., Edelkoort, *Numeri,* p. 151). However, this view rests on a misunderstanding: in Israel, atonement could be effected only by means of blood, except in the case of the offering of flour of the very poor. We are faced here with an ancient concept: the smoke of the incense must hide the assembly from the "wrath" *(qesef)* that "has come out from the LORD" and has thrown itself upon the assembly (cf. e.g., 1:53; 18:5) to do its destructive work. And since this wrath is an expression of the Lord's holiness, we have here a parallel to the burning of incense by the high priest when he enters the Most Holy Place on the Day of Atonement (Lev. 16:12–13), rather than an offering. The verb *kipper,* which we usually translate "to atone," stands here therefore in its original meaning, "to put a cover upon." Aaron obeys Moses' command immediately and runs "into the midst of the assembly," where he places incense on the fire from the altar that has been put in the censer, so that the smoke from the incense will form a dense cloud. And so, standing "between the living and the dead" (v. 48), he lays a cover over the people. And he stays there until the plague stops, or rather, is stayed because of the covering cloud of incense smoke. This is another testimony to the authority of Aaron's priesthood (cf. v. 18).

There is no indication as to how long the "plague" lasted. But its duration cannot be measured by the time it took Aaron to run (as e.g., Baentsch suggests), but rather by the length of Moses' prayer (see commentary on 16:22). This explains the large number (14,700) in verse 49, to which is added that this figure does not include those who had died with Korah. This is a reminder of the ever-increasing severity of the punishment for continuing failure to hear and obey the Lord (Lev. 26:14ff.).

J. *The Budding of Aaron's Staff* (17:1–13)

17:1–11 *The LORD said to Moses, "Speak to the Israelites and get twelve staffs from them, one from the leader of each of their ancestral tribes. Write the name of each man on his staff. On the staff of Levi write Aaron's name, for there must be* *one staff for the head of each ancestral tribe. Place them in the Tent of Meeting in front of the Testimony, where I meet with you. The staff belonging to the man I choose will sprout, and I will rid myself of this constant grumbling against you by the Israelites.''*

So Moses spoke to the Israelites, and their leaders gave him twelve staffs, one for the leader of each of their ancestral tribes, and Aaron's staff was among them. Moses placed the staffs before the LORD in the Tent of the Testimony.

The next day Moses entered the Tent of the Testimony and saw that Aaron's staff, which represented the house of Levi, had not only sprouted but had budded, blossomed and produced almonds. Then Moses brought out all the staffs from the LORD's presence to all the Israelites. They looked at them, and each man took his own staff.

The LORD said to Moses, ''Put back Aaron's staff in front of the Testimony, to be kept as a sign to the rebellious. This will put an end to their grumbling against me, so that they will not die.'' Moses did just as the LORD commanded him.

Twice Aaron's priesthood has clearly been shown to be based solely on the Lord's will and choice. Now the Lord wants to make it clear one more time that only Aaron has been chosen and that only *his* descendants may hold the priestly office in Israel, in order to silence any further opposition on the part of Israel's leaders. This time the Lord uses a means that will be a permanent ''sign to the rebellious'' (v. 10) and cannot slip away into the past as did the judgments of chapter 16. The purpose of this sign is not the impression it makes when it is given, but rather its future witness.

The Lord tells Moses to get a staff from each of the tribal leaders and to write the name of the tribe each one represents on his staff. Since the same word *(matte)* can be used for both ''tribe'' and ''staff'' (as is also true of the other word that could have been used, *šebet*), the author avoids any possible misunderstanding by using a word for ''tribe'' that is otherwise always used to indicate a tribal subunit or ''clan.'' There must, of course, also be a staff for the tribe of Levi; Moses must write Aaron's name on it. Each tribe is thus represented by a staff, the symbol of the ruler (cf. Gen. 38:18; 49:10; Num. 21:18). This means that there were thirteen staffs in all, since, unlike the other twelve tribes (see 1:4–16), Levi does not belong to the ''children of Israel'' (1:47–54). The Vulgate has clarified this by rendering verse 6b, ''there were twelve staffs besides the staff of Aaron.'' This is not an exact translation of the Hebrew text, but it accurately expresses its intention: if Levi were included in the twelve, the statement ''and Aaron's staff was among them'' would be superfluous. Verse 3 correctly refers to the ''staff of Levi'' rather than to the ''staff of Aaron.'' This does not imply, however, as has been suggested, that these verses originally spoke of the priestly prerogative of the tribe of Levi, which is then supposed to have been changed later to Aaron's prerogative. Apart from the view of the Scriptures behind this view, it goes counter to the entire historical development of the relationship between the Aaronic priesthood and the Levites: the Levites become increasingly prominent and their position is more and more on a level with, rather than under, the priests (see 2 Chron. 30:17–18; 35:3–6). Furthermore, in verses 6 and 10 Aaron functions not as the representative of the priestly segment of the tribe of Levi, but as the representative of the entire tribe, as the tribal leader (cf. vv. 2, 8).

These thirteen staffs are placed in the Tent of the Testimony; this name is also used in 9:15; 18:2; 2 Chronicles 24:6, since the "two tablets of the Testimony" (see Exod. 31:18; 32:15; 34:29; cf. 25:16) had been placed in the ark, which is therefore also called "the ark of the Testimony" (Exod. 25:22; 26:33f.; 30:6, 26; 39:35; et al.). "Before the LORD" does not necessarily mean that the staffs were placed in the Most Holy Place, as Exodus 30:36 and 40:5 show. The expression can also mean "in the Holy Place," but close to the curtain that closed off the Most Holy Place. Verse 4 proves that the latter is intended here: "where I meet with you." This cannot refer to the Most Holy Place, since only the high priest could enter it, and then only on the Day of Atonement. But the staffs are placed close to the ark so that they can undergo the full life-giving power of the "living God" (Deut. 5:23; 2 Kings 19:4) who dwells above it.

When Moses enters the Holy Place the next morning, he sees that something miraculous has happened to the staff of the tribe of Levi, which bears Aaron's name. It has gone through all the stages of development of the almond tree: buds, blossoms, and even fruit. The budding staff apparently speaks very clearly to Israel; when Moses brings out the twelve staffs and Aaron's staff each man (except, of course, Aaron) takes his staff back. This can only mean that they all acknowledge that Aaron is the man of God's choice, that the priesthood belongs to him alone.

The rationalists have sought for an explanation of this event that would eliminate the need for the Lord's power to perform a miracle. Aaron's staff then is an almond branch that had already budded; these buds then opened in one night. But this is an explanation that does not explain much: it does not take into consideration the fruit, nor does it give a reason why it happened only and precisely to Aaron's staff.

The acknowledgment of Aaron's priesthood by the other tribal leaders because of what happened to Aaron's staff has been interpreted by some as proof that Israel believed in rhabdomancy (e.g., Baentsch, *Numeri,* pp. 551f.). But rhabdomancy is something entirely different: divination by means of the greening or wilting of trees or shoots, which was widely

practiced in the ancient Near East and was familiar to many in Ephraim in
Hosea's time (Hos. 4:12). There is no divination involved here. A better
parallel would be Hercules' club, which budded when placed next to the
pillar of the god Hermes; or the lance Romulus hurled at the Palatine in
Rome, which became a sacred tree; or Polycarp's stick, which turned into a
terebinth (also a sacred tree!) in Smyrna; or the legend that the terebinth of
Abraham in Hebron sprang from the staff of the angel who appeared to the
patriarch there. But all those stories prove is that it was widely believed
that special divine powers were able to bring new life to dead wood. Here
we find something different: not only is it predicted that one of the thirteen
staffs will sprout, but it is also made clear that this will be the result of the
Lord's elective choice (v. 5). And the vitality that is revealed during that
night ends immediately afterward: although the staff retains its buds, blossoms, and fruit, it remains a staff. It is to be a "sign" to the rebellious,
i.e., an object that can be seen with the natural eye, an object to which a
miracle has happened and that can thus for the person who thinks logically
be the means to no longer doubt the truth of the Lord's word (see e.g.,
Judg. 6:36–40). Aaron's budding staff must therefore not be placed *in* the
ark (Heb. 9:4), but in its old place "in front of the Testimony," so that it
can be seen and thus "put an end to" all the grumbling about the priesthood of Aaron and his descendants. If the grumbling continues, the rebellious will die.

17:12–13 *The Israelites said to Moses, "We will die! We are lost, we are all lost!
Anyone who even comes near the tabernacle of the LORD will die. Are we all going
to die?"*

The last two verses of this chapter report the impression these final
words, combined with the repeated revelation of the Lord's power, make.
These verses reflect the fear that fills the Israelites: the continued presence
of the Lord's Tent, from where such terrible judgments come over the
people, will be their death. This is expressed by means of three verbs,
gawa‘, 'abad, and *mut.* The last of these *(mut)* is the general word for
"dying"; it is used in verse 10b, and in verse 13 ("will die"). *Gawa‘*
means "to breathe out," "to expire," and is used in verse 12 ("We will
die!") and in verse 13 ("Are we all going to die?"). *'Abad,* "perish" (cf.
KJV) is used in verse 12, where the NIV renders it "we are lost."

I do not agree with those who claim that these verses are out of place
here and would fit better after verse 35 (e.g., Heinisch, p. 70). This
language of desperation is caused by the tremendous clash between Israel
and the Lord and His two servants, Moses and Aaron, a clash that involved

not only Korah, Dathan, and Abiram, but also the many unknown Israelites who were felled by the plague, and that led to such awesome manifestations of the Lord's holy anger. It is the rapid succession of these manifestations that makes Israel deeply aware of their own guilt and the resultant danger to their lives.

Duties and Income of the Priests and Levites
(18:1–32)

1. The Duties of the Priests and Levites (18:1–7)

18:1–7 *The Lord said to Aaron, "You, your sons and your father's family are to bear the responsibility for offenses against the sanctuary, and you and your sons alone are to bear the responsibility for offenses against the priesthood. Bring your fellow Levites from your ancestral tribe to join you and assist you when you and your sons minister before the Tent of the Testimony. They are to be responsible to you and are to perform all the duties of the Tent, but they must not go near the furnishings of the sanctuary or the altar, or both they and you will die. They are to join you and be responsible for the care of the Tent of Meeting—all the work at the Tent—and no one else may come near where you are.*

"You are to be responsible for the care of the sanctuary and the altar, so that wrath will not fall on the Israelites again. I myself have selected your fellow Levites from among the Israelites as a gift to you, dedicated to the Lord to do the work at the Tent of Meeting. But only you and your sons may serve as priests in connection with everything at the altar and inside the curtain. I am giving you the service of the priesthood as a gift. Anyone else who comes near the sanctuary must be put to death."

These verses, which describe the relationship between the priests and Levites once again (see 1:50–53; 3:5–10, 38), are undoubtedly related to the attempt of Korah and his followers to be allowed to share in the priesthood (16:10), and to the fear of the Israelites after the judgments of chapter 16 that approaching the Tent would endanger their lives (17:12–13). In this chapter the Lord addresses Aaron directly (vv. 1, 8, 20). He does this only here and in Leviticus 10:8; otherwise Moses is always the mediator (v. 25 and e.g., Lev. 8:1; 16:2; 21:1; Num. 6:22–23; 8:1–2).

The Lord first impresses on Aaron the dangers connected with the priesthood, which requires a daily handling of the holy things of the Lord. Because it is the service of the holy God who, because of His holiness, must punish any shortcomings (Lev. 10:1–7), it is the priest who in Israel must bear the consequences of any ''offenses against the sanctuary'' and ''against the priesthood.'' This is on the one hand what Exodus 28:38 has

160

in mind: the priest must bear any guilt attached to the offerings brought by Israel. On the other hand, it means that all his actions at the altar and in the sanctuary must be in full accord with what the Lord requires of his priests in these matters. Aaron and his sons must bear the full responsibility for this, as well as his "father's family," i.e., the Levites. The Lord wants the Levites to "join" the priests—a beautiful play on words (*lewi,* Levite, and *lawa,* "to join") which is also found in Genesis 29:34. But the Levites may only assist: the ministry "before the Tent of the Testimony" is the prerogative of the priests (v. 2b reads lit., "and minister to you, but [or: and] you and your sons before the Tent of the Testimony"). Should the Levites attempt to take over any priestly duty, they are to be put to death, along with the priest who did not prevent them. I see in verse 3b an allusion to Aaron's weak attitude toward Korah (16:11). The Levites must be well aware that they are "unauthorized" (vv. 4, 7); "altar" and "sanctuary" are strictly the domain of the priests. If they forget this, the Lord's wrath will fall again on Israel (v. 5; see 16:46). This is why verse 6 once again reminds them of what had been said before on several occasions (3:9; 8:16, 19): the Levites are essentially a "gift"—they are the *nethinim,* the temple servants (see my commentary on Ezra 2:43–63), whose only duty is to await instructions. Only they who have been charged with the priesthood by the Lord Himself may issue orders and may serve at the altar and "inside the curtain," i.e., in the Most Holy Place (Exod. 26:33; Lev. 16:12). Anyone else, whether "layperson" (v. 5) or Levite (v. 7) is unauthorized because he is not chosen.

2. *The Income of the Priests* (18:8–19)

18:8–19 *Then the LORD said to Aaron, "I myself have put you in charge of the offerings presented to me; all the holy offerings the Israelites give me I give to you and your sons as your portion and regular share. You are to have the part of the most holy offerings that is kept from the fire. From all the gifts they bring me as most holy offerings, whether grain or sin or guilt offerings, that part belongs to you and your sons. Eat it as something most holy; every male shall eat it. You must regard it as holy.*

"This also is yours: whatever is set aside from the gifts of all the wave offerings of the Israelites. I give this to you and your sons and daughters as your regular share. Everyone in your household who is ceremonially clean may eat it.

"I give you all the finest olive oil and all the finest new wine and grain they give the LORD as the firstfruits of their harvest. All the land's firstfruits that they bring to the LORD will be yours. Everyone in your household who is ceremonially clean may eat it.

"Everything in Israel that is devoted to the LORD is yours. The first offspring of

> *every womb, both man and animal, that is offered to the LORD is yours. But you must redeem every firstborn son and every firstborn male of unclean animals. When they are a month old, you must redeem them at the redemption price set at five shekels of silver, according to the sanctuary shekel, which weighs twenty gerahs.*
>
> *"But you must not redeem the firstborn of an ox, a sheep or a goat; they are holy. Sprinkle their blood on the altar and burn their fat as an offering made by fire, an aroma pleasing to the LORD. Their meat is to be yours, just as the breast of the wave offerings and the right thigh are yours. Whatever is set aside from the holy offerings the Israelites present to the LORD I give to you and your sons and daughters as your regular share. It is an everlasting covenant of salt before the LORD for both you and your offspring."*

Then follows a brief listing of the priests' share of the "holy offerings" (lit. "holy things") of Israel, to the extent that these are *teruma,* or dedicated to the Lord and not burned on the altar. This *teruma* (KJV: "heave offering"), the portion of Israel's offerings demanded by the Lord, is now turned over by the Lord to His priests. That portion is then immediately defined, apparently to avoid any arbitrariness on the part of the priests (cf. 1 Sam. 2:13–16). These verses thus are a compilation of what was previously commanded in other laws concerning the priests' share. This list is comparable to the Punic list of offerings from about 300 B.C., found in Marseille in 1845; to the list of the charges for the various offerings from Carthage, found in 1858 and 1872; and to the cultus list of Sippar (column V) from the ninth century B.C. Our list is thus by far the oldest, but also the most complete (for details, see Jirku, *Altorientalischer Kommentar,* pp. 112–13).

The priests' income falls into five categories. (1) They receive "the most holy offerings" (the grain, guilt, and sin offerings), except of course those parts that had to be burned on the altar; in the case of the sin offerings this includes the restrictions of Leviticus 4:12, 21. But, because they are "most holy," they may only be eaten in a "most holy" place by ceremonially clean male members of the priestly families (vv. 9–10; cf. Lev. 6:16, 26, which refer to a "holy place"). Only the men may eat of it, since the women and daughters did not participate in the cultus.

(2) The priests also receive those offerings that are merely "holy." These can be eaten by the whole priestly household, including the women, insofar as they are ceremonially clean, i.e., have not been excluded from the cultic life for some reason (cf. Lev. 15; 22:3ff.; 1 Sam. 21:4); they must be eaten in a ceremonially clean, rather than a "holy" place (v. 11). These gifts for the priests are here called *teruma,* "the portion set aside from a gift or offering" (KJV—incorrectly—"heave offering"), i.e., that portion of their offering that the Israelites set aside to be dedicated to the

Lord in the form of a "wave offering" (see my commentary on Lev. 7:28–34). This thus refers to the fellowship offerings, the most common of Israel's offerings, which always culminated in the offering meal (see my commentary on Lev. 3:1–17). The breast and the right thigh of the fellowship offering are the priests' portion (Lev. 7:31–34). The priests' share of the "holy offerings" also includes the "finest" (lit. "fat") of the olive oil, new wine, and grain (v. 12); the choice of words indicates that this refers only to portions of the new harvest, already mentioned in 15:17–21. The "finest" is further described as "the first" *(rešit),* which contains the most vitality and is therefore the choicest portion. The amounts to be given to the priests are not specified here or in Deuteronomy 18:4.

(3) The priests are to receive "all the land's firstfruits" (*bikkurim,* v. 13). Deuteronomy 26:1–11 indicates that these firstfruits were brought to the sanctuary with a rather formal ceremony, in contrast to the *rešit,* which were simply turned over to the priests as a contribution (cf. Exod. 23:19; 34:26, which speaks of the *rešit* of the *bikkurim*). In the days of Nehemiah the *rešit* and the *bikkurim* both became a kind of tax (Neh. 10:35–39).

(4) The priests received everything that is "devoted to the LORD" (v. 14), which, according to Leviticus 27:28–29, means that which has been given over to the Lord in such a way that it can neither be sold nor redeemed. This is in contrast to the spoils of war, which were also given over to the Lord, but had to be utterly destroyed (21:2; Deut. 7:1–2; Josh. 6:17; 1 Sam. 15:3).

(5) And finally, in verses 15–18, we hear of the first offspring of every womb, both man and animal. This refers, of course, to male offspring (3:40ff.; see also Exod. 13:12–13, 15; 34:19–20; Deut. 15:19). Here it is restated that the firstborn son must be redeemed, at the rate set in Leviticus 27:6: five shekels for a person between one month and five years (see commentary on 3:47; the price for the redemption of a female is not mentioned, since it does not apply here). The statement in Exodus 22:29b, "You must give me the firstborn of your sons" has led some to defend the idea that human sacrifices were known in Israel, at least in very ancient times. But the special value attached to the firstborn (see e.g., Gen. 49:3) proves that this was not true even in ancient times and that Exodus 22:29b is a general formula that must be understood in the light of Exodus 13:13. The firstborn of Egypt were killed, but not those of Israel; consequently, the latter belong to the Lord and are to be dedicated to Him out of gratitude for the past deliverance (see also Exod. 34:19). The redemption now takes place in the form of payment of a price, as in the case of the firstborn of unclean animals for which there is no place on the Lord's altar either. In

practice this was limited to the firstborn of the donkey, the domestic animal of that time; hence Exodus 13:13 and 34:20, which specify that the donkey must be redeemed with a lamb. Leviticus 27:27 presents the case of someone who dedicates the young of an unclean animal to the Lord by a vow (even though the individual knows that it is a firstborn young and thus cannot be given to the Lord again, since it already belongs to Him), then the set value increased by one-fifth must be given. This determination of the monetary value of the young donkey is simply presupposed in verse 15.

The meat of the firstborn of clean animals (those that are suitable for offerings: ox, sheep, and goat) belongs to the priests. Its blood must be sprinkled (*zaraq,* see my commentary on Lev. 1:5) on the altar and its fat burnt "as an offering made by fire" (v. 17). Verse 18 states that the meat of the firstborn of clean animals, like the breast and the right thigh of the fellowship offering, may be eaten by the entire priestly household if they are ceremonially clean (cf. Lev. 10:14). Others interpret verse 18b to refer to the breast and the right thigh of the meat referred to in verse 18a; verse 18a is then assumed to be a later addition, made by someone who missed the fellowship offering in this list and added these words in the margin of the manuscript, from where they were later inserted (in the wrong place at that!) in the text. But this overlooks two things: (1) the original marginal notation would have specified "breast and right thigh of the fellowship offering"; and (2) both verse 13 and verse 18 must have stated who may eat the meat of the firstborn clean animals. I would therefore translate, "it will be to you as the breast of the wave offering and the right thigh" (cf. NIV).

The list concludes with a restatement of the assurance of verse 8 that this is to be "an everlasting covenant" (v. 19), made more emphatic by the addition "of salt before the LORD" (cf. 2 Chron. 13:5). It is therefore inviolable, because between the Lord's priests and Israel is "salt" (Lev. 2:13) and the Lord is witness (cf. Wellhausen, *Reste des Arabischen Heidentums,* p. 124).

This list is not complete. Verses 25–28 speak of the tithes the Levites must present to the priests, and 31:28ff. refer to the priestly portion of the booty. And finally, 5:6–8 specify that restitution for what had been wrongly taken must be made to the priests if it cannot be made to the owner because the latter has died. We do not hear in this section of the right of the priests to eat the bread set before the Lord (Lev. 24:9), nor of the priests' right to the hide of the burnt offering (Lev. 7:8). These omissions can easily be explained from the fact that this list deals only with those offerings and gifts of which a portion was given to the Lord. Thus, this list also omits any reference to the burnt offerings and the sin offerings of Leviticus 4:12, 21 of which no part was to be eaten.

3. *The Income of the Levites* (18:20–24)

18:20–24 *The LORD said to Aaron, "You will have no inheritance in their land, nor will you have any share among them; I am your share and your inheritance among the Israelites.*

"I give to the Levites all the tithes in Israel as their inheritance in return for the work they do while serving at the Tent of Meeting. From now on the Israelites must not go near the Tent of Meeting, or they will bear the consequences of their sin and will die. It is the Levites who are to do the work at the Tent of Meeting and bear the responsibility for offenses against it. This is a lasting ordinance for the generations to come. They will receive no inheritance among the Israelites. Instead, I give to the Levites as their inheritance the tithes that the Israelites present as an offering to the LORD. That is why I said concerning them: 'They will have no inheritance among the Israelites.'"

This section opens with a concept that applies to both the priests and the Levites: the Lord, who called them into His service and thereby also assumed responsibility for their livelihood, is their share and their inheritance; this means that the priests and Levites will have no need to own land in Canaan. Therefore, Aaron is here not the representative of the priests as in both preceding sections, which speak of Aaron and his sons (vv. 2, 7–9, 11, 19), but of the tribe of Levi as a whole.

The principle of verse 20 is applied specifically to the Levites in verses 21–24: the Levites (here called "the sons of Levi," which excludes the priests; cf. "tribe of Levi" in v. 2 KJV) cannot have an "inheritance," i.e., own land, in Canaan (Deut. 10:9; 12:12; 18:12; Josh. 13:14; et al.). Their means of support is now determined; this will be "a lasting ordinance" as in the case of the priests (v. 23, cf. v. 19). For their support they will receive the tithes that are given by Israel. This represents a very ancient custom, honored not only in Israel but also among other nations of antiquity. The giving of one-tenth can be a sign of respect (Gen. 14:20), but also a gift to the Deity (Gen. 28:22); it applies to "everything," both livestock and fields. The giving of tithes in Israel is dominated by the idea that man is only a tenant (Lev. 25:23) and that the rich proceeds from field and flock speak of the Lord's goodness. This is why man gives a portion of it to the divine Owner (Lord, *'adon, baal*), after which he can freely enjoy the yield of field and flock without sinning (see v. 32).

The tithe of both field and flock are mentioned in Leviticus 27:30–33 and 2 Chronicles 31:6; but Deuteronomy 14:22–29; 26:12–15; Nehemiah 10:37b, 39a; 13:5–12 speak only of the tithe of the field. Numbers 18:27, 30 indicate that only the latter is seen in verses 20–24. The historical development of the tithe is not entirely clear. Deuteronomy 12:6, 11,

17–19; 14:22–27 state that the tithe of the field must be taken to the sanctuary, if necessary in the form of its monetary equivalent, to be enjoyed there in the presence of the Lord. And every third year, according to Deuteronomy 14:28–29, the tithe of the field is to be distributed locally among the Levites, the aliens *(gerim),* the fatherless, and the widows. There the tithe is considered a type of subsidy or aid, while after the captivity the tithes of both field and livestock become more like a tax for the support of the temple servants (Neh. 10:38–39; 13:5, 10), as is also true here in verse 21. This indicates in my opinion that the income of the Levites was gradually increased, as was probably also true of the income of the priests. The growth of the tribe of Levi and the increased standard of living were probably factors in this increase. But lack of data in the historical writings of the Old Testament make it impossible for us to form a clear picture. Later Judaism knew of a triple tithe (Mishna tracts *Ma'aserot, Ma'aser šeni,* and *Pe'a;* see also Josephus, *Antiquities,* IV, 8. 8, 22; Tobit 1:7–8).

After the statement of the general principle in verse 21a the reason is given in verses 21b–22: the tithes are in return for the work of the Levites; their work at the Tent of Meeting will prevent Israel from suffering again under the Lord's wrath. The allusion to the rebellion of Korah and his followers is evident (16:46ff.). This, of course, does not imply that in the days of Korah the common Israelite was allowed to approach the Tent of Meeting and to serve in it (Wiener). The rebellion itself proves that this was not the case. But verse 22 emphasizes how dangerous it is for the "unauthorized" individual to come in close contact with the holy things. The Levites must keep this in mind as well (v. 23): they are allowed to serve, but only as servants of the priests. And as such they will "bear the responsibility for offenses against it" (lit. "and they shall bear their iniquity," cf. KJV), i.e., they must at all times be mindful of the dangers involved in dealing with the holy things, in approaching through these holy things the Holy One. The Levites, like the priests (see v. 2), are responsible for the tasks they have been assigned, and they must bear the consequences of any shortcomings in the execution of these tasks.

4. *The Tithe of the Levites* (18:25–32)

18:25–32 *The LORD said to Moses, "Speak to the Levites and say to them: 'When you receive from the Israelites the tithe I give you as your inheritance, you must present a tenth of that tithe as the LORD's offering. Your offering will be reckoned to you as grain from the threshing floor or juice from the winepress. In this way you also will present an offering to the LORD from all the tithes you receive from the Israelites. From these tithes you must give the LORD's portion to Aaron the priest. You must present as the LORD's portion the best and holiest part of everything given to you.'*

> *"Say to the Levites: 'When you present the best part, it will be reckoned to you as the product of the threshing floor or the winepress. You and your households may eat the rest of it anywhere, for it is your wages for your work at the Tent of Meeting. By presenting the best part of it you will not be guilty in this matter; then you will not defile the holy offerings of the Israelites, and you will not die.'"*

Verses 1–24 were addressed to Aaron; these verses are spoken to Moses, since Aaron is directly involved in this matter. Verse 24 states again that the Levites will "have no inheritance" in Canaan. Consequently, they will not be able to present the firstfruits of field and flock to the Lord, i.e., to His priests, like the other Israelites. Yet they have the same obligation—otherwise they could retain their full income and thus have an advantage over the rest of Israel. They must fulfill this obligation by giving one-tenth of the tithes they receive to the priests. And, even as Israel has to present the best portion to the priests (v. 12), they must give "the best and holiest part" (v. 29). If the Levites do this it will be "reckoned . . . as the product of the threshing floor or the winepress," and the Levites and their households may freely enjoy the remainder of what Israel has given them in accordance with the Lord's instructions.

But if they fail to give the tenth they "defile the holy offerings of the Israelites," because (see Lev. 22:9) the Lord's offerings must be considered holy and His command must not be treated with contempt. Becoming guilty in this matter means signing one's own death warrant.

The Water of Cleansing
(19:1–22)

This section deals with the preparation of the water of cleansing, which served to "purify" someone who had become ceremonially unclean by touching a dead body, and who could therefore not actively participate in Israel's religious life. This chapter is clearly a composite—verse 10b is the subscript, verses 11–13 supplement verses 2–10a, while verses 14–22 supplement verses 11–13.

The Pentateuch refers to the touching of a dead body in several instances (Lev. 11:31ff., 39f.; 21:1–2; Num. 5:2; 6:9; 9:10; 31:19ff.; cf. also Ezek. 44:25; Hag. 2:13; 2 Kings 23:14). Anything connected with death and burial, even the eating of "the bread of mourners," i.e., the bread eaten during the time of mourning for a dead person (Hos. 9:4), excludes an individual temporarily from the Lord's service. In Israel's thinking, sickness and death involve demonic forces.[4]

Leviticus 11:31, 39–40, which deal with contact with the carcass of an

---

[4]See Publisher's Note.

animal, states that the individual is unclean until evening; his clothes (in practice only the *kuttonet* or undergarment; see my commentary on Lev. 8:7–9) must be washed. Numbers 31:19 calls for purification on the third and seventh days after a battle (see 19:19). Numbers 6:9 requires that the Nazirite who has inadvertently become unclean by contact with someone who suddenly died in his presence shave his head on the day of his cleansing, i.e., the seventh day, following his purification. The other references contain no indication as to the duration of the uncleanness or the method of purification.

1. The Preparation of the Water of Cleansing (19:1–10)

19:1–10 *The LORD said to Moses and Aaron: "This is a requirement of the law that the LORD has commanded: Tell the Israelites to bring you a red heifer without defect or blemish and that has never been under a yoke. Give it to Eleazar the priest; it is to be taken outside the camp and slaughtered in his presence. Then Eleazar the priest is to take some of its blood on his finger and sprinkle it seven times toward the front of the Tent of Meeting. While he watches, the heifer is to be burned—its hide, flesh, blood and offal. The priest is to take some cedar wood, hyssop and scarlet wool and throw them onto the burning heifer. After that, the priest must wash his clothes and bathe himself with water. He may then come into the camp, but he will be ceremonially unclean till evening. The man who burns it must also wash his clothes and bathe with water, and he too will be unclean till evening.*

"A man who is clean shall gather up the ashes of the heifer and put them in a ceremonially clean place outside the camp. They shall be kept by the Israelite community for use in the water of cleansing; it is for purification from sin. The man who gathers up the ashes of the heifer must also wash his clothes, and he too will be unclean till evening. This will be a lasting ordinance both for the Israelites and for the aliens living among them.

Moses is instructed to ask the Israelites for "a red heifer without defect or blemish" that is still so young that it has never worked and thus "has never been under a yoke." The rabbis took "a heifer, red, a perfect one" in the sense of "a perfectly red heifer"; but Leviticus 22:21 proves that "perfect" or "without defect" must be connected with "without blemish," as the NIV clearly brings out. The heifer must be red, since this is the color of blood and thus of life, and only "life" can destroy "uncleanness," i.e., the power of death; this concept is found throughout the world of antiquity. The red animal must be a heifer because the sin offering (see v. 9) requires a female animal (Lev. 4:28; 5:6; 14:10; Num. 6:14). It must be without defect, since it is to serve an especially holy purpose (see also Lev. 22:20; Deut. 17:1). It must never have been under a yoke, which means that it is to be young and at the peak of its strength and has never been used for a profane purpose (1 Sam. 6:7; Deut. 21:3; cf. also Deut. 15:19); the Greeks and Romans had the same requirement for their sacrificial animals.

Eleazar must take the heifer—not Aaron, because what has to be done with the heifer brings "ceremonial uncleanness" with it, and the high priest must therefore not be involved (Lev. 21:11). The heifer, like the sin offering of the high priest, must be taken outside the camp by someone (a "layperson"), and slaughtered and burned: the sanctuary and the camp must be kept far from all ceremonial uncleanness (5:1–4; see also Lev. 4:12, 21). The latter indicates also that the words "it is for the purification from sin" (v. 9) are a correct rendering of *hatta'at* (the word for "sin offering"), because this is not a true sin offering; if it were, the heifer would have to be slaughtered at the altar (Lev. 4), and then of course not by a layperson. It is therefore incorrect to speak of "the offering of the red heifer" (thus e.g., J. Scheftelowitz, ZAW, 1921, pp. 113–23). The only connection between this red heifer and a sin offering lies in the fact that the purpose of both is the deliverance from demonic forces. Later Judaism required that the slaughtering of this heifer take place on the Mount of Olives; this on the basis of verse 4, which, of course, does not imply this.

After the heifer has been slaughtered Eleazar must sprinkle some of the blood with his finger seven times (the number of completeness or totality) toward the front of the sanctuary (which faced east), as was also done in the case of the sin offering for the high priest and for the congregation (Lev. 4:6, 17). This sprinkling (*hizza*, see my commentary on Lev. 1:5) dedicates this blood, so to speak, to the Lord. Only then is the entire animal, hide, flesh, blood, and offal, burned to ashes. The priest must supervise this burning (v. 5) as he did the slaughtering (v. 3). He throws cedar wood, hyssop, and scarlet wool onto the burning animal, so that they mix with the ashes of the heifer and, as it were, pervade them. This is reminiscent of the pronouncing clean of a leper and of a house contaminated by mildew, which involved the same three ingredients: cedar wood, hyssop, and scarlet yarn (Lev. 14:4–6, 49ff.). Among many nations of the Euphrates-Tigris valley cedar wood played a prominent role in cleansing rituals. Thus, a text describing the preparation of magic water says, "Fill a vessel with water, add cypress and cedar wood, pronounce the incantation of Eridu over it, and sprinkle the man with this water." It is also known that cedar wood, hyssop, and crimson played a role in ancient medicine, which was entirely geared toward exorcism (see my commentary on 2 Chron. 16:11–14). In the case of the water of purification these materials serve to intensify the "purifying" power. The wool thread probably was used to tie the cedar and hyssop together, here not for the purpose of making a brush (Exod.

12:22; Lev. 14:4), but to be burned along with the wood.

The supervising priest and the man who took care of the burning have become ceremonially unclean (vv. 7–8). This is not quite the same as what happens to the man who sends the scapegoat into the desert and to him who burns the bull and the goat of the sin offering on the Day of Atonement (Lev. 16:26, 28): they actually touch the animals that carry the sins. Here, however, the two individuals come in contact with an animal whose ashes are to deliver someone from ceremonial uncleanness that resulted from touching a dead body. The idea is apparently that so much uncleanness attaches to this animal that it contaminates its whole environment (see below). This contamination also affects the man who gathers the ashes of the red heifer in a "ceremonially clean place" (see Lev. 4:12), so that the ashes will be ready for use outside the camp (v. 10a). All three men remain ceremonially unclean until evening, the shortest period of cultic uncleanness (see e.g., Lev. 11:24ff.; 15:5ff.). But they differ in the degree of their uncleanness, since the first two must not only wash their clothes, but also bathe with water, i.e., wash their bodies. The same thought is also found elsewhere. Thus, we know that a Greek who touched an offering that served to still the wrath of the gods had to take a bath and wash his clothes in running water.

The ashes of the red heifer are used to make "the water of cleansing"; we are not told how this water was prepared. "The water of cleansing" is literally "water of impurity" *(nidda); nidda* was used originally to refer to the monthly period of women (see my commentary on Lev. 16:19–30) and to idolatry (2 Chron. 29:5; Ezra 9:11). It indicates the highest degree of impurity. The water is called "water of *nidda,*" not because it was originally water mixed with menstrual discharge (Eerdmans, *Theologisch Tijdschrift,* 1908, pp. 234ff.), but because it must serve to remove *nidda,* just as the "water of cleansing" (8:7) removes the sin that is perceived as attaching itself to the body. The "water of *nidda*" is thus the "water for the removal of *nidda.*" The elements it contains guarantee to Israel's way of thinking its efficacy: the *red* heifer, which has not been in contact with anything profane; the *red* blood; the *medicinal* cedar wood and hyssop; the *scarlet* wool; and the *living* water. Everything here speaks of the restoration of life.

The concept that underlies the preparation of this water of cleansing stems from the same dynamistic sphere of thought[5] as the "bitter water" of the law of jealousy (5:11ff.) and the ceremony with which a leper or a "leprous" house is pronounced clean (Lev. 14:4–5, 49–52). We have

---

[5]See Publisher's Note.

here (as perhaps also in Exod. 32:20, the drinking of the water mixed with the statue ground into powder) remnants of a very ancient practice, which we still encounter in full force in religions oriented toward magic, and which in Israel dates from the time when the "forefathers . . . lived beyond the River" (Josh. 24:2). This water of cleansing was probably used frequently, although it is never mentioned in the historical books of the Old Testament. Thus, 31:19 speaks of "purifying" on the third and seventh days (see commentary on v. 12 above), and 6:9 refers to the cleansing of the Nazirite on the seventh day. The method of cleansing is not specified in either case and is thus assumed to be known. Leviticus 11:31, 39–40 speaks only of being unclean until evening after touching the carcass of an animal; this may well be explained by the fact that this was a situation that could occur with some frequency in any household, so that a time consuming cleansing procedure was impossible for practical reasons. Israel's lawgiver had to take into consideration the demands of everyday life (see my commentary on Lev. 11:34–38).

Later Judaism deals with this "water of cleansing" at length. The Mishna devotes a separate, twelve-part tract to it, *Para* ("Heifer"), and Maimonides (1135–1204) wrote a lengthy treatise on the topic. Mohammed was also familiar with the Jewish custom and speaks of it in his second sura, which is therefore called *Heifer* (see Geiger, *Was hat Mohammed aus dem Judenthum genommen?*, p. 172).

2. *Situations in Which the Water of Cleansing Is to Be Used* (19:11–22)

19:11–13 *"Whoever touches the dead body of anyone will be unclean for seven days. He must purify himself with the water on the third day and on the seventh day; then he will be clean. But if he does not purify himself on the third and seventh days, he will not be clean. Whoever touches the dead body of anyone and fails to purify himself defiles the LORD's tabernacle. That person must be cut off from Israel. Because the water of cleansing has not been sprinkled on him, he is unclean; his uncleanness remains on him.*

For people whose thinking is dynamistically oriented, as was true of the entire world of antiquity, including Israel, anything connected with death and burial is a source of cultic uncleanness; this is especially true of contact with a dead body. This was so self-evident to Israel that it is simply presupposed (see Lev. 21; 22:4; Num. 5:1–4); it is therefore incorrect to connect the promulgation of this law with the divine judgments of 16:35 and 16:48–49. All that is stated here is the minimum duration of the resulting uncleanness and the means of cleansing: the water is to be used twice, on the third and on the seventh day. Only then is the person pronounced ceremonially clean. Such uncleanness, lasting seven days, was also known in Babel (Jirku, *Altorientalischer Kommentar*, p. 114). Verse 19 indicates how this purification takes place; the fact that the water is applied twice shows how serious the contamination by a dead body was considered to be. This is why it is striking that, in contrast to 5:2 and 31:19, the requirement that the unclean individual leave the camp during the period of his cleansing is absent here. This is perhaps taken for granted and, like the offering of Leviticus 5:1–13, is not mentioned in order to focus all attention on the water of cleansing itself. Anyone who refuses to purify himself and who (presumably) continues to participate in the cultic life, must be put to death. He has brought the uncleanness that clings to him into the Lord's sanctuary, which must be safeguarded against any uncleanness (Lev. 15:31; 16:16; 20:3); he has thereby disclosed a source of uncleanness and thus hindered the life-giving working of Israel's cultic activity; he has thus broken Israel's communion with the Holy One.

19:14–16 *"This is the law that applies when a person dies in a tent: Anyone who enters the tent and anyone who is in it will be unclean for seven days, and every open container without a lid fastened on it will be unclean.*

"Anyone out in the open who touches someone who has been killed with a sword or someone who has died a natural death, or anyone who touches a human bone or a grave, will be unclean for seven days."

Verses 14–16 present some special applications of the general rule of verses 11–13. Anyone who is in, or enters, a tent where a person dies will be unclean for seven days; the same is true of every open container in the tent (vv. 14–15, see Lev. 11:32). Similarly, anyone who touches in the open field a person who has died a violent death or of natural causes, or anyone who touches human remains or a grave (v. 16) will be unclean for seven days. We must remember that graves were usually very shallow; hence the later custom of whitewashing graves (Matt. 23:27).

19:17–19 *"For the unclean person, put some ashes from the burned purification offering into a jar and pour fresh water over them. Then a man who is ceremonially clean is to take some hyssop, dip it in the water and sprinkle the tent and all the furnishings and the people who were there. He must also sprinkle anyone who has touched a human bone or a grave or someone who has been killed or someone who has died a natural death. The man who is clean is to sprinkle the unclean person on the third and seventh days, and on the seventh day he is to purify him. The person being cleansed must wash his clothes and bathe with water, and that evening he will be clean."*

Verses 17–19 further specify the manner in which an individual who has thus become unclean is to be purified. Some ashes from the red heifer (see also Lev. 14:5–6, 50–52) are mixed with "fresh" (lit. "living"), i.e., running or spring water (see Gen. 26:19; Lev. 14:5; Song of Songs 4:15; Zech. 14:8; John 4:10–11; 7:38; Rev. 7:17). A man who is ceremonially clean then takes a bundle of hyssop, dips it into the mixture and sprinkles *(hizza)* twice whatever and whoever has become ceremonially unclean, on the third and on the seventh day (v. 19). The person who has been sprinkled then washes his body and his clothes (see 31:24), which marks the end of the period of uncleanness (cf. the Sumerian ritual, pp. 170–71).

19:20–22 *"But if a person who is unclean does not purify himself, he must be cut off from the community, because he has defiled the sanctuary of the LORD. The water of cleansing has not been sprinkled on him, and he is unclean. This is a lasting ordinance for them.*

"The man who sprinkles the water of cleansing must also wash his clothes, and anyone who touches the water of cleansing will be unclean till evening. Anything that an unclean person touches becomes unclean, and anyone who touches it becomes unclean till evening."

The chapter ends with a restatement of the warning of verse 13 against him who does not purify himself in this manner (v. 20), and the permanent validity of the purification ceremony is again emphasized (v. 21a). Finally, the dual effect of the water of cleansing is indicated (vv. 21b–22): on the one hand it purifies the ceremonially unclean, on the other hand it makes the person who performs the purification ritual unclean, as is true of anyone who touches the water. The uncleanness is of short duration, however: until evening (see vv. 7, 10). This is a concept we find difficult to understand, but which was common in all of antiquity and is still found in underdeveloped cultures: "holy" and "unclean" have more than one point of contact—both are dangerous. This is the taboo which has continued to find expression in Judaism: the name of Jahweh is taboo and must not be pronounced, while touching the letters of the "holy" text makes a person "unclean" *(Judaim* 3. 5; 4. 5–6). The taboo concept explains also the sequence in Leviticus 10:10,[6] which to our way of thinking is wrong: "holy and the profane, unclean and the clean."

Hebrews 9:11ff. refer to the ashes of the heifer and draw a parallel between the water of cleansing and the cleansing blood of the Savior. Some of the church fathers saw in the slaughtering of the red heifer outside the camp a type of Christ's death on the cross, and in the water of cleansing a type of baptism, which is somewhat far-fetched.

---

[6]See Publisher's Note.

Miriam's Death and Moses' Sin at Meribah
(20:1–13)

1. *Miriam's Death* (20:1)

20:1 *In the first month the whole Israelite community arrived at the Desert of Zin, and they stayed at Kadesh. There Miriam died and was buried.*

This pericope, which reports first Miriam's death and then Moses' sin, clearly is intended as a transition to the third main part of Numbers, which deals with the journey from Kadesh to the Transjordan region. It must also explain why neither Moses nor Aaron could enter the Promised Land.

The chronology here presents problems. The date of Miriam's death is not given. The indication of the year that followed the words "in the first month" has dropped out, and we are thus limited to speculation. But a comparison of 20:22 and 33:38–39 shows that Aaron died in the fifth month of the fortieth year of the wanderings, after Israel had left Kadesh and had traveled east in the direction of Edom (20:22). Furthermore, 33:36–37 indicates that the stay at Kadesh preceded the journey to Edom. And finally, verse 3 speaks of those who earlier "fell dead before the LORD," which probably includes more than only those mentioned in 16:19, 35, 48. This makes it in my opinion probable that Miriam's death should be placed in the beginning of the final year of the wanderings. Aaron then dies next, and finally Moses. Others place Miriam's death in the third year of the wanderings on the basis of 10:11–12, where we also hear of an arrival in the Desert of Paran (i.e., Kadesh, according to 13:26), approximately one year after the departure from Sinai. The first thirteen verses of this chapter are then placed after chapter 12, and are considered a parallel account to chapters 13–14. However, this means that the author of the Pentateuch incorrectly placed Miriam's death in chapter 20 and transferred her death to the fortieth year. According to this view the original text read "the first month of the third year," and the author purposely omitted "of the third year." And finally, the implication of this view is that the story of Exodus 17 is the same as that of Numbers 20. I can, of course, not go into detail here; suffice it to say that I consider these suppositions to be unfounded.

A final note: no mention is made of mourning following Miriam's death, in contrast to Aaron's death (v. 29) and Moses' death (Deut. 34:8).

2. *Moses' Sin at Meribah* (20:2–13)

20:2–12 *Now there was no water for the community, and the people gathered in opposition to Moses and Aaron. They quarreled with Moses and said, "If only we*

---

*had died when our brothers fell dead before the L*ORD*! Why did you bring the L*ORD*'s community into this desert, that we and our livestock should die here? Why did you bring us up out of Egypt into this terrible place? It has no grain or figs, grapevines or pomegranates. And there is no water to drink!"*

*Moses and Aaron went from the assembly to the entrance to the Tent of Meeting and fell facedown, and the glory of the L*ORD *appeared to them. The L*ORD *said to Moses, "Take the staff, and you and your brother Aaron gather the assembly together. Speak to that rock before their eyes and it will pour out its water. You will bring water out of the rock for the community so they and their livestock can drink."*

*So Moses took the staff from the L*ORD*'s presence, just as he commanded him. He and Aaron gathered the assembly together in front of the rock and Moses said to them, "Listen, you rebels, must we bring you water out of this rock?" Then Moses raised his arm and struck the rock twice with his staff. Water gushed out, and the community and their livestock drank.*

*But the L*ORD *said to Moses and Aaron, "Because you did not trust in me enough to honor me as holy in the sight of the Israelites, you will not bring this community into the land I give them."*

The grammatical structure of verse 2 indicates that verses 2–13 do not follow chronologically after verse 1, at least not immediately; I would therefore translate verse 2, "Once there was no water. . . ."

Again, lack of water causes Israel to gather in opposition to Moses and Aaron (cf. 16:3, 42). They envy their brothers who had died earlier "before the LORD" (i.e., by a plague, 14:37), and who had thus been delivered from the miseries of the desert (v. 3). Israel once again calls both of their leaders to account in their old manner with their double "Why?" (cf. 11:5; 14:2–4; 16:12–14). They call themselves again "the LORD's community" (16:3) in order to highlight the evil perpetrated by Moses and Aaron; their use of this term insinuates that Moses and Aaron have actually sinned against the Lord Himself. These complainers see the covenant relationship between the Lord and Israel strictly as a source of blessings. They feel that as "the LORD's community" they are entitled to better treatment. The place where they are now is a "terrible place" (lit. "evil place"). The latter proves that this event did not take place at Kadesh (where those things which they now lack were found), but elsewhere in the Desert of Zin (cf. Num. 27:14; Deut. 32:51).

And again both leaders, who are themselves also worn out by the miseries of the desert (see Exod. 17:1ff.), cast themselves upon the Lord; they fall facedown at the entrance to the tabernacle (14:5; 16:4). And the Lord answers. His glory appears to them and He speaks to them (14:10; 15:19, 42ff.). Moses is told to take "the staff" (v. 8), which was "in the LORD's presence" (lit. "before the LORD"; v. 9, cf. KJV). This faces us with the problem which staff this is: the staff of Moses (Exod. 4:2ff., 17, 20; 7:15, 17, 20; 9:23; 10:13; 14:16–18; 17:5f.), or Aaron's staff, which had been placed "in front of the Testimony," according to 17:10. Verse 11 does not help us, since "the staff" becomes automatically "his staff" when Moses picks it up. The LXX and the Vulgate speak of "the staff" in verse 11, and give the impression that they want to avoid any implication that this is Moses', rather than Aaron's, staff, which is in my opinion indeed the author's intention. Otherwise it would have been superfluous to point out in verse 9 that the staff in question is the staff that was "in the LORD's presence," which was true of Aaron's, but not of Moses' staff. These words in verse 9 are therefore considered a later addition by those who want to see here a reference to Moses' staff (e.g., Heinisch, p. 78). It is understandable that Aaron's staff must be used in this situation. Moses can fulfill the command the Lord will give only if he has unshakable confidence in the Lord's unlimited power to perform miracles (see below). Which staff would be more appropriate to provide support in this situation than Aaron's staff, which had budded, bloomed, and produced fruit in a single night? It was not the Lord's intention, therefore, that this staff should be used to strike. It served only to give Moses support in circumstances that required a very special act of faith.

Moses and Aaron must gather "the assembly" together at the rock and simply command the rock to give water. This is thus different from what is recorded in Exodus 17:1–7. There Moses was told to strike the rock; here he must merely speak to it. Here it is not the force of the blow, but the power of the word. We must remember that to the Oriental a word is not a series of sounds, as it is to us, but an act that reveals itself in sounds, a "word-thing" or "thing-word," a reality that comes up out of the heart of the speaker, out of the "workshop" where one's actions are born. The word is, as it were, "charged," and will have a greater "charge" as the one from whom the word goes out has more power or, as the Polynesians would say, more *mana*.

What is asked here of Moses when he is told to command the rock to give up its water is nothing less than to stand in the unshakable certainty of faith that the Lord's word, which is taken to the rock through Moses' mediation, has so much power that it will force the rockwall to open up and release its water on behalf of the thirsty Israelites. He is asked to have the faith of Psalm 33:9; Isaiah 55:11; Matthew 17:20.

"The rock" must refer to the only rock in that area. At Ain Qadeis a chasm is shown from which water bubbles up; this is supposed to be the result of Moses' sin. But those who have seen "the inn of the good Samaritan" between Jerusalem and Jericho, or "the house of Mary and

Joseph'' in Nazareth will be less than impressed by this.

Moses (with the staff) and Aaron gather "the assembly together in front of the rock," as they have been instructed. And though they do not realize it, the moment that will be decisive for the course of the rest of their lives has come. Moses speaks when he should have been silent; he strikes the rock twice when he should have spoken once. He speaks in his own name, and strikes in his own strength. His words are in the first place an expression of the revulsion he feels when he sees "the assembly," and of the bitterness that fills his soul when he remembers what he has had to endure from them for so many years. "You rebels," you people who are always in opposition because you think only of yourselves and measure others by your standards, even the Lord. After this reproach, which was unquestionably deserved but misplaced here because it was not part of the Lord's instructions, comes a question. Not a command to the rock in the name of the Lord, but a question addressed to the "rebels": "Must we bring you water out of this rock?" The unique characteristics of the Hebrew idiom make three renderings of the six Hebrew words possible. The meaning of the phrase is determined by one word, *nosi'*. The possibilities are: (1) shall we, (2) must we, or (3) can we bring you water out of this rock? The first rendering would indicate a hesitation on Moses' part, the second would reflect reluctance, while the third would indicate doubt. The whole picture changes, depending on our choice here. I finally chose "must we" (so also NIV), because it reflects the same aversion implicit in his earlier "you rebels." Yet, I do not want to deny that the emphatic position of the words "from this rock" (lit. "from this rock *nosi'* for you water?") also seems to express a great deal of doubt concerning the possibility of doing this. But the rendering "can we . . . ?" would only express doubt and eliminate the aversion that seems so clearly implied. Psalm 106:33 says that "rash words came from Moses' lips." Moses thus fell into the snare of sin because of his negative feelings toward his rebellious people (cf. Lev. 5:4): he fails to do what he was told and does what he was not commanded to do. He strikes the rock, twice, and . . . the water "gushed out." However, for Israel this gushing water is now no longer a special miraculous act of God on Israel's behalf; it is not the Lord who has given them water from the rock but "we," i.e., Moses and Aaron. And they used a staff that had proven to be the bearer of special powers by budding and producing blossoms and fruit in one night.

This puts an end to the opposition against Moses and Aaron; man and beast drink and are happy. "But the LORD said"—He sheds His light on their act and announces His punishment. "You did not trust in me" and consequently "you did not honor me as holy" (lit. "sanctify me'');

"enough" is not in the Hebrew text). The first statement means, you did not believe Me to be the trustworthy One on whose word man can always and under all circumstances depend; thus you have robbed Me of My honor, and put Me on the same level as "the other gods," on whose word man cannot depend either. And consequently "you did not honor me as holy"; "holy" *(kadosh)* means "separated," essentially different from any other, living by His own law, Lord and Master of His own territory. To "sanctify" ("honor as holy") the Lord thus means to acknowledge His otherness, to live out of this reality and to show by word and deed that He is the wholly other, who cannot even come close to being compared to other gods. The Lord had only said, "Speak." Had Moses obeyed before the eyes of all of Israel, the exceptional power of Him who can force a rock to release its water simply by His word would have been made manifest. Then it would once again have been made clear to Israel that the Lord simply cannot be compared to "the other gods." He does not need magical formulas. His word does not need the support of mysterious manipulations, not even of *any* accompanying act. His word itself is an act. It will accomplish *all* that He desires (Isa. 55:11).

Thus Moses and Aaron stood in the Lord's way. They deprived their people of the opportunity to gain a profound insight into the Lord's power, and they deprived themselves of the fruit of their forty-year-long struggle to reach Canaan. They "did not trust" (v. 12), they "rebelled" (v. 24; 27:14), i.e., they did not "obey" Him (1 Sam. 12:15), they did not keep the Lord's command (1 Kings 13:21). Many have claimed that there is a clear distinction between "not trusting" and "rebelling," following Cornill (ZAW, 1891, pp. 20–34). The words "Listen, you rebels" (v. 10b) are then supposed to be part of the Lord's words to Moses and Aaron (v. 12), moved to their present position by a reader who was offended by this characterization of the great leaders, and put in Moses' mouth. But, apart from the view of the Scriptures reflected in this supposition, it is based on error.

Moses and Aaron failed the test of which Deuteronomy 33:8 speaks and to which all of Israel was subjected during the wilderness journey (Deut. 8:2). At the crucial moment they did not trust their Sender. Yet He did not abandon them, His envoys. The rock did give the water Israel needed. Ultimately it is not the envoy who is important, but only the purpose the Lord wants to achieve by sending him.

20:13 *These were the waters of Meribah, where the Israelites quarreled with the Lord and where he showed himself holy among them.*

Verse 13 specifies where the preceding event took place: "These were the waters of Meribah" ("Quarreling"). The word *Meribah,* which is also found in Genesis 13:8 to describe the argument between Abraham and Lot, has nere become a proper noun: here the Israelites "quarreled" (*rib,* see v. 3) with the Lord. Then is added that here "he showed himself holy [*hit-qaddeš*] among them," clearly an allusion to Kadesh *(Qadeš).*

Meribah and Kadesh are sometimes combined in a genitival relationship. We hear of Meribah Kadesh in Deuteronomy 32:51; Ezekiel 47:19; 48:28. The last two references state that this Meribah Kadesh will be on the southern border of Israel, which will run from Tabat via Meribah Kadesh to the Mediterranean. The name Meribah Kadesh (which does not necessarily mean "Meribah, that is, Kadesh"), indicates that Israel wanted to distinguish this Meribah (also mentioned in 20:24; Pss. 81:7; 106:32) from another Meribah. This is similar to the distinction made between Mizpah in Moab (1 Sam. 22:3) and Mizpah in Gilead (Judg. 11:29), between Gibeah in Benjamin (1 Sam. 13:15), Gibeah of Saul (1 Sam. 11:4), and Gibeah of Phinehas (Josh. 24:33), and between Ramah in the Negev (Josh. 19:8) and Ramoth Gilead (1 Kings 4:13). The other Meribah is known from Exodus 17:7, where we hear of a place near Rephidim, called Massah and Meribah after the events that took place there. This Meribah is mentioned together with Massah in Deuteronomy 33:8 and Psalm 95:8 (only Massah is mentioned in Deut. 6:16; 9:22).

The need to distinguish this second Meribah from the first by adding "Kadesh" points, apart from various exegetical considerations, clearly to the fact that Exodus 17:1–7 and Numbers 20:1–13 do not speak of the same event, as is usually assumed today (e.g., Böhl, *Exodus,* p. 136). The ancient Jewish exegetes concluded from the fact that both chapters speak of a Meribah, that "the rock" with its miraculous provision of water continuously accompanied Israel, like "the cloud." Paul refers to this curious view in 1 Corinthians 10:4 when he speaks of Christ as Israel's spiritual rock from which they all drank on their journey through the wilderness.

Part Three

From Kadesh to the Fields of Moab
(20:14–36:13)

The Journey to the Transjordan Region
(20:14–21:9)

1. Edom Refuses Passage (20:14–21)

20:14–21 *Moses sent messengers from Kadesh to the king of Edom, saying:*

"This is what your brother Israel says: You know about all the hardships that have come upon us. Our forefathers went down into Egypt, and we lived there many years. The Egyptians mistreated us and our fathers, but when we cried out to the LORD, *he heard our cry and sent an angel and brought us out of Egypt.*

"Now we are here at Kadesh, a town on the edge of your territory. Please let us pass through your country. We will not go through any field or vineyard, or drink water from any well. We will travel along the king's highway and not turn to the right or to the left until we have passed through your territory."

But Edom answered:

"You may not pass through here; if you try, we will march out and attack you with the sword."

The Israelites replied:

"We will go along the main road, and if we or our livestock drink any of your water, we will pay for it. We only want to pass through on foot—nothing else."

Again they answered:

"You may not pass through."

Then Edom came out against them with a large and powerful army. Since Edom refused to let them go through their territory, Israel turned away from them.

After the experience gained in their attempt to invade Canaan from the south (14:39–45), Israel will now try to enter Canaan from the east. But they must first go south to the northern tip of the Gulf of Aqaba, then east along the southern border of Edom, and finally north along the eastern borders of Edom and Moab toward the Arnon in order to reach the Jordan from the east (cf. Judg. 11:17–18). This was a long and roundabout way, which could be shortened considerably if Israel could travel through the heavily wooded mountains of Seir, the region that lies south of Palestine and west of the present Wadi el-Arabah. Since these mountains are under Edom's control, Moses tries to negotiate with Edom (and according to Judg. 11:17–18 also with Moab) for passage for Israel.

C. F. Lehmann-Haupt (*Israel,* 1911) has tried to show that this narrative, which probably takes us back to the fifteenth century B.C., cannot be historical, because Edom was still nomadic at that time and could therefore not have controlled this territory. This claim is based on the following: an Egyptian border official from the time of Pharaoh Merneptah states that he gave permission to the ''Bedouins'' of the *Atuma* to enter Egypt and to go to the marshes of Pithom in order to keep themselves and their flocks alive. The assumption is that this *Atuma* is Edom, which was then (between 1255 and 1215 B.C.) still nomadic. But this *Atuma* refers to the Etham of Exodus 13:20 and Numbers 33:6, which was not a border fortress, as Böhl claims (*Exodus,* p. 125), but a region north of the Red Sea.

Verse 14 states that Edom had a king at that time. But in Genesis 36:31–39 we find a list of the kings of Edom, which speaks of eight kings ''who reigned in Edom before any Israelite king reigned'' (see my commentary on 1 Chron. 1:43–51). If this list is complete, we must take ''king'' in verse 14 in the sense of ''ruler'' or ''chief,'' since eight kings cannot fill the centuries from Moses to David; Genesis 36:15–19 lists no fewer than fourteen ''chiefs,'' while verses 40–43 list another eleven.

Moses asks this ''chief'' of Edom for free passage for his people. He bases his request on the fact that Israel is Edom's ''brother''; they belong to the same tribe (cf. Deut. 2:4; 23:7; Obad. 10, 12; Amos 1:11). Without (wisely!) stating the purpose of Israel's journey, he explains why Israel has left the region west of the Egyptian border, an area coveted by Bedouins: mistreatment at the hands of the Egyptians. His words ''our forefathers . . . and we'' convey that they left Egypt only after a long period of oppression. Without elaborating on the power of Egypt, of which Edom was of course well aware, Moses hastens to impress on Edom the power of Israel's God: the sending of His ''angel'' or ''messenger'' was sufficient to break Egypt's resistance and to liberate Israel. Moses thus implies that Israel is backed by a strong God and that Edom should think twice before refusing its request. To make it easier for Edom to give Israel permission to travel through Edom's territory from Kadesh, Moses adds the solemn promise that Israel will not be a burden to Edom. Israel will not touch Edom's fields and vineyards, something they would have done had they considered Edom to be conquered territory. Rather, they will follow the "king's highway," one of the wide overland routes that today are still called "sultan's roads." These roads were marked by slabs of slate placed in the ground on both sides of the road, and were made suitable for transport in such a way that not only caravans, but also armies could use them. Traces of such "king's highways" have been found on the Carmel and in the region of Moab (Jirku, *Altorientalischer Kommentar,* p. 114). Paved roads probably did not exist until the time of the Romans.

Edom bluntly refuses passage and adds the threat of armed resistance. Yet Israel makes a second attempt to persuade Edom. It even promises to pay the regular price for anything they may need for themselves and their livestock.

The second request is also refused, in spite of the assurance, "we only want to pass through on foot—nothing else" (cf. Deut. 2:28). The seriousness of Edom's refusal is made clear to Israel when Edom marches to its western border "with a large and powerful army."

Moses is anxious to avoid a repetition of what happened at Hormah (14:39–45). Israel therefore turns away without pressing the issue. The list in chapter 33 gives further details of this journey.

Deuteronomy 2:1–8 does not mention this incident. There Israel travels north along Edom's border. But this omission does not make Deuteronomy 2:1–8 "an entirely different story," as Edelkoort claims (*Numeri,* p. 164).

2. *Aaron's Death* (20:22–29)

20:22–29 *The whole Israelite community set out from Kadesh and came to Mount Hor. At Mount Hor, near the border of Edom, the LORD said to Moses and Aaron, "Aaron will be gathered to his people. He will not enter the land I give the Israelites, because both of you rebelled against my command at the waters of Meribah. Get Aaron and his son Eleazar and take them up Mount Hor. Remove Aaron's garments and put them on his son Eleazar, for Aaron will be gathered to his people; he will die there."*

Moses did as the LORD commanded: They went up Mount Hor in the sight of the whole community. Moses removed Aaron's garments and put them on his son Eleazar. And Aaron died there on top of the mountain. Then Moses and Eleazar came down from the mountain, and when the whole community learned that Aaron had died, the entire house of Israel mourned him for thirty days.

The answer to the question in which direction Israel traveled after it "turned away" (v. 21) hinges on the location of Mount Hor. Verse 23 and 33:37 place it "near" or "on" the border of Edom, which of course does not help us any. Tradition locates it "near Petra," where travelers are still shown Aaron's grave on a mountain called Nebi Harun (see e.g., Forder, *Petra, Perea, Phoenicia,* 1923, pp. 50–51). This would contradict the statement that Mount Hor is "near the border of Edom," since Petra lies in the heart of Edom's territory. F. J. Abel (*Géographie de Palestine,* I, 1933, pp. 386–89) points to the Wadi Haruni, ten miles northeast of Kadesh; H. C. Trumbull (*Kadesh Barnea,* 1886, pp. 128ff.) also thinks of a mountain northeast of Kadesh, Madara, which sounds somewhat like Moserah, the place where Aaron died according to Deuteronomy 10:6. Numbers 33:30–31 mentions Moseroth, located between Hashmonah and Bene Jaakan, which is also unknown to us. Nor does Abel's assumption that, as Nebo is one of the peaks of the Abarim mountains, so Hor is one of the peaks of the Moseroth mountains shed any light on the question. Given this uncertainty it appears to me that it is risky to maintain that, after leaving Kadesh, Israel went north rather than south, all the more so since attempts at locating Mount Hor somewhere north of Kadesh are actually based solely on the words "the king of Arad" in 21:1, which, going by Hebrew idiom, are undoubtedly a later addition (see commentary on 21:1). I believe that we must therefore assume that Israel, after leaving Kadesh, did not travel in a northeasterly direction, where the route to the Transjordan region was blocked, but rather in a southeasterly direction toward the Gulf of Aqaba, to Elath and Ezion Geber. A Mount Hor is also mentioned in 34:7–8, but this mountain lies in the Lebanon region.

Because of the sin he and Moses committed at Meribah (20:2–13), Aaron will not go with Israel on the rest of the journey to Canaan, but will die here. According to 33:38 his death takes place on the first day of the fifth month of the fortieth year after the Exodus. At the Lord's command Aaron and his son Eleazar, who is the eldest surviving son after the death of Nadab and Abihu (Lev. 10), and thus Aaron's successor, go up Mount Hor with Moses, who is in charge. On the mountain the ceremony of the transfer of the garments takes place, a ceremony performed by Moses. Verses 26 and 28 speak of Aaron's "garments." These may be his regular clothes, or the "sacred garments" of Exodus 28:2, the official high-priestly garments. We cannot make a definitive choice here; 1 Kings 19:19 indicates that in Israel's thinking regular, everyday garments absorbed the personality of the wearer to such an extent that his special powers were, so to speak, automatically transferred to him who received those garments. The question must thus remain open.

In accordance with the Lord's command the three men go up the mountain in the sight of "the whole community." We are not told what this brief journey meant to these men; Edelkoort says, "There a man lost his life's ideal, a son lost his father, a brother his faithful helper, the people one of its pioneers." It is a mystery to me how some of the rabbis could have arrived at the idea that Moses killed his brother Aaron. How Aaron died is not stated; he was "gathered to his people" (v. 26), which, according to Genesis 15:15 is not the same as "buried" but speaks of belief in a continued existence in the realm of the dead. Aaron was 123 years old when he died (33:39).

Israel legitimately honored Aaron's contributions to his people by mourning him for thirty days, as it would also do later when Moses died (Deut. 34:8). Jacob's sons mourned their father for seven days (Gen. 50:10).

3. *The Canaanite Attack* (21:1–3)

21:1–3 *When the Canaanite king of Arad, who lived in the Negev, heard that Israel was coming along the road to Atharim, he attacked the Israelites and captured some of them. Then Israel made this vow to the LORD: "If you will deliver these people into our hands, we will totally destroy their cities." The LORD listened to Israel's plea and gave the Canaanites over to them. They completely destroyed them and their towns; so the place was named Hormah.*

These verses speak of an attack on Israel by the Canaanites of the Negev after Israel had taken "the road to Atharim." In the present MT the attacker is called "the king of Arad." But Hebrew idiom makes it clear beyond doubt that "the king of Arad," both here and in 33:40, was originally written in the margin of the manuscript and later transferred to the text by mistake. The marginal notation was added by some reader who felt justified in his identification because in Judges 1:16–17 Arad (the present Tell 'Arad, approximately eighteen miles south of Hebron? Cf. Garstang, *Joshua-Judges,* 1931, p. 357) is linked with Hormah. However, Judges 1:16–17 speaks of Zephath (the present es-Sbeita between Kadesh and Beersheba?), and states that the Israelites called it Hormah (see commentary on 14:45).

We know nothing more about the "road to Atharim," which is mentioned only here. The ancient versions already had problems with it. The Targum, Peshitta, Onkelos, Vulgate, and also the KJV, and ASV margin omit the *'alef* and read "the way of the spies," referring back to chapter 14. Dillmann believes it to be the name of the regular caravan route leading to Arad through the Negev. The Canaanites would then have interpreted

Israel's traveling along this road as a hostile act and therefore staged a counterattack. But this can hardly be correct, since according to verse 2 Israel considers the attack an act of perfidy to which they respond by vowing that they will "totally destroy their cities" (see NIV margin). Hence also the statement that the Canaanites "captured some of them," which is found only here. The LXX and a number of exegetes take Atharim to be a proper noun, which is probably correct, but does not offer any help in determining where this attack took place.

In verse 4 we find Israel again at Mount Hor, where Aaron had died. From there it travels south. There is thus no indication that Israel made use of the victory that led to the complete destruction of the Canaanites and their cities. This has led Wiener to surmise that 21:1–3 originally preceded chapter 13, and that 14:39–45 relates how Israel had to give up the conquered territory ("The Exodus and the Southern Invasion," *Nieuwe Theologische Studiën*, 1927, pp. 1–81). But Wiener forgets to explain how these verses strayed to their present position between 20:29 and 21:4, and overlooks the fact that 14:39–45 do not speak of giving up conquered territory, but of a failed attempt to invade Canaan from the south. It also escapes Wiener that in 33:40 this event is placed between Aaron's death and Israel's departure from Mount Hor, exactly as it is here. And finally, if the victory over the Canaanites of the Negev had indeed preceded chapter 13 chronologically, then both the language of the spies and the fact that Joshua and Caleb do not mention this victory are inexplicable.

Several exegetes (e.g., Strack) are of the opinion that Israel's victory of verse 3 is the same as that mentioned in Judges 1:17. But Hebrew idiom does not support this view, and we might then also expect a further indication in Judges as to when this took place. Furthermore, in Judges 1 Israel attacks from the north, while here it responds to an attack from the north.

This is a treacherous attack, repulsed in a most bloody manner by the Israelites camped at Mount Hor. The Israelites, however, cannot exploit this military success, since they are moving south after Edom's refusal.

4. *The Bronze Snake* (21:4–9)

21:4–9 *They traveled from Mount Hor along the route to the Red Sea, to go around Edom. But the people grew impatient on the way; they spoke against God and against Moses, and said, "Why have you brought us up out of Egypt to die in the desert? There is no bread! There is no water! And we detest this miserable food!"*

Then the LORD sent venomous snakes among them; they bit the people and many Israelites died. The people came to Moses and said, "We sinned when we spoke against the LORD and against you. Pray that the LORD will take the snakes away from us." So Moses prayed for the people.

The LORD said to Moses, "Make a snake and put it up on a pole; anyone who is bitten can look at it and live." So Moses made a bronze snake and put it up on a pole. Then when anyone was bitten by a snake and looked at the bronze snake, he lived.

After Aaron's death and the defeat of the Canaanites of the Negev, Israel continues its southward journey "along the route to the Red Sea." This means the present Gulf of Elat, as indicated by the following statement that Israel planned "to go around Edom" after the refusal of 20:21. They travel through the desolate Araba region, where once again the people experience the hardships of life in the desert. Again the people grow "impatient" (lit. "their souls became short," cf. Judg. 16:16; Zech. 11:8) and again they speak "against God and against Moses" with bitter complaints and accusations (cf. Exod. 14:11; 17:3; Num. 11:4ff.; 14:12ff.; 16:13; 20:4). To give at least the appearance of legitimacy to their complaints they speak again contemptuously of the manna: "this miserable food!" (cf. 11:6). They are without food or water—all that is left for them is death in the desert! They would rather have stayed in Egypt!

Moses' reaction to these complaints is not recorded (cf. 16:15), nor is the fact that the Lord's anger is aroused (cf. 11:1). We are only told of the result of the Lord's anger: venomous snakes are sent (lit. "fiery serpents," cf. KJV; their bite caused the burning sensation of a serious infection). Many kinds of snakes whose bite is dangerous to man and beast are still found in the Sinai peninsula and in the desert south of Palestine. The author considers them to be so well-known that he simply refers to them as *"the venomous snakes."* Among the venomous snakes is also the "flying serpent" of Isaiah 14:29; 30:6 (NIV: "darting serpent"), a tree serpent that is still found in Arabia and Egypt, and which in the popular imagination has become some kind of dragon. The Assyrian king Essarhaddon (681–668 B.C.) also speaks of such serpents in the report of his march through the Syrian desert on his way to Egypt: "double-headed serpents . . . I trampled them." And in a report on his campaign against the Arabian Bazu tribe (Buz, Gen. 22:21) he speaks of a region full of snakes and scorpions that "cover the ground like ants." The suffering of the many dying Israelites, whose misery is intensified by burning thirst, causes the people to repent. Again they say, "we have sinned" (see 14:40; cf. 12:11) and ask for Moses' intercession. And again the plague is lifted, but this time only for those who prove in deed that they trust the Lord's faithfulness. The Lord promises that anyone who "looks" (vv. 8–9; two different verbs are used), i.e., anyone who directs his attention in hopeful expectation, will live. Moses must make a bronze snake, a replica of the "venomous

186

snakes'' that caused many Israelites to die (v. 6). He must put this bronze snake, which symbolizes the Lord's victory (cf. Exod. 17:15) on a pole, which is the signal to rally around the Victor (Isa. 5:26; 11:10, 12). Thus, the animal that brought destruction now speaks of life graciously given back.

The serpent played a prominent role in the thinking of the ancient Near Eastern world (B. Rentz, *Der Orientalische Schlangendrache,* 1930). On the one hand it was feared as the monster from the nether world that guards its gates, on the other hand it was worshiped as representing life. The latter is expressed in an ancient Babylonian text: ''If a serpent falls on a sick person, who has been ill for many days, the sick person will live long.'' On a vase of Gudea of Lagash (ca. 2600 B.C.) we find a staff in the form of a serpent, flanked by two demons; this staff was dedicated by Gudea to the prolongation of his life (Gressmann, *Altorientalische Bilder zum Alten Testament,* 2nd ed., p. 106, ill. 367). In Beit Mirsim in southern Canaan (probably Kiriat-Sefer; see M. G. Kyle, *Excavating Kirjath-Sefer's Ten Cities,* 1934) Albright discovered a bas relief depicting a snake goddess whose upper torso unfortunately has been destroyed, but around whose feet snakes are coiled. Similar representations of the snake goddess, worshiped in Babylonia under the name Shachan, have also been found in Beth Shemesh and in a cave near Atlit. The city of Beth Shean appears to have been a center of snake worship (see e.g., J. Simons, *Opgravingen in Palestina,* 1935, pp. 370ff.).

In this section the snake is on the one hand the carrier of evil that kills many, on the other hand it represents life. But this duality is very different from that generally found in the ancient Near East: the life-giving aspect of the serpent is not inherent in the animal itself. The snake on the pole can give life only because of the Lord's gracious will, and its curative effect is experienced only by those who see in this snake the symbol of the Lord's grace that forgives and delivers from death. Only thus could the snake point forward to the coming Christ (John 3:14–15; 1 Cor. 10:9).

This bronze snake played a large role in Israel's religious life until the days of Hezekiah (2 Kings 18:4). Israel fell back into the ancient Near Eastern way of thinking and worshiped the bronze snake as the bearer of life, and thus as worthy of divine honor. Israel did with the snake as Gideon did with the ephod (Judg. 8:27): they came to see the carrier of power as autonomous and made it into a god. (Concerning snake charming, see Jer. 8:17.)

The Journey to Moab; Sihon and Og Defeated
(21:10–22:1)

1. *The Journey to Moab* (21:10–20)

21:10–13 *The Israelites moved on and camped at Oboth. Then they set out from Oboth and camped in Iye Abarim, in the desert that faces Moab toward the sunrise. From there they moved on and camped in the Zered Valley. They set out from there and camped alongside the Arnon, which is in the desert extending into Amorite territory. The Arnon is the border of Moab, between Moab and the Amorites.*

The Israelites are now east of the Araba (see commentary on 20:14) and continue their journey in a northerly direction along the eastern border of Moab's territory (Deut. 2:19; Judg. 11:18). They cross the upper reaches of the Arnon and then go toward Mount Pisgah in the Abarim range. Peor (23:28), Nebo (Deut. 34:1ff.), and Pisgah are the best-known peaks in this range, which rises up east of the northern tip of the Dead Sea. Chapter 21 lists the following campsites after the departure from Mount Hor: Oboth, Iye Abarim, the Zered Valley, Arnon, Beer, Bamoth, "the valley in Moab where the top of Pisgah overlooks the wasteland." The list in Numbers 33:41ff. is somewhat different: Zalmonah, Punon, Oboth, Iye Abarim, Dibon Gad, Almon Diblathaim, and the mountains of Abarim. In Deuteronomy 2:8, 13 we find Elath, Ezion Geber, the Desert of Moab, the Zered Valley. Perhaps we must explain these differences by assuming that Israel traveled north in two groups (Heinisch, *Numeri*, p. 83). It is in any case clear that Israel's journey along the western border of Edom took it to the northern tip of the Gulf of Elat, where the well-known port Ezion Geber was located (1 Kings 9:26; 22:49). It is largely impossible to identify these campsites. Thus, Zered is identified with the Wadi es-Sultani by some, with the Wadi el-Rasa-sared by others, or also with the Wadi el-Kerak; this el-Kerak is probably the site of the ancient Kir Moab (Kir Hareseth, 2 Kings 3:25; Isa. 16:7, 11; Jer. 48:31). The Arnon ("Swift") is now called the Wadi el-Modshib. It rushes down the mountains on the eastern shore of the Dead Sea with many waterfalls. Since Deuteronomy 2:19 and Judges 11:18 specifically state that Israel traveled along the eastern border of Moab, we must think here of the upper reaches of the Arnon. The river has cut a deep valley in the plateau, thus forming a natural border between first the Moabites and Amorites, and later between the Moabites and the Israelites (cf. Judg. 11:22; Isa. 16:2; Jer. 48:20). Mention of the Arnon provides the author with an opportunity to quote from *The Book of the Wars of the Lord,* apparently an ancient collection of stories and poems dealing with Israel's struggle for the possession of Canaan (cf. 1 Sam.

18:17; 25:28). This is the only reference to this book; according to some (e.g., P. Heinisch, p. 83) it may be the same as *The Book of Jashar* (or *The Book of the Upright;* Josh. 10:13; 2 Sam. 1:18), but this assumption is in my opinion unfounded.

21:14–15 *That is why the Book of the Wars of the LORD says:*
". . . Waheb in Suphah and the ravines,
  the Arnon and the slopes of the ravines
that lead to the site of Ar
  and lie along the border of Moab."

The quotation begins with an accusative case and lacks a verb. Those who believe this to be a song celebrating the conquest of the places mentioned here (in my opinion correctly so) add "we captured." The location of Waheb and Suphah is unknown. Ar ("city") is most likely Moab's ancient capital (see Deut. 2:9, 18, 29), which is also called Ar Moab ("Ar of Moab," 21:28; Isa. 15:1). It is usually thought to have been located on the middle reaches of the Arnon; for some time it was incorrectly identified with Rabbat Ammon, which is located much farther south on the road from Diban to el-Kerak (because of this incorrect identification it was called Areopolis; the name has been changed again to Rabba).

The Amarna letters (two hundred letters from Palestinian city-kings to Amenhotep III and IV of Egypt; first half of the fourteenth century B.C.) do not mention a Moabite state. This has led Edelkoort (*Numeri,* pp. 166–67; *Uittocht en Intocht,* 1924, p. 97) to assume that it no longer existed at that time and that its "restoration was due to a joint [!] march of Israel and Moab from the desert." This view has at least two problems: (1) the Amarna letters deal exclusively with the region west of the Jordan, and primarily with the coastal region to which Egypt's power was largely limited; and (2) this view presents as historical fact something that squarely contradicts the testimony of the Old Testament, which never mentions such a joint action of Moab and Israel.

21:16–18 *From there they continued on to Beer, the well where the LORD said to Moses, "Gather the people together and I will give them water."*
  Then Israel sang this song:
    "Spring up, O well!
      Sing about it,
    about the well that the princes dug,
      that the nobles of the people sank—
      the nobles with scepters and staffs."
  Then they went from the desert to Mattanah.

From the Arnon Israel travels north to Beer, which is frequently identified with the Beer Elim of Isaiah 15:8; some place it in the Wadi et-Themed, others in el-Mdejjene. Beer means "well"; wells were usually made of masonry and covered with flat rocks, which were then covered with dirt to keep strangers from using the well. The author then leads into a second quotation by reporting a command of the Lord to Moses: "Gather the people together and I will give them water." It is not possible to determine whether a complaint similar to those of Exodus 17:2 and Numbers 20:2 preceded this giving of water. The song that follows clearly reflects the joy over the discovering or uncovering of such a well. To the Bedouins water is a gift from God, which is why they like to sing while drawing water (E. Littmann, *Neuarabische Volkspoesie,* 1902, pp. 81, 92, 154). Wellhausen believed that this song referred to the taking of a city rather than to the digging of a well; but Budde made a good case for the possibility that the princes and nobles lifted the cover of the rediscovered well with their "scepters and staffs," the symbols of their dignity (*Preussische Jahrbücher,* 1895, pp. 491ff.). It is also possible that the interpretatation should be based on the fact that in the desert water often lies close to the surface and can be discovered with relative ease by an expert, after which the sand is removed with a stick (J. A. Montgomery, *Arabia and the Bible,* 1934, p. 8, n. 14). The Hebrew manuscripts separate the last line from the rest of the song, since it was felt that the words *umimmidbar mattana* refer to two campsites, the desert and Mattanah (so English versions). But this is not possible, since in verse 16 Israel is in Beer (the LXX reads *beer* not *midbar* for this reason); so I translate the last line of verse 18, "a gift from the wilderness." Jewish exegetes believe that this is again a reference to the water from the rock (Exod. 17 and Num. 20:7–13) that, according to the Haggadah, followed Israel (see commentary on 20:13).

21:19–20 *From Mattanah to Nahaliel, from Nahaliel to Bamoth, and from Bamoth to the valley in Moab where the top of Pisgah overlooks the wasteland.*

Bamoth is probably the same as Bamoth Baal, according to Joshua 13:17 located between Dibon and Beth Baal Meon; some identify it with the Beth Bamoth to which the Mesha inscription refers (line 27). It is usually thought to be located near Mount Attarus, just north of the Arnon and close to the Dead Sea. *Hagaj* can mean "valley" (thus NIV), but here it apparently is the name of a peak of the Pisgah mountains (see above). The wilderness above which it rises is probably the Ghor-el-belqa, the wild region along the northeastern shore of the Dead Sea. Israel has now come close to the Jordan and can actually see Canaan.

2. *The Victory Over Sihon* (21:21–31)

21:21–26 *Israel sent messengers to say to Sihon king of the Amorites:*

"Let us pass through your country. We will not turn aside into any field or vineyard, or drink water from any well. We will travel along the king's highway until we have passed through your territory."

But Sihon would not let Israel pass through his territory. He mustered his entire army and marched out into the desert against Israel. When he reached Jahaz, he fought with Israel. Israel, however, put him to the sword and took over his land from the Arnon to the Jabbok, but only as far as the Ammonites, because their border was fortified. Israel captured all the cities of the Amorites and occupied them, including Heshbon and all its surrounding settlements. Heshbon was the city of Sihon king of the Amorites, who had fought against the former king of Moab and had taken from him all his land as far as the Arnon.

These verses take us back to before verses 16–20, since the southern border of Sihon's territory lies near the Arnon, rather than close to Mount Pisgah. Sihon's small state, situated between the Arnon and the Jabbok, was one of the last remnants of the large territory once controlled by the Amorites. Edward Meyer even believed that the realm of the Amorites included not only Egypt and Syro-Palestine, but also the Euphrates-Tigris Valley and even the Aegean islands (see my *Gods Woord,* pp. 257ff.). The Amorites were gradually robbed of their power, on the one hand by the peoples we collectively call the Hittites, on the other hand by the revival of Egypt, which under the pharaohs of the Eighteenth Dynasty increasingly concerned itself with the Syro-Palestinian region. The Amorites were, however, able to maintain their own dynasty for some time east of the Jordan; under Sihon[1] they not only succeeded in subduing the Ammonites, but also in driving the Moabites, who had occupied the land between Arnon and Jabbok (see v. 26; Judg. 11:23–24; my *Gods Woord,* p. 363), back south beyond the Arnon. We can no longer determine when this happened. In any case, Sihon feels that he is strong enough to refuse Moses' request to allow Israel to pass through his country (see also Deut. 2:26). The wording of the request is similar to that made to Edom (20:17); the response is also very similar. But this time Israel does not "turn away" (20:21), and a battle ensues at Jahaz (cf. Isa. 15:4; Jer. 48:34; and the Moabite Stone, lines 19–20). The Onomasticon, a list of Palestinian place

---

[1]The bas-relief of Shichan (south of Diban and east of the Dead Sea), presently in the Louvre, which dates according to R. Dussaud from the time of Rameses II, depicts such an Amorite ruler in Hittite-Egyptian style; this clearly indicates a Hittite culture in the Transjordan region and also proves that at that time the Amorites were in control south of the Arnon. See e.g., Kittel, *Geschichte des Volkes Israel,* I, 1916, p. 573, n. 2.

names drawn up by Eusebius of Caesarea (d. 339) and translated by Jerome (d. 419/420), places Jahaz between Medeba and Dibon, i.e., just north of the Arnon; Jahaz later belonged to the territory of Reuben. Sihon is utterly defeated and his small state collapses. Later Reuben and Gad will occupy the land between the Arnon and the Jabbok (ch. 32). "As far as the Ammonites" (v. 24) defines the eastern border of the territory occupied by Israel. Jazer[2] was located here, still in Amorite territory according to verse 32; the Onomasticon places Jazer between Sihon's capital Heshbon (now Hesban, fifteen miles east of the northern end of the Dead Sea) and Rabbat-Ammon (now Amman, fourteen miles northeast of Heshbon). Jazer is usually identified with the present Khirbet-Sar in the Wadi es-Sir west of Rabbat-Ammon; but there may be more reason to identify it with el-Jadude south of Rabbat-Ammon (see F. Schulz, *Palästinajahrbuch 1932*, pp. 18-80). We do not know why Jazer did not fall together with "all the cities" (v. 25); the list of cities, which may have been the same as that in 32:34-36, has been omitted here. Deuteronomy 2:34 states that they were completely destroyed, "men, women and children"; but "the livestock and the plunder from the town we had captured we carried off for ourselves," even though this is contrary to the nature of the "ban," the irrevocably giving over to the Lord (cf. Josh. 6:18-19, 25; 7:1, 11; 1 Sam. 15:3, 9).

21:27-31 *That is why the poets say:*
"Come to Hesbon and let it be rebuilt;
let Sihon's city be restored.

"Fire went out from Heshbon,
a blaze from the city of Sihon.
It consumed Ar of Moab,
the citizens of Arnon's heights.
Woe to you, O Moab!
You are destroyed, O people of Chemosh!
He has given up his sons as fugitives
and his daughters as captives
to Sihon king of the Amorites.
"But we have overthrown them;
Heshbon is destroyed all the way to Dibon.
We have demolished them as far as Nophah,
which extends to Medeba."

So Israel settled in the land of the Amorites.

---

[2]Noordtzij adopts the LXX reading *Jazer* instead of the MT reading *'az* ("strong") in verse 24; the end of verse 24 then reads, "because Jazer was the border of the Ammonites." (tr.)

Verse 26 pointed out that the territory Israel took from Sihon belonged originally to Moab (see above), which leads into the quotation of a song of rejoicing. This song is undoubtedly also the basis for Jeremiah 48:45–47. Several exegetes have followed H. Ewald and have taken this to be a satire on the Amorites (thus e.g., Keil and Heinisch), but this interpretation requires quite a few textual emendations. Furthermore, verse 29 clearly states that it is Moab that is mocked here, and "Sihon's city" (v. 27) is in juxtaposition to "the cities of Moab"[3] (v. 28b). Meyer and Stade see this as a song of rejoicing over Omri's victory over Moab, of which the Moabite Stone speaks. But they can maintain this interpretation only by eliminating verse 29c, where Sihon is said to be the victor. We undoubtedly have here a song of victory, sung by the Amorites on the occasion of Moab's defeat. The purpose of the quotation is clear: it wants to put in perspective the magnitude of Israel's victory over Sihon. The man who defeated Moab is destroyed in one blow (see also W. Rudolph, "Zum Text des Buches Numeri," ZAW, 1934, pp. 113–20). It is unfortunate that the text has been transmitted poorly, so that we are frequently forced into conjecture.

The song begins with an exhortation by the Amorite singer to his fellow countrymen to come to Heshbon and to help build the walls of the city that is now "Sihon's city" (cf. "David's city," 2 Sam. 5:7). The city is in need of work, but not because it has been destroyed, as is usually assumed. If this were the case, verse 28a would have to read "fire went *up* from Heshbon" (cf. Josh. 8:20). But Judges 9:15, 20; Ezekiel 19:14 (see also Lev. 10:2; Num. 16:35) show that Heshbon must have been the source of the fire, as verse 28b implies. Heshbon, as Sihon's royal city, now rules over a large territory and its buildings must therefore reflect its important status. It has acquired this new status because "it consumed Ar of Moab, the citizens [or, lords] of Arnon's heights."[4] These "heights" are probably the sanctuaries of Chemosh. As the Philistines were later to destroy Shilo to demonstrate the superiority of Dagon over Israel's God, so also do the Amorites destroy the places of worship of the god of Moab. Hence the poet's "Woe!" addressed to Moab, which is here purposely called "people of Chemosh" (cf. also Jer. 48:46), in order to show that the god perishes with his people, since no one is left to worship him. "He" in verse 29 cannot refer to Chemosh; if Sihon's victory were the result of Chemosh's anger against his people, the importance of the victory of the Amorites would be negated. However, "his" ("his sons . . . his

---

[3]Noordtzij reads *'are,* "cities," instead of *'ar;* no reason for this emendation is given. (tr.)

[4]Noordtzij emends the text to read "consumed the cities of Moab and devoured Arnon's heights" (*bl'h* instead of *bl'j,* cf. LXX) (tr.)

daughters'') does refer to Chemosh. This use of ''sons'' and ''daughters'' for the Moabites is in line with the thinking of the ancient Near East that is also found in the Old Testament (Deut. 14:1; 32:5; Isa. 1:2; 30:1, 9; Jer. 3:14; also Hos. 11:1; Ps. 80:16). Hence also names like Abibaal (''My father is Baal'') and Abihu (''My father is Jahweh'').

Verses 29b and 30 indicate how complete Sihon's victory was: the young men fled, the young women were made captives, i.e., slaves, or at best concubines.

The text of verse 30 is badly mutilated, so that we are limited to conjecture. My own translation is therefore subjective: ''Their offspring perished, from Heshbon to Dibon, their women as far as Nophah, and their men as far as Medeba.'' If I understand verse 30 correctly, it speaks of the complete destruction of Moab throughout the territory they had occupied, since Heshbon lies east of the northern end of the Dead Sea, while Dibon lies just north of the Arnon. Mesha occupied Dibon and made it his capital (Moabite Stone, lines 19–20). Medeba (now Madeba) lies halfway between Heshbon and Dibon. Nophah is not mentioned elsewhere and its location is unknown.

This victory over Sihon is mentioned a number of times in the Old Testament (Num. 32:33; Deut. 1:4; 2:24–36; 3:2, 6; 4:46; 29:7; 31:4; Josh. 2:10; 9:10; 12:2; Judg. 11:19; Pss. 135:11; 136:19), which is understandable. It was Israel's first victory over an organized state. As such it contained an unmistakable promise for the coming conquest of Canaan. The door is now open. The suggestion that Israel would have gained this victory in cooperation with Moab (Edelkoort) is in direct contradiction to the facts.

3. *The Victory Over Og* (21:32–22:1)

21:32–35 *After Moses had sent spies to Jazer, the Israelites captured its surrounding settlements and drove out the Amorites who were there. Then they turned and went up along the road toward Bashan, and Og king of Bashan and his whole army marched out to meet them in battle at Edrei.*

The LORD said to Moses, "Do not be afraid of him, for I have handed him over to you, with his whole army and his land. Do to him what you did to Sihon king of the Amorites, who reigned in Heshbon."

So they struck him down, together with his sons and his whole army, leaving them no survivors. And they took possession of his land.

The destruction of Sihon opened up the northern part of the Transjordan region to Israel. First, Israel travels east toward Jazer (see commentary on v. 24), which is captured. This brings it close to the Jabbok, across which lies the land of Og of Bashan, which, like Sihon's domain, was a sad remnant of the territory once controlled by the Amorites.

The Old Testament does not provide an exact definition of Bashan's territory. In the narrower sense Bashan is bounded by the Yarmuk to the south, the Hermon to the north, the Sea of Gennesaret to the west, and the Hauran to the east. But according to Deuteronomy 3:12–13 the area between the Jabbok and the Yarmuk can also be considered part of Bashan. Salecah (the present Salchad, south of the Hauran mountains) marks the eastern border (Deut. 3:10; Josh. 13:11; cf. 1 Chron. 5:11). Bashan thus covered primarily the region now known as en-Nukra, "the hollow hearth," an exceptionally fertile area.

Given these data it is of course very difficult, even impossible, to determine the exact extent of Og's territory; it is usually thought to have been the region between the Jabbok and the Hermon. In any case, the center of his power was located in Bashan proper between the Yarmuk and the Hermon, since his capital, Ashtaroth, which is called the city of Og in Joshua 9:10, was located north of the Yarmuk (unless it is to be identified with Tell Ashtara or el-Muserib). According to Joshua 12:4; 13:11, 13 Og's territory was separated from the Jordan valley by Geshur and Maacah. I conclude from the fact that Moses needs encouragement before the battle at Edrei (v. 34) that Og's power was considerably greater than that of Sihon.

As soon as Israel moves in the direction of Bashan they encounter Og, who engages them in battle at Edrei. This is undoubtedly the present Der'a, under which a veritable labyrinth of subterranean dwellings has been found. Encouraged by the Lord, Moses utterly defeats Og and treats him as he treated Sihon and his territory. Deuteronomy 3:11 further illustrates the magnitude of this victory by stating that Og belonged to the Rephaites (incorrectly rendered "giants" in the KJV), who at one time controlled the entire Transjordan region together with the Emites (the territory later held by Moab; Deut. 2:11) and the Zamzummites (the later territory of Ammon; Deut. 2:20); concerning these tribes, see J. H. Kroeze, *Genesis XIV*, 1937, pp. 51ff.

Numbers 21:33–35 is found almost verbatim in Deuteronomy 3:1–3. The command, "do to him what you did to Sihon" (v. 34b and Deut. 3:2b) makes sense only in the context of Deuteronomy 3, since there it refers back to 2:34–35 where Sihon's people and his cities are utterly destroyed; Numbers 21:24 does not mention this. The only possible conclusion is that Numbers 21:33–35 has been taken from Deuteronomy 3:1–3 and added here in order to present a complete picture of the events that took place in the Transjordan region, especially since Sihon and Og are always mentioned in the same breath (Num. 32:33; Deut. 1:4; 4:46f.; 29:7; 31:4; Josh.

2:10; 9:10; 12:2, 4; 13:10, 12, 21, 30; 1 Kings 4:19; Neh. 9:22). Edel-koort, Eduard Meyer, Steuernagel, Sellin, and others have proposed that after the destruction of Sihon Israel's army was divided into two contingents; one remained north of the Dead Sea and went from there across the Jordan to attack Jericho and then to Shechem via Michmash and Ai, while the other did battle with Og and thus reached the Hermon. The majority of the northern army then made the crossing to the plains of Jezreel, while the rest (especially Reuben) preferred to stay in the newly occupied territory. This view is based on the reasoning that *if* all of Israel (but is this what vv. 33–35 say?) went so far north that it found itself north of the Yarmuk, it is difficult to understand why it would then retrace its steps in order to force a crossing of the Jordan at Jericho. I disagree with this view because it squarely contradicts the picture presented in Joshua, which knows only of Israel acting as a unified whole under Joshua's leadership, and because it also disagrees with the unanimous Old Testament tradition, which speaks only of one conquest (de Groot appropriately labels the above view "an abstract product of the study"; *Jozua,* 1931; pp. 14f.).

22:1 *Then the Israelites traveled to the plains of Moab and camped along the Jordan across from Jericho.*

This verse takes us back to the same location as 21:20, and is a transition to the Balaam story (22:2–24:25). Balaam's encounter with Israel takes place "in the fields of Moab," where Israel camped near the northern slope of the mountains; the name "fields of Moab" is retained because Moab ruled this region before Sihon. The location is further described as being "across the Jordan-of-Jericho"; the same expression is also found in 26:3, 63; 31:12; 33:48, 50; 35:1; Joshua 13:32; 16:1. Some feel that since this refers to the region east of the river Jordan, the author must have lived west of the Jordan, as other statements in the Pentateuch also indicate (e.g., Gen. 50:1–11; Num. 32:32; 34:15; 35:14; Deut. 1:1, 5; 3:8; 4:46; but see also Num. 32:19; Deut. 3:20, 25; 11:30).

Balaam's Encounter With Israel
(22:2–24:25)

The story of Balaam occupies a unique position among the historical sections of the Old Testament. While elsewhere in the Old Testament events in Israel's history are recorded in which Israel always plays an active role, here an event is recorded which, of course, involves Israel (otherwise it would not have been reported), but in which Israel not only plays an inactive role, it is not even directly involved.

The purpose of Balak's meeting with Balaam is to turn Israel's initial success around by overwhelming Israel with Balaam's curse and by thus breaking the flow of the Lord's blessing that is active in Israel. Israel is here therefore passive rather than active. We are not told how Israel learned of the conversations between these two men and about Balaam's oracles.

Verses 2–3a (not only v. 2, as is usually assumed) connect the Balaam story with the report of Israel's victory over Sihon (21:21–31), not with the report of Israel's battle with Og (21:32–22:1), which immediately precedes it. This is proven by the fact that only the Amorites are mentioned here; Og is never called an Amorite in 21:33–35, but Sihon is (21:21, 26, 34). This indicates once again that 21:33–35 is a later addition (see above). Verses 2–3a, therefore, take us back to before the battle with Og, which must of course have taken quite some time. It is therefore irrelevant to calculate whether someone coming from the Euphrates could have arrived in time, or whether Balak's messengers used fast camels that (as e.g., Heinisch claims; p. 86) could make the journey in less than a week, so that all the traveling back and forth would have taken only forty days. The situation is thus that, while a larger or smaller contingent of Israel's army was busy taking care of Og, Israel's camp remained in the same place where it was before the battle with Sihon: in the valley in Moab (21:20). At that point Balak could not yet know whether, and to what extent, his kingdom is endangered by the invading Israelites. He only knows that they are engaged in battle with his former opponent Sihon, and that in this battle military success is on their side. Balak's fear is aroused precisely by the fact that this people appears to be stronger than Sihon, and thus *a fortiori* stronger than Moab. He therefore takes timely measures in cooperation with his Midianite neighbors, who also feel threatened (22:4, 7). The latter, however, adopt a neutral stance as soon as it becomes apparent that they are not in danger.

Verses 2–3a, since they are connecting verses, only give the name of the man who was the instigator of the events that follow: Balak, the son of Zippor, whose relationship with Moab is briefly indicated, but whose position is not further specified. The author who established the connection between Israel's battle with Sihon and Balak's attempt to safeguard Moab did not consider it necessary to provide this detail, since it is given in the opening verses of the Balaam section itself (v. 4c).

Balak's name (which has also been found on an Egyptian-Aramean papyrus) means "he [the deity] has destroyed," a statement of what the father expected from his son: destruction of the enemy (Sihon?). Zippor is the masculine form of the name of Moses' wife, Zipporah ("a small song bird").

197

Attempts have been made to make Balak a king of Edom, based on the consideration that a king of Moab would have been delighted with Sihon's demise. This would mean that throughout the story "Edom" has been consistently changed to "Moab." But this view appears to assume that it is peculiar to our own time that a war tends to expand, while in "the good old days" national frontiers were never endangered. I feel that we cannot give any more credence to this view than to the many other conjectures proposed by the same school of thought, such as, the idea that Balak is simply the name of the region in which this story is set, which is called Belka by the Arabs (thus S. Mohwinkel, "Der Ursprung der Bileamsage." ZAW, 1930, pp. 233–71).

1. *Balak Summons Balaam Twice* (22:2–21)

22:2–6 *Now Balak son of Zippor saw all that Israel had done to the Amorites, and Moab was terrified because there were so many people. Indeed, Moab was filled with dread because of the Israelites.*

The Moabites said to the elders of Midian, "This horde is going to lick up everything around us, as an ox licks up the grass of the field."

So Balak son of Zippor, who was king of Moab at that time, sent messengers to summon Balaam son of Beor, who was at Pethor, near the River, in his native land. Balak said:

"A people has come out of Egypt; they cover the face of the land and have settled next to me. Now come and put a curse on these people, because they are too powerful for me. Perhaps then I will be able to defeat them and drive them out of the country. For I know that those you bless are blessed, and those you curse are cursed."

The story begins with a description of the fear that grips Moab when they sees how swiftly Israel destroys the man who had taken the whole area between the Arnon and the Jabbok from Moab. Moab, like Egypt (Exod. 1:12) some forty years earlier, is "filled with dread" because of Israel; they suffer from an anxiety psychosis. Being dependent primarily on livestock (2 Kings 3:4), they fear in the first place that Israel's herds will take over all available grassland. Of course, they could not know that Israel was to avoid any battle with Moab (Deut. 2:8). They speak of their fear to Midian (v. 4a), the seminomadic people in the southernmost part of the Transjordan region (cf. Gen. 36:35), who also possessed large herds (Judg. 6:5). They apparently expect their neighbors to the east to understand their fear, and they are not disappointed, as the joint delegation shows (v. 7). But the initiative remains with Moab, which feels threatened most directly, now that Israel is camped just north of its territory.

In the ancient Near East it was believed that an enemy could be combatted in two ways: with arms or by means of incantations, and if possible by means of a combination of the two. The incantations are based on the concept that a people and its deity constitute a unit; they seek to force, by means of various kinds of magic, the deity of the enemy to withhold his power from his people. Thus the enemy will be powerless and become an easy prey for the opponent. Moab does not dare use the first means, since Israel has already proven to be superior in military power to Sihon, whom Moab had been forced to acknowledge as their superior in the past. This leaves only the second means; they must find the kind of man who in the Euphrates-Tigris valley is called a *baru* (''seer''). The *baru* belongs to the priestly class, and his specialty is ''seeing'' what will happen on the basis of phenomena that escape the common person, but are found e.g., in the liver of a ritually slaughtered animal, or in the configuration of drops of oil on water, or in the stars, or in the shape of the clouds. Such *baru*s were believed to be able to influence the will of the gods because of their secret knowledge and mysterious manipulations, and to force the gods to do, or not to do, a given thing (see e.g., Jastrow, *Religious Belief in Babylonia and Assyria,* 1911, pp. 162ff.). Moab thus seeks a man (in Israel called a *qosem,* ''diviner,'' or *jid'oni,* ''one who knows'') capable of destroying the ''flow of blessing'' that is active in Israel with his ''curse.'' It seeks one of those men who is inspired by higher powers and who speaks the ''language of the gods,'' who makes this his profession and whose magically active pronouncements of curse or blessing are available to those who, in exchange for money or honor, ask for his assistance.

Balak believes to have found his man in Balaam, the son of Beor. An interesting Jewish interpretation of the name Balaam is ''destroyer of the people'' (*bala',* ''to destroy,'' *'am,* ''people''), based on Numbers 31:16; but we can credit this view as little as the idea, still in vogue, that the name Jordan means ''descending from Dan'' *(jored middan).* The former view is already found in the Targum Jonathan and is derived from the LXX, which renders the Hebrew *bil'am* ''Balaam.'' Because Balaam is supposed to mean ''devourer,'' some have wanted to identify him with the pre-Islamic prophet Lokman, mentioned in the Koran (Sura 31. 11), whose name has the same meaning. Others follow Nöldeke, who identified Balaam with Bela, son of Beor, king of Edom (Gen. 36:32), or see in Balaam an Edomite or an Edomite sage. In that case ''Aram'' (23:7a) must of course be changed to ''Edom.'' But that would also mean that 23:7b must be changed, since it states that Balaam came from ''the eastern mountains,'' while Edom lies south, rather than east of Moab. A third view sees in Balaam an Ammonite, which necessitates changing *'mw* (''his people'') in

22:5 to *'mwn* ("Ammon"); the "eastern mountains" are then the Hauran north of Moab.

Earlier exegetes saw in Balaam's statements, which imply that Jahweh was willing to communicate with him and even that Balaam considered Jahweh his own *'elohim* ("god"), a reflection of his personal conviction, and thus took these statements seriously (22:18; but see below); they therefore preferred to see in Balaam a Midianite, so that he could be considered a descendant of Abraham on the basis of Genesis 25:2; they claimed that in Balaam's circle the memory of Abraham's God had been kept alive, and that he and his people still served that God, albeit not exclusively. But this view is based strictly on fantasy (see also commentary on 22:3–9).

Balaam is said to have lived in "Pethor, near the River." Except in Isaiah 19:5, where it refers to the Nile, "the River," with or without the qualification "great," always refers to the Euphrates (Gen. 31:21; Exod. 23:31; Deut. 11:24; 2 Sam. 8:3; Isa. 8:7, 11:15; et al.). We are also familiar with a city called Pitru, mentioned by the Assyrian king Shalmaneser II in the report of his first campaign against Damascus (854 B.C.). He states that Pitru is the Hittite name of the city Ashur-uttir-asbat; the latter name may have been given to the city after Tiglath-Pileser I (ca. 1100 B.C.) had settled colonists in the city. The Egyptian pharaoh Thutmose III (ca. 1480 B.C.) also mentions it in his so-called Naharin-list (see W. M. Mueller, *Asien und Europa,* pp. 98, 267). This city was located just south of Carchemish along the great, centuries-old military road that connected Mesopotamia and the Syro-Palestinian countries. Strictly speaking, the city was not on the Euphrates, but on one of its tributaries, the present Sadshur, near their confluence. Many have—in my opinion correctly so—identified this Pitru as the home of Balaam (cf. W. F. Albright, "The Home of Balaam," *Journal of the American Oriental Society,* 1917, pp. 386–90); this also agrees with Deuteronomy 23:4, which states explicitly that Pethor was in Aram Naharaim (see also Num. 23:7), which stretched from the Orontes valley eastward to beyond the Euphrates. Pethor was thus some 600 km. (360 mi.) from Moab.

But others feel that Balaam must have lived much closer to Moab, on the basis of (a) verses 20–25, and (b) the time it would take to travel from Moab to the Euphrates and back (these arguments are valid only if it is assumed that 22:2 follows chronologically immediately after the defeat of Og of Bashan). They then identify Pethor with the Egyptian city Pitara on the Nile, this in spite of the fact that Balaam arrives "at the Moabite town on the Arnon border" (22:36), i.e., from the north. But it is clear that Isaiah 19:5, where the Nile is called "the river," does not provide sufficient support for this view. Others, therefore, who want to seek Balaam's home still closer to Moab, think of a city in Edom or in the territory of the Ammonites; the latter view necessitates changing (with the Samaritan Pentateuch, the Peshitta, and the Vulgate) "in his native land" to "in the land of the sons of Ammon" (see below). We are then faced with the curious fact that Israel would have given the name it gave to the Euphrates and the Nile, "the River," also to some entirely unknown wadi; this much resembles sifting the gnat and swallowing the camel—the "gnat" in this case being the expression "in the land of the sons of *'mw'*" (NIV: "In his native land"). This *'mw* was read as *'ammo* in very early times (thus the MT, the LXX, and the Targum Onkelos). This reading gives the meaning "in the land of the sons of his people" (cf. Gen. 23:11). However, this would be a rather meaningless addition on the part of the author. One thing is, in my opinion, certain: the author did not add "in the land of the sons of *'mw'*" to clarify to his readers which river is meant here; as stated above, "the River," with or without the modifier "great," always refers to the Euphrates (except in Isa. 19:5), and no geographical clarification is ever added. The words "in the land of the sons of *'mw'*" are thus added to describe the person of Balaam and to give his readers a better idea of what kind of man he is. I see therefore every reason to suggest another possibility, proposed by A. T. Sayce (*Higher Criticism,* 1894, p. 275). According to Sayce *'mw* should not be vocalized *'ammo* ("his people"), and certainly not changed to *'mwn* ("Ammon"), but should be read Amu or Ammu, which then refers to a god worshiped by the Arameans of the region in which Pethor was located. An Amorite god of that name, who was worshiped in the northern part of the Syrian desert, is indeed known (see *Reallexicon der Assyriologie,* I, 1929, pp. 98f.). It is possible that this name, Amu or Ammu, is also contained in names such as Amminadab, Ammiel, Ammihud, etc. It is entirely in keeping with ancient Near Eastern thinking to call a people "sons" of a god (cf. "people of Chemosh," Jer. 48:46; "Israel my . . . son," Exod. 4:22). The addition "in the land of the sons of Amu" thus characterizes Balaam as a worshiper of the god Amu, as someone far removed from the God of Israel.

I realize that this does not resolve all problems, but this solution seems to me to be more tenable than the assumption that the original text read "sons of Ammon." The latter expression occurs so frequently that it is incomprehensible that a copyist would not have recognized it immediately, but replaced it with "the sons of *'mw,*" even if he vocalized this to read *'ammo,* which would have resulted in an expression unique in the entire Old Testament: "sons of his people."

The messengers sent by Balak, according to verse 7 not only Moabites but also Midianites, are instructed to summon Balaam to curse a people that has "come out of Egypt" and that is a danger to them because they "cover the face of the land" (this cannot be Moab's territory because of the following "have settled next to me"); these people are too powerful to make it advisable for Balak to attack them with his army. The "curse" Balaam is asked to pronounce must therefore serve to render the people, not mentioned by name, powerless. The fact that Israel is not mentioned by name argues against the supposition, stated above, that Balaam was an Edomite or a Moabite. Both the Edomites and the Moabites had had sufficient contact with Israel to know its name; but there would be no sense in Balak's speaking of "Israel" to a man living near the Euphrates who had never heard of Israel.

What does Balak mean when he asks Balaam to "put a curse" on Israel? Two verbs are used in this story, *'arar* and *qabab*. The first delegation (v. 6) uses *'arar*, Balaam himself *qabab* (v. 11). The second delegation, however, uses *qabab* (v. 17), as does Balak in the rest of the story (23:11, 13, 25, 27; 24:10); Balaam himself uses both *'arar* (23:7; 24:9) and *qabab* (23:8). It is impossible to determine the exact distinction that may have existed between these two verbs. Both are, of course, connected with a series of mysterious manipulations, reinforced by the incantations that are pronounced in the required tone, whose purpose is to separate an individual, or group, or nation from its god. This will reduce its vitality and make it a victim of the sinister forces and demons that always lie in wait to assail man, that torture and finally destroy him when he lacks divine protection. "Curse" is thus the opposite of "bless" (*berek;* see commentary on 6:22–23), which involves increasing the soul's vitality, a renewal of the unfolding of life. "To curse" thus means to unleash destructive forces that will result in loss of strength (1 Sam. 17:43; 2 Sam. 16:5; Prov. 3:33).

Only thus can we understand Balak's hope ("perhaps," v. 6) that after a curse is put on Israel he will be able to defeat them with the sword and drive them away. "Perhaps" does not reflect doubt as to the disruptive power of any curse Balaam may pronounce (cf. v. 6b), but rather his uncertainty as to the ability of Israel's God to resist the curse (cf. also J. Hempel, "Die israelitischen Anschauungen von Segen und Fluch im Lichte altorientalischer Parallelen," *Zeitschrift der Deutschen Morgenländischen Gesellschaft,* 1925, pp. 20–110).

A. *The first delegation* (22:7–14)

22:7–14 *The elders of Moab and Midian left, taking with them the fee for divination. When they came to Balaam, they told him what Balak had said.*

"Spend the night here," Balaam said to them, "and I will bring you back the answer the LORD gives me." So the Moabite princes stayed with him.

God came to Balaam and asked, "Who are these men with you?"

Balaam said to God, "Balak son of Zippor, king of Moab, sent me this message: 'A people that has come out of Egypt covers the face of the land. Now come and put a curse on them for me. Perhaps then I will be able to fight them and drive them away.'"

But God said to Balaam, "Do not go with them. You must not put a curse on those people, because they are blessed."

The next morning Balaam got up and said to Balak's princes, "Go back to your own country, for the LORD has refused to let me go with you."

So the Moabite princes returned to Balak and said, "Balaam refused to come with us."

The elders (cf. v. 15) of Moab and Midian go to Pethor; they take, of course, the "fee for divination" with them, because priests, seers, and in general anyone who stands in a close relationship with the deity, must be paid in advance for their services (see also 1 Sam. 9:8; 1 Kings 13:7; 2 Kings 5:5–6; Amos 7:12; Mic. 3:5). Only after giving Balaam the fee do they convey Balak's words. If Balaam had said to them, I do not know the God of this people, I do not know His name, i.e., His essence, and have therefore no power over Him and cannot force Him to withdraw from Israel, then he would not have received the additional reward for a successful curse (22:37; 24:11). The messengers then would have turned to another *baru*. Balaam thus gives the impression that he has such a close relationship with Israel's God that he can speak with Him any time he wants to, by means of a dream at night, since the gods live in the darkness and speak at night (Gen. 20:3; 28:12).

In reading verses 8–13 carefully it strikes us that Balaam speaks of Jahweh (vv. 8, 13), while the author uses *'elohim* (vv. 9, 10, 12). Anyone enamored of the school of Wellhausen will see this as proof that two sources are combined here, the Jahwist and the Elohist. But in my opinion the solution lies in the thinking of the ancient Near East. Balaam must give the impression (see above) that he knows Jahweh, while the author wants to make it clear that he does *not*. Balaam says that he will speak with Jahweh (v. 8), and claims that Jahweh does not want him to go with the messengers (v. 13); he will continue to play this game (vv. 18–19; 23:3, 12; 24:13). But the author says that Balaam did not meet Jahweh, but *'elohim* (vv. 9–10, 12, 20). We assume that both are the same: Jahweh=*'elohim* and *'elohim*=Jahweh, and translate *'elohim* as "God" (capitalized). But this is not necessarily accurate. Israel was part of the ancient Near Eastern world, which spoke of all kinds of *ilani* (the Hebrew *'elohim*): forces of the invisible realm, both good and evil. But Israel has come to know the Lord (Jahweh) through His self-revelation. Jahweh ranges Himself among the large number of *'elohim* (in whose "assembly" He stands, Ps. 82:1, unequaled in the "council of the holy ones," Ps. 89:7) by revealing himself to Moses in the burning bush as the *'elohim* of his father and of the patriarchs (Exod. 3:6, 13, 15) and then as "Jahweh, the *'elohim* of the Hebrews" (Exod. 3:18), because He has adopted Israel as His people that He might be their *'elohim*. This is why He says at Sinai, "You shall have no other *'elohim* before me" (Exod. 20:3). Jahweh thus begins by being an *'elohim* insofar as Israel's understanding is concerned. Do other gods exist beside Him? This is neither stated nor denied—but Israel must not have any other gods than Jahweh. The further self-revelation of the Lord will inevitably clarify what Israel must think of the other *'elohim*. Only the progression of the divine revelation will show that *this 'elohim* is *the 'elohim* (Deut. 4:35; 1 Kings 18:37), and that apart from Him there is no *'elohim* (Isa. 45:5). The kingdom of heaven is like yeast, also with respect to the self-revelation of Jahweh (Matt. 13:33).

The meaning of verses 8–13 becomes clear when we keep all this in mind. Balaam gives the impression that he knows the God of Israel (whose name the elders of Moab and Midian have told him, and who to them and to Balaam is Israel's *'elohim* in the same sense that Chemosh is Moab's *'elohim* and Milkom is the *'elohim* of Ammon) so well that a dream like the one Jacob had at Bethel (Gen. 28:11–12) will enable him to establish contact with Him. But the sacred author indicates that Balaam does not meet Jahweh at all. It is *'elohim* (which is rendered "God" in the English versions, but which could with equal justification be rendered "god") who speaks to him. It is impossible to make this distinction entirely clear in a translation. I only caution the reader not to conclude that because verses 9, 10, 12 mention "God," this refers necessarily to Jahweh (the Lord). I sense an undertone of holy mockery when the author counters Balaam's pretense that he will get in touch with Jahweh, and has been in touch with Him, with the assurance that the one who spoke to Balaam was *not* Jahweh, but merely an *'elohim*. That *'elohim* refuses Balaam permission to go with the elders, because Israel is "blessed" (see commentary on 6:22–23) and this blessing must not be hindered, let alone be destroyed, by the opposing force of a curse.

But when the elders return to Balak with the message that Jahweh has forbidden Balaam to go with them (v. 13), they see in Balaam's response merely an excuse; they relay Balaam's response as a refusal on his part (v. 14). Balak agrees with their assessment and immediately makes a second attempt, this time with a larger and more prominent group of men

(v. 15), and with an explicit description of the riches that await Balaam *if* he puts a curse on Israel (v. 17). These verses provide a beautiful insight into the reputation of such *barus:* they are available for any task, as long as the price is right.

B. *The second delegation* (22:15–21)

22:15–21 *Then Balak sent other princes, more numerous and more distinguished than the first. They came to Balaam and said:*

"This is what Balak son of Zippor says: Do not let anything keep you from coming to me, because I will reward you handsomely and do whatever you say. Come and put a curse on these people for me."

But Balaam answered them, "Even if Balak gave me his palace filled with silver and gold, I could not do anything great or small to go beyond the command of the LORD my God. Now stay here tonight as the others did, and I will find out what else the LORD will tell me."

That night God came to Balaam and said, "Since these men have come to summon you, go with them, but do only what I tell you."

Balaam got up in the morning, saddled his donkey and went with the princes of Moab.

Balak's messengers return to Balaam, again, of course, with the "fee for divination," although this is not mentioned. But this time they let Balaam feel the importance of their sender's position; their message is introduced with an official formula: "This is what Balak son of Zippor says" (v. 16; KJV: "Thus saith Balak, the son of Zippor"; cf. "Thus saith the LORD"). And the message is sent by one who can richly reward Balaam and for whom no demand Balaam makes is impossible to grant (v. 17). What could possibly keep Balaam from coming? But Balaam does not let himself be caught that easily. Balak must not think that he, the well-known *baru,* can be bought with money; not even a palace filled with gold and silver would be enough, a claim that may contain an invitation to Balak to try it. And now Balaam boasts in his relationship with Jahweh, since he knows that this is precisely what motivates Balak to insist on Balaam's coming; Balak is powerless against Israel without a man who knows Jahweh well and who can therefore influence Him. Balaam impresses this fact on Balak by saying, "Jahweh my *'elohim,"* indicating the close relationship between himself and Jahweh, and, by implication, the value of a curse put on Israel by him in Jahweh's name (v. 18). Balaam himself is certainly willing to come. One night is enough for him to get in touch with Jahweh. But this time it is "what else the LORD will tell me" (v. 19), implying that Balaam now expects to have a conversation with Jahweh; he maintains the tone of his earlier statement, "Jahweh, my *'elohim."*

But once again the author shows us the emptiness of Balaam's pretension: not Jahweh, but an *'elohim* comes to him. And this *'elohim* gives him permission to go with "these men," albeit with the express condition, "do only what I tell you" (v. 20). We are not told how Balaam relayed this to Balak's messengers; he undoubtedly claimed again to have spoken with Jahweh. Only the result is given: Balaam goes to Balak (v. 21).

2. *The Angel of the Lord Meets Balaam* (22:22–35)

22:22–35 *But God was very angry when he went, and the angel of the Lord stood in the road to oppose him. Balaam was riding on his donkey, and his two servants were with him. When the donkey saw the angel of the Lord standing in the road with a drawn sword in his hand, she turned off the road into a field. Balaam beat her to get her back on the road.*

Then the angel of the Lord stood in a narrow path between two vineyards, with walls on both sides. When the donkey saw the angel of the Lord, she pressed close to the wall, crushing Balaam's foot against it. So he beat her again.

Then the angel of the Lord moved on ahead and stood in a narrow place where there was no room to turn, either to the right or to the left. When the donkey saw the angel of the Lord, she lay down under Balaam, and he was angry and beat her with his staff. Then the Lord opened the donkey's mouth, and she said to Balaam, "What have I done to you to make you beat me these three times?"

Balaam answered the donkey, "You have made a fool of me! If I had a sword in my hand, I would kill you right now."

The donkey said to Balaam, "Am I not your own donkey, which you have always ridden, to this day? Have I been in the habit of doing this to you?"

"No," he said.

Then the Lord opened Balaam's eyes, and he saw the angel of the Lord standing in the road with his sword drawn. So he bowed low and fell facedown.

The angel of the Lord asked him, "Why have you beaten your donkey these three times? I have come here to oppose you because your path is a reckless one before me. The donkey saw me and turned away from me these three times. If she had not turned away, I would certainly have killed you by now, but I would have spared her."

Balaam said to the angel of the Lord, "I have sinned. I did not realize you were standing in the road to oppose me. Now if you are displeased, I will go back."

The angel of the Lord said to Balaam, "Go with the men, but speak only what I tell you." So Balaam went with the princes of Balak.

These verses are often viewed as a record of Balaam's journey, and various conclusions are then drawn as to its duration. But this interpretation misses the point. A parallel is found in the account of Jacob's experience at Bethel (Gen. 28:11–22), which records a single event in Jacob's journey from Beersheba to Haran. Neither this segment of the Balaam story, nor the account of Jacob at Bethel, is intended to report an entire journey. Rather, even as the rest of Jacob's life cannot be understood apart from Bethel, so also Balaam's behavior cannot be understood apart from his encounter with the Angel of the Lord.

It has been claimed that verses 22–35 are not a continuation of what precedes them, because in verse 35b Balaam is still at the point where he was in verse 21. But I refer to Genesis 22:6b, 8b, where the phrase "the two of them went on together" is found twice, yet no one claims that in verse 8b Abraham and Isaac are still in the same place as in verse 6b. It is precisely the repetition of the words "Balaam went with the princes of Moab" that intensifies the description of Balaam's actions: he has joined his fate to that of the Moabite princes.

Another claim is that "Jahweh's anger" in verse 22a contradicts *'elohim's* permission of verse 20b. As has been made clear, this is a problem only if Jahweh and *'elohim* are believed to be the same, which is not the case. Similarly, the problem that Balaam's confession that he has sinned in going with the princes of Moab (v. 34) does not make sense after the permission given in verse 20b disappears when Jahweh and *'elohim* are distinguished. Another, older interpretation that has no basis in the narrative itself is that Jahweh is angry not because Balaam went to Balak, but because he did so for the sake of money (e.g., Keil).

We can only see a contradiction between the statement in verse 22b that Balaam went with his two servants and the fact that in verse 21b Balaam went with the princes of Moab if we assume that Moab's princes also traveled without servants.

In verses 22–35 man is no longer at the center, but the Lord and His Angel, i.e., Jahweh, the God of Israel and the Angel of Jahweh. The NIV follows the MT in verse 22: "And God ['*elohim*] was very angry." There would indeed be a contradiction between verses 20 and 22 if the reading *'elohim* were correct. But the Samaritan Pentateuch and several important MSS of the LXX read here correctly "the LORD [Jahweh] became very angry." It would be difficult to understand how an author whose narrative is dominated by the distinction between Jahweh and *'elohim*, could here suddenly lose sight of this distinction and thus create a contradiction that he cannot have intended. Two things are expressed in Jahweh's anger: (1) that Jahweh occupies a unique position among the *'elohim* and does not allow Himself to be brought under the influence of some *baru*, so that the latter may impose his will on Him, as he would with other *'elohim;* and (2) that He opposes any attempt to thwart His plan and purpose for Israel. Especially when Israel is about to enter Canaan it must be clear to all that she is inviolable and that Jahweh stands behind her. The appearance of the Angel

207

of the Lord is closely connected with Jahweh's anger. "The angel of the LORD" (called "the angel of God"—at least in the MT—in Gen. 21:17 and Judg. 13:9) is also mentioned in Genesis 16:7; 22:11, 15; Exodus 3:2; Judges 2:1; 6:11ff.; Zechariah 3:1ff. A careful reading of these references will show that this Angel of the Lord is so intimately connected with Jahweh Himself that He refers to the words and acts of Jahweh as His own (Judg. 2:1–3); thus, in Judges 6:11ff., the expression "the angel of the LORD" (vv. 11–12) goes over into "the LORD" (vv. 14, 16), as is also the case in Exodus 3:2ff. and in Zechariah 3:1ff. He is Israel's Protector (Exod. 14:19; 2 Kings 19:35), which is why He is called "the angel of the covenant" (or, "messenger of the covenant") in Malachi 3:1. Hence His resistance to Balaam's attempt to put a curse on Israel, and His appearance to Balaam (lit.) "as an enemy against him" (v. 22, cf. KJV; NIV: "to oppose him"). The word for "enemy" is *satan,* which later became a proper noun for *the* enemy and opponent of mankind (see my *Gods Woord,* pp. 152ff.). The Angel awaits Balaam, a drawn sword in his hand as a sign of his intention to destroy Balaam if he refuses (cf. Josh. 5:13; 1 Chron. 21:16). Balaam is traveling south, accompanied by two servants (cf. Abraham, Gen. 22:3); he rides on a donkey, the common mode of transportation (cf. Judg. 5:10; 2 Kings 4:22). We are not told where this encounter took place; "a field" (v. 23; Exod. 23:16 and Num. 20:17 indicate that this refers to land used for agriculture) and the "two vineyards" (v. 24) indicates that we are here not in the desert, but in a cultivated region, probably not far from their destination, i.e., in the Transjordan region. Another touch of sacred irony: the donkey sees the Angel of the Lord standing in the road, but the man who claims to know Jahweh so well that he can meet with Him whenever he wants (see above) does not see the Angel! To say that the donkey saw the Angel because animals have much stronger premonitions of various natural phenomena such as earthquakes and storms (e.g., Hengstenberg, Keil) is of course incorrect for the simple reason that this is not a "natural phenomenon." Such an explanation amounts to rational apologetics—but there is nothing to "apologize" for here! The world of the invisible God shows itself to whomever He wills. The donkey evades the Angel by leaving the road and going into the field (v. 25). But now the Angel awaits Balaam "in a narrow path between two vineyards." The word *miš'ol* may mean "hollow path," in this case a path between the stone walls that were built around vineyards (Prov. 24:30–31; Isa. 5:5). The donkey again tries to evade, this time by pressing close to the wall, so that Balaam's leg is painfully jammed between the wall and his donkey (v. 25). Only then does the inevitable happen: the Angel of the Lord takes up a position where there is no room for any evasive maneuver. When the donkey lies down, Balaam, who is not used to this kind of behavior from his donkey (v. 30c), becomes angry and beats the animal with his riding stick (v. 27). Only then does the Angel act, first by opening the donkey's mouth (v. 28), and then by opening Balaam's eyes (v. 31). The author uses two different verbs that are eminently suitable to describe what happened. In the case of the donkey the verb is *patach,* indicating the making of an opening so that something or someone can pass through it; but in Balaam's case it is *gilla,* the removal of something that covers and prevents that which is covered from fulfilling its natural function. The result is a double dialogue, one between the donkey and Balaam (vv. 28–30), the other between the Angel of the Lord and Balaam (vv. 31–35a).

The first of these two dialogues has especially been the focus of attention. In it the donkey reproaches Balaam for his treatment of her, and Balaam acknowledges that she has indeed never before behaved in this way, which implies that the reason for her behavior must be something very unusual. However, we know that a conversation between an animal and a human being is impossible, if only because animals are structurally different from human beings and have no developed vocal cords. The Scriptures' statement that such a discussion did indeed take place has elicited three basic responses. Most interpreters have simply declared the narrative to be legendary, and have pointed out that animals who observe apparitions and carry on conversations are also found in the popular belief of other nations. They point to the speaking horse of Achilles in Homer's *Iliad,* and to the talking ox of Livy, and the Egyptian story of "the two brothers," in which a cow tells her keeper that his brother is about to kill him (A. de Buck, *Egyptische verhalen,* 1928, pp. 128ff.). Others agree that this is not a historical event, but view it as the casting of a profound idea in a form that could be understood by the people of antiquity: he who deliberately resists God's command and follows his own will loses his spiritual discernment and becomes less than an animal (e.g., Edelkoort, *Numeri,* p. 174). But they lose sight of the fact that according to the author *'elohim* is not the same as Israel's God (see above); and even if my explanation of verses 7–20 is not accepted, there is no question of Balaam resisting God's command, because *'elohim* (who is then no other than Jahweh Himself) gave him permission to go with the princes of Moab. The Lord's anger and the resultant encounter with the Angel of the Lord are then only the result of the revocation of a permission granted earlier.

And finally, a third group of exegetes does not deny the historicity of the conversation between the donkey and Balaam. Some among this group feel that we are faced here with some internal, subjective experience on Balaam's part, who then merely heard the donkey talk while he was in a visionary or dream state (Maimonides, Hengstenberg, Strack). But it is clear that this introduces an element foreign to the text, and it also disregards the statement that "the LORD opened the donkey's mouth." Others, however, including Calvin, place full emphasis on the miracle recorded here, and even discuss the question whether the donkey's vocal cords were changed so that it could utter human sounds, this on the basis of 2 Peter 2:16, which states that the donkey "spoke with a man's voice."

In all this three things are certain. In the first place, all civilizations of antiquity and uncivilized peoples of today speak of talking animals. Second, the speaking of the donkey is explained as being the result of the opening of the animal's mouth by the Lord, and Balaam does not appear to be surprised. And third, the self-revelation of the Lord, when directed toward a specific individual, utilizes the means that by its very nature will make the deepest impression on that person and will initiate the change in him that will make him suited to the purpose the Lord intended to achieve with His self-revelation.

In this case, the purpose can have been no other than to give this man such a surpassing impression of Israel's God that he will surrender himself to His guidance and, setting aside his own goals (improving his reputation and finances), be willing to do what will be asked of him: to present Israel as a nation chosen by the Lord and thus richly blessed and consequently invincible, and to thwart Balak's plan to take away Israel's power by putting a curse on her and pushing her back into the desert.

We must not forget that the Lord's revelatory acts are not isolated, independent acts, but that they are interrelated and present a historical sequence because they are part of the execution of His divine plan and purpose, to which they are subservient. And at this point His plan is that Israel shall enter Canaan, radiating, so to speak, an aura of unfathomable strength and power, so that the resistance of the rulers of Canaan's cities will be broken before Israel reaches their territory, and they will be in the grip of the defeatism to which Rahab's words (Joshua 2) and the behavior of the Gibeonites (Joshua 9) witness. This requires the cooperation of a man like Balaam. In order to force him to cooperate, the Lord uses a means that is appropriate for Balaam and his way of thinking, but that also, because of its exceptional nature, reflects the working of a power that has thus far been unknown to him, a Power over which Balaam has no control whatsoever and that is able to impose its will on him.

The speaking of the donkey convinces Balaam that he is surrounded by as yet invisible powers who have forced his donkey into such uncharacteristic behavior, and himself into an admission of his wrong reaction. And now is the time for the Angel of the Lord to open Balaam's eyes to His presence, and to force Balaam to submit to His divine will and to do only that which the hitherto Unknown (in spite of his claims to the contrary —vv. 13, 19—Balaam has never yet encountered the Lord) will command him.

The conversation between the Angel of the Lord and Balaam (vv. 31–35) takes the donkey's first question as its starting point (v. 32a, cf. v. 28b). The Angel, who identifies Himself with the Lord, explains that it is He and not the donkey who is interrupting Balaam's journey, and that Balaam is not only the inferior of his donkey because she saw what he, the *baru,* did not see, but that his life has been saved by his donkey's reactions. The Angel has come to oppose him because Balaam's ''path'' is against the Lord; these words indicate not only that Balaam did indeed intend to make use of the permission granted by the *'elohim* (v. 20), in accordance with Balak's wishes, but also that the Lord's Angel protects Israel against any attack.

Only now does it appear what kind of impression the speaking of the donkey and the self-revelation of the Angel of the Lord have made on Balaam. He is deeply aware that this time a Power—he would say, one of the gods—from the realm of the invisible, with which he always attempted to make contact by virtue of his occupation, has appeared, against whose will he is powerless. And thus awakens in his soul the desire not to lend himself to Balak's plan, but to return as quickly as possible to Pethor. ''I have sinned'' (v. 34): the verb must not be understood in the sense of our word ''sin,'' but rather in the sense of Exodus 9:27, ''I am in the wrong,'' I have acted incorrectly, which is why it is followed by an expression of his willingness to return and to sever all ties with Balak. This implies, as the words ''if you are displeased'' indicate, a submission of Balaam's will to the will of the Angel of the Lord. But now that Balaam asks what the Angel wants him to do (cf. Acts 9:6 KJV), the time has come for the Angel to use the words spoken earlier by the *'elohim:* ''Go with the men, but speak only what I tell you'' (v. 35; cf. v. 20, ''go with them, but do only what I tell you''). Balaam may continue his journey, no longer by permission of the *'elohim,* but of Jahweh, the God of Israel, whom he has met here for the first time, and whose power he has experienced.

3. *Balaam Meets Balak* (22:36–40)

22:36–40 *When Balak heard that Balaam was coming, he went out to meet him at the Moabite town on the Arnon border, at the edge of his territory. Balak said to Balaam, ''Did I not send you an urgent summons? Why didn't you come to me? Am I really not able to reward you?''*

"Well, I have come to you now," Balaam replied. "But can I say just anything? I must speak only what God puts in my mouth."

Then Balaam went with Balak to Kiriath Huzoth. Balak sacrificed cattle and sheep, and gave some to Balaam and the princes who were with him.

These verses are not a continuation of verse 21, as the school of Wellhausen claims, but of verse 35. They describe Balak's reception of Balaam. As soon as Balak hears that Balaam is coming he travels to "the Moabite town" to meet Balaam. The location of *"Ar Moab"* is unknown, but it was probably situated on the middle reaches of the Arnon (see 21:14b). Balak goes out to meet Balaam, not to honor the powerful *baru,* whose curse he so urgently needs, but to accomplish his plan against Israel as quickly as possible. Israel is at this point camped north of the Arnon, near the Jordan (22:1).

The reception is cool. Balaam's apparent hesitation before coming is construed by Balak as an insult. Balak knows that any *baru* is available for money, and he sees in Balaam's hesitation the suspicion that he (the king of Moab!) would not be able to give Balaam an ample reward for his services (v. 37). I mention in passing that a number of adherents of the school of Wellhausen have concluded from verse 37 that Balak did not say these words to Balaam when the latter arrived in "the Moabite town," but in his house in Pethor, where Balak supposedly went when the second delegation was also unsuccessful. But this kind of conclusion can be reached only if verse 37 is taken out of its context. Apart from the fact that this is an inappropriate procedure, verse 37 states only that Balak and Balaam met, not where that meeting took place.

Balaam rejects Balak's reproach with the observation that his coming proves the opposite of Balak's suspicion. But he hastens to add that he is not at all sure what he will be able to do for Balak. Balak must not have any illusions: Balaam can say only that which the *'elohim* puts in his mouth—*'elohim,* the common Near Eastern term for the gods, which in the context should perhaps more appropriately be rendered "the deity" rather than "God" (see pp. 203–04). With this statement Balaam maintains his independence from Balak; the latter must not think that the fact of Balaam's coming will automatically mean that Israel will be cursed—it will depend on the diety. In other words, Balaam is not Balak's servant. If I read this correctly, Balaam's statement reflects the pride of the *baru,* which has been hurt by Balak's barely concealed accusation that Balaam is after a large sum of money. This pride is also shown in his attitude later on (23:1, 3, 15, 29). The king and the *baru* clash repeatedly; the latter knows that the king needs him, and the king is finally forced to abandon his initial reproachful attitude toward Balaam (22:37; 23:11) and to change from giving orders (23:25) to making a humble request (23:27).

Balaam's arrival is festively celebrated in Kiriath Huzoth (location unknown) where, in keeping with the ancient Near Eastern custom, a sacrificial meal is prepared in order to make sure that the deity will be favorably disposed toward what is to follow shortly. And according to ancient custom, which requires that honored guests are given special treatment (see also Gen. 43:34; 1 Sam. 9:23–24; Neh. 8:12), special portions are given to Balaam and "the princes who were with him." The latter is not entirely clear: are these the same princes of verses 21 and 35?

The suggestion that Balak would also have given Balaam the intestines of the slaughtered animals, and especially the liver, to determine whether the omens were favorable, seems to me to run ahead of the story (cf. Von Gall, *Zusammensetzung und Herkunft der Bileam-Perikope in Numeri 22–24*). Balaam has not yet reached that stage in the process.

This concludes the first half of the story (22:2–40), which speaks of Balak's attempts, initially unsuccessful, to move Balaam to put a curse on Israel, and of the intervention of the Angel of the Lord, who makes Balaam's going to Balak subservient to His own purpose. Now the second part (22:41–24:25) begins, which will tell of Balak's increasing failure to achieve what he desires with such intensity: the putting of a curse on Israel, which is turned into a blessing by the Lord's power.

4. Balak's First Attempt to Make Balaam Curse Israel (22:41–23:6)

22:41–23:6 *The next morning Balak took Balaam up to Bamoth Baal, and from there he saw part of the people.*

Balaam said, "Build me seven altars here, and prepare seven bulls and seven rams for me." Balak did as Balaam said, and the two of them offered a bull and a ram on each altar.

*Then Balaam said to Balak, "Stay here beside your offering while I go aside. Perhaps the L*ORD *will come to meet with me. Whatever he reveals to me I will tell you." Then he went off to a barren height.*

God met with him, and Balaam said, "I have prepared seven altars, and on each altar I have offered a bull and a ram."

*The L*ORD *put a message in Balaam's mouth and said, "Go back to Balak and give him this message."*

So he went back to him and found him standing beside his offering, with all the princes of Moab.

The next morning Balak takes Balaam farther north, toward Israel's camp. The MT reads "Bamoth Baal," which is usually identified with the

Bamoth of 21:19 and Joshua 13:17 and with the Bamoth of the Mesha stele (line 27). I prefer the reading, also adopted by the KJV, "the high places of Baal," i.e., one of the many sacred locations in Moab dedicated to Baal (cf. Isa. 15:2; 16:12; Jer. 48:35; Mesha stele, line 3). We are not told exactly where these "high places" were located. But from the fact that Balaam could see Israel's camp from there follows that it must have been in the Abarim range, and more specifically on one of the northern peaks that overlook the Jordan region. This is a characteristic choice for a polytheist, to whom all gods were comparable, and who always recognized his own gods in those of other nations. It never occurred to Balak that the Lord, Israel's God, had only one "holy place" where He caused His name to dwell (Deut. 12:11; 14:23; et al.). Balak chooses the spot deliberately so that Balaam can see "part of the people" (KJV "the utmost [part] of the people"; RSV "the nearest of the people"). Many, including the NIV, take the phrase to mean "only the extreme part of the people," i.e., only a small part of Israel (since Balaam might have been too impressed when he saw the people all at once), but 23:13 indicates that the intended meaning is "the whole people," i.e., "to the farthest end"; in other words, not the extreme edge of the camp closest to him, but rather that farthest away from him. This is also supported by 23:9. The assumption is, of course, that Balaam must see all the poeple; he must, so to speak, be able to pour his curse over all, whereby I again remind you of the fact that to the Oriental a word is not merely a series of sounds, but something charged with a certain power, a power determined on the one hand by the meaning of the words, and on the other hand by the power of the one who pronounces them. A sequence of words can be hurled through space as if it were matter, and attaches itself to the person to whom it is directed in order to achieve there its inherent effect.

From here on Balaam is in the foreground. "Cursing" is not the work of a king, but of a *baru,* who stands in a close relationship with, and knows exactly how to approach, the deity. Balaam treats Balak, therefore, as his subordinate and issues orders that are carried out promptly and to the letter.

Balaam orders Balak to build seven altars of earth and unhewn stones (cf. Exod. 20:24–25). The reason for the offerings is, on the one hand, to make the deity favorably disposed, on the other hand to obtain from the sacrificial animals themselves (especially from the liver and intestines) various mysterious indications, known only to the *baru,* which reveal the will of the deity. Balak must build seven altars, because to the Semite "seven" is the number of perfection and as such has magical powers (see J. Hehn, "Zur Bedeutung der Ziebenzahl," in Marti-Budde, *Vom Alten Testament,* 1925, pp. 131ff.). This is also why seven rams and seven bulls are offered; these are thus all male animals, which are not only more expensive, but also more efficacious. Israel's concept is similar (see my commentary on Lev. 1:3–9). As soon as the animals have been cut into pieces in the traditional manner and have been placed on the altars (cf. Lev. 1:6ff.), and, I surmise, it has been determined that the omens provided by these animals indicate that the deity is favorably disposed, Balaam instructs Balak to stand beside his offering. They are his offerings because he, as the king, is the one who has the right to bring offerings for his people, a right he usually transfers to his priests, he himself being the chief priest. Especially in this instance does he function as the one who brings the offerings, because they are for the sake of his people. He must therefore stand watch (cf. vv. 6, 15, 17), not only because this is what an offerer is supposed to do, but also to prevent any contamination of the offering (cf. Gen. 15:11). In the meantime, Balaam wants to retire in solitude because "perhaps the LORD [Jahweh] will come to meet with me" (v. 3). We find here a somewhat different expression than in Exodus 3:18; 5:3, which speak of a meeting between the Lord and Moses and Aaron; here the phrase indicates an approaching on the part of Jahweh. I suspect that this reflects Balaam's conviction that the gods are attracted by offerings (see my *Gods Woord,* p. 178). Of course, Balaam now refers to "Jahweh," because the curse is to be put on His people, and He is therefore involved. The offering must help channel His will in the direction Balak desires. Balaam goes to "a barren height," without water or grass (cf. Isa. 41:18; 49:9; Jer. 14:6). This is usually understood to mean that he went there to have an unimpeded view to observe various natural phenomena; but 24:1 indicates, in my opinion, a different purpose. I suspect, with Kuenen, that the original reading was *lkšfjw* rather than *šfj* ("barren place"; the word immediately preceding, *wjlk,* "and he went," ends in *lk,* which was then read only once instead of twice). If we accept this emendation, then Balaam "went to his sorceries" (cf. 24:1); the word collectively refers to various practices designed to influence the will of the deity (cf. Jezebel, 2 Kings 9:22, and Babylon, Isa. 47:9, 12). First, the *'elohim* meets with him, whom Balaam tells what he has done: seven altars have been built and two animals have been offered on each (v. 4). But before the *'elohim* can give Balaam further instructions as to what he must do next, the Lord (Jahweh) acts and puts the message in Balaam's mouth that he must relay to Balak (v. 5; cf. 22:35). With this charge Balaam returns to Balak, who is waiting with the princes of Moab beside the altars.

5. *Balaam's First Oracle* (23:7–10)

The word "oracle" *(mašal)* is used to characterize this and Balaam's subsequent pronouncements, (23:7, 18; 24:3, 15; also 24:20, 21, 23). A *mašal* is either a shorter or longer pronouncement, poetic in form, with a deep meaning or with more or less cryptic allusions, which is easily memorized because of its form, and creates curiosity and stimulates reflection because of its content. The word *mašal,* however, is never applied to the pronouncements of Israel's prophets or to the Psalms, even though the latter, and frequently the former, are poetic in form. This is, in my opinion, a hint on the part of the author of the Pentateuch that (in spite of 24:2, see below), he does not want to place a man like Balaam in the same category as Israel's messengers of God. The structure of these oracles in Hebrew is striking: each sentence consists of two short, related clauses. Much of the poetic form is, of course, lost in translation.

23:7 *Then Balaam uttered his oracle:*
  "Balak brought me from Aram,
    the king of Moab from the eastern mountains.
  'Come,' he said, 'curse Jacob for me;
    come, denounce Israel.'"

In his first oracle Balaam begins by stating the reasons for his being here. Balak, Moab's king, brought him here from Aram. Aram is "the country of Aram" (Hos. 12:12; kjv "field of Aram"), elsewhere called Aram Naharaim ("Aram of the two rivers," see Gen. 24:10; Deut. 23:4; et al.), or Paddan Aram (perhaps "Plain of Aram," see Gen. 25:20; 28:2; et al.), "the land of the sons of the east," of the nomadic tribes that live between the Syro-Palestinian countries and the Euphrates (Judg. 6–8; Jer. 49:28; Ezek. 25:4, 10). The "eastern mountains" thus are the high mountain range of the Syrian desert, visible from afar in the direction of Sadshur and the Middle Euphrates, which cuts through these mountains near Pethor. Those who see in 22:22–35 primarily a record of Balaam's journey and consequently believe Balaam to be an Edomite (see pp. 200–01) read here, of course, Edom (*'dm*) instead of Aram (*'rm*), while the "eastern mountains" then are to be sought east of Edom.

Then Balak's purpose is stated: to put a curse on Israel (see p. 202); the parallel clause uses "denounce," or, "to make one's anger felt by someone," which includes the use of deprecations (see also Prov. 24:24). This cursing and denouncing must be directed against Jacob and Israel; these two names are used in parallel constructions in 23:10, 21, 23; 24:5, 17–19. The same parallel use is found seventeen times in Isaiah 40–55, and four times in Micah 1–3; those who forget that poetic language has a preference for archaic forms and terminology see in this proof of a recent redaction of Numbers 23–24. I disagree with this conclusion.

23:8 *"How can I curse*
    those whom God has not cursed?
How can I denounce
    those whom the Lord *has not denounced?"*

But Balaam immediately continues with the assurance that for the carrying out of Balak's instructions he is entirely dependent on the *'elohim,* among whom he gives a special position to Jahweh, because it is His people that must be cursed and denounced. Balaam's cursing and denouncing must be preceded by a cursing and denouncing on the Lord's part (cf. 22:38). And thus far there are no indications whatsoever that He will do this. Note that Balaam does not say that he does not *want* to curse, but only that at this point he *cannot* do it. I see in this an attempt to play up to Balak.

23:9–10a *"From the rocky peaks I see them,*
    from the heights I view them.
I see a people who live apart
    and do not consider themselves one of the nations.
Who can count the dust of Jacob
    or number the fourth part of Israel?"

Balaam then explains why he cannot curse Israel: it is because of the impression that seeing Israel (all of Israel, not just a part; see commentary on 22:41) makes on him. Israel lives "apart," which, according to Deuteronomy 33:28; Jeremiah 49:31; Micah 7:14 means "safe, undisturbed"; in those days this was the incontrovertible evidence of exceptional power, the result of the working of the blessing of the deity that dwelt in its midst.

"[They] do not consider themselves one of the nations": "nations" is not used here in the sense of pagan, unclean nations, a use of *'am* not found until the Books of Ezra, Nehemiah, and Esther (Ezra 3:3; 10:2, 11; Neh. 10:29ff.; Esth. 8:17). The kjv rendering "shall not be reckoned among the nations" is incorrect, since the words immediately preceding indicate that Israel is a nation to be reckoned with. The niv and rsv correctly translate this phrase as an expression of Israel's self-awareness, which reflects the same divine blessing as its "living apart." Israel knows that it is a unique people as the result of a special relationship with the Lord (Exod. 19:5; Deut. 7:6; 10:14–15; 14:2; et al.). Consequently they are blessed in a special way, as their large numbers indicate; Jacob's offspring has become "like the dust of the earth," as was promised (Gen. 13:16;

28:14), so that its "countless thousands" (cf. 10:36) cannot be numbered. The MT of verse 10a is problematic: "and a number, the fourth part of Israel"; I would be inclined to follow the LXX: "and who shall number the families of Israel?"

23:10b *"Let me die the death of the righteous,*
and may my end be like theirs!"

Balaam sees the divine blessing that rests on Israel as surpassing anything he has seen thus far: he would consider it his good fortune to die as the children of Israel can die, not only because his own death would then not be premature and violent (cf. Job 4:7), but also because he would then have the assurance that his offspring would belong to a blessed nation and would continue to live in safety and peace, a blessing that was even rarer then than it is in our own time. He calls them "the righteous *(jšr),* a play on words with "Israel" *(jšrl),* which is also found in the title *The Book of Jashar* (the Book of the Upright, Josh. 10:13; 2 Sam. 1:18), and in the name Jeshurun for Israel (Deut. 32:15; 33:5, 26; Isa. 44:2). Those who want to see a later redaction here claim, of course, that the "righteous" of verse 10b replaces another word on the basis of "Jeshurun" in the above references in Deuteronomy and Isaiah. The question is, however, why the redactor then changed the original word to "Jashar" instead of "Jeshurun."

The final clause of verse 10 does not, as was assumed in the past, reflect Israel's belief in a life beyond the grave, surrounded by divine blessing. Balaam merely expresses his hope that henceforth his life may be different, and that his coming years may reflect the rest and security that Israel enjoys. He speaks of his "end" in the sense of Job 42:12.

6. *Balak Is Disturbed and Wants to Make a Second Attempt* (23:11–17)

It is fully understandable that Balak is disturbed when he hears Balaam's first oracle. Although it is not correct that Balaam has done "nothing but bless them," it is true that he has only mentioned the blessing that rests on Israel and given this as the reason why he cannot curse Israel as Balak wanted him to do. For "blessing" and "curse" are opposing forces, and it is impossible to generate a curse-flow when the flow of blessing is so powerful.

23:11–12 *Balak said to Balaam, "What have you done to me? I brought you to curse my enemies, but you have done nothing but bless them!"*
He answered, "Must I not speak what the LORD puts in my mouth?"

Balaam responds to Balak's blunt reproach out of the awareness of his importance as a *baru:* he is indispensable, even for a king. He, and only he. stands in a relationship with Jahweh, and as *baru* he can, of course, say nothing but the words He gives him. Ultimately it all depends on the Lord: Israel is His people, and thus He must first decrease the flow of blessing before the curse desired by Balak can gain a foothold in Israel.

23:13 *Then Balak said to him, "Come with me to another place where you can see them; you will see only a part but not all of them. And from there, curse them for me."*

But Balak is not yet ready to give up. As an Oriental he knows—or at least thinks he knows—that the success of an undertaking such as the one for which he called on Balaam depends on a variety of relatively small details such as the ritual correctness of the offerings and the choice of location. Balaam's first oracle was given on Bamoth Baal. Perhaps the choice of this location was a mistake, not, of course, because this site was dedicated to the worship of Baal, but rather because from this vantage point Balaam was bound to get an overwhelming impression of the nation camped down below and could not but conclude that this nation was under a powerful blessing from the Lord (v. 13b). Balak therefore wants to take Balaam to a different place, from where he can only see "a part" of the people; he takes him to "the field of Zophim on the top of Pisgah" (v. 14a), which, like Nebo, is part of the Abarim range in the northwestern part of the plateau of Moab, northeast of the Dead Sea (see 21:20; Deut. 3:17, 27; 4:49; et al.). The name may have survived in the present Fesha, one of the front ranges. The name Zophim ("Watchers") not only indicates that this field provided a wide view, but also that experience (which is the only decisive criterion in polytheism, which is faced with the riddle of the gods) had proven this field to be eminently suited to all kinds of occult practices. This is therefore also "sacred" ground where the deity had repeatedly provided indications of its presence. And thus Balaam has here the right atmosphere for his work.

23:14–17 *"So he took him to the field of Zophim on the top of Pisgah, and there he built seven altars and offered a bull and a ram on each altar.*

Balaam said to Balak, "Stay here beside your offering while I meet with him over there."

The LORD *met with Balaam and put a message in his mouth and said, "Go back to Balak and give him this message."*

So he went to him and found him standing beside his offering, with the princes of Moab. Balak asked him, "What did the LORD *say?"*

Again, the first step is to build the required seven altars and to sacrifice the two times seven animals. Again Balaam asks the king (and, according to v. 17b, the princes of Moab with him) to stand guard by the altars, while he is to "meet with him over there" (v. 15b). Balaam literally says "I shall let myself be met," a typical statement for a *baru* such as Balaam, who believes that his practices can move the deity, and can force the deity to enter into a conversation with him. Neither here nor in the following verses do we hear of a meeting between Balaam and *'elohim* such as the one described in 23:4. The Lord Himself is dominant in the narrative from here on. As in verses 5ff., the Lord "put a message [lit. 'word'] in his mouth" with the command to relay only this message. When Balaam returns, Balak asks him a question he did not ask the first time: "What did *the LORD* say?" Balak is clearly anxious, but he shows that he has fully grasped from Balaam's first oracle that the issue of curse or blessing depends solely on the Lord (23:8); it is impossible for us monotheists to determine exactly what this meant for a polytheist. The answer follows immediately.

7. *Balaam's Second Oracle* (23:18–24)

23:18–20 *Then he uttered his oracle:*
> *"Arise, Balak, and listen;*
> *hear me, son of Zippor.*
> *God is not a man, that he should lie,*
> *nor a son of man, that he should change his mind.*
> *Does he speak and then not act?*
> *Does he promise and not fulfill?*
> *I have received a command to bless;*
> *he has blessed, and I cannot change it."*

By beginning with "Arise" Balaam indicates that he is about to speak a divine oracle, which requires that man stand (see Judg. 3:20b). Balak must not only "listen" but also "hear" (lit. "give ear"). Then follow the words that put an end to Balak's expectations. Balak had hoped that this second attempt would achieve his goal. He expected to be able to force the will of the deity into a different direction, used as he is to seeing only a difference in gradation between men and the gods, who are essentially nothing but *Uebermenschen*, "supermen" (see my *Gods Woord*, pp. 258ff.). And here, suddenly, Balaam's words establish a deep chasm between God and man. The Hebrew word translated "God" in verse 19 is *'el*, the equivalent of the Assyrian *ilu*, the most general term for what we would call the "deity." Israel used this word to refer to either God or a god; the plural (*'elim*, Assyrian *ilanu*) is used to refer to "the gods" (Exod. 15:11; Deut.

11:16; et al.). We cannot determine what Balaam himself meant by '*el* (God, god, or the deity); personally I believe that, given Balaam's personality, he referred to "the deity" rather than to the God of Israel. In his role of *baru* it is all-important to him that Balak does not doubt the importance of his pronouncements. Balaam must not in any way support the idea, which again and again finds expression in Balak's words (22:11, 17; 23:11), that a *baru* can do whatever he wants. The fact that Samuel later applied these words to the Lord Himself (1 Sam. 15:29; cf. Mal. 3:6) does not imply, of course, that this was also Balaam's intended meaning.

But even if it were not, it would not detract from the truth of Balaam's statement. His words correctly express a concept that in the world of the ancient Near East could only have been born out of the Lord's self-revelation. In this revelation man is not the product of the eternally active matter from which gradually even the gods developed (cf. the Babylonian creation epic; my *Gods Woord*, pp. 122, 139), but rather the result of the creative act of God. This is why there cannot be any intermediate forms between God and man, as is believed elsewhere: there is no line that connects God and man (cf. Isa. 31:3; Hos. 11:9)! God is the opposite of unreliable ("lie") and the opposite of fickle ("change his mind"). He never goes back on His word. Therefore he who, like Balaam, speaks on His behalf can only repeat the message '*el*, the deity, has given him. God told Balaam to bless Israel, and Balaam must carry this out faithfully: it is irrevocable (v. 20).

23:21 *"No misfortune is seen in Jacob,*
no misery observed in Israel.
The LORD their God is with them;
the shout of the King is among them."

The KJV and RSV make the Lord the subject of verse 21a: "He has not beheld . . . nor has he seen." But this contradicts verse 21b, which gives the reason for the parallel statements in verse 21a: the Lord is with Israel. The NIV, in my opinion, correctly takes the subject to be impersonal, as do also the LXX and the Vulgate: "one sees . . . one observes," which is then idiomatically changed to the passive "is seen . . . (is) observed." "One" sees no "misfortune," no "misery" in Israel; these two words are found together also in Psalm 90:10 and Job 5:6 (where they are rendered "trouble and sorrow" and "hardship and trouble" respectively); in Habakkuk 1:3 they are further explained as "destruction and violence." Calvin thought here of "evil and injustice." That which is found among other nations to such a high degree cannot be found in Israel, because the Lord "is with them''; He is on their side, and His power protects them from all misfortune and misery (v. 21b; cf. 14:43). Balaam's words deliver the final blow to Balak's expectations—they are exactly the opposite of what he wanted to hear and on which he had built his hopes: the possibility of separating the Lord from His people and of being thus able to generate a curse-flow in Israel that would render it powerless. But the bond between the Lord and His people is too strong, and the "shout of the King" (lit. "shout of a king") is among them. This has been seen as a reference to an earthly king, David or Jeroboam II, or also to the messianic King. But both the parallelism and the context eliminate any doubt that this "king" refers to the Lord Himself (cf. Exod. 15:18; Deut. 33:5; Judg. 8:23; 1 Sam. 8:7; Isa. 33:22), whom Israel can acclaim and honor as its King (cf. 1 Sam. 4:5; 2 Sam. 6:15).

23:22 *"God brought them out of Egypt;*
   they have the strength of a wild ox."

Verse 22 further illustrates the power of this King of Israel: it reminds of the deliverance from Egypt, which is *the* central fact in Israel's history, to which the Scriptures refer again and again (cf. Jer. 2:6; 11:7; 16:14; 23:7; and many other references). The rendering "God brings them out of Egypt" (RSV) is more accurate than the past tense, "God brought them out of Egypt" (NIV), as the participle indicates: only when Israel enters the Promised Land shall the "bringing out" be completed. But Israel is not in danger: the power of Israel's God is as the power (lit. "the horns," RSV) "of the wild ox," the *re'em,* the untamable animal with its mighty horns of which Job 39:9–10 speaks. The KJV follows the LXX and renders *re'em* "unicorn" (cf. also Deut. 33:17; Ps. 22:21).

23:23–24 *"There is no sorcery against Jacob,*
   no divination against Israel.
It will now be said of Jacob
   and of Israel, 'See what God has done!'
The people rise like a lioness;
   they rouse themselves like a lion
that does not rest till he devours his prey
   and drinks the blood of his victims."

Verse 23 does not say that there is no sorcery or divination in Israel, as the LXX, the Vulgate, and Luther read; this meaning would require *'en,* rather than *lo'* to express the negation. It does say, however, that *nachaš* and *qesem* are powerless against Israel. These two words comprise what we would call magic and divination; the secret arts that seek to lift the veil of the future, and that are used for one's own benefit and to the detriment of others by exerting influence on the will of the gods (cf. Deut. 18:10–11; 2 Kings 17:17). For Balak this means that he may as well give up any hope of using these means in any way against Israel (and Balaam realizes that Balak has no other means at his disposal!). Israel's God is too powerful! This power of the Lord, so evident in Israel, gives Balaam the right to speak now of the great things Israel will be able to do in the future. Israel will be like a lioness, like a lion that crushes all resistance with claw and tooth (Gen. 49:9, 27) and will rest again only after devouring its prey and drinking its blood. Balak will be wise, Balaam implies, not to antagonize Israel: soon it will be Balak's neighbor!

8. *Balak's Third Attempt* (23:25–24:2)

23:25–30 *Then Balak said to Balaam, "Neither curse them at all nor bless them at all."*

Balaam answered, "Did I not tell you I must do whatever the LORD says?"

Then Balak said to Balaam, "Come, let me take you to another place. Perhaps it will please God to let you curse them for me from there." And Balak took Balaam to the top of Peor, overlooking the wasteland.

Balaam said, "Build me seven altars there, and prepare seven bulls and seven rams for me." Balak did as Balaam had said, and offered a bull and a ram on each altar.

The Moabite king, highly irritated by Balaam's attitude, which he fails to understand, is close to severing any connection with Balaam—but not quite yet (see 24:11). He merely tells Balaam what he is *not* to do: he must neither curse nor bless Israel, although Balak does not specify what Balaam is allowed to do. This illustrates an attitude typical of someone who sees all his expectations shattered, yet does not dare to give up because he is afraid what will happen then. This is the next-to-the-last conflict between king and *baru;* the latter repeats the fact that from the very beginning (22:38) he has claimed to be able to say nothing but what the deity (then *'elohim,* now, after 23:18, *Jahweh*) tells him. This is a renewed attempt on Balaam's part to maintain his dignity as *baru* over against Balak (cf. 23:3, 12).

But Balak wants to make one final attempt. The message of 23:19 has bypassed him, which is not difficult to understand if we remember that Balak is a polytheist. This time he takes Balaam "to the top of Peor." They stay in the Abarim range, of which Pisgah is also a part and from where Israel's camp can be seen, the absolutely necessary condition for pronouncing a curse on Israel. Hence the reiteration of the phrase of 21:20, "overlooking the wasteland." This is also a sacred mountain, as the name indicates. It is the mountain of Peor, one of the many Baals of Moab's religion, whose worship was especially characterized, according to 25:18; 31:16; Joshua 22:17, by sexual acts. Nearby lies Beth Peor (Deut. 3:29; 4:46; 34:6; Josh. 13:20), although we can no longer determine its exact location.

Balaam lends himself without hesitation to Balak's third attempt, proof that, in spite of his assertion of verse 26, he wants to oblige Balak as much as he can. Again, seven altars are built on Balaam's instructions and two animals are prepared and offered on each (vv. 29–30); here the narrative is somewhat more detailed than in verse 14. Missing here is, on the other hand, what was included in verse 15: Balaam's charge to Balak to stay beside the altars. It is clear that this does not necessarily imply different authorship, as the school of Wellhausen claims.

24:1–2 *Now when Balaam saw that it pleased the Lord to bless Israel, he did not resort to sorcery as at other times, but turned his face toward the desert. When Balaam looked out and saw Israel encamped tribe by tribe, the Spirit of God came upon him.*

But Balaam's approach changes: he no longer goes out to "meet with the Lord" as in 23:3, 15, which, as 24:1 bluntly states, meant resorting "to sorcery" (see commentary on 23:3, 23). We are also given the reason for this change: Balaam is now deeply aware of what he must do. While in the first two oracles he witnessed to the blessing that rested on Israel, he now must perform a positive act: he must bless Israel. This means that the continued urging of the Lord has finally conquered Balaam's inner resistance. He no longer tries to influence the Lord's will by means of "sorcery," but rather places himself under His will. This is why he simply stays near the altars with "his face toward the desert," the same desert as in 21:1, 13 (also Judg. 11:22) of which the plains of Moab were a part (22:1) and where Israel was encamped (21:20). Balaam wants to let the impression that Israel's camp was bound to make on the observer work on him once more (v. 2a). The claim that Balaam sees Israel's camp "apparently for the first time" in verse 2a is "apparent" only to those who are convinced that we are dealing here with a separate tradition. And now something happens to Balaam that has not happened to him before: the "Spirit of God" comes on him (v. 2b), as happened later to Samson (Judg. 14:6, 19) and Saul (1 Sam. 10:6, 10; 19:20, 23). He thus becomes an "inspired man" (Hos. 9:7; rsv: "man of the spirit"), so that he is now equipped with exceptional powers and gifts (cf. Exod. 31:3; Judg. 3:10; 1 Sam. 16:13; et al.). His statements henceforth begin with *ne'um* ("the oracle"; vv. 3b, 15b), as is also true of David in his ecstasy (2 Sam. 23:1) and of Agur (Prov. 30:1). Elsewhere, *ne'um* (a passive participle meaning "whispered in") is always followed by the name of the Lord as the One who is the source of the "whispering"; *ne'um Jahweh* is then rendered "declares the LORD" (KJV: "saith the LORD"; e.g., Gen. 22:16; Amos 2:11; 6:8; Zech. 12:1; et al.). This being seized by the Spirit of the Lord is reflected in the opening lines of Balaam's next two oracles, where Balaam appeals to this ecstasy, his awareness of the presence of the Lord's Spirit, to support his statements. In this he distinguishes himself, incidentally, from Israel's prophets, who never appeal to the presence of the Spirit. This ecstasy is apparently an entirely new experience for Balaam.

9. *Balaam's Third Oracle* (24:3–9)

24:3–4 *And he uttered his oracle:*
  "The oracle of Balaam son of Beor,
    the oracle of one whose eye sees clearly,
  the oracle of one who hears the words of God,
    who sees a vision from the Almighty,
    who falls prostrate, and whose eyes are opened."

Balaam now knows himself to be, as it were, a new person, filled with a power ("the Spirit of God") entirely different from that under whose influence he performed his sorcery. Like David and Agur, he begins by stating his name and presenting himself as an ecstatic. He knows himself to be the man whose eyes have been opened and whose ears hear, so that he can now see and hear what cannot be perceived by the ordinary mortal: the words (lit. "thing-words," hence seeing and hearing) of God. Thus he can now claim to know as much as the Most High[5] and to see what the Almighty sees ("sees the vision of the Almighty," RSV), because, prostrate in his ecstasy, he has eyes that have been freed from all impediments that would hinder him from seeing the unseeable. Balaam describes himself as a "seer," who in ecstasy receives his revelation from a higher power. His condition is thus essentially different from that of Israel's prophets, but similar to Saul's experience (1 Sam. 10:10–11; 19:24).

It is not certain whether the translation of verses 3b–4 is correct. The two Hebrew words rendered "whose eye sees clearly" in the NIV are

---

[5]Noordtzij adds "who has knowledge from the Most High" after "who hears the words of God" in verse 4a, on the basis of verse 16 (tr.).

translated "who sees in truth" in the LXX, the result of a different word division. Others follow the Vulgate and read "whose eye is closed" (cf. RSV margin), which would create a very subtle contrast with verse 4b, which then refers to the spiritual eye; however, this contrast is stated in Job 10:4 in a very different and much more readily understood manner. Jewish tradition says that Balaam was blind in one eye, since verse 3b speaks of "eye" rather than "eyes" (*Sanhedrin*, 105a), while Rashi claims that one eye had been put out. This is an interesting example of eisegesis, as is the claim of the Targum Onkelos that Balaam received his visions only at night, based on the "prostrate" of verse 4b (but see Exod. 21:18).

It is striking that Balaam here speaks not only of *'elohim* (God), and thus uses the general Semitic word, *ilu*, but also of "the Most High" *('elion,* v. 4a,[6] v. 16) and "the Almighty" *shaddai*). In the past, prior to our increased knowledge of the ancient Near East, this has led to a variety of conjectures concerning Balaam's concept of God, since in a number of instances in the Old Testament the Lord is called *'el 'eljon* (Gen 14:18ff.; Ps. 78:35) or *'eljon* (Pss. 83:18; 97:9; et al.), while *'el shaddai* is the name under which the Lord made Himself known to the patriarchs (Gen. 17:1; 28:3; 35:11; Exod. 6:3; et al.). There can be no doubt, however, that already before 1200 B.C. a monarchic polytheism had gained ground in the Syro-Palestinian region, which placed over the plurality of the gods a surpreme god, who was referred to not only as "the lord of the gods," but also as *'eljon*. Concerning *shaddai*, it seems highly likely to me that Balaam did not say *shaddai (šdi),* but *shadu (šdw),* a name of honor (lit. *shadu rabu,* "the great mountain"), used by the Babylonians and Assyrians, as well as by the Amorites for their supreme god (see e.g., J. Hehn, *Babylonische und Israelitische Gottesidee,* pp. 265ff.). Balaam's use of these two names does therefore not necessarily imply any kind of Israelite concept of God on his part.

24:5-6 *"How beautiful are your tents, O Jacob,*
  your dwelling places, O Israel!
"Like valleys they spread out,
  like gardens beside a river,
like aloes planted by the LORD,
  like cedars beside the waters."

After this introduction Balaam describes the impression the sight of Israel's camp makes on him (v. 5); this verse is addressed to Israel. He compares the rows of Israel's tents (v. 6a) to valleys with streams and

---

[6]See footnote on p. 225.

abundant plant life, to gardens where water is plentiful and fruit thus abundant (cf. Ps. 1:3); these are, according to Isaiah 58:11, proofs of God's blessing (for the opposite, cf. Isa. 1:30). Israel is also compared to aloes; this tree was not known in Israel—it is native to southeast Asia—but its fragrant wood was well-known (cf. Ps. 45:8; Prov. 7:17; Song of Songs 4:14). The comparison involves exceptionally strong trees, because the Lord Himself planted them (cf. Ps. 104:16; Jer. 2:21; et al.). And finally, Balaam compares Israel to cedars which, although they grow on mountain slopes, still need ground water. Balaam presents a simile and not, as some think, a description of the fertility of the Promised Land. He sees Israel as a nation, strong and growing in numbers, to which the future belongs.

24:7 *"Water will flow from their buckets;*
their seed will have abundant water.
Their king will be greater than Agag;
their kingdom will be exalted."

In verses 7–9b Balaam no longer speaks to, but rather about Israel. Baentsch saw in verse 7a (both parts!) a description of the abundance of water in Israel's future territory. But, apart from the fact that Balaam had no knowledge of the Lord's promises to Israel concerning Canaan, this explanation is very improbable because Balaam's oracle deals with the impression the *present* Israel makes on him. Nor does verse 7a speak of Israel's numerous descendants, and even less of the coming Messiah (LXX, Syriac, Targums). It appears to me that the first line of verse 7a depicts Israel's prosperity under the image of a man returning from his abundantly flowing well with overflowing buckets. In the second line of verse 7a I would read the four consonants *zr'w,* which the MT reads as *zar'o* ("his seed"), as *zero'o* ("his arm"), and with the Targums I would read *b'mjm (be'ammim,* "against nations") instead of *bmjm (bemajim,* "in water"), which gives the meaning "and his arm is against many nations" (thus Buchanan Gray in his commentary). This then marks the beginning of the description of what Israel's neighbors can expect from a nation so richly blessed by God, a typically Oriental train of thought, which sees great vitality manifested only in military force and political power. Balaam fails to see that Israel is to be a nation whose greatness lies only in the fullness of the blessing that rested on it, a blessing that would later spread to the nations (Gen. 12:2–3).

Verse 7b also speaks of military power. The vision of Israel as a kingdom is entirely in keeping with the conditions of that time, when each city had its own king. Israel's king will be more powerful than Agag. This presents us with a problem, because we know Agag only as the king of the

Amalekites in the days of Saul (1 Sam. 15:8). The latter can of course not be the one of whom Balaam speaks; this Agag must have been known to his hearers (unless, of course, v. 7b is taken as proof of a later recension, which eliminates the problem). But the question is whether this Agag is a proper noun, like the Assyrian Agigu, in which case it may be a recurring royal name of the Assyrians, or a title meaning "the mighty one" (cf. the Assyrian *agagu*, "to rage"). In the latter case it must be the title of the ruler of a nation greatly feared by the Moabites (Amalek?). The Samaritan Pentateuch and the four Greek versions (LXX, Aquila, Symmachus, and Theodotion) speak here of Gog, the enemy referred to in Ezekiel 38–39 (see also 24:23), a change apparently based on an incorrect exegesis.

24:8–9 *"God brought them out of Egypt;*
they have the strength of a wild ox.
They devour hostile nations
and break their bones in pieces;
with their arrows they pierce them.
Like a lion they crouch and lie down,
like a lioness—who dares to rouse them?
May those who bless you be blessed
and those who curse you be cursed!"

In verse 8 Balaam speaks of the source from which so much vitality flows for Israel: Israel's God. Balaam does not draw this conclusion on the basis of any special knowledge of the covenant relationship into which the Lord has entered with Israel; rather, it reflects the general ancient Near Eastern concept that such a strong nation must have a strong God. To Him Israel owes her deliverance from Egypt (see 23:22) and her ability to utterly destroy her opponents. Balaam uses a verb (*'akal,* "to eat") that evokes the image of an animal. He continues in the same vein when he speaks of breaking "their bones in pieces," and he returns almost naturally to the image of the lion that no one dares to rouse (cf. 23:24).

He ends his oracle with the assurance that whoever blesses Israel will himself be blessed, while anyone who curses Israel will be cursed (v. 9b). This again does not prove that Balaam was familiar with God's plan for Israel's future (Gen. 12:1–3), or specifically with the words "I will bless those who bless you, and whoever curses you I will curse" (see also Gen. 27:29). But Balaam wants to say that such a powerful flow of blessing is at work in Israel that those who, by showing honor and respect, manifest an awareness of the power of that blessing will themselves participate in the blessing, while those who attempt to unleash a curse in Israel will find that the blessing throws the curse back on those from whom it went out.

10. *Balak's Displeasure and Balaam's Excuse* (24:10–14)

24:10–14 *Then Balak's anger burned against Balaam. He struck his hands to-gether and said to him, "I summoned you to curse my enemies, but you have blessed them these three times. Now leave at once and go home! I said I would reward you handsomely, but the LORD has kept you from being rewarded."*

Balaam answered Balak, "Did I not tell the messengers you sent me, 'Even if Balak gave me his palace filled with silver and gold, I could not do anything of my own accord, good or bad, to go beyond the command of the LORD—and I must say only what the LORD says'? Now I am going back to my people, but come, let me warn you of what this people will do to your people in days to come."

It is understandable that this undisguised revelation of the fullness of Israel's blessing, and of the consequent danger to anyone who would attempt to change this blessing into a curse, makes Balak angry—he sends Balaam packing. Balak, used as he is to the idea that a *baru* (if paid well, since here the principle also applies that one gets what one pays for) can do anything, including forcing the will of the deity to submit to his will by the secret means of sorcery, finds what is happening incomprehensible. Balaam's coming indicated that he was willing to help Balak and to render Israel powerless by cursing it, and thus to make it possible for Moab to expel Israel from the land it still considered its territory, even though Moab temporarily had to surrender control of it to Sihon (i.e., the land between Arnon and Jabbok, see commentary on 21:21–31). But Balaam has done nothing but bless Israel, i.e., speak of the fullness of Israel's blessing and of the power that flows from this blessing! Balak strikes his hands together, not in amazement, but as a sign of contempt (cf. Job 27:23; Lam. 2:15), all that is left for a *baru* who has so little power over the deity that he does exactly the opposite of that which could have brought him so much "honor" (KJV) or monetary reward. Balak has only one piece of advice for Balaam: leave quickly as a fugitive, as someone who has been utterly defeated (Amaziah's advice to Amos, see Amos 7:12). He adds with a mocking laugh: the God of Israel, whom Balaam claimed to know so well (22:8, 18–19; 23:3, 15) and whose mouthpiece Balaam turned out to be, He is the cause of Balaam's leaving without any reward, without any payment.

Balaam's only response is that which he had already told the second delegation (22:18): he is totally dependent on the Lord (Jahweh), whose power he now has experienced, however, in a different manner and meas-ure than he could suspect back then. I see in this answer, therefore, not proof of Balaam's willing submission to the Lord's will, but rather of his professional pride as a *baru:* he does not want to encourage the idea that his sorcery is nothing but clever fraud.

Balaam is entirely willing to depart without reward, but he does not want to leave without a new oracle that will make clear to Balak what he and his people can expect from this blessed nation Israel "in days to come" (lit. "in the end of the days"); this expression does not refer to "the latter days" (KJV, RSV) in the eschatological sense (see L. Dürr, *Die Stellung des Propheten Ezechiel in der Israelitisch-Jüdischen Apokalyptik,* 1923, pp. 100ff.), but rather to that portion of the future that falls within the scope of the speaker's perspective (cf. Gen. 49:1). Balaam feels himself insulted by Balak and wronged by him. Therefore, he will force Balak to hear how the curse he wanted to direct against Israel is now mobilized against his own people.

11. *Balaam's Fourth Oracle* (24:15–19)

24:15–19 *Then he uttered his oracle:*

> *"The oracle of Balaam son of Beor,*
>> *the oracle of one whose eye sees clearly,*
> *the oracle of one who hears the words of God,*
>> *who has knowledge from the Most High,*
> *who sees a vision from the Almighty,*
>> *who falls prostrate, and whose eyes are opened:*
> *I see him, but not now;*
>> *I behold him, but not near.*
> *A star will come out of Jacob;*
>> *a scepter will rise out of Israel.*
> *He will crush the foreheads of Moab,*
>> *the skulls of all the sons of Sheth.*
> *Edom will be conquered;*
>> *Seir, his enemy, will be conquered,*
>> *but Israel will grow strong.*
> *A ruler will come out of Jacob*
>> *and destroy the survivors of the city."*

This oracle begins with the same description of the seer as the third oracle (vv. 3b–4[7]). And then Balaam suddenly speaks of Israel, not as it is now camped near the Jordan, at most a threat to Moab, but as it will be later. Balaam sees into the future. On the horizon of his vision he sees someone. But he is aware of the distance both in time ("not now") and space ("not near") that separates him from the one he sees. However, he sees him sufficiently clearly to be able to say that he is a "star" and a "scepter" that rises out of Israel. In Isaiah 14:12 the king of Babel is

---

[7]See footnote on p. 225.

referred to as the "morning star." In the Arabic language rulers are also on occasion called "stars." In the ancient Near East it was common for a king to call himself the "sun" of his land, a custom found not only in the Tigris-Euphrates region, but also among the Hittites of Asia Minor and in Egypt, and in Rome (Nero and Caligula). It is thus clear that the designation "star" has no reference to the divine origin of the one so designated. The scepter is the insignia of the ruler since ancient times, as the ancient Near Eastern representations of kings and rulers with crook or club show (see also Gen. 49:10; Ps. 45:6; Amos 1:5, 8). There can be no question, therefore, that Balaam here speaks of a king who shall come out of Israel.

Both the Targum Onkelos and the Targum Jonathan show that rabbinical Judaism was convinced that Balaam here spoke of the Messiah. Onkelos paraphrases, "The king rises out of Jacob and the Anointed One [Messiah] of Israel becomes great, and he slays the mighty men of Moab and rules over all the children of men." This view is also reflected in the name, given by Rabbi Akiba to the pseudo-Messiah of the days of emperor Hadrian (A.D. 132), Bar Kochba, "Son of the Star." This view was introduced into the church by Justin Martyr, Irenaeus, and Cyprian, and was for centuries considered the only correct exegesis of verse 17. While the Jewish exegete Rashi already expressed his conviction that the "star" of verse 17 refers to David, who made subjects of Moab and Edom (2 Sam. 8:2), it was not until the publication of Verschuir's *Dissertatio de Oraculis Bileami* in 1773 that the identification of the star with the Messiah came to be increasingly questioned (for a detailed survey of the various interpretations of v. 17 up to his own day, see L. Reinke, *Beiträge zur Erklärung des Alten Testaments IV,* 1885, pp. 179–284).

It appears to me that we do not have a direct messianic prophecy here, in which Balaam saw the blessed person of the Savior arise. Neither the expression in verse 14, "days to come," nor the fact that no mortal king of Israel ever subjugated Israel's neighbors as completely as verses 17–19 indicate, support the interpretation of these verses as a messianic prophecy. Nor does it find support in the fact that the "scepter" is also mentioned in Genesis 49:10 (Heinisch, *Numeri,* p. 98). A more solid basis for seeing in these verses a messianic prophecy would be found in the connection Israel's prophets see between the destruction of Moab and Edom and the coming of the Messiah (Isa. 11:14; 25:9–11; Ezek. 35:1–14; Amos 9:12; Zeph. 2:8–11)—but these prophets lived many centuries later!

In my opinion, Balaam saw a royal figure, recognizable by the scepter, arise in Israel, but not a specific king; he wanted to show that Israel would owe the full development of its power to its kings, which would lead to the demise of Moab and Edom—only these two are mentioned, since in

Balaam's day they were the two powers that were a threat to Israel. Only in the later development of Israel as a kingdom would it become clear that Israel's kings would not fulfill the expectation expressed here; the great prophets would turn Israel's eyes toward "the Coming One," "to whom [the scepter] belongs" (Gen. 49:10), "to whom it rightfully belongs; to him I will give it" (Ezek. 21:27; "it," viz. the destroyed Davidic kingdom and the destroyed city of David; see my commentary on Ezek. 21:27). Only with Him will come "*the* star" and will Israel receive "*the* scepter"! Balaam's oracle is thus messianic only when viewed in the light of the later unfolding of God's revelation.

In typically ancient Near Eastern fashion, all Balaam sees of the work of the "star" is the destruction of Israel's enemies. First this will affect Moab, whose "foreheads" (lit. "corners," KJV, i.e., "temples," incorrectly understood metaphorically as "leaders") will be crushed as those of a man lying powerlessly on the ground. The following words also relate to Moab; the NIV reading, "skulls," is an emendation of the MT, based on the Samaritan Pentateuch and on Jeremiah 48:45 (*qodqod* instead of *qarqar*, "destroy," KJV; cf. NIV margin). The Moabites are here called "the sons of Sheth"; I prefer the rendering "sons of tumult" or "war-minded," which reflects Moab's pride of which Isaiah 16:6; 25:11; and Zephaniah 2:10 speak. In contrast to the preceding oracles the future destruction of Edom is mentioned here along with that of Moab. Those who believe that Balak was originally an Edomite king (see p. 200) are, of course, of the opinion that verse 17b, which mentions Moab, is a later addition from the hand of the redactor who (on what grounds?) made Balak a king of Moab. Others, on the other hand, are convinced that verses 18–19 are a more recent addition. In my opinion both views are purely subjective suppositions. After Edom's treatment of Israel (20:14–21) there was every reason to refer to Edom's future demise. Even though the text here is rather mutilated, the sense is clear: Edom will be powerless against the coming display of Israel's power. Although it does not fully share in Moab's lot, it will nevertheless lose its independence.

As we summarize the four oracles we see that all four are rhythmic, since the rhythmic phrase is the natural form of expression of the ecstatic. It made a great impression on the people of antiquity and was seen by them as the carrier of exceptional power. The structure of all four oracles is reminiscent of the curse songs and curse formulas of the ancient Arabs, which were believed to have magical powers and were therefore feared; these songs and formulas were hurled against the enemy by the "seer" of the tribe.

The sequence of the four oracles leads toward a distinct climax. The first one expresses the thought that it is impossible to curse Israel because its camp proves that a great blessing rests on it (23:7–10). The second oracle explains why it is futile to curse Israel: Israel's God maintains the blessing once bestowed, and thus protects His people against all sorcery (23:18b–24). The third oracle speaks of Israel's inner strength that dooms any attack on it to failure (24:3b–9). And the fourth oracle, finally, presents Israel as the future conqueror of Moab and Edom (24:15–19).

This climax would be sufficient reason not to assign different authorship to the last two oracles, as Wellhausen did; a study of the content of the four oracles provides adequate grounds why we should not consider them descriptive statements dating from a much later time (the time of David? Jeroboam II? after the captivity? of Jesus?), put in Balaam's mouth in the form of prophetic sayings *(vaticinia ex eventu)*. Only of the fourth oracle can it be said that it predicts something; the other three speak only of the admiration that filled Balaam when he saw Israel's camp. Also, we must not forget that Balak lived strictly for the present: all he wanted to hear from Balaam was that his curse had separated Israel from its God, so that Israel was rendered powerless and Balak could proceed to the attack. Balak would have had no use for prophecies. A prediction of the future can be given only after Balaam has been sent home by Balak without any reward—*then* Balak must know what awaits him from the side of Israel.

12. *Three Additional Oracles* (24:20–25)

The last three oracles have nothing in common with the preceding four, except their introduction, "Balaam . . . uttered his oracle." The first two of these final oracles are also preceded by the words "Then Balaam saw Amalek" and "Then he saw the Kenites." Concerning verse 23, see below. But the "seeing" of the two nations here is of a different nature than the "seeing" of Israel in 22:41; 23:9, 13; 24:3. Now it is not a seeing with the natural eye, but rather a "spiritual" seeing (in a different sense than in v. 17). Furthermore, the final three oracles, unlike the first four, do not arise out of the present situation; neither Israel nor Moab are involved. And finally, their content also points to a different time, which is especially obvious in the final oracle. In my opinion, these last three oracles were inserted here later, since they deal with nations with which Israel was involved in the later course of its history.

24:20 *Then Balaam saw Amalek and uttered his oracle:*
"Amalek was first among the nations,
but he will come to ruin at last."

The first oracle of the last three concerns Amalek, with which Israel had done battle before (Exod. 17:8ff.; Num. 14:43, 45). Here Amalek is called the "first among the nations," and is thus considered a very ancient nation (see also Gen. 14:7, where we must probably read "Amalek's rulers," rather than "Amalek's field," *šrj* instead of *šdh*). But this nation shall also perish. The oracle does not say when, or by whose hand. I note that in 1 Samuel 30 Amalek is still so powerful that it dares to attack Ziklag. But in 1 Chronicles 4:43 we hear of its destruction by the Simeonites, although it is not known when this happened.

24:21–22 *Then he saw the Kenites and uttered his oracle:*
> *"Your dwelling place is secure,*
> *your nest is set in a rock;*
> *yet you Kenites will be destroyed*
> *when Asshur takes you captive."*[8]

The oracle against the Kenites presents several problems. We know very little about these people. Moses' father-in-law is called "priest of Midian" in Exodus 3:1, and a "Midianite" in Numbers 10:29, but his son Hobab is called a Kenite in Judges 1:16; 4:11. We also know that part of the Kenites joined Judah (Judg. 1:16), while Judges 4:11 speaks of Kenites in the territory of Naphtali, and 1 Samuel 15:6 of Kenites who live among Amalek. Verse 21 reads "when he saw *the* Kenites"; does this mean that the oracle speaks of the Kenites in a time when they were still undivided and lived as nomads side by side with Midian and Amalek in the Sinai peninsula? Whatever the answer, the references mentioned above prove with sufficient certainty that Eduard Meyer was in error when he claimed that the Kenites were an Edomite tribe (*Die Israeliten und ihre Nachbarstämme,* 1906, pp. 393ff.). They were undoubtedly of Arabian origin and closely related to the Midianites.

Both the KJV and the NIV render *qajin* in verse 22 "Kenites." I prefer the more obvious rendering "Cain" (cf. RSV); this oracle is then built around a play on words: *qeni* (Kenite), *qajin* (Cain), and *qen* (nest). We are not told where this "nest" is. Those who believe that the Kenites of this verse must be identified with the later Nabataeans, an Arabian tribe that conquered Edom's territory in postexilic times and suffered much at the hands of the Seleucids, seek this "nest" in Petra (but see below). Like Amalek, the Kenites will not escape destruction (v. 22a). The MT of verse 22b reads "For how long? Asshur shall take you away captive" (cf. RSV). This "how

---

[8]Noordtzij emends the text of verse 22 to read, "yet Cain will be destroyed, your dwelling shall become a rubble- and trash-heap."

long'' is problematic. Whenever the expression is used it reflects impatience (Pss. 4:2; 74:9; 79:5; 89:46). This cannot be the case here, because the question then would be ''for how long will this destruction last,'' while the following words, which speak of a complete destruction of the Kenites' existence as a nation, would not fit the question. Some exegetes therefore want to render the rest of verse 22 ''until Asshur shall take you away captive'' (cf. KJV). But this is against Hebrew usage and idiom. Those who consider this oracle to be of recent origin identify Asshur with the Assyrian empire that extended into this region around 700 B.C., or are of the opinion that this refers to the eastern half of the Greek empire; but both these views lack convincing proof (see below). It appears to me that instead of the MT reading of verse 22b (''For how long? Asshur shall take you captive'') we should read ''your dwelling shall become a rubble- and trash-heap'' (*'arema we'aspot mosabekha;* cf. W. Rudolph, ZAW, 1934, p. 115). Judgment shall also fall on the Kenites, in spite of Cain's seemingly unassailable position.

24:23–24 *Then he uttered his oracle:*
> *"Ah, who can live when God does this?*
> *Ships will come from the shores of Kittim;*
> *they will subdue Asshur and Eber,*
> *but they too will come to ruin."*

We are not told to whom the final oracle is addressed. The LXX begins verse 23 with the words, ''And seeing Gog''; it also substitutes ''Gog'' for ''Agag'' in verse 7. The Itala and the Greek versions of Aquila, Symmachus, and Theodotion make the same changes. But this cannot be correct: Gog is a person, the ruler of the peoples of the north that from 1000 B.C. onward caused the Assyrian empire much trouble (see my commentary on Ezek. 38:2). We would expect the name of a nation here; and the oracle undoubtedly began at one time with a specific name that has dropped out of the text.

The MT of verses 23–24 is in poor condition. The second part of verse 23 is impossible to translate with any degree of certainty; most English versions read ''Alas, who shall live when God does this?'' or a close parallel. The next line, which reads literally ''and ships from the coast of Kittim,'' seems to be suspended in midair and can be salvaged only by an exclamation point (thus the Dutch NBG version) or by inserting ''will come'' (as the English versions do). Much ingenuity has been expended on this text, but the conclusions do not go beyond conjecture. With W. Rudolph (see above) I would change the last two words of verse 23 and the first word of verse 24 to *miqqumo 'el yosi'em* and translate ''Woe! who shall live when he arises whom God shall cause to come out from the side of Kittim?'' This derives some support from the fact that the Samaritan Pentateuch and the LXX read ''he makes to come forth'' *(yšjm)* instead of ''and ships'' *(wšjm)*.

If we accept this emendation, which I fully recognize to be conjectural, then this oracle speaks of an event that will have a catastrophic character for many (''who shall live?''): an invasion of Canaan by sea-faring people who deal death and destruction, and who come from the direction of Kittim. There is no doubt that this ''Kittim'' is a Hebraicized form of the name of a Phoenician colony, called ''Kittion'' by the Greeks, situated on the eastern shore of Cyprus. This colony gave its name to the entire island, which is referred to as ''the land of Kittim'' in Isaiah 23:1 (KJV, NIV margin). And because Cyprus was always the first port of call on the Phoenicians' travels westward, Cyprus and the islands west of it (perhaps as far as Sicily?) were called collectively ''the isles of Kittim'' (KJV; NIV; RSV: ''coasts of Kittim''; Jer. 2:10; Ezek. 27:6; Dan. 11:30). The danger thus comes from the Mediterranean. With F. Hommel (*Die Altisraelitische Ueberlieferung,* pp. 245ff.) I see in this a reference to the great movement of the ''sea people'' who gave the rulers of the Nile valley so much trouble for more than a century, from the time of Seti I (1318–1298 B.C.) until Rameses III (1198–1167 B.C.); Ramses II (1298–1231 B.C.) called them ''the strangers from the north, the Temhu (rulers of Lybia), the warriors of the great ocean of the north.'' This was a mixture of Indo-European peoples and tribes, migrating south from the Balkans and from the plains north of the Black Sea. They overran Greece, conquered Crete, and overpowered Libya. In Asia Minor the Hittite empire of Boghazkoy fell under their onslaught, and they conquered Cilicia and Syria. In ''the land of the Amorites'' (Canaan?) they established a camp from where they went out to destroy ''land and inhabitants.'' Finally, in conjunction with a naval attack, they attempted an invasion of Egypt under the leadership of several Greek tribes and of a people that, coming from Crete, made the name of the Philistines feared for many centuries. ''They drive fire before them,'' Rameses III said, who, after an immense struggle, succeeded in dealing their army and their fleet a resounding defeat, and who thereby halted their movement in the direction of Egypt.

Only such a major migration, which also deeply affected Palestine, could justify an exclamation such as that in verse 23, ''Woe! who shall live?'' The oracle does not specify who will be the victims of this catastrophe. We hear of only two peoples or tribes, which fall within the speaker's perspective: Asshur and Eber. Since the migration stopped at Egypt's borders, we must probably identify Asshur with the north Arabian tribe of the Asshurites, mentioned in Genesis 25:3 and in south Arabian inscriptions. For a considerable period of time this tribe appears to have given its name to the entire northern half of the Sinai peninsula west of Edom (see F. Hommel, *Grundriss der Geographie und Geschichte des Alten Orients,* II, 1926, p. 612). Eber then is probably Ibr Naharan, which is mentioned along with Asshur in a south Arabian manuscript.

It is much more obvious that we see in verses 23–24 a reference to this migration than to the failed campaign of the Syrian king Antiochus Epiphanes against Egypt in 168 B.C. (H. Winckler, *Alttestamentliche Forschungen,* 2nd series, vol. 3, pp. 421ff.), in which case Asshur and Eber would be the eastern and western half of Antiochus' kingdom; this view lacks proof. Others have thought of the destruction of the Persian empire by Alexander the Great (333 B.C.), or of the Seleucid empire by the Romans (93 B.C.). It is difficult to accept the fact that those events would have been of such great importance to the nations and tribes of Canaan!

24:25 *Then Balaam got up and returned home and Balak went his own way.*

This verse, which followed immediately after verse 19 before the final three oracles were inserted here, concludes the narrative of Balak's and Balaam's joint attempt to give Moab the opportunity to render Israel powerless and to push it back into the wilderness. Through the intervention of the Angel of the Lord Balak has heard exactly the opposite of what he wanted to hear, and Balaam has not only lost the reward he had hoped to receive, he also failed to find the inner peace of him who serves the Lord wholeheartedly. Although he was very much aware that Israel's God had taken him into His service, he nevertheless tried to turn this service into material gain for himself. His ambivalence proved fatal. The Talmud tract *Sanhedrin* (106b) claims that he died at age 33; the *Pirke Abot* (5:19) says that, like Doeg, Ahithophel, and Gehazi, he will not have part in "the age to come," and that he who follows him shall enter Gehenna.

Israel's Sin and Phinehas's Zeal
(25:1–18)

This is clearly a much abridged narrative. Without being told whether or how Moses' command of verse 5 is executed, we hear in verse 6 suddenly of *"the* Midianite woman," although she has not been mentioned in the preceding verses (the English versions render the definite article as an indefinite article: "a"). Furthermore, verse 9 speaks of "the plague," of which the preceding verses make no mention. But this does not point to two separate narratives, the first one (vv. 1–5) taking place in Moab, the second one (vv. 6–18) in Midian, whereby the second narrative would chronologically precede chapter 20; this is one of those conjectures of the school of Wellhausen that lack proof. The more extensive narrative probably told how Balaam, after the failure of his attempt to separate the Lord from Israel by means of his "sorceries," advised Balak to attempt to separate Israel from the Lord by seducing Israel into participating in the sensual worship of the Baal of Peor. This would destroy Israel's power and achieve Balak's goal (cf. 31:8, 16; also Rev. 2:14).

Chronologically chapter 25 fits in with the three preceding chapters, where we found Israel in "the plains of Moab" across from Jericho; here Israel is in Shittim ("Acacia"), according to 33:49 a shortened form of Abel Shittim ("Acacia Meadows"), from where Israel went across the Jordan to enter Canaan (Josh. 2:1; 3:1). On the authority of Josephus (*Antiquities,* IV, 9. 1; V, 1. 1) many are inclined to identify Shittim with Abila, a city that has not yet been rediscovered, but must have been about sixty stadia (seven miles) east of the Jordan; the name, however, points to a region, rather than a city. Others, with more justification, seek Shittim in the oasis Kefrin, directly across from Jericho (see Buhl, *Geographie,* pp. 116, 265).

1. *Israel Seduced to Worship the Baal of Peor* (25:1–5)

25:1–5 *While Israel was staying in Shittim, the men began to indulge in sexual immorality with Moabite women, who invited them to the sacrifices to their gods. The people ate and bowed down before these gods. So Israel joined in worshiping the Baal of Peor. And the LORD's anger burned against them.*

The LORD said to Moses, "Take all the leaders of these people, kill them and expose them in broad daylight before the LORD, so that the LORD's fierce anger may turn away from Israel."

So Moses said to Israel's judges, "Each of you must put to death those of your men who have joined in worshiping the Baal of Peor."

Israel begins to "indulge in sexual immorality" with "Moabite women." From this the (unnecessary) conclusion has been drawn that, according to verses 1–5, the Arnon was not the northern border of Moab's kingdom (see 21:13; 22:36). The fact that Sihon took the territory between the Arnon and the Jabbok from the king of Moab does not necessarily imply that he also killed the entire population of that area, which apparently consisted of Moabites and Midianites. Although the verb rendered "to indulge in sexual immorality" is often used in the sense of cultic or religious sexual immorality connected with the worship of "other gods" (e.g., Isa. 57:3; Jer. 2:20; Ezek. 16:15; Hos. 2:7), in the Pentateuch it is used in this sense only when it is followed by a prepositional phrase referring to the "other god" (e.g., "they prostituted themselves *to their gods*," Exod. 34:15f.; cf. Lev. 17:7; 20:5; Deut. 31:16). In my opinion this verse refers therefore strictly to sexual deviation, followed as an almost natural outgrowth of the worship of the love goddess Baalat, Astarte, Ashera, or by whatever other name she was known, since sexual immorality was an integral part of that worship (see my *Gods Woord,* pp. 351ff.). This is also reflected in verse 2, which states that the Israelites were invited to participate in the sacrificial meals in honor of "their *'elohim.'*" This is usually rendered "their" gods; but *'elohim* can also refer to a single god (Judg. 11:24; 1 Sam. 5:7; 1 Kings 11:33) or goddess (1 Kings 11:5, 33; there is no Hebrew word for "goddess"). I therefore believe that verse 2 refers to the love goddess, who in verse 3 recedes behind her "husband," Baal Peor, who, even as his "wife," had his own devotees, young men and women who in honor of their god gave their bodies over to all kinds of immoral acts and became "temple prostitutes" (see Hos. 4:13; 9:10; according to König's *Wörterbuch* the meaning of the name Peor supports this: "*Aufsperrung, Auseinanderspreizung im obszönen Sinne*"). (For Baal Peor, cf. 23:28; 31:16; Deut. 4:3; Josh. 22:17; Hos. 9:10; Ps. 106:28; 1 Cor. 10:8.) His worship, like that of the other Canaanite gods, was centered on "the heights," usually under the open sky ("on every high hill and under every spreading tree," 1 Kings 14:23; 2 Kings 17:20; Jer. 17:2); it consisted of cultic dances, performed by naked men and women, followed by drinking and sexual debauchery. These celebrations took place mostly during the agricultural festivals, which were the high points of the Canaanite "religious" life. "Israel joined in worshiping the Baal of Peor" (v. 3), lit. "yoked themselves to [the wagon of] the Baal of Peor," a sarcastic description on the part of the sacred author, also found in Psalm 106:28.

Israel's ingratitude for the Lord's fatherly protection in the face of the danger that threatens from the side of Balaam and Balak rouses the Lord's anger. This is an anthropomorphic description of the opposition of the holy God against any attempt to put Him on the same level as the "other gods," which attacks the very heart of the covenant He gave to Israel. This time the Lord's anger is directed against "all the leaders of these people." We must not conclude from this that they were the ones who set the example in "bowing down" before the Baal of Peor, although this was probably true of some of them, as it had been in other instances. Nor can we agree with Dillmann and Baentsch (who find support in the Samaritan Pentateuch) that "them" (v. 3) originally did not refer to the leaders but to the guilty ones, while the leaders were instructed to punish them. To the Near Eastern mind, the head of the tribe or clan is the representative, the embodiment, as it were, of the entire tribe or clan. His death therefore is punishment for the people as a whole.

The type of punishment that awaits the leaders is mentioned only in verse 4 and in 2 Samuel 21:6, 9. Its nature is not entirely clear. The LXX speaks of "making an example of," or also "exposing to the sun"; the Vulgate refers here to "hanging," and in 2 Samuel 21 to "crucifying." We probably are to think of the punishment mentioned frequently in the Assyrian inscriptions and depicted in their works of art: the individual who has been condemned to death is placed on his stomach on top of a tall, pointed pole, and thus sinks slowly to his death. The execution is to take place in public, "in broad daylight" (lit. "before the sun"), "before the LORD." The latter phrase indicates the special nature of this punishment: it has, as it were, a religious character—every execution is like an offering brought to the Lord's violated honor (see also 2 Sam. 21:6, 9; cf. Josh. 6:17). Moses charges "Israel's judges" with the execution; their position is not entirely clear to us. In Deuteronomy they are sometimes mentioned along with the priests (19:17), sometimes with the elders (21:2) or the officials (16:18). On the basis of Exodus 18:25–26 I suspect that each of these judges was responsible for the administration of justice among a specific group of the Israelites, while the leaders of Israel also fell under their jurisdiction. No mention is made of the execution itself.

2. *Phinehas's Act and His Reward* (25:6–15)

Instead, we hear of Phinehas's reaction to the moral degeneration among his people, and of the reward the Lord gives him for his action. The fact that this involved a Midianite woman has led some interpreters to conclude that the event of verses 6–15 cannot have taken place at the same time as verses 1–5, but rather earlier, when Israel was camped south of Canaan, prior to the journey around Edom, i.e., before chapter 20. But this is incorrect. As stated in connection with 22:4, the Midianites as well as the Moabites belonged to the inhabitants of the southern portion of the Transjordan region; the Midianites thus did not live only in the northern area of the Sinai peninsula. They had close ties with the Moabites, as is evident from 22:4, 7.

There are, in my opinion, two reasons why the author selected this particular event from the larger narrative at his disposal (see above) for special emphasis. In the first place, he wanted to show to what extent the moral and spiritual degeneration had affected Israel's leaders specifically, and how great a danger lay in this for Israel (see also vv. 16–18); and second, to clarify the special position of the descendants of Phinehas within the circle of the Aaronites.

25:6–9 *Then an Israelite man brought to his family a Midianite woman right before the eyes of Moses and the whole assembly of Israel while they were weeping at the entrance to the Tent of Meeting. When Phinehas son of Eleazar, the son of Aaron, the priest, saw this, he left the assembly, took a spear in his hand and followed the Israelite into the tent. He drove the spear through both of them— through the Israelite and into the woman's body. Then the plague against the Israelites was stopped; but those who died in the plague numbered 24,000.*

Up to this point the men of Israel at least respected the purity of Israel's camp (5:1–4) and of family life; but now one of the leaders of Simeon (v. 14) takes a Midianite woman into his tent (the Hebrew says "the Midianite woman," indicating that she has been mentioned before in the larger narrative). He does this "right before the eyes of Moses and the whole assembly of Israel." By his action he indicates that this woman is henceforth to be considered his wife. He does this while Moses and the whole assembly are weeping before the Lord about their worship of the Baal of Peor and about the plague that resulted (v. 8)! A stronger proof of rebellion against the Lord's demand (Exod. 20:3), and a greater contempt for the required purity of Israel's camp are hardly possible.

As soon as Aaron's grandson Phinehas (a name of Egyptian origin, *pe-nhes,* "dark-skinned") sees this happen, he jumps up from the weeping assembly in holy anger, takes his spear, and goes after the Simeonite. The latter thinks himself to be safe in the *qubba* (v. 8; NIV "tent," RSV "inner room," ASV "pavilion"). This word is found only here in the Old Testament. In the Mishnah the word means "bordello," but this cannot be its meaning here, since the man takes the Midianite woman "to his brothers" (NIV "to his family," v. 6). On the basis of the Arabic *al-kobbat* (whence our word "alcove," cf. ASV margin) I suspect, as do many other exegetes, that this word refers to the women's section of the tent in which, of course, no other man was allowed to enter (cf. Judg. 4:18ff.). But Phinehas follows him into this normally forbidden area and kills both the Simeonite and the Midianite woman with a single thrust of his spear. That single thrust is emphasized by the addition "and the woman through her belly" (NIV "into the woman's body"). The word for "belly," *qeba,* also provides a play on words (*qubba, qeba,* see above), which the Easterner would readily recognize.

"Then the plague against the Israelites was stopped," after 24,000 (1 Cor. 10:8 says 23,000) Israelites had died. Concerning this figure I refer back to my comments on the Hebrew *'elef* (commentary on 1:20–46). "The plague" indicates here (as in 14:37; 16:48; but cf. Exod. 9:14; 2 Chron. 21:14) a fatal disease that suddenly breaks out among the people (cf. 31:16; 1 Sam. 6:4; 2 Sam. 24:21).

25:10–13 *The LORD said to Moses, "Phinehas son of Eleazar, the son of Aaron, the priest, has turned my anger away from the Israelites; for he was as zealous as I am for my honor among them, so that in my zeal I did not put an end to them. Therefore tell him I am making my covenant of peace with him. He and his descendants will have a covenant of a lasting priesthood, because he was zealous for the honor of his God and made atonement for the Israelites."*

These verses show the causal relationship between Phinehas's act and the cessation of the plague on the one hand (vv. 10–11), and the reward Phinehas received for his zeal on the other (vv. 12–13). Phinehas "was as zealous as I am" (lit. "was zealous with My zeal"). This "zeal" is the active resistance that has its source in the Lord's Being, against anything that is contrary to that Being. It burns like a fire that destroys (cf. Isa. 26:11; Ezek. 36:5; Zeph. 1:18; 3:8); in Deuteronomy 29:20 the Lord's zeal and His wrath are parallel. Phinehas's revulsion, evoked by the Simeonite's deed, was as destructive as the Lord's zeal over Israel's sin and sexual immorality. Phinehas felt the dishonor brought on the Lord's name by the Simeonite so deeply that he saw it as having been done against him personally; only death could eliminate the shame and dishonor. And in response to this burning love for the Lord and His service revealed in Phinehas's act, which prevented the destruction of all Israelites by the Lord's burning zeal (v. 11), the Lord gives Phinehas the assurance of his continued priesthood. The expression "covenant of peace" is also found in Isaiah 54:10; Ezekiel 34:25; 37:26; Malachi 2:4ff.; it implies the assurance of a continual relationship of peace with God, from which relationship then will flow the blessings implicit in it. For Phinehas and his descendants this will mean an uninterrupted priesthood.

It has been thought strange that the hereditary priesthood is so strongly emphasized here, since Phinehas, as Eleazar's son, was entitled to this by birth; Kuenen concluded that these verses were inserted here to legitimize the priestly rights of the Zadokites, from whom the high priest was chosen after the demise of the house of Eli. Apart from the underlying view of the Scriptures, which I do not share, this view overlooks the fact that verse 13 apparently points to the link between the high-priestly office and the house of Eleazar-Phinehas, which bypasses all other branches of the Aaronic family tree (cf. Lev. 10:6, 12, 16; Num. 3:2, 4; 1 Chron. 24:1ff.; Ezra 8:2). Furthermore, 20:25–26 indicates that the high priest did not have the right to appoint his successor, so the fact that Phinehas was Eleazar's son did not necessarily mean that he would also be high priest. Phinehas is thus called "the priest" in Joshua 22:13, 30ff. Also, the suggestion that Exodus 6:24 and 1 Chronicles 6:4, 50 would indicate that Phinehas was Eleazar's only son is certainly incorrect, unless it is assumed that all subsequent generations also had only one son each (cf. the genealogies in 1 Chron. 6). The need for an organization of the priests into divisions during David's time (1 Chron. 24) proves the opposite. In verse 13 the line of priests traced by Ezekiel from Levi via Zadok begins (cf. Ezek. 44:15–16 and my commentary on those verses).

25:14–15 *The name of the Israelite who was killed with the Midianite woman was Zimri son of Salu, the leader of a Simeonite family. And the name of the Midianite woman who was put to death was Cozbi daughter of Zur, a tribal chief of a Midianite family.*

Phinehas's act is given added relief by the mention of the names of the two people he killed. Both were of noble descent. The father of the woman was Zur, called here "head of the *'ummas* in Midian." In Genesis 25:16 *'umma* is used in connection with the Ishmaelites ("according to their nations," KJV; "according to their tribes," RSV); in Psalm 117:1b it is used in a parallel construction with "nations." We do not know the exact meaning of the word; it was apparently unknown to the Israelite reader in relatively early times, as indicated by the marginal addition of the Hebrew word for "family" in the MT. In 31:8 Zur is counted among the kings of the Midianites.

3. *No Peace With the Midianites* (25:16–18)

25:16–18 *The LORD said to Moses, "Treat the Midianites as enemies and kill them, because they treated you as enemies when they deceived you in the affair of Peor and their sister Cozbi, the daughter of a Midianite leader, the woman who was killed when the plague came as a result of Peor."*

Even as after the experience at Rephidim an oath was sworn that peace between Israel and Amalek would never again be possible (Exod. 17:16), so here the same is said with regard to Israel and Midian. The further addition of verse 18 shows the great danger to which Israel exposed itself by bowing down before the Baal of Peor (v. 3). On Midian's part it was a *seror,* a display of enmity under the guise of friendliness, in this case by inviting Israel to participate in the offering meal. Midian "deceived" Israel. The first battle between Israel and Midian is described in chapter 31.

The Second Census
(26:1–65)

1. *The Census Commanded* (26:1–4a)

26:1–4a *After the plague the L*ORD *said to Moses and Eleazar son of Aaron, the priest, "Take a census of the whole Israelite community by families—all those twenty years old or more who are able to serve in the army of Israel." So on the plains of Moab by the Jordan across from Jericho, Moses and Eleazar the priest spoke with them and said, "Take a census of the men twenty years old or more, as the L*ORD *commanded Moses."*

The first census, organized by Moses and Aaron, is recorded in chapter 1. The arrangement of the camp in chapter 2 is based on this census. In chapter 26 we find the second census, this time carried out by Moses and Eleazar, who had succeeded his father after the latter's death (20:22–29). According to verse 63, the second census is held "on the plains of Moab," i.e., when Israel is about to enter Canaan. This census must provide the basis for the future division of the land (vv. 52–56). In verse 1 the census is said to take place "after the plague"; this does not, however, establish a causal connection between the plague and the census, as if the census would have been necessitated by the plague (Edelkoort, *Numeri*, p. 187). Although the number 24,000 in 25:9 is a round figure, the results of the plague were sufficiently well-known not to require a new census. No census was needed after the plague of 16:49, nor after that of 11:33. But, as stated, a new census is needed because of what is about to take place in Canaan. The statement "after the plague" merely fixes the time of the census, and chapter 26 is thus linked with 22:1. We are not told where the census took place until verses 63–65.

As was the case in 1:2–3, all men "twenty years old or more who are able to serve in the army of Israel" are to be counted by families. Many have translated the verb *paqad* (vv. 7, 18, et al.) in the sense of "muster"; but this would give the word a military connotation, while verses 52–56 indicate that the purpose was not military in nature. I therefore prefer here, as in chapter 1, the rendering "number." In chapter 1 twelve family heads were to help Moses and Aaron with the census; this is not mentioned here, but we cannot conclude from this omission that Moses and Eleazar performed the task by themselves.

2. *The Results of the Census* (26:4b–51)

26:4b–51 *These were the Israelites who came out of Egypt:*

The descendants of Reuben, the firstborn son of Israel, were:
  through Hanoch, the Hanochite clan;
  through Pallu, the Palluite clan;
  through Hezron, the Hezronite clan;
  through Carmi, the Carmite clan.

These were the clans of Reuben; those numbered were 43,730.

  *The son of Pallu was Eliab, and the sons of Eliab were Nemuel, Dathan and Abiram. The same Dathan and Abiram were the community officials who rebelled against Moses and Aaron and were among Korah's followers when they rebelled against the L*ORD*. The earth opened its mouth and swallowed them along with Korah, whose followers died when the fire devoured the 250 men. And they served as a warning sign. The line of Korah, however, did not die out.*

The descendants of Simeon by their clan were:
  through Nemuel, the Nemuelite clan;
  through Jamin, the Jaminite clan;
  through Jakin, the Jakinite clan;
  through Zerah, the Zerahite clan;
  through Shaul, the Shaulite clan.
These were the clans of Simeon; there were 22,200 men.

The descendants of Gad by their clans were:
  through Zephon, the Zephonite clan;
  through Haggi, the Haggite clan;
  through Shuni, the Shunite clan;
  through Ozni, the Oznite clan;
  through Eri, the Erite clan;
  through Arodi, the Arodite clan;
  through Areli, the Arelite clan.
These were the clans of Gad; those numbered were 40,500.

Er and Onan were sons of Judah, but they died in Canaan.
The descendants of Judah by their clans were:
  through Shelah, the Shelanite clan;
  through Perez, the Perezite clan;
  through Zerah, the Zerahite clan.
  The descendants of Perez were:
    through Hezron, the Hezronite clan;
    through Hamul, the Hamulite clan.
These were the clans of Judah; those numbered were 76,500.

The descendants of Issachar by their clans were:
  through Tola, the Tolaite clan;
  through Puah, the Puite clan;
  through Jashub, the Jashubite clan;
  through Shimron, the Shimronite clan.
These were the clans of Issachar; those numbered were 64,300.

The descendants of Zebulun by their clans were:
  through Sered, the Seredite clan;
  through Elon, the Elonite clan;
  through Jahleel, the Jahleelite clan.
These were the clans of Zebulun; those numbered were 60,500.

The descendants of Joseph by their clans through Manasseh and Ephraim were:

The descendants of Manasseh:
  through Makir, the Makirite clan (Makir was the father of Gilead);
  through Gilead, the Gileadite clan.
  These were the descendants of Gilead:
    through Iezer, the Iezerite clan;
    through Helek, the Helekite clan;
    through Asriel, the Asrielite clan;
    through Shechem, the Shechemite clan;
    through Shemida, the Shemidaite clan;
    through Hepher, the Hepherite clan.
    (Zelophehad son of Hepher had no sons; he had only daughters, whose names
    were Mahlah, Noah, Hoglah, Milcah and Tirzah.)
These were the clans of Manasseh; those numbered were 52,700.

These were the descendants of Ephraim by their clans:
  through Shuthelah, the Shuthelahite clan;
  through Beker, the Bekerite clan;
  through Tahan, the Tahanite clan.
  These were the descendants of Shuthelah:
    through Eran, the Eranite clan.
These were the clans of Ephraim: those numbered were 32,500.

These were the descendants of Joseph by their clans.

The descendants of Benjamin by their clans were:
  Through Bela, the Belaite clan;
  through Ashbel, the Ashbelite clan;
  through Ahiram, the Ahiramite clan;
  through Shupham, the Shuphamite clan;
  through Hupham, the Huphamite clan.
  The descendants of Bela through Ard and Naaman were:
    through Ard, the Ardite clan;
    through Naaman, the Naamite clan.
These were the clans of Benjamin; those numbered were 45,600.

These were the descendants of Dan by their clans:
  through Shuham, the Shuhamite clan.
These were the clans of Dan: All of them were Shuhamite clans; and those num-
bered were 64,400.

The descendants of Asher by their clans were:
  through Imnah, the Imnite clan;
  through Ishvi, the Ishvite clan;
  through Beriah, the Beriite clan;
  and through the descendants of Beriah:
    through Heber, the Heberite clan;
    through Malkiel, the Malkielite clan.
  (Asher had a daughter named Serah.)
These were the clans of Asher; those numbered were 53,400.

The descendants of Naphtali by their clans were:
  through Jahzeel, the Jahzeelite clan;
  through Guni, the Gunite clan;
  through Jezer, the Jezerite clan;
  through Shillem, the Shillemite clan.
These were the clans of Naphtali; those numbered were 45,400.

The total number of the men of Israel was 601,730.

The results of the census are introduced by the words "These were the Israelites who came out of Egypt" (v. 4b). This has been taken as proof that chapter 26 is a parallel account to chapter 1, the report of the census at Sinai, which was then later transposed to the plains of Moab. This, however, overlooks the fact that the emphasis here is not on the number of individuals, but rather on the tribes and their structure. The total for each tribe is given only because the size of each tribe would later determine the allotment of a proportional section of Canaan (cf. vv. 52–56).

The tribes are listed in the same order as in chapter 1, except for Manasseh and Ephraim, who have here exchanged places (cf. 1:32, 34 and 26:29, 35). But, for the reason already stated, chapter 26 differs from chapter 1 in that the various clans in each tribe are here also listed.

Comparison of the names of the clans of the various tribes with the names of the children of Jacob's sons in Genesis 46:9–25 (for Reuben and Simeon, see also Exod. 6:14–15) reveals several differences. Missing in Numbers 26 are Ohad (Simeon), Ezbon (Gad), Beker and Gera (Benjamin; in Gen. 46:21 we should probably read with Kittel, *Biblia Hebraica*, 3rd ed., "Ahiram," "Shupham," and "Hupham" instead of "Ehi, Rosh, Muppim, and Huppim"), and Ishvah (Asher), while the tribes of Manasseh and Ephraim are of course missing in Genesis 46. There has thus apparently been some fluctuation in the structure of the tribes. This is also the impression we get when we compare Numbers 26 and 1 Chronicles 2ff., where only the tribal structures of Reuben, Issachar, and Naphtali are the same. Differences that are merely the result of alternate spellings of the same name (e.g., Jemuel-Nemuel) can, of course, be ignored.

247

A comparison of the totals for each tribe in chapter 1 and chapter 26 shows that the grand totals of the two censuses are approximately the same (a decrease of 1,820, or about .3 percent), but that the strength of the individual tribes fluctuated rather markedly:

	chapter 1	chapter 26	increase	decrease	% change
Reuben	46,500	43,730	—	2,770	− 6 %
Simeon	59,300	22,200	—	37,100	−63 %
Gad	45,650	40,500	—	5,150	−11 %
Judah	74,600	76,500	1,900	—	+ 3 %
Issachar	54,400	64,300	9,900	—	+18 %
Zebulon	57,400	60,500	3,100	—	+ 5 %
Manasseh	32,200	52,700	20,500	—	+64 %
Ephraim	40,500	32,500	—	8,000	−20 %
Benajmin	35,400	45,600	10,200	—	+29 %
Dan	62,700	64,400	1,700	—	+ 3 %
Asher	41,500	53,400	11,900	—	+29 %
Naphtali	53,400	45,400	—	8,000	−15 %
Totals	603,550	601,730	59,200	61,020	− .3%

Any attempt to explain these differences is futile; we simply do not have any further data. But one thing is certain: the totals are round figures, as the absence of tens and units indicates. Concerning the size of these numbers I refer back to my comments on 1:20–46.

The structure of Manasseh and Ephraim is, of course, not given in Genesis 46. In Numbers 26:29 Makir is called (lit.) the son of Manasseh (cf. Josh. 17:1; 1 Chron. 7:14), and Gilead the son of Makir; in verses 30–32 several descendants (lit. "sons") of Gilead are listed. This is, of course, nothing more than a genealogical description of historical events. Except in Judges 5:14, Makir is always the representative of East Manasseh, which settled very early in Bashan and Gilead (32:33ff.; Deut. 3:13–14; Josh. 13:29ff.). The "sons" of Gilead of verses 30–32 are called "sons" of Manasseh in Joshua 17:2 (Iezer of v. 30 there is called, probably more correctly, Abiezer); in 1 Chronicles 7:19 Shechem is called the "son" of Shemida, while both are here "sons" of Manasseh. This indicates that over the years quite a few changes took place within eastern Manasseh, which is hardly surprising in a region where the Aramaic influence was increasingly felt (cf. Manasseh's Aramean concubine, 1 Chron. 7:14). I point out that Shechem is undoubtedly the well-known city of Shechem, west of the Jordan, while in Judges 6:11 we hear of a clan of Abiezer (Iezer, see above) among West Manasseh. This indicates that at the time of the census of Numbers 26 the division of Manasseh had not yet taken place.

Three Ephraimite clans are mentioned in verses 35–36, while a fourth one, the Eranite clan, was apparently of lesser importance, since it is listed as the "descendants" of one of the first three. An entirely different picture of the structure of Ephraim is presented in 1 Chronicles 7:20–29, probably because its author wanted to emphasize the genealogy of Joshua (see my commentary on 1 Chron.). The author has incorporated several "footnotes" in the report of the second census that are not of direct relevance to the census itself: verses 5a, 9–11, 19, 33, 46. Verses 9–11 and 33 relate to the contents of Numbers: the former to the rebellion of Korah (chs. 16–17), the latter to 27:1–11 and chapter 36, the daughters of Zelophehad. The fact that Reuben was Jacob's eldest son (v. 5a) serves here, as in 1:20, to justify his position at the head of the list of tribes. The comment in verse 19 is derived from Genesis 46:12, that in verse 46 from Genesis 46:17; I have no idea why these two comments are incorporated here.

3. *The Future Division of Canaan* (26:52–56)

26:52–56 *The Lord said to Moses, "The land is to be allotted to them as an inheritance based on the number of names. To a larger group give a larger inheritance, and to a smaller group a smaller one; each is to receive its inheritance according to the number of those listed. Be sure that the land is distributed by lot. What each group inherits will be according to the names for its ancestral tribe. Each inheritance is to be distributed by lot among the larger and smaller groups."*

The land of Canaan is to be "allotted to them" (v. 53), i.e., to the recounted twelve tribes, not including Levi. This division is to be based on two principles: the distribution must be by lot, and it must be based on the numerical strength of each of the tribes. The specific manner in which this distribution is to be decided, however, is not mentioned here, nor in 33:54, where the subject is again brought up in passing. It is possible (although this is strictly conjectural) that lots were first cast to decide whether a given tribe would settle in the north, east, south, or west of Canaan, without defining the territory. A second casting of lots would then further determine the general location of each tribe within the region. Only after this had been accomplished could the specific boundaries be determined in accordance with the size of each tribe. And finally, a third casting of lots would assign a specific territory to each clan. This process would undoubtedly involve quite a number of practical problems, and many have consequently questioned the feasibility of this method. But there was no choice; without the casting of lots Israel would immediately have disintegrated because the stronger tribes would have crowded out the weaker ones, and intertribal conflict would have been unavoidable.

The time of the actual distribution by lot, whether it took place before or after the conquest, is not indicated. But the land was divided in this manner, at least the land west of the Jordan (Josh. 14:1–5); Eleazar and the heads of the tribal clans were in charge of the allocation process. We do not hear anything about the division of the Transjordan region. Joshua 13:15–33 states only that Moses "gave" certain areas to the various tribes (vv. 15, 24, 29, 32); but lots were undoubtedly also cast in this instance, since Israel, like all nations of antiquity, perceived in the lot the voice of the deity (Prov. 16:33), whose decision, of course, brooked neither resistance nor appeal. Thus, each tribe received its inheritance, as it were, directly from the Lord. Psalm 16:5–6 and Micah 2:4–5 show how deeply the concept of dividing land by lot was embedded in Israel's life. Even today a number of Bedouin tribes still divide available land by lot.

4. *The Counting of the Levites* (26:57–65)

26:57–58b *These were the Levites who were counted by their clans:*
through Gershon, the Gershonite clan;
through Kohath, the Kohathite clan;
through Merari, the Merarite clan.
These also were Levite clans:
the Libnite clan,
the Hebronite clan,
the Mahlite clan,
the Mushite clan,
the Korahite clan.

Again, as in the first census (1:47ff), the Levites are counted separately, but this time for a different reason. At Sinai it was because the Levites served at the tabernacle, here it is because they are not involved in the division of the land (v. 62).

This section begins (v. 57) with a listing of the three main clans of the Levites, rather than with the sons of Levi (3:17). These clans and their subdivisions were presented in 3:17–33 (cf. also chapter 4 and Exod. 6:16–19) as follows:

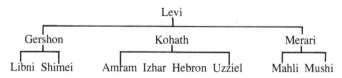

But instead of the eight clans of chapter 3, chapter 26 lists only five: four of the clans of chapter 3 (Libni, Hebron, Mahli, and Mushi) and the "Korahite clan." The latter is, according to Exodus 6:21, 24, a subdivision of the clan of Izhar, and is not mentioned in chapter 3. I do not know the reason for the addition of the Korahite clan, nor for the omission of Shimei, Amram, Izhar, and Uzziel, especially since the last four are mentioned in 1 Chronicles 23:7; 26:23; 23:18, 20 respectively. Verse 58 has its own superscription ("These also were Levite clans," lit. "These are the clans of the Levites"), while verse 58c is, so to speak, a footnote to verse 57. I would conclude, with Strack and Heinisch, that verse 58a, b were inserted by a later redactor, who added the Levite clans that were most prominent in his own day. In any case, this list of five Levite clans is found nowhere else.

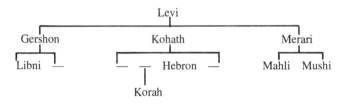

26:58c–61 *(Kohath was the forefather of Amram; the name of Amram's wife was Jochebed, a descendant of Levi, who was born to the Levites in Egypt. To Amram she bore Aaron, Moses and their sister Miriam. Aaron was the father of Nadab and Abihu, Eleazar and Ithamar. But Nadab and Abihu died when they made an offering before the LORD with unauthorized fire.)*

These verses are a brief excursus, based on Exodus 6:20, 23ff., and are related to verse 57 only to the extent that Moses and Aaron belonged to the Kohathite clan through their father Amram. Again (cf. 3:2) a list of Aaron's sons is given, and the death of Nadab and Abihu is mentioned (see Lev. 10).

26:62 *All the male Levites a month old or more numbered 23,000. They were not counted along with the other Israelites because they received no inheritance among them.*

This verse refers back to verse 57; the total number of Levites is one "thousand" *('elef)* higher than the total in 3:39. It is emphasized that the Levites were counted separately "because they received no inheritance among them."

26:63–65 *These are the ones counted by Moses and Eleazar the priest when they counted the Israelites on the plains of Moab by the Jordan across from Jericho. Not one of them was among those counted by Moses and Aaron the priest when they counted the Israelites in the Desert of Sinai. For the LORD had told those Israelites they would surely die in the desert, and not one of them was left except Caleb son of Jephunneh and Joshua son of Nun.*

While 26:1 stated only that the census took place "after the plague," here the location is given: "on the plains of Moab by the Jordan across from Jericho." Furthermore, it is emphasized that of all those counted in the first census at Sinai only Caleb and Joshua are still alive: the judgment of 14:28ff. has been fulfilled.

Zelophehad's Daughters
(27:1–11)

1. The Legal Question (27:1–4)

27:1–4 *The daughters of Zelophehad son of Hepher, the son of Gilead, the son of Makir, the son of Manasseh, belonged to the clans of Manasseh son of Joseph. The names of the daughters were Mahlah, Noah, Hoglah, Milcah and Tirzah. They approached the entrance to the Tent of Meeting and stood before Moses, Eleazar the priest, the leaders and the whole assembly, and said, "Our father died in the desert. He was not among Korah's followers, who banded together against the LORD, but he died for his own sin and left no sons. Why should our father's name disappear from his clan because he had no son? Give us property among our father's relatives."*

A legal issue is raised by the five daughters of Zelophehad. The name Zelophehad is probably of very ancient origin, at least if it means, as is supposed, "Protection is the One to be Feared" (i.e., God; see Gen. 31:42, 53: "the Fear of Isaac"). The census of chapter 26 included only male Israelites ("Israelite community," 26:2, is literally, "all the congregation of the sons of Israel") and the assumption thus was that only male members of a family could own land. Zelophehad's daughters fear that, since their father has died without any male offspring, they will be excluded when the land is divided; this means that Zelophehad's name will "disappear from his clan," while they themselves will be absorbed into the clans of their husbands.

The fact that they decide to bring this question to Moses and the other authorities indicates again (cf. ch. 12) that the position of women, including that of unmarried women, was entirely different then than it was later, and still is, in the Orient. Although the woman's position in Israel was no longer what it was in Babylonia in the third millennium B.C., when the woman was in every respect the equal of the man and her right of succession was secure (see also Job 42:15), nevertheless she is not yet considered inferior. She still has the right to bring legal matters before the court, and her vows can still be legally binding (cf. ch. 30). Only, she has lost her right of succession (see Deut. 21:15ff.; 25:5ff.).

Since the question raised by the daughters of Zelophehad is a legal question that affects the entire community, they bring it before the body that has the authority to settle legal matters: Moses, the high priest, the leaders, and the whole assembly (see commentary on 1:16 and 16:21). This body sits at the entrance to the Tent of Meeting, because ultimately justice comes from the Lord. In Israel every judicial decision is an oracle, a divine decision.

The manner in which they present their question is in more than one respect remarkable. First, because of what they say about their father: they emphasize that, although many of the leaders followed Korah (16:1–2), their father had not supported him, even though he was one of the leaders according to 26:33. The fact that he has died toward the end of the wilderness journey is, they say, unrelated to the judgment of God on Korah and his followers. He died "for his own sin," i.e., he has fallen under the general judgment on rebellious Israel (14:18ff.; see also Deut. 24:16). There is thus no special reason why Zelophehad's name should "disappear" (lit. "be taken away," used in this sense only here; "erased," Exod. 17:14; Deut. 9:14; et al.; "blotted out," Deut. 25:6; 29:20). This statement reflects the importance placed on a name, not only in Israel, but in the entire ancient Near East. A name is not merely a designation, but an integral part of existence: only that which has a name exists. The perpetuation of a name is therefore a matter of importance; only a son can ensure that a name will not "disappear" (cf. Deut. 25:6ff.), because only a son has the right of succession. The name of a man who has no son will be "remembered no more" (Jer. 11:19), because it has ceased to be connected with an inheritance. This reflects a concept that was prominent in Israel: a name is linked with landownership, and it is therefore important to prevent any land from being removed from the family, clan, or tribe to which it originally belonged (cf. Lev. 25:8ff.; 1 Kings 21; Isa. 5:8; Jer. 32:6ff.; Mic. 2:2–3; see also Deut. 25:5–10). Since Zelophehad had only daughters, and thus no heir, his family could not receive any land when Canaan was divided, and consequently his name would no longer exist in the Israelite community. His daughters now ask that they be allowed to inherit.

2. *The Divine Decision* (27:5–11)

27:5–11 *So Moses brought their case before the L*ORD *and the L*ORD *said to him, "What Zelophehad's daughters are saying is right. You must certainly give them property as an inheritance among their father's relatives and turn their father's inheritance over to them.*

*"Say to the Israelites, 'If a man dies and leaves no son, turn his inheritance over to his daughter. If he has no daughter, give his inheritance to his brothers. If he has no brothers, give his inheritance to his father's brothers. If his father had no brothers, give his inheritance to the nearest relative in his clan, that he may possess it. This is to be a legal requirement for the Israelites, as the L*ORD *commanded Moses.' "*

This important legal issue could not have arisen before. Neither in Egypt nor in the desert was landownership possible. It is thus a new case, and everyone realizes that the decision will have far-reaching consequences. If the request is denied and daughters cannot inherit, then the possibility exists that land assigned by lot, i.e., by divine choice, can later go over into other hands; this would open the way for "landlordship," i.e., large landholdings by a few individuals. If, on the other hand, the request is granted, the right to inherit is given to those who previously did not have it. It is not surprising that Moses takes the case before the Lord. We are not informed how he does this, as was also true in the cases mentioned in Leviticus 24:12–13 and Numbers 15:34–35; verses 5–6 probably follow the pattern set forth in 12:8.

The Lord decides in favor of Zelophehad's daughters. They are given the right to receive their father's inheritance when the land in Canaan is distributed, and may thus own land. This decision does not apply to this case only, but will henceforth be a legal principle. The decision has an implication that is not brought up here: if the daughter who has inherited land marries a man from a different tribe, her property would go over to her husband's tribe, since the woman becomes part of that tribe. This problem will require a separate decision later (see ch. 36). A special case that is dealt with here is that of the man who dies without any offspring at all. The same principle on which the previous decision was based is applied: the inheritance is to remain in the clan of the deceased. It goes to his brothers, or his paternal uncles, or to his nearest relatives, i.e., to the nearest living male relative on his father's side. Male maternal relatives cannot inherit, since they belong to a different clan, which the woman left when she married.

This decision, which does not invalidate the general rule that women cannot inherit, but rather makes provision in a special case where landownership is involved, is henceforth upheld by Israel as the legal norm. See also chapter 36.

Joshua to Succeed Moses
(27:12–23)

The Lord's command to Moses to go up into the Abarim range to die there is contained twice in the Pentateuch as it lies before us: here and in Deuteronomy 32:48–52, where Moses is also told that he will see Canaan, but will not be allowed to enter it. It is, of course, not possible that this command was given twice, since it would imply that a repetition was necessary because Moses delayed obeying the first command. The only possible solution is that the author of the Pentateuch derived this chapter from a different account than that on which Deuteronomy 32:48–52 is based, while this account is inserted here because 32:28 and 34:17 clearly speak of Joshua as Moses' appointed successor.

1. *Moses' Death Imminent* (27:12–17)

27:12–17 *Then the Lord said to Moses, "Go up this mountain in the Abarim range and see the land I have given the Israelites. After you have seen it, you too will be gathered to your people, as your brother Aaron was, for when the community rebelled at the waters in the Desert of Zin, both of you disobeyed my command to honor me as holy before their eyes." (These were the waters of Meribah in Kadesh, in the Desert of Zin.)*

Moses said to the Lord, "May the Lord, the God of the spirits of all mankind, appoint a man over this community to go out and come in before them, one who will lead them out and bring them in, so the Lord's people will not be like sheep without a shepherd."

The Abarim range (see commentary on 21:20; also 33:47–48; Deut. 32:49) lies on the edge of the plains of Moab, and from there descends into the Jordan valley close to the northeastern point of the Dead Sea. Mount Pisgah (21:20) is in this range, as is Nebo, which, according to Deuteronomy 32:49 and 34:1 is the mountain on which Moses died. From one of these peaks (approx. 4,000 ft. high) Moses is allowed to see the land from Hebron to Galilee, the land he and Aaron would never enter because of their lapse into sin. Once he ascends this mountain Moses will not descend again. He will be "gathered to his people," an expression that reflects the belief that the dead find a place in the realm of the dead according to families and clans (Gen. 25:8; 35:29; 49:29, 33; Deut. 32:50; see also commentary on 20:26). Moses does not have to be reminded of the specifics of his and Aaron's disobedience. The end of verse 14 is therefore not part of the Lord's words to Moses, but has been added by the author for the benefit of his readers; the NIV appropriately puts it in parentheses. Concerning the incident at Meribah in Kadesh, see 20:7–11; concerning Aaron's death, see 20:23ff.

Moses, who has known what his fate would be ever since Kadesh, bows without questioning under the Lord's will; the Lord is "the God of the spirits of all mankind" (lit. "of the spirits of all flesh," KJV), the omnipotent God in whose hands is the disposition of man's life (cf. 16:22). Moses therefore does not think of himself, but rather of the people whom he has led for several decades, and whose virtues and weaknesses he knows so well. The people need a young man, strong in body and spirit, who will be eminently capable of leading them. This new leader must not be limited in his ability to go with the people when they "go out and come in." This phrase has strong military overtones (Deut. 31:2–3; Josh. 14:11; 1 Sam. 18:13, 16; 29:6; 1 Kings 3:7), although it is not an exclusively military expression (2 Kings 11:9; 1 Chron. 27:1). In the near future, more than ever before, Israel's leader must be present where the decisive events take place: on the battlefield. Otherwise, the people would be "like sheep without a shepherd" (cf. 1 Kings 22:17; Ezek. 34:6; Zech. 11:8; 13:7). I see in this prayer of Moses an awareness of his own shortcomings during the battle with Sihon and Og, which were the result of his advanced age. It is, of course, entirely possible, and even probable, that Moses had Joshua in mind when he prayed. But it is incorrect to see in this narrative a different presentation of the course of events than that given in Deuteronomy 3:21, 28; 31:14–15.

2. *Joshua Becomes Moses' Successor* (27:18–23)

27:18–23 *So the L*ORD *said to Moses, "Take Joshua son of Nun, a man in whom is the spirit, and lay your hand on him. Have him stand before Eleazar the priest and the entire assembly and commission him in their presence. Give him some of your authority so the whole Israelite community will obey him. He is to stand before Eleazar the priest, who will obtain decisions for him by inquiring of the Urim before the L*ORD*. At his command he and the entire community of the Israelites will go out, and at his command they will come in."*

*Moses did as the L*ORD *commanded him. He took Joshua and had him stand before Eleazar the priest and the whole assembly. Then he laid his hands on him and commissioned him, as the L*ORD *instructed through Moses.*

Moses then receives from the Lord the command to solemnly appoint his faithful servant, Joshua, the son of Nun (cf. Exod. 17:9ff.; 24:13; 32:17), as his successor. Joshua is a man "in whom is the spirit"; in Deuteronomy

34:9 this spirit is called "the spirit of wisdom," i.e., of ability. Joshua is thus capable of choosing the appropriate means to achieve the intended purpose (cf. Gen. 41:38). Moses must lay his hand on Joshua, which is in one sense a sign of blessing (cf. Gen. 48:14), on the other hand a sign of dedication (of man or beast) to a given purpose (Lev. 1:4; 24:14; Num. 8:10; see also Acts 6:6). In the presence of Israel's lawful representatives (cf. v. 2), Moses must "commission" Joshua (v. 22), which, according to 1 Samuel 13:14; 25:30; 2 Samuel 6:21; Deuteronomy 3:28 means that he must "install" him; the laying on of hands is the symbol of investiture with authority, which now goes from Moses to Joshua. "Authority" is literally "honor" (cf. KJV) or "majesty," with which also the Lord Himself and Israel's kings are invested (1 Chron. 29:25; Pss. 8:2; 21:6; 45:4; 96:6; 104:1; 111:3; 148:13; Jer. 22:18; Dan. 11:21; Hab. 3:3). Although Joshua becomes Moses' successor, he does not become his equal. Only a portion of Moses' authority is given to Joshua (v. 20). The implication is given in verse 21: while Moses received his instructions directly from the Lord (cf. Exod. 25:22; Lev. 24:12; Num. 9:8; 15:34–35), Joshua will receive them through the mediation of the high priest, who is to use the sacred lots, the Urim and Thummim, for this purpose (Exod. 28:30; Lev. 8:8). The nature and appearance of these lots are completely unknown, but according to 1 Samuel 14:41–42 they served to make known the Lord's will in a given case. Joshua thus will not be able to do without the intermediary of the high priest, and will thus not be a "prophet" like Moses (Deut. 34:10). Joshua will be the leader, but the Lord (to whom the "his" in v. 21b refers) will always determine the "how" and "when" through the high priest. However, we do not hear of the use of the Urim and Thummim in the Book of Joshua, although we do read that the Lord "speaks" with Joshua (1:1; 3:7; 4:1; 7:10; 8:1, 8; 10:8; et al.).

Verses 22–23 emphasize the fact that Moses carried out the Lord's instructions to the letter. Joshua is now commissioned, and knows what task awaits him.

New Laws
(28:1–30:17)

1. *Daily Offerings and Festival Offerings of the Community* (28:1–29:40)

Neither this law, nor the law in chapter 30 fits in the context of the narrative of Numbers. Both contain regulations that relate to the organization of Israel's life in Canaan. This law gives, sometimes very extensive, regulations for the offerings that Israel as a community must bring daily (vv. 1–8), on the Sabbath (vv. 9–10), monthly (New Moon, vv. 11–15), and on the annual festivals (Passover, Feast of Weeks, Feast of Trumpets, Day of Atonement, Feast of Tabernacles; 28:16–29:11). The offerings for the Feast of Tabernacles are especially treated in great detail (29:12–40). These chapters differ from the calendar of feasts in Leviticus 23 in that there a chronological list is given of "the appointed feasts of the LORD," which were to be accompanied by a *miqra' qodeš,* a "holy convocation" (cf. RSV; see my commentary on Lev. 23:1–2). This is why in Leviticus 23 the offerings to be brought on the feast days are presupposed, rather than spelled out (see vv. 27, 36, 37–38), except in the case of the Firstfruits (vv. 11ff.) and the Feast of Weeks (vv. 16ff.). In Numbers 28–29 the offerings are central. Leviticus 23 thus presupposes Numbers 28–29, while both are based on an older calendar of feasts. Furthermore, Numbers 28–29 presupposes the laws of the offerings in Leviticus 1–7, 16, 23, as well as Numbers 15:1–12.

These two chapters begin with a superscription (28:1–2), and end with a subscript (29:39–40). The superscription eliminates the possibility of any arbitrariness on Israel's part in the bringing of offerings as a community. The offerings are to be brought "at the appointed time" *(mo'ed),* a word that derives its meaning from Genesis 1:14 and originally referred to the constellations as the determinants of time. Arbitrariness is not allowed, since Israel's offerings are not a favor bestowed by the people on their God, but rather "the food for my offerings made by fire," i.e., the Lord's rightful property. To the other Semites offerings were gifts to a hungry and thirsty god, who is dependent on his people for sustenance; this is not the case here. The offerings in Israel depend on God's gracious will, through which He has entered into a covenant relationship with His people—they are His (cf. 9:7, 13; 31:50; also Lev. 23:14). Concerning *qorban* ("offering"), see my commentary on Leviticus 1:2. Yet the lawgiver does not hesitate to call the Lord's offerings "food," "the food of their God" (Lev. 21:6, 8, 17, 21–22; 22:25), "food, an offering made to the LORD by fire" (Lev. 3:11, 16; cf. Num. 28:24). The offerings are also repeatedly characterized as "a pleasing aroma," or, more accurately, "an aroma of satisfaction," i.e., of the stilling of God's anger (see my commentary on Lev., Introduction, §VII). I note here that the usual rendering "an offering made by fire," which assumes that *'išše* is derived from *'eš* ("fire"), is incorrect. The word *'išše* rather characterizes the offering as the means by which it is possible to enjoy God's benevolence. Of course, this and other terms are remnants of the ancient priestly language from the time when the forefathers "lived beyond the River" (Josh. 24:2) and still believed that the gods did indeed eat and drink (Judg. 9:13). See my commentary on Leviticus, Introduction, §VII.

A. *The daily offerings* (28:1-8)

28:1-8 *The LORD said to Moses, "Give this command to the Israelites and say to them: 'See that you present to me at the appointed time the food for my offerings made by fire, as an aroma pleasing to me.' Say to them: 'This is the offering made by fire that you are to present to the LORD: two lambs a year old without defect, as a regular burnt offering each day. Prepare one lamb in the morning and the other at twilight, together with a grain offering of a tenth of an ephah of fine flour mixed with a fourth of a hin of oil from pressed olives. This is the regular burnt offering instituted at Mount Sinai as a pleasing aroma, an offering made to the LORD by fire. The accompanying drink offering is to be a fourth of a hin of fermented drink with each lamb. Pour out the drink offering to the LORD at the sanctuary. Prepare the second lamb at twilight, along with the same kind of grain offering and drink offering that you prepare in the morning. This is an offering made by fire, an aroma pleasing to the LORD.' "*

The requirements for the *tamîd,* the "regular offering" or "continual offering" (KJV, RSV), to be brought by Israel as a community twice daily, are given first. The wording is reminiscent of Exodus 29:38-42. This is the foundation for all the offerings Israel is to bring, the center of Israel's regulated worship. The other communal offerings are accurately described in Judaism as *musaf-*offerings, i.e., added offerings. While elsewhere the word *tamîd* is always preceded by "burnt offering" or "grain offering," Daniel (8:11-13; 11:31; 12:11) speaks of the *tamîd* without any qualification: the cessation of the *tamîd* means nothing more or less than the rendering inoperative of the Lord's covenant with Israel. The *tamîd* must be brought twice daily: in the morning and "between the two evenings," i.e., at twilight (see commentary on 9:3). Even as in Exodus 29:38-42 (cf. v. 6, which is omitted in the LXX), the *tamîd* must always consist of a lamb one year old and a grain offering of a tenth of an ephah (approximately two quarts) of *solet* (coarse flour or groats, the heart of the wheat kernel, at one time thought to refer to fine flour, cf. the English versions), mixed with a fourth of a hin (approximately one quart) of "beaten oil" (KJV, RSV), i.e., oil made from olives in a mortar rather than in a press (contrary to the NIV rendering: see Gispen's commentary on Exod. 27:20 in this series), accompanied by a drink offering of one-fourth of a hin (again, approximately one quart) of fermented drink. Except for the fermented drink that is to be poured out at the sanctuary (v. 7; the offering was to be poured out around the altar, *not* in the Holy Place; according to Ecclesiasticus 50:15 and Josephus, *Antiquities,* III, 9. 4 *on* the altar of burnt offering, in which, according to a more recent Jewish tradition, special tubes were installed for this purpose), the *tamîd* is to be burned entirely on the altar as a sign of

Israel's full dedication to the Lord's service. The bringing of the *tamîd* is the most important task of the priests. The "fermented drink" in verse 7 is *šekar,* lit. "strong drink," which is the traditional but less accurate rendering of the word (see commentary on 6:3). Because wine was always required with the offerings, here (in contrast to v. 14) *šekar* probably refers to some kind of grape juice. In Deuteronomy 14:26; 29:6; et al. both wine and *šekar* are used. The NIV rendering "fermented drink" is probably correct, since it avoids the incorrect connotation of our term "strong drink."

The bringing of the *tamîd* is also mentioned in 1 Kings 18:29, 36 and 2 Kings 16:15, and is alluded to in Hebrews 7:27; 10:11. In Ezekiel 46:13–15 only the morning burnt offering is mentioned, and there the requirement is a one-year-old lamb and a grain offering of one-sixth of an ephah of *solet* mixed with one-third of a hin of oil, larger quantities than are required here. The drink offering of fermented drink is omitted by Ezekiel, for reasons I do not know.

B. *Sabbath offerings* (28:9–10)

28:9–10 *" 'On the Sabbath day, make an offering of two lambs a year old without defect, together with its drink offering and a grain offering of two-tenths of an ephah of fine flour mixed with oil. This is the burnt offering for every Sabbath, in addition to the regular burnt offering and its drink offering.' "*

In addition to the *tamîd* an offering identical to it must be brought on behalf of the Israelite community on the Sabbath. This offering is not mentioned in Leviticus 23:3, but Ezekiel refers to this special Sabbath offering in 45:17 and 46:4–5, although there the quantities are again different: six lambs and a ram, which undoubtedly symbolize the week (see v. 13), while to the ram is added a grain offering of one ephah of *solet,* mixed with one hin of oil. The grain offering added to each of the six lambs could be determined by the prince himself in proportion to his gratitude for the blessings bestowed by the Lord in the week past. Concerning the Sabbath, see my commentary on Leviticus 23:3.

C. *Monthly offerings* (28:11–15)

28:11–15 *" 'On the first of every month, present to the LORD a burnt offering of two young bulls, one ram and seven male lambs a year old, all without defect. With each bull there is to be a grain offering of three-tenths of an ephah of fine flour mixed with oil; with the ram, a grain offering of two-tenths of an ephah of fine flour mixed with oil. This is for a burnt offering, a pleasing aroma, an offering made to*

---

the Lᴏʀᴅ by fire. With each bull there is to be a drink offering of half a hin of wine; with the ram, a third of a hin; and with each lamb, a fourth of a hin. This is the monthly burnt offering to be made at each new moon during the year. Besides the regular burnt offering with its drink offering, one male goat is to be presented to the Lᴏʀᴅ as a sin offering.'"

Israel's calendar was based on the moon. A new month *(chodeš)* began when according to the witness of reliable people the new moon *(chodeš)* was visible in the sky. This was also the sign for the "New Moon Festival," mentioned frequently in the Old Testament (1 Sam. 20:5ff.; Amos 8:5; et al.), an indication of the importance Israel attached to this feast, as was indeed true throughout the ancient Near East. Ezekiel 46:6–7 also speaks of the offering to be brought on this day in addition to the *tamîd*; but while we hear here of two young bulls, one ram, and seven male lambs one year old, Ezekiel only mentions the ram, one young bull, and six lambs. The additional grain offerings are also different. Ezekiel does not mention the sin offering, which speaks of the confession of unconscious transgression (see my commentary on Lev. 4:1ff.); I do not know the reason for these differences.

D. *The Passover* (28:16–25)

28:16–25 *" 'On the fourteenth day of the first month the Lᴏʀᴅ's Passover is to be held. On the fifteenth day of this month there is to be a festival; for seven days eat bread made without yeast. On the first day hold a sacred assembly and do no regular work. Present to the Lᴏʀᴅ an offering made by fire, a burnt offering of two young bulls, one ram and seven male lambs a year old, all without defect. With each bull prepare a grain offering of three-tenths of an ephah of fine flour mixed with oil; with the ram, two-tenths; and with each of the seven lambs, one-tenth. Include one male goat as a sin offering to make atonement for you. Prepare these in addition to the regular morning burnt offering. In this way prepare the food for the offering made by fire every day for seven days as an aroma pleasing to the Lᴏʀᴅ; it is to be prepared in addition to the regular burnt offering and its drink offering. On the seventh day hold a sacred assembly and do no regular work.'"*

This section actually concerns two feasts, the Passover and the *Massot* feast; the two feasts came to be considered a unit, however, to such an extent that Ezekiel can speak of a Passover of seven days (Ezek. 45:21; cf. Deut. 16:1–2), while we hear elsewhere of a *Massot* feast (Feast of Unleavened Bread) that includes the Passover (2 Chron. 30:13, 21; Ezra 6:22). See also my commentary on Leviticus 23:4–8. It strikes us immediately that, while in verse 16 the Passover is set for the fourteenth day of the first month, no indication is given as to how and when the Passover lamb was to be eaten; and also that, while in Exodus 23:15; 34:18; Leviticus 23:6; and Deuteronomy 16:16 the feast that Israel must celebrate from the fifteenth to the twenty-first day of the first month is called the "Feast of Unleavened Bread," here it is not given a specific name. The lawgiver limits himself to stating that the *massot,* the unleavened, round loaves of bread must then be eaten. This indicates that both the details concerning the Passover lamb and the name of the Feast of Unleavened Bread were considered to be so well-known that they did not need further elaboration.

The lawgiver focuses here on the keeping of the "sacred assembly" on the first (v. 18) and on the seventh day (v. 25) of the *Massot* feast, and on the offerings that are to be brought during this feast. The "sacred assembly" (*miqra' qodeš,* KJV: "holy convocation") refers to the call (*qr',* "to call") that goes out on this day; it is "holy" *(qodeš),* which marks it as a special day, set apart from all other days by the Lord as *His* festival. On that day all *regular* work is prohibited, in contrast to the Sabbath, when *any* kind of work is prohibited (see my commentary on Lev. 23:3).

The offerings to be brought on each of the seven feast days are identical to those that are required on the first day of every month (vv. 11–15). This brings us to a total of no fewer than seventy animals for burnt offerings. Although it goes without saying, verse 23 nevertheless emphasizes that all these offerings are to be brought in addition to the *tamîd*; only the morning *tamîd* is mentioned here, since the festival offerings were brought in the morning. Ezekiel 45:23–24 mentions a burnt offering of seven young bulls and seven rams with their accompanying grain offerings, and a male goat for a sin offering, not mentioned in Numbers 28; again, I cannot explain these differences.

E. *The Feast of Weeks* (28:26–31)

28:26–31 " 'On the day of firstfruits, when you present to the LORD an offering of new grain during the Feast of Weeks, hold a sacred assembly and do no regular work. Present a burnt offering of two young bulls, one ram and seven male lambs a year old as an aroma pleasing to the LORD. With each bull there is to be a grain offering of three-tenths of an ephah of fine flour mixed with oil; with the ram, two-tenths; and with each of the seven lambs, one-tenth. Include one male goat to make atonement for you. Prepare these together with their drink offerings, in addition to the regular burnt offering and its grain offering. Be sure the animals are without defect.' "

"Day of firstfruits" is the name, found only here, of a feast that is called the "Feast of Harvest" in Exodus 23:16, and the "Feast of Weeks" in

Exodus 34:22 and Deuteronomy 16:10; the latter name is alluded to here in the word *bešabu 'otekem,* "in your weeks," rendered "during the Feast of Weeks" in the NIV (KJV: "after your weeks"). We call this feast Pentecost because it is to be celebrated on the fiftieth day (*pentekostē,* Acts 2:1ff.) after the sheaf of the first grain is presented (Lev. 23:9–14), that is, at the official end of the harvest, which lasted from mid-April until mid-June. The Feast of Weeks is thus essentially a day of thanksgiving for the harvest. The offering to be brought in addition to the *tamîd* is again identical to that of the New Moon festival (vv. 11–15) and of the *Massot* feast (vv. 16–25). Concerning the differences between these verses and Leviticus 23:18ff., see my commentary on Leviticus 23:15–22.

F. *The Feast of Trumpets* (29:1–6)

29:1–6 *" 'On the first day of the seventh month hold a sacred assembly and do no regular work. It is a day for you to sound the trumpets. As an aroma pleasing to the LORD, prepare a burnt offering of one young bull, one ram and seven male lambs a year old, all without defect. With the bull prepare a grain offering of three-tenths of an ephah of fine flour mixed with oil; with the ram, two-tenths; and with each of the seven lambs, one-tenth. Include one male goat as a sin offering to make atonement for you. These are in addition to the monthly and daily burnt offerings with their grain offerings and drink offerings as specified. They are offerings made to the LORD by fire—a pleasing aroma.' "*

The number "seven," the ancient Oriental number of perfection, occupied an important place in Israel's thinking, not only in the bringing of the offerings (28:11, 19, 27), et al.), but also in the structure of their calendar. The seventh day, the seventh month, the seventh year, and the year of Jubilee, to be celebrated after seven "weeks of years," are holy to the Lord. Thus, the beginning of the seventh month must be celebrated with special ceremony. It is a "sacred assembly commemorated with trumpet blasts" (Lev. 23:24), a "day to sound the trumpets" (Num. 29:1). This is the sounding of the *shofar,* the rams horn with its deep, majestic sound. At least since the time of the Seleucids Judaism has celebrated this day as New Year's day, the *Rosh Hashana,* and an entire tract was later devoted to it. But we are not certain that this was already true in ancient Israel (see my commentary on Lev. 23:23–25). Ezekiel 45 also speaks of the special character of this day; there we find a cycle of feasts that includes two semiannual days of atonement that mark the beginning of the two halves of the religious year. The first one is to be held on the first day of the new year, the second one on the first day of the second half of the year[9] (Ezek. 45:20). Concerning the many questions involved, see L. I. Pap, *Das israelitische Neujahrsfest,* pp. 18–33.

This day must, of course, also be dedicated to the Lord by the bringing of offerings, once again identical to those of the previous three feasts. "As specified" (v. 6; "according to the ordinance for them," RSV) is a clear reference to 28:7, 14 and 15:1–12.

G. *The Day of Atonement* (29:7–11)

29:7–11 *"'On the tenth day of this seventh month hold a sacred assembly. You must deny yourselves and do no work. Present as an aroma pleasing to the LORD a burnt offering of one young bull, one ram and seven male lambs a year old, all without defect. With the bull prepare a grain offering of three-tenths of an ephah of fine flour mixed with oil; with the ram, two-tenths; and with each of the seven lambs, one-tenth. Include one male goat as a sin offering, in addition to the sin offering for atonement and the regular burnt offering with its grain offering, and their drink offerings.'"*

Concerning the nature of this day and the offerings required for it, see Leviticus 16. In Leviticus 23:26–32 only the command to fast and the prohibition of work on that day are given. Reference is made here only in passing to the offerings of Leviticus 16 with the words "the sin offering for atonement" (v. 11). The special offering (vv. 8ff.) is again the same as those for the previous feasts.

H. *The Feast of Tabernacles* (29:12–40)

29:12–40 *"'On the fifteenth day of the seventh month, hold a sacred assembly and do no regular work. Celebrate a festival to the LORD for seven days. Present an offering made by fire as an aroma pleasing to the LORD, a burnt offering of thirteen young bulls, two rams and fourteen male lambs a year old, all without defect. With each of the thirteen bulls prepare a grain offering of three-tenths of an ephah of fine flour mixed with oil; with each of the two rams, two-tenths; and with each of the fourteen lambs, one-tenth. Include one male goat as a sin offering, in addition to the regular burnt offering with its grain offering and drink offering.*

"'On the second day prepare twelve young bulls, two rams and fourteen male lambs a year old, all without defect. With the bulls, rams, and lambs, prepare their grain offerings and drink offerings according to the number specified. Include one male goat as a sin offering, in addition to the regular burnt offering with its grain offering, and their drink offerings.

"'On the third day prepare eleven bulls, two rams and fourteen male lambs a

---

[9]I.e., on the first day of the seventh month, rather than on "the seventh day of the month" (NIV). (Tr.)

year old, all without defect. With the bulls, rams and lambs, prepare their grain offerings and drink offerings according to the number specified. Include one male goat as a sin offering, in addition to the regular burnt offering with its grain offering and drink offering.

"'On the fourth day prepare ten bulls, two rams and fourteen male lambs a year old, all without defect. With the bulls, rams and lambs, prepare their grain offerings and drink offerings according to the number specified. Include one male goat as a sin offering, in addition to the regular burnt offering with its grain offering and drink offering.

"'On the fifth day prepare nine bulls, two rams and fourteen male lambs a year old, all without defect. With the bulls, rams and lambs, prepare their grain offerings and drink offerings according to the number specified. Include one male goat as a sin offering, in addition to the regular burnt offering with its grain offering and drink offering.

"'On the sixth day prepare eight bulls, two rams and fourteen male lambs a year old, all without defect. With the bulls, rams and lambs, prepare their grain offerings and drink offerings according to the number specified. Include one male goat as a sin offering, in addition to the regular burnt offering with its grain offering and drink offering.

"'On the seventh day prepare seven bulls, two rams and fourteen male lambs a year old, all without defect. With the bulls, rams and lambs, prepare their grain offerings and drink offerings according to the number specified. Include one male goat as a sin offering, in addition to the regular burnt offering with its grain offering and drink offering.

"'On the eighth day hold an assembly and do no regular work. Present an offering made by fire as an aroma pleasing to the Lord, a burnt offering of one bull, one ram and seven male lambs a year old, all without defect. With the bull, the ram and the lambs, prepare their grain offerings and drink offerings according to the number specified. Include one male goat as a sin offering, in addition to the regular burnt offering with its grain offering and drink offering.

"'In addition to what you vow and your freewill offerings, prepare these for the Lord at your appointed feasts: your burnt offerings, grain offerings, drink offerings and fellowship offerings.'"

Moses told the Israelites all that the Lord commanded him.

The name of this feast, which was to be celebrated "at the end of the year" (Exod. 23:16) or "at the turn of the year" (Exod. 34:22) is not given here, nor is the living in booths mentioned. All that is said is that the feast is to begin on the fifteenth day of the seventh month and is to last seven days. In both references in Exodus the feast is called "the Feast of Ingathering," but its length is not specified, nor the living in booths. In Leviticus 23 and Deuteronomy 16:13–15; 31:9–13 it is called the "Feast of Tabernacles" and its duration is set at seven days. Ezekiel 45:25 does mention the seven days, but not the name of the feast, nor the living in booths, in contrast to Nehemiah 8:14ff. See also my commentary on Leviticus 23:33–36.

Verses 12–39 deal extensively with the offerings that are to be brought on each of the seven days. On the first day the offering consists of thirteen bulls, two rams, and fourteen lambs. Each subsequent day the number of bulls is reduced by one, but the number of rams and lambs remains the same. This comes to a total of seventy bulls, fourteen rams, and ninety-eight lambs in addition to the regular *tamîd*; each of these totals is divisible by seven, the number of perfection.

Added to these seven days, of which the first one is a "sacred assembly," is an eighth day, mentioned only here and in Nehemiah 8:18. On that day one bull, one ram, and seven lambs are to be offered, while the day itself is marked by the holding of an *'etseret,* a "solemn assembly" (KJV), a special festive gathering of which we know nothing more. This eighth day is thus apparently not part of the feast itself.

This chapter deals only with those offerings that are to be brought by Israel as a community, i.e., the offerings of the official cultus, financed by the whole community. This means that the offerings brought by individuals were added to these. How numerous these offerings could be is indicated in e.g., 2 Chronicles 29:21; 32–33; 34:7–9; Ezra 8:35. The large number of "official" offerings shows that this feast was for Israel indeed the feast par excellence (1 Kings 8:2; 12:32; Ezek. 45:25).

2. *The Legal Validity of Vows Made by Women* (30:1–16)

It is curious that this section is introduced with the words "Moses said," rather than "The LORD said," and is addressed not to "the Israelites," but to "the heads of the tribes of Israel." The closest parallels to "Moses said" are Exodus 16:15, 32; 35:4; Leviticus 8:5; 9:6; 17:2, while the expression "the heads of the tribes" is elsewhere found only in 1 Kings 8:1 (= 2 Chron. 5:2). The latter are, of course, the same as "the family heads of the Israelite tribes" in 32:28; Joshua 14:1; 21:1.

A. *Vows and their obligation* (30:1–2)

30:1–2 *Moses said to the heads of the tribes of Israel: "This is what the LORD commands: When a man makes a vow to the LORD or takes an oath to obligate himself by a pledge, he must not break his word but must do everything he said."*

Two issues are involved here: first, the making of a vow, which is the product of a generally observable human tendency to support, as it were, prayer by conditionally promising either oneself or part of one's possessions; second, the assumption of an obligation to abstain, in case of answered prayer, from something that is in itself permissible, e.g., from wine (the Nazirite vow, ch. 6), food (1 Sam. 14:24; Acts 23:14), or sleep (Ps. 132:3–4). These two aspects are thus closely related, but the first one is "positive," the second one "negative."

In Israel, as elsewhere, the making of a vow or the taking on of an obligation to abstain from something was frequently abused as a means to influence God's actions, after which the vow or obligation was not carried out (see my commentary on Lev. 27). A number of passages are directed against this tendency, such as Leviticus 22:21–22; 27:1ff.; Deuteronomy 23:22ff., which point out that it is no sin not to make a vow, but that once a vow has been made it must be kept (see also Prov. 20:25; Eccl. 5:3–4; Mal. 1:14).

The law in this chapter deals specifically with the question of the legal validity of vows and pledges made by unmarried and married women. But first, Israel is impressed with the very serious nature of vows and pledges in general, and with the demand that any vow or pledge made to the Lord must be kept. But such a vow becomes binding only when the intention has been expressed in words (vv. 2, 6, 12), whereby I once again point out that to the Israelite a word is not merely a series of sounds, but a reality that has an existence of its own, a "word-thing" or "thing-word" (see commentary on 20:2ff.). And because this "word-thing" is directed to the Lord, and has thus entered the sphere of the holy, it must be kept. Such a spoken word is binding (see 32:24; Judg. 11:35–36; Ps. 66:13–14; Jer. 44:17). Breaking a vow is nothing less than desecrating the "word-thing": it is withdrawn from the sphere of the holy and becomes profane (see A. Wendel, *Das israelitisch-jüdische Gelübde,* 1931).

B. *Vows of unmarried women* (30:3–5)

30:3–5 *"When a young woman still living in her father's house makes a vow to the* LORD *or obligates herself by a pledge and her father hears about her vow or pledge but says nothing to her, then all her vows and every pledge by which she obligated herself will stand. But if her father forbids her when he hears about it, none of her vows or the pledges by which she obligated herself will stand; the* LORD *will release her because her father has forbidden her."*

Since in a polygamous society marriage is, of course, more common than in a monogamous one, and because marriage, furthermore, was seen in a religious light in Israel, the unmarried woman referred to here is probably the young marriageable woman. The girl who has not yet reached puberty is in any case excluded here, because she was not considered to have the right to make a vow. The Talmud tract *Nedarim* (47b) attempted to harmonize verses 3–5 with the later rule that when a woman has reached puberty her father no longer has authority over her. It did this by limiting "youth" (v. 4, "in her father's house in her youth," KJV) to the prepubescent years; but this contradicts the Hebrew word used here, *ne'urim*. What is stated here is that the vow or pledge of an unmarried woman who lives in her father's house, and is thus subject to his authority, is legally valid only to the extent that her father does not object. If the father objects, he must express his veto *as soon as* he finds out about it ("hears," v. 4, cf. v. 7). Verse 15 indicates that he must object immediately—if the father is silent, his silence constitutes agreement with his daughter's vow, and the vow or pledge must be kept.

C. *Vows of married women* (30:6–16)

30:6–8 *"If she marries after she makes a vow or after her lips utter a rash promise by which she obligates herself and her husband hears about it but says nothing to her, then her vows or the pledges by which she obligated herself will stand. But if her husband forbids her when he hears about it, he nullifies the vow that obligates her or the rash promise by which she obligates herself, and the LORD will release her."*

Two cases are distinguished here. Verses 6–8 deal with a situation where the marriageable woman marries during the period when her vow or pledge is still in force, and she is under obligation to keep her vow or pledge, lest she sin. When she marries she exchanges the authority of her father for that of her husband, and it will depend on the latter whether her vow or pledge continues to be legally binding. If he is silent when he hears about the vow then his silence constitutes his authorization for his wife to continue to fulfill her obligation. But if he expresses his veto, her vow, which derived its legal status only from her father's authority to which she is no longer subject, has ceased to be legally binding; the Lord will then forgive her because someone who has authority over her has made it impossible for her to fulfill her obligation. Note that in verses 6 and 8 the vow made by the woman is called a "rash promise," the result of insufficient reflection. References such as Proverbs 20:25; Ecclesiastes 5:2, 4–6; Ecclesiasticus 18:23 show how frequently this happened in Israel: the Mishnah tracts *Nazir* and *Nedarim* also refer to this. But rashness does not exempt one from fulfilling the assumed obligation (cf. Lev. 5:4).

30:9 *"Any vow or obligation taken by a widow or divorced woman will be binding on her."*

A number of exegetes (e.g., Heinisch) wrongly consider this verse a later addition. An incorrect conclusion might be drawn from verses 6–8. Israelite jurisprudence places a widow under the authority of her eldest son, if of age, and otherwise under the authority of her family. Thus, the vow of a widow could, strictly speaking, remain in force only if the eldest son of the family did not object. The same would also be true of the woman who was rejected by her husband: she once again came under the authority of her father. But verse 9 states clearly that these conclusions, while logically correct, do not apply. The vow of both the widow and the rejected woman must be fully kept, and cannot be nullified. The widow and the divorced woman thus occupy a unique position in Israel's law.

30:10–16 *"If a woman living with her husband makes a vow or obligates herself by a pledge under oath and her husband hears about it but says nothing to her and does not forbid her, then all her vows or the pledges by which she obligated herself will stand. But if her husband nullifies them when he hears about them, then none of the vows or pledges that came from her lips will stand. Her husband has nullified them, and the LORD will release her. Her husband may confirm or nullify any vow she makes or any sworn pledge to deny herself. But if her husband says nothing to her about it from day to day, then he confirms all her vows or the pledges binding on her. He confirms them by saying nothing to her when he hears about them. If, however, he nullifies them some time after he hears about them, then he is responsible for her guilt."*

These are the regulations the LORD gave Moses concerning relationships between a man and his wife, and between a father and his young daughter still living in his house.

These verses concern the woman who makes a vow *while* she is married. In that case the legal validity of the vow depends on her husband. This is entirely in agreement with verses 3–5, since the married woman is under the authority of her husband even as the unmarried woman is under her father's authority. If the husband does not speak up when the woman makes her vow, then the vow or pledge is legally binding. But if he forbids her to keep the vow, then it is not binding and the Lord will forgive her for not keeping it, because she was unable to do so. But the husband must act immediately; he cannot go back on his tacit approval afterward. If he nevertheless does this, then he "is responsible for her guilt," i.e., he is obligated to fulfill what she promised, and if the vow is not kept he, rather than his wife, is guilty.

Vengeance on the Midianites
(31:1–54)

1. *Israel's Glorious Victory* (31:1–12)

31:1–12 *The LORD said to Moses, "Take vengeance on the Midianites for the Israelites. After that, you will be gathered to your people."*

So Moses said to the people, "Arm some of your men to go to war against the Midianites and to carry out the LORD's vengeance on them. Send into battle a thousand men from each of the tribes of Israel." So twelve thousand men armed for battle, a thousand from each tribe, were supplied from the clans of Israel. Moses sent them into battle, a thousand from each tribe, along with Phinehas son of Eleazar, the priest, who took with him articles from the sanctuary and the trumpets for signaling.

They fought against Midian, as the LORD commanded Moses, and killed every man. Among their victims were Evi, Rekem, Zur, Hur and Reba—the five kings of Midian. They also killed Balaam son of Beor with the sword. The Israelites captured the Midianite women and children and took all the Midianite herds, flocks and goods as plunder. They burned all the towns where the Midianites had settled, as well as all their camps. They took all the plunder and spoils, including the people and animals, and brought the captives, spoils and plunder to Moses and Eleazar the priest and the Israelite assembly at their camp on the plains of Moab, by the Jordan across from Jericho.

Had it been the author's purpose to give a description of Israel's military exploits against the Midianites, not only would this chapter have been placed immediately after chapter 25 (see vv. 17–18), but it would also have provided more details. As it stands, the chapter is incorporated in one of the legal sections of Numbers and deals at length and in detail with the necessary cleansing of an army returning from battle (vv. 13–24), and with the laws that are to govern the division of the spoils (vv. 25–47). These matters had to be regulated at this point because Israel was about to enter Canaan, where their life would initially be dominated by warfare. We do not know how these matters were dealt with after the victories over Sihon and Og. It is possible that the experience following those victories had impressed on Israel the need for a clear regulation of the division of the spoils, and that the first opportunity that presented itself was used to settle the matter. Also for Israel experience was the best teacher.

From these considerations I conclude that the author has considerably shortened the military portion of a more extensive narrative: the actual battle is summarized in three (Hebrew) words, "and killed every man" (v. 7b). This appears to be a reference to the "ban" (*herem*, cf. 21:2 NIV margin). But the focus falls entirely on the regulations that are instituted after the battle against Midian. The author thus limits himself to a brief reference to 25:17–18 (v. 2a), while the dating of the event also takes few words (v. 2b, an allusion to 27:12–14).

First of all, it is made clear that the battle with Midian is nothing more or less than vengeance: for Israel (v. 2), vengeance for the snare that Midian had set on Balaam's advice (see commentary on 25:1), which had caused Israel to suffer the miseries of "the plague" (v. 16); for Israel's God (v. 3), vengeance for the infringement on His honor in the breaking of the covenant that was the result of Israel's seduction by the Midianites. The entire event is thus seen in a religious light, and the battle with Midian is in fact an application of the "ban" (*herem,* see above), although the word is not used here. Israel's whole army must not go into battle; twelve thousand men are sufficient to defeat Midian. This must make the power of Israel's God manifest to all. We must remember that in the ancient Near East, and in Israel, war between two nations was considered to be ultimately a battle between the gods of those nations (see also below).

The army is accompanied by Phinehas, rather than by his father Eleazar, the high priest; the reason for this may lie in the function the latter had to fulfill with Moses after the battle (v. 21). Phinehas must take with him the "trumpets for signaling" (see 10:9), as well as the "articles from the sanctuary" (KJV: "holy instruments," RSV: "vessels of the sanctuary"); it is not entirely clear what the latter included. In 3:31; 4:15; 18:3 the phrase refers to all the furnishings of the sanctuary, as is also true in 1 Kings 8:4. It seems to me unlikely that the phrase here refers to the priestly garments. More likely, it refers to the Urim and Thummim, with which the son of the high priest would be able to answer all kinds of questions that might arise during such a campaign. The fact that a priest accompanies the army makes sense in light of the contemporary understanding of war, which saw it as a cultic, even a religious act: "the wars of the LORD" (cf. 21:14). A priest always accompanied the army in war (see e.g., 1 Sam. 14:18; 23:2).

We are not told where Israel meets Midian, but considering the close contact between Moab and Midian (22:4, 7; 25:17–18), it is most likely in the region east of Edom and south of Moab. Nor are we informed of the duration of the war. In view of the overwhelming results I get the impression that it was an entirely successful surprise attack. In my opinion, v. 7b does not imply that the entire population of Midian was killed. The size of the territory occupied by Midian (towns and tent camps, v. 10) and the high degree of mobility of such a nomadic people force us to think of the usual restriction when reading the last words of verse 7: to the extent that they fell into Israel's hands. In Judges 6 we hear again of the Midianites. The Midianites apparently tried to resist: no fewer than five of their "kings" are slain. We must not take the title "king" in too strict a sense (cf. commentary on 20:14); in Joshua 13:21 the "kings" are called literally "princes of Sihon," i.e., vassals of Sihon, while one of them, Zur, is merely called a "tribal chief of a Midianite family" in 25:15. I see the hopelessness of their resistance in the fact that the Midianites had already experienced Israel's superiority when they fought alongside Sihon (Josh. 13:21). Balaam also perishes in this attack. It may be surprising to find Balaam among the Midianites after 24:25, but it certainly does not prove that Balaam lived in Midian: our utter ignorance of the sequence of events after Balaam's attempt to curse Israel forces us to greater modesty than such a conclusion would reflect.

The Israelites capture a large number of women and children (the word used in vv. 9, 17–18, *taf,* forces us to think of prepubescent children; the older girls, v. 18, fall under the general designation "women"). Equally considerable are the herds and flocks (specified in vv. 32ff.) that are taken as plunder, and the other possessions of the Midianites (cf. v. 50), the latter being proof that it is incorrect to think of the Bedouins as poor people (see also Judg. 8:24–26). With these spoils the victors return to Israel's camp, which is still located across from Jericho by the Jordan (v. 12).

2. *The Treatment of the Captives and the Purification of the Army* (31: 13–24)

31:13–18 *Moses, Eleazar the priest and all the leaders of the community went to meet them outside the camp. Moses was angry with the officers of the army—the commanders of thousands and commanders of hundreds—who returned from the battle.*

"Have you allowed all the women to live?" he asked them. "They were the ones who followed Balaam's advice and were the means of turning the Israelites away from the LORD in what happened at Peor, so that a plague struck the LORD's people. Now kill all the boys. And kill every woman who has slept with a man, but save for yourselves every girl who has never slept with a man."

Moses and his immediate circle (Eleazar and the leaders of the community) go out to meet the returning army. Their purpose is not so much to welcome them as to prevent defilement of the camp: the soldiers have, of course, become unclean in many ways—if only by contact with dead bodies, cf. chapter 19—and cannot simply re-enter the camp (5:1–4). Moses immediately observes how the officers have failed in their duty: although they knew that their campaign was to carry out "the LORD's vengeance" (v. 3), which means the "ban" *(herem),* and in spite of the fact that they had witnessed the great danger for Israel in contact with

Midianite women, they have, notwithstanding the command of 25:17–18, spared the women and children. Moses' anger is aroused; he reminds the officers of the misery they have experienced so recently, and underlines Balaam's role and the deepest cause of their action (*ma'al*, "trespass, infidelity," v. 16). It is not contact with non-Israelite women per se that is dangerous to Israel (see Deut. 21:10–14)—but Midian has proven itself to be a special danger to Israel's faithfulness to the Lord. The officers of the army have seriously failed in their duty in this matter. Moses now commands them to do what they should have done in the first place: kill the male children, in order to break Midian's strength, and also all women who had slept with a man, and who could therefore still become mothers. Only the prepubescent girls are allowed to live; i.e., these girls can become slaves or concubines (v. 18; cf. Deut. 21:10–14; Judg. 21:10–14).

31:19–20 *"All of you who have killed anyone or touched anyone who was killed must stay outside the camp seven days. On the third and seventh days you must purify yourselves and your captives. Purify every garment as well as everything made of leather, goat hair or wood."*

Moses adds a second command: the army with all its captives and its spoils must remain outside the camp for seven days (cf. 19:16–17; also Lev. 12:7; 13:5–6, 21, 26, 32–34; 15:24). They must purify themselves twice, on the third and on the seventh day, with the "water of cleansing" (19:12–13; see also v. 23). This purification is a purely cultic act, and the "sin" of which they are to be cleansed is to be understood strictly in terms of ceremonial uncleanness, which was the result of contact with dead bodies. The purification ritual includes, according to the regulation of 19:14–15, their clothing and, according to Leviticus 13:49ff. anything made of leather; furthermore, anything made of goat hair, probably because according to 1 Samuel 19:13, 16 this was generally used to make blankets; and finally, anything made of wood, since "sin"—which was seen as something material by ancient Israel[10]—attaches itself so easily to it. The weapons of the army are not mentioned specifically.

31:21–24 *Then Eleazar the priest said to the soldiers who had gone into battle, "This is the requirement of the law that the LORD gave Moses: Gold, silver, bronze, iron, tin, lead and anything else that can withstand fire must be put through the fire, and then it will be clean. But it must also be purified with the water of cleansing. And whatever cannot withstand fire must be put through that water. On the seventh day wash your clothes and you will be clean. Then you may come into the camp."*

---

[10]See Publisher's Note.

Eleazar now adds further specific regulations to the general command, by virtue of his priestly authority to give *tora,* i.e., instruction (Deut. 33:10). He requires that all noncombustible items (which would include not only captured items but also their weapons) must first be put through the fire, so that the "sin" will, as it were, be burned out of them, and then purified with the "water of cleansing" (19:9). Anything combustible must be put "through the water" (NIV "through that water," i.e., the water of cleansing), which means that it must be washed off thoroughly. Eleazar finally repeats what Moses has already said concerning their clothing (v. 24, cf. v. 20). In 19:7 we also hear of the requirement that an individual bathe himself as part of the purification ritual; but this rule applies only in the case of an individual and is not mentioned here.

3. *Division of the Livestock* (31:25–47)

31:25–30 *The* Lord *said to Moses, "You and Eleazar the priest and the family heads of the community are to count all the people and animals that were captured. Divide the spoils between the soldiers who took part in the battle and the rest of the community. From the soldiers who fought in the battle, set apart as tribute for the* Lord *one out of every five hundred, whether persons, cattle, donkeys, sheep or goats. Take this tribute from their half share and give it to Eleazar the priest as the* Lord'*s part. From the Israelites' half, select one out of every fifty, whether persons, cattle, donkeys, sheep, goats or other animals. Give them to the Levites, who are responsible for the care of the* Lord'*s tabernacle."*

After this purification they can proceed with the division of the livestock under the direction of Moses and his immediate circle. The livestock is divided into two equal parts: one half for the army, the other half for those who remained in the camp, a rule later also enjoined by Joshua (Josh. 22:8) and applied by David (1 Sam. 30:24, see also De Groot on 1 Sam. 30:24). But in addition, we hear here of a tribute for the cultus, to be given by the army to the priests, and by those who stayed behind to the Levites. Justifiably, the latter are to give more (one out of every fifty, or 2 percent) than the soldiers (one out of every five hundred, or .2 percent). The Levites thus receives much more than the priests, as is also true of the tithes (18:25ff.), probably because of the larger number of Levites. Later, Mohammed even required 20 percent of the spoils to be given to Allah's messenger, relatives, orphans, the poor, and wanderers. Mesha of Moab and Asshurbanipal of Assyria also speak of similar gifts to their gods (Jirku, *Altorientalischer Kommentar,* p. 116).

31:31–47 *So Moses and Eleazar the priest did as the* Lord *commanded Moses.*

The plunder remaining from the spoils that the soldiers took was 675,000 sheep, 72,000 cattle, 61,000 donkeys and 32,000 women who had never slept with a man. The half share of those who fought in the battle was:

337,500 sheep, of which the tribute for the LORD was 675;
36,000 cattle, of which the tribute for the LORD was 72;
30,500 donkeys, of which the tribute for the LORD was 61;
16,000 people, of which the tribute for the LORD was 32.

Moses gave the tribute to Eleazar the priest as the LORD's part, as the LORD commanded Moses.

The half belonging to the Israelites, which Moses set apart from that of the fighting men—the community's half—was 337,500 sheep, 36,000 cattle, 30,500 donkeys and 16,000 people. From the Israelites' half, Moses selected one out of every fifty persons and animals, as the LORD commanded him, and gave them to the Levites, who were responsible for the care of the LORD's tabernacle.

Then the final count of the captured livestock and people is given with great precision, as well as the share each party receives. Verse 32 specifically states that this concerns only the plunder "remaining from the spoils"; losses are attributable not only to what the army used for food during the campaign, but also to death during the journey (cf. Gen. 33:13). The "tribute for the LORD" includes, besides sheep, cattle, and donkeys also thirty-two women (v. 40), who became what is later called "temple servants" (1 Chron. 9:2; Ezra 2:43; Neh. 3:26; et al.); they are to work as slaves at the sanctuary.

4. *The Tribute of the Officers* (31:48–54)

31:48–54 *Then the officers who were over the units of the army—the commanders of thousands and commanders of hundreds—went to Moses and said to him, "Your servants have counted the soldiers under our command, and not one is missing. So we have brought as an offering to the LORD the gold articles each of us acquired— armlets, bracelets, signet rings, earrings and necklaces—to make atonement for ourselves before the LORD."*

Moses and Eleazar the priest accepted from them the gold—all the crafted articles. All the gold from the commanders of thousands and commanders of hundreds that Moses and Eleazar presented as a gift to the LORD weighed 16,750 shekels. Each soldier had taken plunder for himself. Moses and Eleazar the priest accepted the gold from the commanders of thousands and commanders of hundreds and brought it into the Tent of Meeting as a memorial for the Israelites before the LORD.

The officers begin by giving Moses a report; they are able to state that a count of the men under their command indicates that no one has fallen in action (v. 49). This is rather surprising, even if Strack's supposition is correct that besides the twelve thousand men of verse 5 many others also joined in the campaign and that the casualties were among the latter. The officers therefore want to give all the captured gold ornaments "to make atonement for ourselves before the LORD" (cf. Lev. 4:20). The question here relates to the intent of this statement. It seems to me that Heinisch's view that the counting of the men was displeasing to the Lord, so that the tribute is essentially a penance, is untenable, for several reasons: (1) the counting is not a census; (2) there is no reason to assume that Israel would never have determined the number of men in an army that went on a campaign (cf. v. 4); (3) if a counting or census were forbidden in principle, the census of chapter 1 and chapter 26 would not have been commanded. Nor can there be any connection between this tribute and the "atonement money" of Exodus 30:11–16 (Dillman). It appears to me that this tribute of the officers was based on considerations common to all tributes of this nature: an acknowledgment that during the campaign much had happened that·was contrary to God's law, and an attempt to receive forgiveness for these actions by increasing the temple treasure. The introduction in verse 49 and the statement "not one is missing" serve to indicate the special reason for the giving of this tribute. It is therefore clear that no special significance should be attached to the statement "not one is missing," since it appears to be more a formula than a factual statement.

The tribute consists exclusively of gold objects (v. 50b), further described as "crafted articles" (v. 51; KJV "wrought jewels"). The exact meaning of the words is not entirely certain; the "armlets" were probably ornaments of the aristocracy, worn around the upper arm (2 Sam. 1:10), as were the "signet rings," worn on the finger (Gen. 41:42; Esther 3:10, 12; 8:2). The exact meaning of the word rendered "necklaces" (KJV "tablets," RSV "beads") is unknown.

All these ornaments constitute an enormous weight: 16,750 shekels, i.e., about 420 pounds, of gold. Added to this should also be the gold ornaments captured by the rank and file of the army (v. 53). We must probably remember what was said about the *'elef* in chapter 1 when looking at these totals; otherwise, the spoils would have been exceptionally large for a semi-nomadic tribe (cf. Judg. 8:26).

The Division of the Transjordan Territory
(32:1–42)

In chapter 21 we were told that Israel, after Sihon refused passage through his territory, had to use force to make its way to the Jordan, which included the battle with Og of Bashan. Here we hear that this land, suited for livestock and famous for its fertility and excellent pastures (especially between the Jabbok and the Arnon), has aroused the desire of the tribes of Reuben and Gad, who turn to Moses with the request that they be allowed to occupy it, and to be discharged from their obligation to take part in the battle against the Canaanites with the other tribes.

1. *Moses' Initial Refusal of Gad's and Reuben's Request* (32:1-15)

32:1-2 *The Reubenites and Gadites, who had very large herds and flocks, saw that the lands of Jazer and Gilead were suitable for livestock. So they came to Moses and Eleazar the priest and to the leaders of the community, and said.*

In verse 1 the Reubenites are mentioned first, reflecting Reuben's status as the firstborn. In the rest of the chapter we hear of "the Gadites and Reubenites," which indicates the relative importance of the two Transjordan tribes (cf. Deut. 33:21). As Deuteronomy 33:6 clearly shows, Reuben was unable to stand up to the pressure of the Moabites, who would soon push forward again (Judg. 3:12ff.), followed later by the Midianites (Judg. 6). Reuben would soon fall into decline, so that the Moabite king Mesha, a contemporary of Ahab (ca. 850 B.C.) makes no mention of it at all. Gad, on the other hand, was the prominent tribe in the Transjordan region. The well-known inscription of Mesha still mentions "the men of Gad," who "since ancient times lived in the land Ataroth" (line 10). The overwhelming superiority of Damascus finally overpowers Gad (2 Kings 10:32f.).

The Gadites and Reubenites "had very large herds and flocks" (v. 1a), a fact they bring up in their request to stay in the Transjordan region (v. 4). This does not necessarily imply of course that they had larger herds and flocks than the other tribes. The predominantly pastoral character of these two tribes in the time of the judges (Judg. 5:16-17a) was the result of their settling in this land, so eminently suitable for cattle raising.

32:3-5 *"Ataroth, Dibon, Jazer, Nimrah, Heshbon, Elealeh, Sebam, Nebo and Beon—the land the LORD subdued before the people of Israel—are suitable for livestock, and your servants have livestock. If we have found favor in your eyes,"* they said, *"let this land be given to your servants as our possession. Do not make us cross the Jordan."*

They address their request (vv. 3-5) to Moses and his immediate circle (31:13). They make it very clear that they want to settle down and do not want to continue the journey with the other tribes; they mention several places that are also found in verses 34-38. The location of some of these can be determined with great accuracy. The best-known is Heshbon,

Sihon's capital (21:26), the present Chesban, east of the northern tip of the Dead Sea. Dibon is the present Diban, just north of the Arnon (21:30). Northwest of Dibon is Ataroth, also mentioned by King Mesha (see above), the present Attarus, just north of the Herodian Machaerus. Northeast of Ataroth is Baal Meon,[11] elsewhere called Beth Meon or Beth Baal Meon, probably the present Khirbeth Main; Mesha also mentions this place (line 30). Nebo was probably near the mountain of the same name, i.e., southwest of Heshbon. About one half hour to the north of Heshbon lies Elealeh, the present El-Al, and west of this, toward the Jordan, lies Nimrah, called Beth Nimrah in verse 36, perhaps the present Tell Nimrin. Sebam is usually thought to be southwest of Heshbon in the present Sumeye (Sibmah, Isa. 16:9, famous for its vineyards). Of all these places Jazer was the northernmost, at least if its identification with the present Beit-Zera is correct. See also commentary on verses 34–36. We are not told here from whom Israel captured these places between the Arnon and the Jabbok, nor by what name this region was known. This information is given later in verses 27, 29 and in verse 33 (see commentary on those verses).

32:6–15 *Moses said to the Gadites and Reubenites, "Shall your countrymen go to war while you sit here? Why do you discourage the Israelites from going over into the land the LORD has given them? This is what your fathers did when I sent them from Kadesh Barnea to look over the land. After they went up to the Valley of Eshcol and viewed the land, they discouraged the Israelites from entering the land the LORD had given them. The LORD's anger was aroused that day and he swore this oath: 'Because they have not followed me wholeheartedly, not one of the men twenty years old or more who came up out of Egypt will see the land I promised on oath to Abraham, Isaac and Jacob—not one except Caleb son of Jephunneh the Kenizzite and Joshua son of Nun, for they followed the LORD wholeheartedly.' The LORD's anger burned against Israel and he made them wander in the desert forty years, until the whole generation of those who had done evil in his sight was gone.*

"And here you are, a brood of sinners, standing in the place of your fathers and making the LORD angry with Israel. If you turn away from following him, he will again leave all this people in the desert, and you will be the cause of their destruction."

The request of the Gadites and Reubenites arouses Moses' anger and he responds in terms that do not allow for misunderstanding. To grant their request would mean nothing less than destroying Israel's unity (v. 6), a fear that was later proved justified (cf. Judg. 5:15a–17a), and would have the

---

[11]On the basis of verse 38, Noordtzij emends the text to read "Baal Meon" instead of "Beon," as do the Samaritan Pentateuch and the LXX (tr.).

immediate effect of ''discouraging'' the rest of Israel from crossing the Jordan as well (v. 7a). This would break Israel's strength and therefore (chs. 13–14!) render any attack on the feared Canaanites hopeless from the start. Furthermore, the Lord's promise speaks only of Canaan, i.e., the land west of the Jordan, as the language of the Old Testament and of the Egyptian inscriptions prove (see below).

This ''discouraging'' of the Israelites, which would make them unwilling to go on, reminds Moses immediately of what happened in Kadesh (called here Kadesh Barnea; cf. 34:4; Deut. 1:2, 19; 2:14; 9:23; Josh. 10:41; 14:6–7; 15:3; see ch. 13). There Israel was also kept from unconditionally trusting the Lord's promise and entering Canaan at His command without hesitation, which resulted in the forty years of wandering in the wilderness. Moses refuses the request of Gad and Reuben because of the consequences he foresees: Israel would refuse a second time to enter Canaan, which would of necessity result in another outburst of the Lord's anger.

It is striking that Moses does not point out to these two tribes that it is impossible to grant their request because the Lord's promise to Abraham and his seed speaks only of Canaan. The language of the Old Testament shows that this includes only the land west of the Jordan (vv. 30, 32; 32:21; 34:2, 29; 35:10; cf. also Gen. 12:5; 23:2, 19; 35:6; 48:3, 7; 49:30; Exod. 16:35; Deut. 32:49; Josh. 5:12; 14:1; 21:2; 22:9–11, 32; 24:3; Judg. 21:12; and also the well-known list of the inhabitants of Canaan, all of whom live west of the Jordan: Exod. 3:8; 13:5; 33:2; Josh. 3:10; 11:3; 24:11). The Egyptian inscriptions of the so-called New Empire (after 1580 B.C.) and the Amarna letters (fourteenth century B.C.) also refer only to the land west of the Jordan when speaking of Canaan. This is understandable, since the Transjordan region does not form a geographical unit with Canaan proper: between the two lies a chasm up to twelve miles wide, in which the Jordan has cut a double bed, and whose walls are 3280 to 4593 feet high on both sides. Consequently, there is little or no contact between the two sides.

Moses was well aware that the Lord's promise concerned only the land west of the Jordan, and that therefore *all* the tribes had to settle there (cf. vv. 7, 9, 11, 30, 32; also 13:17). Yet he does not say this to Gad and Reuben. He is only disturbed by the possibility that the other tribes will be discouraged from entering Canaan, which would result in the Lord's anger against Israel. Moses is therefore forced to give in when Gad and Reuben can show that Moses' fear is groundless.

The second point that strikes us is that Moses who, whenever he is faced with difficult decisions, takes them before the Lord, does not do so in this case. He negotiates directly with the representatives of Gad and Reuben and places himself, in spite of his detailed reminiscences of what happened at Kadesh (vv. 6–15), in a position that will ultimately force him to give in. Moses clearly shows Gad and Reuben how he *will* be able to grant their request. I have therefore the strong impression that we are faced here with a weak moment in Moses' life. He gives in where he should have refused, and it does not take him long to realize this; hence his repeated "taken" in 34:14f. (NIV "received"), which implies the acknowledgment on his part that he was wrong in giving in to their pressure (see commentary on 34:14).

2. *Gad and Reuben Are Insistent* (32:16–19)

32:16–19 *Then they came up to him and said, "We would like to build pens here for our livestock and cities for our women and children. But we are ready to arm ourselves and go ahead of the Israelites until we have brought them to their place. Meanwhile our women and children will live in fortified cities, for protection from the inhabitants of the land. We will not return to our homes until every Israelite has received his inheritance. We will not receive any inheritance with them on the other side of the Jordan, because our inheritance has come to us on the east side of the Jordan."*

Both Gad and Reuben realize that they have gone too far with their request to remain in the Transjordan region, and that they will not be given permission if they pursue this approach. Yet they have not heard a categorical refusal in Moses' words, stern as they may sound. Rather, they see—and correctly so—in his words an indication of the way in which their request may be granted. The unity of Israel must be maintained when it invades Canaan; all tribes without exception must participate. Therefore, before their request can be considered, it must be established that they are willing to take part in the conquest. Moses and his circle, as well as the leaders of Gad and Reuben, realize, of course, that this will mean leaving the women and children behind, and that in a recently acquired territory!

Nevertheless, Gad and Reuben approach the matter from this angle, which was so clearly suggested to them. They declare themselves willing to leave their families and cattle and to assist vigorously in the conquest of Canaan. Only after the conquest is complete will they return to the Transjordan region. They even have the kindness (!) to assure Moses that they will not lay claim to any part of Canaan, since they already consider the east side of the Jordan their legitimate inheritance. Thus, they take into consideration only the present and the immediate future. They are not concerned with the fact that the Jordan will effectively divide Israel, and they do not consider the question whether a divided Israel will in the future be able to maintain control over Canaan.

3. *Moses' Permission* (32:20–27)

32:20–24 *Then Moses said to them, "If you will do this—if you will arm yourselves before the* LORD *for battle, and if all of you will go armed over the Jordan before the* LORD *until he has driven his enemies out before him—then when the land is subdued before the* LORD*, you may return and be free from your obligation to the* LORD *and to Israel. And this land will be your possession before the* LORD.

"But if you fail to do this, you will be sinning against the LORD*; and you may be sure that your sin will find you out. Build cities for your women and children, and pens for your flocks, but do what you have promised."*

Since Gad and Reuben have taken the approach indirectly suggested by Moses himself, Moses no longer has any reason to refuse. He merely restates the condition on which they will receive the land east of the Jordan: they must vigorously assist in the conquest of Canaan, and only afterward can they return to "this land." Three times (vv. 20–22a) he points out the religious basis of Israel's military campaign against Canaan: it is to be done "before the LORD." Thus, the Lord is drawn into an agreement reached between these two tribes and the other ten. If they renege on their commitment they sin against the Lord; in that case their sin "will find them out," a curious expression that ascribes to sin an independent existence, which enables it to carry out its own duty (cf. Gen. 4:7). What takes place here is thus nothing more or less than the making of a covenant (although the word is not used) "before the LORD."

Only after the condition has been set do Gad and Reuben receive permission to take care of their women, children, and flocks (v. 24; as in v. 16, "women and children" is lit. "little ones"). But Moses concludes his official permission by reminding them of their obligation to keep their promise (cf. 30:2).

32:25–27 *The Gadites and Reubenites said to Moses, "We your servants will do as our lord commands. Our children and wives, our flocks and herds will remain here in the cities of Gilead. But your servants, every man armed for battle, will cross over to fight before the* LORD*, just as our lord says."*

The leaders of Gad and Reuben repeat Moses' condition that they leave their families and flocks and help the other tribes in the conquest of Canaan to show that they fully understand what they promise.

4. *The Agreement Is Confirmed and Implemented* (32:28–38)

The negotiations with Gad and Reuben apparently took more time than would appear on the surface from verses 1–27. The leaders began by bringing their request before Moses and his immediate circle, but as the negotiations progress, the circle recedes into the background and is informed only after the agreement has been reached.

32:28–32 *Then Moses gave orders about them to Eleazar the priest and Joshua son of Nun and to the family heads of the Israelite tribes. He said to them, "If the Gadites and Reubenites, every man armed for battle, cross over the Jordan with you before the LORD, then when the land is subdued before you, give them the land of Gilead as their possession. But if they do not cross over with you armed, they must accept their possession with you in Canaan."*

The Gadites and Reubenites answered, "Your servants will do what the LORD has said. We will cross over before the LORD into Canaan armed, but the property we inherit will be on this side of the Jordan."

Because Moses knows that he is nearing the end of his life (27:12–14; 31:2) and that he will not live to see the implementation of the agreement, he reports to Eleazar, Joshua, and the family heads what has been agreed upon and what must be done with Gad and Reuben if they keep their promise (v. 29c), or if they fail to do so (v. 30). In the latter case they must "accept their possession with you in Canaan"; the verb implies that they must be forced to accept. If they keep their promise they must be given "the land of Gilead" (see below). Gad and Reuben on their part repeat what they already said to Moses: they will cross over with the rest of Israel, but they also expect the other ten tribes to keep their part of the agreement.

32:33–38 *Then Moses gave to the Gadites, the Reubenites and the half-tribe of Manasseh son of Joseph the kingdom of Sihon king of the Amorites and the kingdom of Og king of Bashan—the whole land with its cities and the territory around them.*

The Gadites built up Dibon, Ataroth, Aroer, Atroth Shophan, Jazer, Jogbehah, Beth Nimrah and Beth Haran as fortified cities, and built pens for their flocks. And the Reubenites rebuilt Heshbon, Elealeh and Kiriathaim, as well as Nebo and Baal Meon (these names were changed) and Sibmah. They gave names to the cities they rebuilt.

The implementation of this agreement is recorded in verses 33–38, which are a more recent addition. Gad and Reuben are given the areas listed in verses 34–38. Later it will be clarified that Reuben receives the land between the Arnon and Elealeh along the eastern shore of the Dead Sea, while Gad receives the land north of the Jabbok, the best land. But verse 33 suddenly faces us with the curious fact that besides the two tribes mentioned in the preceding section a third tribe, the "half-tribe of Manasseh," also appears to be interested in the land east of the Jordan. We are not told which part this half-tribe receives; in verses 39–42 we are merely told how various groups of Manassites—Makir, Jair, and Nobah—were able to capture areas that apparently did not as yet belong to Israel. Three times the word "capture" is used, while Gad and Reuben are merely said to have "built," i.e., they fortified their territory and restored what had been destroyed (see 1 Kings 16:34; Isa. 58:12; 61:4; Ezek. 36:36; Amos 9:14; also the Mesha inscription, lines 9, 27).

We find a similar phenomenon in Joshua 22, where we hear of the return of the Transjordan tribes. While verses 25 and 32–34 speak only of Reuben and Gad (Reuben first, as in Num. 32:1), verse 1 also mentions the "half-tribe of Manasseh" as inhabiting the Transjordan region, a fact that is explained in verse 7: Moses had given them the land in Bashan.

There can be no doubt that since Moses' time half of Manasseh was settled in the Transjordan region north of Gad (Deut. 3:12–15; 4:43; 29:7–8; Josh. 12:6; 13:29, 31; 14:3; 18:7). But this does not mean that this should also have been mentioned in Numbers 32. I am convinced that the words "and [to] the half-tribe of Manasseh, the son of Joseph" (v. 33) were inserted by a later reader who missed them here because of what is said concerning the Manassites in verses 39–42. However, these verses are not part of Moses' negotiations with Gad and Reuben, but were added by the author of the Pentateuch for the sake of completeness.

We encounter several problems when we attempt to decide on the basis of verses 34–38 exactly what territory was assigned to Gad and Reuben respectively. Gad was given Dibon (near the Arnon), Ataroth (northwest of Dibon), Aroer (south of Dibon near the Arnon, the present Arair), Atroth Shophan (mentioned only here; location unknown); all of these lie in the territory usually ascribed to Reuben. Also Jazer (north of Elealeh), Jogbehah (the present Adshbehat, northwest of Amman-Rabba or Rabbat-Ammon, thus northeast of Jazer), Beth Nimrah (perhaps the present Tell Nimrin northwest of Heshbon), and Beth Haran (called Beth Haram in Josh. 13:27; perhaps the present Tell er-Rame just north of the Dead Sea). Only these last four are located in the territory we usually consider Gad's.

Conversely, the places assigned to Reuben constitute a territory that cannot be clearly distinguished from that of Gad. Reuben receives Heshbon (north of the places mentioned in vv. 34–35a), Elealeh (just north of Heshbon), Kiriathaim (also mentioned by Mesha, line 10, the present Kurejat, thus between Ataroth and Dibon, which belonged to Gad), Nebo (near Heshbon by Mount Nebo), Baal Meon (south of Nebo), Musaboth-Shem,[12] and finally Sibmah (southwest of Heshbon).

---

[12]Noordzij takes this to be a place name, although he adds, "a strange name for a place: 'change of name.'" English versions see this as a historical footnote: "these names were changed" (NIV), "their names being changed" (KJV), "their names to be changed" (RSV) (tr.).

When we compare verses 34–38 with Joshua 13:15–28, where we have a very detailed statement of the territory assigned to each of the two tribes, we find that Aroer and Dibon, here assigned to Gad, are there listed as belonging to Reuben. Joshua 13 does not mention Ataroth, Atroth Shophan, or Jogbehah, here given to Gad, nor Elealeh and Nebo, here assigned to Reuben. In Joshua 13 we thus find Gad north, and Reuben south of Heshbon, while in Numbers 32 their territories are not clearly separated. This seems to indicate that over the years Reuben was assimilated into Gad, as also happened to Simeon and Judah, and that the picture in verses 34–38 represents a later period, as the "building" of these cities would also lead us to believe. This means that these verses, as well as verses 39–42, were added later. The original narrative thus ends with verse 33.

5. *The Half-tribe of Manasseh* (32:39–42)

32:39–42 *The descendants of Makir son of Manasseh went to Gilead, captured it and drove out the Amorites who were there. So Moses gave Gilead to the Makirites, the descendants of Manasseh, and they settled there. Jair, a descendant of Manasseh, captured their settlements and called them Havvoth Jair. And Nobah captured Kenath and its surrounding settlements and called it Nobah after himself.*

These verses, added by the author to the narrative of the settling of Gad and Reuben in the Transjordan region in order to complete the history of this region, contain a report of the settling of the half-tribe of Manasseh in the territory north of Gad. In verse 39 this region is called Gilead; it also included the areas occupied by Jair and Nobah (1 Chron. 2:22f.). In Joshua 13:30 it is called Bashan, the old kingdom of Og, while in Deuteronomy 3:14 we read of Argob, the southwestern part of Bashan. In ancient times geographical concepts were rather fluid. Thus, Gilead can sometimes refer to the entire Transjordan region up to the territory of Dan (Deut. 34:1; 1 Kings 4:19), sometimes only to the territory occupied by Israel (Josh. 22:9; Judg. 10:8, 18; et al.); it is also used alongside Bashan (Deut. 3:10, 13; Josh. 12:5; 13:11, 31) and is then limited to the region divided into two parts by the Jabbok, which is why in Deuteronomy 3:13; Joshua 12:5; 13:31 we hear of "half of Gilead" (i.e., the northern half; Deut. 3:13: "the rest of Gilead"), and in Deuteronomy 3:12; Joshua 12:2 also of "half of Gilead" (i.e., the southern half).

Makir was already mentioned in 26:29, where we get the impression that he was the only son of Manasseh. Here we hear of a second son of Manasseh, Jair (v. 41), while in Joshua 17:2 we even find a list of the "sons of Manasseh" (NIV "male descendants of Manasseh"), four of whom we know as place names, and in 1 Chronicles 7:15 still another "son" is mentioned, Zelophehad, who is, however, called Manasseh's great-grandson in Numbers 27:1 and Joshua 17:3. This reminds us of the fact that these and other genealogies reflect many historical events and changes in the relationship of the various clans to one another of which we have no knowledge whatsoever. Our problems relative to the tribe of Manasseh are compounded by the fact that Joshua 13:31 states that only half of Makir settled in Bashan; the other half of Makir consisted of the clan of Zelophehad (Josh. 17:3–6), which settled west of the Jordan. We will have to settle for the fact that Makir is always the representative of Manasseh east of the Jordan, except in Judges 5:14, where Makir represents Manasseh west of the Jordan.

Jair is also mentioned in Judges 10:3–4; there he is called "Jair of Gilead" and is listed among the "minor" judges. Here, as well as in Judges 10 and Deuteronomy 3:14 he is called "son of Manasseh," while 1 Chronicles 2:21–22 identifies him as the great-grandson of Makir. Was Jair a person or a clan? I am inclined toward the former view (see my commentary on 1 Chron. 2:18–24). Also, I do not see any reason to assume that all references to Jair refer to the same individual. Verse 31 then would take us well into the period of the judges, several generations after Moses. The same thing is always said of Jair: "he captured settlements" or tent villages, which he calls Havvoth Jair, "settlements of Jair" (Num. 32:41; Deut. 3:14; Josh. 13:30; 1 Chron. 2:22). In verse 41 these settlements are called "their" settlements, referring back to the Amorites of verse 39. But the Amorites had more than only tent villages, and it is perhaps better to read instead of "their settlements" *(chwtjhm)*, "the settlements of Ham" *(chwt hm)* in verse 41, i.e., the present Tell Ham, three miles south of Irbid. According to Judges 10:4 Havvoth Jair consisted of thirty settlements, according to 1 Chronicles 2:22 of twenty-three, while Deuteronomy 3:4 states that there were "sixty cities" in the territory captured by Jair, which Deuteronomy 3:14 calls Argob. We also find the number sixty in 1 Chronicles 2:23, but there the statement is added that those sixty also included "Kenath with its surrounding settlements." On the other hand, 1 Kings 4:13, whose author clearly distinguishes between Gilead, Bashan, Jair, and Argob (see van Gelderen in this commentary series on 1 Kings 4:13), makes a distinction between "the settlements of Jair son of Manasseh" and "the district of Argob in Bashan" with "its sixty large walled cities with bronze gate bars." This forces us to conclude that we must differentiate between "the settlements of Jair" and "the cities of Argob." The "sixty" of Deuteronomy 3:4 and 1 Chronicles 2:23 are thus confined to what is called Kenath in 1 Chronicles 2:23. Geographical preciseness was apparently not considered overly important in those days. The term "settlements" *(chawwot)* is found only in connection with Jair. The word refers to a "circle of tents," as the Arabic parallel indicates; but the term certainly does not imply that these settlements remained "tent villages." Hasor ("Fence") in northern Galilee retained its name, even though it became a royal city in the fourteenth century according to the Amarna letters, which mention it alongside Sidon.

Nobah is mentioned only here. It is striking that any indication of clan or tribe is lacking. But he was probably a "son of Manasseh," a phrase that may inadvertently have been omitted from the text by a careless copyist. It is said of Nobah that he captured Kenath and named it after himself (cf. Judg. 18:29). In Judges 8:11 we hear that a place named Nobah lay near Jogbehah (see commentary on v. 35). Kenath is perhaps the present Qanawat near the western slope of the Hauran mountains. But more likely is its identification with al-Quneyye, fifteen miles farther to the west, where inscriptions have been found with the name Qanata.

The campaign of Manasseh is directed against "the Amorites" (v. 39). After 21:33–35, where we hear of the destruction of the kingdom of Og of Bashan, this is rather surprising, and the question arises: When do the events of verses 39–42 take place? We cannot give a categorical answer. Deuteronomy 3:13–15 connects the name of Moses with the settlement of the half-tribe of Manasseh in "Gilead and Bashan." Joshua 17:1–6 states that the allotment did not take place until Joshua's time. And finally, Judges 10:3–4 connects the "settlements of Jair" with the judge Jair, who was Jephthah's immediate predecessor. I have therefore the impression that these reports reflect a very gradual process in which the territory was captured over a rather long period of time. Budde and others felt, on the basis of Joshua 17:14–16 and Judges 5:14, that some clans of Manasseh went to Bashan (then not yet occupied by Israel) when they realized that the territory allotted to Ephraim and Manasseh in Canaan was too small for them, and captured Bashan. But this view does not appear to agree with the facts we have at our disposal, which is not to say that the history of the settling of Manasseh is clear to me.

The Stages in Israel's Journey Through the Wilderness
(33:1–49)

33:1–49 *Here are the stages in the journey of the Israelites when they came out of Egypt by divisions under the leadership of Moses and Aaron. At the Lord's command Moses recorded the stages in their journey. This is their journey by stages:*

The Israelites set out from Rameses on the fifteenth day of the first month, the day after the Passover. They marched out boldly in full view of all the Egyptians, who were burying all their firstborn, whom the LORD had struck down among them; for the LORD had brought judgment on their gods.

The Israelites left Rameses and camped at Succoth.

They left Succoth and camped at Etham, on the edge of the desert.

They left Etham, turned back to Pi Hahiroth, to the east of Baal Zephon, and camped near Migdol.

They left Pi Hahiroth and passed through the sea into the desert, and when they had traveled for three days in the Desert of Etham, they camped at Marah.

They left Marah and went to Elim, where there were twelve springs and seventy palm trees, and they camped there.

They left Elim and camped by the Red Sea.

They left the Red Sea and camped in the Desert of Sin.

They left the Desert of Sin and camped at Dophkah.

They left Dophkah and camped at Alush.

They left Alush and camped at Rephidim, where there was no water for the people to drink.

They left Rephidim and camped in the Desert of Sinai.

They left the Desert of Sinai and camped at Kibroth Hattaavah.

They left Kibroth Hattaavah and camped at Hazeroth.

They left Hazeroth and camped at Rithmah.

They left Rithmah and camped at Rimmon Perez.

They left Rimmon Perez and camped at Libnah.

They left Libnah and camped at Rissah.

They left Rissah and camped at Kehelathah.

They left Kehelathah and camped at Mount Shepher.

They left Mount Shepher and camped at Haradah.

They left Haradah and camped at Makheloth.

They left Makheloth and camped at Tahath.

They left Tahath and camped at Terah.

They left Terah and camped at Mithcah.

They left Mithcah and camped at Hashmonah.

They left Hashmonah and camped at Moseroth.

They left Moseroth and camped at Bene Jaakan.

They left Bene Jaakan and camped at Hor Haggidgad.

They left Hor Haggidgad and camped at Jotbathah.

They left Jotbathah and camped at Abronah.

They left Abronah and camped at Ezion Geber.

They left Ezion Geber and camped at Kadesh, in the Desert of Zin.

They left Kadesh and camped at Mount Hor, on the border of Edom. At the LORD's command Aaron the priest went up Mount Hor, where he died on the first day of the fifth month of the fortieth year after the Israelites came out of Egypt. Aaron was a hundred and twenty-three years old when he died on Mount Hor.

> The Canaanite king of Arad, who lived in the Negev of Canaan, heard that the
> Israelites were coming.[13]
> They left Mount Hor and camped at Zalmonah.
> They left Zalmonah and camped at Punon.
> They left Punon and camped at Oboth.
> They left Oboth and camped at Iye Abarim, on the border of Moab.
> They left Iyim and camped at Dibon Gad.
> They left Dibon Gad and camped at Almon Diblathaim.
> They left Almon Diblathaim an camped in the mountains of Abarim, near Nebo.
> They left the mountains of Abarim and camped on the plains of Moab by the
> Jordan across from Jericho. There on the plains of Moab they camped along the
> Jordan from Beth Jeshimoth to Abel Shittim.

The author of the Pentateuch wants to give, as it were, a survey of the in more than one respect dramatic period that marked the beginning of Israel's journey through the centuries. He therefore includes this list of many (not all!) of the places where Israel camped for a shorter or longer time during its wanderings through the Sinai peninsula. Not counting the starting point (Rameses) and the endpoint (the plains of Moab) of Israel's journey, we find forty names, probably in connection with Israel's forty years in the wilderness (although it does not follow that Israel would have spent one year in each place, see below). Wellhausen and Kuenen, and many who followed their lead, have tried to give the impression that this list was put together by the "compiler" of the Pentateuch or by a still later redactor on the basis of Exodus 12–Numbers 22. But the facts speak an entirely different language. In the first place, an Assyrian inscription that has unfortunately survived only in part (see Br. Meissner, *Babylonien und Assyrien,* I, p. 339) proves that such lists with a precise account of the various stages and camps, and even of the travel time between the camps, were certainly not unknown in the ancient world. Second, in Numbers 33 we find no fewer than sixteen places not mentioned elsewhere in the Pentateuch (Dophkah, Alush, v. 13; Rithmah, Rimmon Perez, Libnah, Rissah, Kehelathah, Mount Shepher, Haradah, Makheloth, Tahath, Terah, Mithcah, Hashmonah, vv. 18–30; Abronah, v. 34; and Zalmonah, v. 41). And third, if this list had been compiled on the basis of the Pentateuch, we might expect complete harmony between the sequence of the camps in Numbers 33 and the other, shorter reports of Israel's wanderings that we find elsewhere in the Pentateuch. This is however not the case. Numbers 33:43ff. gives the sequence Oboth, Iye Abarim, Dibon Gad, Almon Diblathaim, mountains of Abarim, and the plains of Moab; Numbers

---

[13]Noordtzij takes "king of Arad" to be a later addition; see commentary on 21:1 (tr.).

21:10–20, on the other hand, lists Oboth, Iye Abarim, the Zered Valley, alongside the Arnon, Beer, Mattanah,[14] Nahaliel, Bamoth, and the valley in Moab where the top of Pisgah overlooks the wasteland. Similarly, Numbers 33:31–33 and Deuteronomy 10:6f. differ. In Numbers 33:31ff. we hear of Moseroth, Bene Jaakan, Hor Haggidgad, and Jotbathah, while Deuteronomy 10:6–7 mentions the wells of the Jaakanites, Moserah, Gudgodah, and Jotbathah. And finally, only verse 8 mentions the Desert of Etham, which is called the Desert of Shur in Exodus 15:22. The claim of the school of Wellhausen, therefore, apart from its underlying view of the Scriptures, does not do justice to the facts. There is no reason whatsoever to doubt the antiquity of this list. The fact that the number of stages has been reduced to forty makes this list no less reliable than e.g., the grouping into three times fourteen generations in the genealogy in Matthew 1.

A closer look at this list shows that Israel's wilderness journey here falls into three sections:

1. from Rameses to the Desert of Sinai, eleven stages (vv. 5–15)
2. from Sinai to Kadesh, twenty-one stages (vv. 16–36)
3. from Kadesh to the plains of Moab, nine stages (vv. 36–49)

Since Israel arrived at Mount Sinai three months after the Exodus (10:11) and stayed there for a full year, the first eleven stages must be spread over that first year. And since the last nine stages must fall in the final year of the wanderings, only twenty-one stages remain for the intervening thirty-nine years. This proves that it was not the author's intention to give his readers the impression that Israel stayed for one year at each of the forty sites.

Furthermore, not all campsites are included in this list, as verse 8 clearly shows: "they . . . traveled for three days" from Pi Hahiroth to Marah, but the intervening stops are omitted. On the other hand, verse 10 speaks of a camp by the Red Sea about which Exodus is silent; the same is true of Dophkah and Alush in verse 13. Also, if the present text of verse 36 is correct (which in my opinion is not the case, see below), the distance between Ezion Geber and Kadesh would be no less than sixty-seven miles; no campsites are given between these two locations, while we hear of no fewer than twenty-one stages between Mount Sinai and Ezion Geber, which are about equally far apart (about eighty-four miles).

I must draw attention to one more point. In verse 31 we find Israel camped in Bene Jaakan. Genesis 36:27 and 1 Chronicles 1:42 indicate that

---

[14]See commentary on 21:16–18.

Jaakan was a Horite clan that lived in, or on the border of, Edom. This means that Israel is near Kadesh. Yet, in verse 36 Israel travels from Ezion Geber to Kadesh. This allows for two possibilities: either Israel stayed in Kadesh twice, or verses 36b–41a belong between verse 30a and verse 30b. In the latter case Israel traveled from Hashmonah via Kadesh and Mount Hor to Moseroth, and hence south toward Moab, as chapter 21 indicates. But if Israel stayed at Kadesh twice, it must have gone in a northeasterly direction from Kadesh through northern Edom and southern Moab to Dibon Gad, which is in direct contradiction to chapter 21 and Deuteronomy 2. I am therefore convinced that for some reason verses 36b–41a have been moved from their proper place and belong between verses 30a and b.

Much effort has been, and is being, expended on the identification of the places mentioned in chapter 33 (cf. e.g., F. M. Abel, *Géographie de Palestine,* I, 1933; F. Hommel, *Ethnologie und Geographie des alten Orients,* 19, pp. 621–34). We can identify with certainty Sinai, Kadesh, Ezion Geber, Dibon Gad, Abarim, and Nebo. Rameses probably refers to *R'-mš-šw* ("House of Rameses"); its exact location is unknown (near Pelusium?); the present Tell Rotab, which used to be identified as Rameses, is probably the location of Pithom (Exod. 1:11). Sukkoth is probably *Tkw(t)* (Zeku), later called Heriopolis, on the present Tell Mashuta in the Wadi Tumilât. Etham was probably one of the Egyptian fortifications at the edge of the desert. Pi Hahiroth is still a mystery, as is Baal Zephon ("Lord of the North": a temple? a mountain?), although both are probably to be sought near the present Suez, even as Migdol ("Fortress"). It is still an open question whether Mara should indeed be placed near the present Spring of Moses, and Elim in the Wadi Gharandel. Punon (v. 42) is probably the present Fenan, north of Petra on the eastern border of Edom, while Almon Diblathaim (v. 46) is probably the same as the Beth Diblathaim of Jeremiah 48:22, located in the territory that later belonged to Moab. Concerning Mount Hor, see 20:22. And finally, Beth Jeshimoth is probably to be identified with the present Khirbet Zuweme, very near the place where the Jordan enters the Dead Sea.

The author of the Pentateuch prefaced the Mosaic list with four verses in which he first describes the nature of the list (v. 1), then identifies its author (v. 2) and fixes the beginning of the journey in terms of both time and place (v. 3), and finally states the circumstances under which the journey began (v. 4). He ends his introduction with a verbatim quote of Exodus 12:12b, where Israel's exodus from Egypt is described as a victory of the Lord over the gods of Egypt, a description that is in full agreement with the ancient Near Eastern concept that a war between two nations is in essence a war between their gods.

The author of the Pentateuch also has added a few historical notes. Only here do we find a statement concerning the time of Aaron's death and his age; verses 38–39 are certainly from the hand of the author of the Pentateuch. The same is true of verse 40, where the response of the Canaanite has been omitted ("king of Aram" is a later addition; see commentary on 21:1).

The Conquest and Division of Canaan
(33:50–34:29)

1. *The Inhabitants of Canaan Must Be Driven Out* (33:50–56)

33:50–56 *On the plains of Moab by the Jordan across from Jericho the* Lord *said to Moses, "Speak to the Israelites and say to them: 'When you cross the Jordan into Canaan, drive out all the inhabitants of the land before you. Destroy all their carved images and their cast idols, and demolish all their high places. Take possession of the land and settle in it, for I have given you the land to possess. Distribute the land by lot, according to your clans. To a larger group give a larger inheritance, and to a smaller group a smaller one. Whatever falls to them by lot will be theirs. Distribute it according to your ancestral tribes.*

" 'But if you do not drive out the inhabitants of the land, those you allow to remain will become barbs in your eyes and thorns in your sides. They will give you trouble in the land where you will live. And then I will do to you what I plan to do to them.' "

At the Lord's command an entirely new chapter in the history of Canaan must begin when Israel enters the land. Every trace of the Canaanite society must be eradicated; its inhabitants must be driven out, and anything connected with their religion—carved images, cast idols, and the high places—must be demolished (cf. Exod. 23:23–24, 27–33; 34:11–26; Lev. 26:1). "The old has gone, the new has come" (2 Cor. 5:17), because Canaan is the Lord's gift to Israel, in which each tribe is to receive an equitable portion "by lot," i.e., according to the Lord's determination (see 26:52–56). This is the command, to which a warning is attached: any transgression of the command will not only result in Israel's shame and harm ("barbs, thorns, trouble," see also Josh. 23:13), but also in the Lord's judgment: Israel itself will be driven out (cf. the Babylonian captivity). In Canaan Israel is to be the Lord's people! But history shows how spiritual sluggishness and military lassitude have hindered the implementation of the Lord's command (see my *Geknecht in eigen land,* 1939), and how Israel was consequently "enslaved" in its own land, until the captivity became necessary.

291

2. The Boundaries of Canaan (34:1–12)

34:1–12 *The* Lord *said to Moses, "Command the Israelites and say to them: 'When you enter Canaan, the land that will be allotted to you as an inheritance will have these boundaries:*

"'Your southern side will include some of the Desert of Zin along the border of Edom. On the east, your southern boundary will start from the end of the Salt Sea, cross south of Scorpion Pass, continue on to Zin and go south of Kadesh Barnea. Then it will go to Hazar Addar and over to Azmon, where it will turn, join the Wadi of Egypt and end at the Sea.

"'Your western boundary will be the coast of the Great Sea. This will be your boundary on the west.

"'For your northern boundary, run a line from the Great Sea to Mount Hor and from Mount Hor to Lebo Hamath. Then the boundary will go to Zedad, continue to Ziphron and end at Hazar Enan. This will be your boundary on the north.

"'For your eastern boundary, run a line from Hazar Enan to Shepham. The boundary will go down from Shepham to Riblah on the east side of Ain and continue along the slopes east of the Sea of Kinnereth. Then the boundary will go down along the Jordan and end at the Salt Sea.

"'This will be your land, with its boundaries on every side.'"

Since the promise of the land concerned Canaan proper (see commentary on 32:6–15), only the boundaries of the territory west of the Jordan, to the extent that this was to belong to Israel, are given here. Even as in Ezekiel 47:15–20, a rectangular area is designated that is to be inhabited exclusively by Israel. The southern boundary, which runs through virtually the same points in Joshua 15:1–4 and Ezekiel 47:19, stretches from the Dead Sea over the pass of Akrabim ("Scorpion Pass," perhaps the present Naqb es-Safa) over Zin (location unknown) in a southwesterly direction to Kadesh Barnea (the present Ain Qadeis), and from there in a northwesterly direction to the Wadi of Egypt (the present Wadi el-Arish).

Because of our inadequate knowledge of the geography involved we are completely in the dark where the northern boundary is concerned. Even the expression "the entrance to Hamath" (Lebo Hamath) is not clear: does this refer to the entrance to the "great Hamath" of Amos 6:2, the present Hama on the Orontes, or to Hamath Zobah of 2 Chronicles 8:3, usually thought to be located south of Mount Hermon? I am inclined toward the latter view (see also 13:21 and my commentary on Ezekiel 47:13–20). I would seek the west end of the northern boundary near the Nahr el-Kasimiye, just north of Tyre; the boundary then runs eastward to the southern slopes of the Hermon, near Banias. The "entrance to Hamath" would then be between the Nahr Litani and the Nahr Hasbani. Others, however, are of the opinion that the northern boundary ran from modern Tripoli to Mount Hor, the present Gebel Akkar, one of the northernmost peaks of the Lebanon, and from there northeastward to the present Restan, twenty miles from Hamat, where the "entrance to Hamath" then would be located. Ziphron (v. 9) then should be identified with the present Za Ferani southeast of Restan, while Hazar Enan would be located in the present Cariates on the road from Damascus to Palmyra; if the latter view is correct, then Israel did fall far short indeed of completing its assigned task!

The eastern boundary runs from Hazar Enan, of which Ezekiel 47:18 says that it lies "between Hauran and Damascus," and which is probably to be sought near the source of the Jordan, southward along the eastern shore of the Sea of Kinnereth and along the river Jordan. Riblah (v. 11) can, of course, not be the well-known Riblah on the Orontes (2 Kings 23:33; 25:6–7, 20–21; Jer. 52:9), northeast of the modern Baalbek. We should very likely read here another name, perhaps with the Samaritan Pentateuch and the LXX the otherwise completely unknown Harbela. Nor can Ain (v. 11) be the present Aiun, east of the southern tip of the Sea of Kinnereth, since the boundary does not reach the northern end of the Sea of Kinnereth until verse 11b. Perhaps Ain refers to the source of the Jordan.

Concerning the western boundary I note that the shore of the Great Sea, i.e., the Mediterranean, was never in Israel's possession. Joppa was not conquered until 144 B.C. by Simon Maccabeus (1 Macc. 14:5). The Philistines and Phoenicians have always occupied the coastal plain during the days of Israel's kingdom, and after the captivity those who returned had to be satisfied at first with the southern half of Canaan, again without the coastal plain.

3. *The Division of Canaan* (34:13–29)

34:13–15 *Moses commanded the Israelites: "Assign this land by lot as an inheritance. The LORD has ordered that it be given to the nine and a half tribes, because the families of the tribe of Reuben, the tribe of Gad and the half-tribe of Manasseh have received their inheritance. These two and a half tribes have received their inheritance on the east side of the Jordan of Jericho, toward the sunrise."*

The territory defined in verses 1–12 must be divided by lot (see 26:52–56; 32:28–33) among "the nine and a half tribes," which are not again identified by name (v. 13). Reuben, Gad, and the half-tribe of Manasseh will already have "received" their inheritance "on the east side of the Jordan of Jericho, toward the sunrise" (vv. 14–15). The verb rendered "receive" *(lakach)* means literally "to take"; these tribes will thus already have "taken" their inheritance. Are the English versions correct when they, like Dillmann, Baentsch, Heinisch, Edelkoort, and Buchanan Gray, translated *lakach* "received," or is a reproach implied? In my opinion the Hebrew idiom does not leave any doubt on this point. The verb *lakach* never loses its meaning "to take." Moses here in fact goes back on his granting of the request of Gad and Reuben (32:33) and indicates that he was wrong in giving in to their pressure. The Transjordan tribes did indeed provide no support whatsoever to Israel; they soon succumbed to the advancing Moabites, Amorites, and Arameans. And most important of all, the settling of the Transjordan territory prevented the complete conquest of Canaan itself.

34:16–29 *The LORD said to Moses, "These are the names of the men who are to assign the land for you as an inheritance: Eleazar the priest and Joshua son of Nun. And appoint one leader from each tribe to help assign the land. These are their names:*

Caleb son of Jephunneh,
  from the tribe of Judah;
Shemuel son of Ammihud,
  from the tribe of Simeon;
Elidad son of Kislon,
  from the tribe of Benjamin;
Bukki son of Jogli,
  the leader from the tribe of Dan;
Hanniel son of Ephod,
  the leader from the tribe of Manasseh son of Joseph;
Kemuel son of Shiphtan,
  the leader from the tribe of Ephraim son of Joseph;
Elizaphan son of Parnach,
  the leader from the tribe of Zebulun;
Paltiel son of Azzan,
  the leader from the tribe of Issachar;
Ahihud son of Shelomi,
  the leader from the tribe of Asher;
Pedahel son of Ammihud,
  the leader from the tribe of Naphtali."
These are the men the LORD commanded to assign the inheritance to the Israelites in the land of Canaan.

Then the names are given of those who are to be in charge of assigning the land to the various tribes and clans: Eleazar and Joshua (the priest is again mentioned first; cf. 32:28; also Josh. 14:1; 17:4; 19:51; 21:1). One leader from each tribe (except Gad and Reuben) is to assist in this task. We are again struck by the fact that none of the names listed here is a composite of Jahweh, which indicates that these names are very old (see 13:4–15).

More than one of these names has also been found among the inhabitants of the Euphrates-Tigris valley, which has, however, not kept the school of Wellhausen from declaring these names purely fictitious. None of these leaders are among those who helped with the census of chapter 1, or (except for Caleb) among the spies of chapter 13, all of whom had fallen under the judgment of 14:29. The order in which the tribes are listed corresponds to their location from south to north.

The Towns of the Levites
(35:1–8)

35:1–8 On the plains of Moab by the Jordan across from Jericho, the LORD said to Moses, "Command the Israelites to give the Levites towns to live in from the inheritance the Israelites will possess. And give them pasturelands around the towns. Then they will have towns to live in and pasturelands for their cattle, flocks and all their other livestock.

"The pasturelands around the towns that you give the Levites will extend out fifteen hundred feet from the town wall. Outside the town, measure three thousand feet on the east side, three thousand on the south side, three thousand on the west and three thousand on the north, with the town in the center. They will have this area as pastureland for the towns.

"Six of the towns you give the Levites will be cities of refuge, to which a person who has killed someone may flee. In addition, give them forty-two other towns. In all you must give the Levites forty-eight towns, together with their pasturelands. The towns you give the Levites from the land the Israelites possess are to be given in proportion to the inheritance of each tribe: Take many towns from a tribe that has many, but few from one that has few."

As was already stated in 18:20, 23–24; 26:62, the Levites—to be understood in the genealogical sense: the tribe of Levi, which thus also includes the priests—are not allowed to "inherit" in the same sense as the other tribes, that is, they are not allowed to have their own tribal territory. By virtue of their work at the central sanctuary—the only sanctuary Israel was permitted to have—they are in the service of Israel as a whole. For this reason they are to live scattered throughout Israel, i.e., they are to live in groups in the various tribal territories. This is regulated in more detail in 35:1–8. The Israelites are to give the Levites a number of towns (forty-eight, v. 7) "to live in," with pasturelands of a precisely determined size. Two conditions must be fulfilled: (1) six of these towns must serve as cities of refuge, further regulated in a separate law (35:6–34); and (2) the size of the territory allotted to each tribe shall determine the number of cities each tribe is to give to the Levites.

Several details are not entirely clear. Verse 4 states that the pasturelands must extend a thousand cubits (approximately 1,500 feet) out from the town wall and must border on that wall. The width of the land is specified in verse 5, which speaks of four parcels of two thousand cubits (approximately 3,000 feet). The total pastureland adjacent to each town thus comes to four parcels of approximately 1,500 by 3,000 feet, a total of about 18 million square feet, or approximately 413 acres. Is this pastureland intended for the exclusive use of the Levites? This question, if asked at all, is usually answered in the affirmative, in my opinion incorrectly so. The same principle that applies to the towns of the Levites also applies to the land: both are given to the Levites. But not only members of the tribe of Levi were allowed to live in the towns; the implementation of this law in Joshua 21 leaves no doubt on this point. Among the cities given to the Levites we find towns such as Hebron, Shechem, Libnah, Gibeon, Gezer, Jokneam, Taanach, and Kadesh; we know that these towns had a very mixed population. It appears to me therefore that, since the towns were not inhabited exclusively by the Levites, the surrounding pastureland was not for their exclusive use either. Rather, we have here something similar to the Hittite "cities of god," which were not populated exclusively by temple servants but were governed by them, and they derived a significant portion of their income from the surrounding land (see A. Götze, *Kleinasien,* 1933, p. 96).

K. H. Graf originated the idea, which has since been repeated consistently by the school of Wellhausen, that this law could be implemented only in the south-Russian steppe or in the (then) still nonsettled regions of North America. But this overlooks the fact that the lawgiver assumed that Israel would carry out the command to drive out Canaan's inhabitants completely and to the letter, so that all the land would be at Israel's disposal (33:52). The lawgiver probably realized that in a mountainous country like Canaan it would not always be possible to find pastureland of the dimensions given in verse 4. He gave a general rule and relied on the practical sense of those whom he entrusted with the implementation of this law.

This implementation is recorded in Joshua 21. Two things emerge from that chapter: (1) the tribes first decided which towns they wanted to become "towns of the Levites" and only then decided by lot to which clan they would be assigned; and (2) among the towns given to the Levites were quite a few that were not as yet in Israel's possession. The latter can be said with certainty of Gezer (Judg. 1:29; 1 Kings 9:16), Taanach (Judg. 1:27), Nahalol (Judg. 1:30), and Rehob (Judg. 1:31). But considering how little we know of the period from Joshua to Saul, there appears to me to be every reason to suspect that the same also applied to many of the other "towns of the Levites.'' Thus we can also explain without difficulty why the picture of the Levites in Judges 17:8 and 19:1ff. does not give the impression of settled town dwellers. It is also striking that neither Nob nor Shiloh, which in Samuel's day were "towns of the priests" (1 Sam. 21:1; 1 Sam. 1–4; Nob is even called specifically "the town of the priests" in 1 Sam. 22:19) are not listed among the towns of the Levites in Joshua 21. And finally, it is difficult to deny that the regulation of verse 8 (the number of towns is to be in proportion to the size of each tribe's territory) was interpreted very loosely. Thus, Naphtali, although it was at that time larger than Ephraim or Gad (see ch. 26), gave three towns, while Ephraim and Gad each gave four. Likewise, Issachar and Dan do not give more towns than Ephraim, even though they were larger (see ch. 26). This law was thus carried out very imperfectly, but we are in the dark concerning many of the details. We only know from 1 Chronicles 13:2 that the Levites lived in certain cities in David's time, while 2 Chronicles 11:13–14 states that in the days of Jeroboam I many Levites left the territory of Ephraim and went to Judah. Ezekiel's description of the kingdom of God (see my commentary on Ezek. 40ff.) reflects the concept that is the basis of this law (45:1–8; 47:8–20): he sees a portion of Israel's land set apart as a "sacred district" for the Lord's temple and its servants, a square area, situated between the territories assigned to Judah and Benjamin. Ezekiel thus envisions the realization of the arrangement of the camp of Numbers 2.

The Cities of Refuge and the Right of Asylum
(35:9–34)

This section, in which verses 16–29 are added on the basis of Deuteronomy 19:1–13, deals with the right of asylum. Because we generally render the Hebrew *go'el hadam* "avenger of blood" (v. 19), the idea is widely held that we have here the regulation of blood revenge, a remnant of barbarism. This is incorrect in more than one respect. In the first place, *go'el* does not mean "avenger." The verb implies the discharge of an obligation that rests on the nearest relative. Examples of this obligation are the levirate (Ruth 3:13), the demanding of payment of a debt owed to a deceased relative (Num. 5:8), the buying back of land sold by a relative who has fallen into poverty, whether during his lifetime (Lev. 25:25) or after his death (Jer. 32:7ff.), or also the redemption (by means of payment) of a poor relative (Lev. 25:48). The *go'el* is thus someone who restores the family and prevents the family from suffering harm in any way. In this case, the family has suffered harm through the death of one of its members, and has thus suffered a diminishing of blood, i.e., of life. The balance must now be restored. The dead person cannot return; therefore, the life of the family of the murderer must also be diminished. This is accomplished by the *go'el hadam,* the so-called "avenger of blood," whose task, however, is the restoration of balance rather than revenge.

From the above follows, secondly, that we have here, even as in Exodus 21:12–27 and Deuteronomy 19:1–13, not blood revenge, but rather the law of retribution, which is a different matter. Blood revenge punishes not only the damage done, but kills "a man for wounding . . . a young man for injuring" (Gen. 4:23). Blood revenge acts without restraint, blindly. Not so the law of retribution, which is based on the principle "an eye for an eye, and a tooth for a tooth" (Exod. 21:23–25; Lev. 24:19–20; Deut. 19:21; 24:16). Blood revenge leads to ever-increasing bloodshed; the law of retribution, on the other hand, is applicable among people where the old tribal relationships still exist, and is the means to normalize the legal relationships in those circles; this is why it still exists among the Bedouins. It therefore does not reflect a primitive concept of justice, as does blood revenge, but is related to the social structure of the tribal community. Consequently, when the law of retribution has virtually disappeared in the Code of Hammurabi it does not prove that the Babylonian concept of justice stood on a higher level than that of Israel, but only that in Babylonia the ancient tribal structure had disappeared and had been replaced by what we call a "state," a phase Israel would not reach until it became a kingdom. In a state the government must punish the guilty. The law of retribution thus relates to social organization rather than to morality and justice. Not morally, but only socially, does the law of retribution stand on a lower plane than a normalized jurisprudence as we know it.

The lawgiver thus found in Israel the law of retribution in conjunction with the ancient tribal organization, and he had to take that which existed as his starting point. But God's intention for Israel was its development into a people in which all parts functioned harmoniously; this included centralized authority, i.e., its development into an ordered state. In the future there would therefore no longer be room for the law of retribution. In order to prepare Israel for this, the foundation is laid with the words "You shall not murder" (Exod. 20:13), the basic concept that must govern the society of those who want to live in accordance with God's law. The Book of the Covenant, the oldest collection of laws incorporated into the Pentateuch (Exod. 20:1–23:33) makes a distinction between murder (intentional) and manslaughter (unintentional); in the case of manslaughter the law of retribution may not be applied, and the guilty person may seek refuge in a place to be designated later (Exod. 21:13). This section then speaks of the designation of these places of refuge and specifies in which situations the seeking and reaching of such a city of refuge is legally valid.

1. *The Six Cities of Refuge* (35:9–15)

35:9–15 *Then the LORD said to Moses: "Speak to the Israelites and say to them: 'When you cross the Jordan into Canaan, select some towns to be your cities of refuge, to which a person who has killed someone accidentally may flee. They will be places of refuge from the avenger, so that a person accused of murder may not die before he stands trial before the assembly. These six towns you give will be your cities of refuge. Give three on this side of the Jordan and three in Canaan as cities of refuge. These six towns will be a place of refuge for Israelites, aliens and any other people living among them, so that anyone who has killed another accidentally can flee there.' "*

These cities are called "cities of refuge for one accused of murder" (lit. "for the slayer") in Joshua 21:13, 21, 27, 32, 38. Three of these cities were to be selected on each side of the Jordan. Not only the Israelites, but also the alien *(ger),* the person of non-Israelite descent who enjoys Israel's hospitality and through marriage can participate in the tribal life with his family, can make use of these cities of refuge, as well as "any other people living among them" *(tošab,* KJV "sojourner"), i.e., those who live in Israel only temporarily (v. 15a). But these cities may be used for refuge only by the individual "who has killed someone accidentally" (vv. 11, 15).

2. *For Whom Are the Cities of Refuge Intended?* (35:16–34)

35:16–29 *" 'If a man strikes someone with an iron object so that he dies, he is a murderer; the murderer shall be put to death. Or if anyone has a stone in his hand that could kill, and he strikes someone so that he dies, he is a murderer; the murderer shall be put to death. Or if anyone has a wooden object in his hand that could kill, and he hits someone so that he dies, he is a murderer; the murderer shall be put to death. The avenger of blood shall put the murderer to death; when he meets him, he shall put him to death. If anyone with malice aforethought shoves another or throws something at him intentionally so that he dies or if in hostility he hits him with his fist so that he dies, that person shall be put to death; he is a murderer. The avenger of blood shall put the murderer to death when he meets him.*
" 'But if without hostility someone suddenly shoves another or throws something at him unintentionally or, without seeing him, drops a stone on him that could kill him, and he dies, then since he was not his enemy and he did not intend to harm him, the assembly must judge between him and the avenger of blood according to these regulations. The assembly must protect the one accused of murder from the avenger of blood and send him back to the city of refuge to which he fled. He must stay there until the death of the high priest, who was anointed with the holy oil.
" 'But if the accused ever goes outside the limits of the city of refuge to which he has fled and the avenger of blood finds him outside the city, the avenger of blood

may kill the accused without being guilty of murder. The accused must stay in his city of refuge until the death of the high priest; only after the death of the high priest may he return to his own property.

"'These are to be legal requirements for you throughout the generations to come, wherever you live.'"

What is meant by "killing someone accidentally" is now specified in more detail. In Exodus 21:13 it is described with the words "God lets it happen," and a number of specific instances are given there. Here other cases are added. It is clear that the question of guilt is determined by the intention of the individual; Israel sees this as the relationship between the act and the acting "soul." Does the act come from the "heart," the "soul," i.e., from the source of human actions, or was it merely "in the vicinity" of the soul? This can be determined by the object used to strike the other person or by the feelings of the murderer when he committed the act: if the weapon is an iron object (v. 16), a stone, or a wooden object "that could kill" (vv. 17–18), or if the act is committed with malice aforethought or hostility (vv. 20–21), the intention and will to kill was present, and the blood avenger must act. The law does not state who is called upon to act as blood avenger, and this was not necessary; the observations concerning the *go'el* (see above) make it clear that the blood avenger is to be the nearest relative of the victim. Furthermore, the wording of verses 16–21 indicates that it is assumed that the killer has fled to one of the cities of refuge. Perhaps he has even sought the protection of an altar, which throughout antiquity provided asylum. But neither the one (Exod. 21:14) nor the other (Deut. 19:12) helps. The murderer *must* be put to death (cf. 1 Kings 2:28–31) as soon as the blood avenger finds him. The guilt of shedding "innocent blood" must be purged, "so that it may go well with you" (Deut. 19:13).

Verse 22 further presents the possibility that someone used a weapon "that could kill," yet had no feelings of hostility or hate, nor sought to harm the other person. There was neither the intention nor the will to kill. Flight to a city of refuge is then, of course, indicated, because the blood avenger goes into action immediately. But in this case the right of asylum in the city of refuge must not be violated. First, the assembly must render a decision as to whether the intention to kill was indeed present. We are not told where this was to be decided, although the words "send him back" (v. 25) indicate that it was not in the city of refuge; most likely the investigation is to be made where the killing took place, because there "the voice of the blood" (Gen. 4:10) is heard. The accused is taken there under the protection of the assembly, which functions here as the court, and, if his innocence is proven, is returned from there to the city of refuge. Nothing is said about the composition of the "assembly." It does not consist of the elders of the city where the accused lives, because all they do is give the blood avenger the opportunity to carry out the verdict already reached (Deut. 19:12). It is probable that the "assembly" consisted of the legal representatives of the district in which the city of refuge is located. In any case, this proves that we are not dealing with a new law, since the lawgiver would then have had to define the "assembly" in more detail.

But if the accused is acquitted of intentional murder, he has not thereby regained his freedom of movement; he must remain in the city of refuge where he has sought asylum "until the death of the high priest [*kohen haggadol;* only here in the Pentateuch!] who was anointed with the holy oil" (v. 25, see also vv. 28, 32). This is not because the death of the high priest would have a propitiating effect, but because it marks the end of an era. A parallel is still found in some countries where a new king will grant amnesty. Concerning the anointing, see Exodus 29:7, 29; Leviticus 8:12. But woe to the accused if he returns to his own land before this time, or if he so much as sets foot outside the realm of the city of refuge: the right of the blood avenger then remains in force, and he can kill the accused without being guilty of murder himself, since he has merely done his duty—the blood he spills is not innocent and therefore does not call for retribution.

35:30–32 "*'Anyone who kills a person is to be put to death as a murderer only on the testimony of witnesses. But no one is to be put to death on the testimony of only one witness.*

"*'Do not accept a ransom for the life of a murderer, who deserves to die. He must surely be put to death.*

"*'Do not accept a ransom for anyone who has fled to a city of refuge and so allow him to go back and live on his own land before the death of the high priest.'*"

In the preceding verses the practice of blood revenge has been limited by specific conditions, to prevent retribution from degenerating into an unrestricted blood feud. These verses present the further condition that no one may be declared guilty except on the testimony of witnesses (v. 30); the minimum acceptable number of witnesses is two (see Deut. 17:6; 19:15).

Another restrictive condition concerns the acceptance of "ransom" *(kofer),* offered by someone who is without question (and apparently without trial) a murderer (v. 31). Such a *kofer* would eradicate the crime (see my commentary on Lev. 1:4): the money would restore the balance (see above). But this would not only give the rich an advantage, since the poor could not afford the *kofer* (Prov. 13:8), it would also turn someone's death into a means of enrichment, which would undermine Israel's concept of the value of human life. The innocent blood would in this case continue to "cry"; this should not be allowed to happen, since it would then not "go well" with Israel (Deut. 19:13).

A further restriction lies in the prohibition of verse 32: like the murderer of verse 31, the person who has been forced to remain in a city of refuge until the death of the high priest because he has unintentionally killed someone must not be allowed to pay a ransom in order to be able to return to his own land before the high priest's death.

35:33–34 *"'Do not pollute the land where you are. Bloodshed pollutes the land, and atonement cannot be made for the land on which blood has been shed, except by the blood of the one who shed it. Do not defile the land where you live and where I dwell, for I, the LORD, dwell among the Israelites.'"*

The law ends by focusing on the purely religious basis for it: the Lord dwells in Israel's land, and Israel must therefore keep the land from being "polluted" (v. 33) and "defiled" (v. 34). "Pollute" *(chanaf)* means making the land something different from what it is intended to be, by transgressing the Lord's law (Isa. 24:5; Jer. 3:1). "Defile" *(timme')* means withdrawing the land from the sphere of holiness in which it is to be if the Lord is to dwell in it, by doing that which precludes the possibility of fellowship with the Lord. The concern here is, of course, exclusively the failure to avenge "innocent blood." Deuteronomy 21:1–9 shows the danger this involves. The pollution and defilement that result from this failure can be prevented only by putting the murderer to death (cf. Gen. 9:5–6).

The Right to Marry of Daughters Who Inherit
(36:1–13)

1. *The Legal Question* (36:1–4)

36:1–4 *The family heads of the clan of Gilead son of Makir, the son of Manasseh, who were from the clans of the descendants of Joseph, came and spoke before Moses and the leaders, the heads of the Israelite families. They said, "When the LORD commanded my lord to give the land as an inheritance to the Israelites by lot, he ordered you to give the inheritance of our brother Zelophehad to his daughters. Now suppose they marry men from other Israelite tribes; then their inheritance will be taken from our ancestral inheritance and added to that of the tribe they marry into. And so part of the inheritance allotted to us will be taken away. When the Year of Jubilee for the Israelites comes, their inheritance will be added to that of the tribe into which they marry, and their property will be taken from the tribal inheritance of our forefathers."*

This law is intended to supplement 27:1–11, where it was determined that in Canaan the land that would have been allotted to the family of Zelophehad, who had died without male offspring, was to be given to his daughters. They would thus be given the legal rights of their deceased father. But the question arises, What will happen to this land if these daughters marry outside their own tribe, since through their marriage they will then belong to the tribe of their husbands? If the land goes over to the other tribe along with the daughters, will the geographical unity of the tribal territory not be destroyed, and families of one tribe then not be given the right to own property in the territory of another tribe?

This question, raised by the family heads of the clan of Gilead, faces Israel's leaders with the implications of an earlier decision, made strictly on behalf of Zelophehad's daughters. The question is all the more serious because, as the Gileadites do not fail to point out, the transfer of the property would be the result of inheritance, rather than purchase, and the law of the Year of Jubilee (Lev. 25:13ff.) would thus not apply. The land (although it would remain in the possession of the descendants of Zelophehad in the female line) would therefore in fact become the property of members of another tribe, and thus be removed from the tribe of Manasseh, and after the Year of Jubilee it would become the permanent possession of the other tribe, because the right of redemption has not been used. This poses a threat to the concept on which Israel's society rested, the inalienability of landownership, which would over the years be gradually lost.

2. *The Lord's Decision* (36:5–13)

36:5–12 *Then at the LORD's command Moses gave this order to the Israelites: "What the tribe of the descendants of Joseph is saying is right. This is what the LORD commands for Zelophehad's daughters: They may marry anyone they please as long as they marry within the tribal clan of their father. No inheritance in Israel is to pass from tribe to tribe, for every Israelite shall keep the tribal land inherited from his forefathers. Every daughter who inherits land in any Israelite tribe must marry someone in her father's tribal clan, so that every Israelite will possess the inheritance of his fathers. No inheritance may pass from tribe to tribe, for each Israelite tribe is to keep the land it inherits."*

So Zelophehad's daughters did as the LORD commanded Moses. Zelophehad's daughters—Mahlah, Tirzah, Hoglah, Milcah and Noah—married their cousins on their father's side. They married within the clans of the descendants of Manasseh son of Joseph, and their inheritance remained in their father's clan and tribe.

This legal question is presented to Moses and his immediate circle; Eleazar and "the whole assembly" are not mentioned (cf. 27:2). Through

Moses' mediation the Lord gives His decision, which applies not only to Zelophehad's daughters, but to all daughters in Israel who inherit. Henceforth the same rule shall apply to all. While their right to inherit if their father dies without male offspring is maintained, they must accept a limitation when they marry: they are allowed to marry only within their own tribe. There can thus be no question of land being transferred to another tribe. Each tribe remains a geographical unit. Verses 10–11 add that Zelophehad's daughters limited themselves even further by marrying within their own clan, and their closest relatives at that: they married their cousins on their father's side.

36:13 *These are the commands and regulations the* Lord *gave through Moses to the Israelites on the plains of Moab by the Jordan across from Jericho.*

Numbers concludes with a subscript similar to Leviticus 7:37–38; 26:46; 27:34, which serves to conclude a collection of laws, in this case those of chapters 28–31 and of 33:50–36:12.